BED AND BREAKFAST
IN THE MID-ATLANTIC STATES

"We've been open long enough to see the impact of Chesler books on the entire guidebook industry. . . . No one does the personalized job that Bernice does— accurate, detailed, helpful—all with follow-up. . . . If we could only be in one book, Chesler would be our choice."
—*Charles (formerly director of convention services, the Washington Hilton Hotel, Washington, D.C.) and Deborah North, The Pineapple Inn, Lewisburg, Pennsylvania*

"I usually do not write fan letters, but I felt you must know that your book kept me up all night. What a delight to read about so many wonderful B&B."
—*Barbara Lincoln Hall, Lincoln, Ltd. B&B Mississippi Reservation Service*

"Easy, fun reading, yet packed with all the necessary details. Highly recommended!"
—*Bed & Breakfast Update*, North Hollywood, California

"Chesler's books are a valuable resource for agents interested in offering bed and breakfasts as an alternative to their clients."
—*Travel Weekly*

"In the world of publishing, she's a central point for the entire concept of Bed and Breakfast."
—*The Tab*, Newton, Massachusetts

"Unprecedented personal and logistical data about the hosts and their accommodations. . . . [Chesler's] style rei. orces the concept of bed & breakfast as a warm, person-to-person accommodation."
—*Shoptalk*

"She's not called the 'queen of B&Bs' for nothing. [Chesler's] books . . . thoroughly cover the B&B scene."
—*The Boston Globe*, Boston, Massachusetts

"After reading your books for hours on end, I realized you are the vehicle to the traveler and educator to the public."
—*The White Pillars Inn*, New York

Other books by Bernice Chesler

Editor and Coordinator
The ZOOM Catalog
Do a ZOOMdo
People You'd Like to Know

Coauthor
The Family Guide to Cape Cod

Author
In and Out of Boston with (or without) Children
Mainstreaming through the Media
Bed & Breakfast Coast to Coast
Bed and Breakfast in New England

BED AND BREAKFAST
IN THE MID-ATLANTIC STATES

Delaware • District of Columbia
Maryland • New Jersey • New York
Pennsylvania • Virginia • West Virginia

Second Edition

by Bernice Chesler

A Voyager Book

The
Globe
Pequot
Press

Chester, Connecticut

Cover photo by Sean Kernon
Cover design by Barbara Marks

Library of Congress Cataloging-in-Publication Data

Chesler, Bernice.
    Bed and breakfast in mid-Atlantic states: Delaware, District of Co-
lumbia, Maryland, New Jersey, New York, Pennsylvania, Virginia, West
Virginia / by Bernice Chesler.—2nd ed.

    000p. 00 cm.
    "A Voyager book."
    Includes index.
    ISBN 0-87106-606-8
    1. Bed and breakfast accommodations—Middle Atlantic States—
Guide-books. I. Title.
TX907.3.M53C48   1989
647.9475'03—dc19
                                           89-31210
                                            CIP

Manufactured in the United States of America
Second Edition/Second Printing

CONTENTS

to David

Introduction

Bed and breakfast is the hottest travel trend in America. Long established in Europe, it is a personalized style of travel that has flourished on this side of the Atlantic during the 1980s. As the number of B&Bs has multiplied, so have the variations.

All those variations and the people who run the B&Bs are what this book is all about. What accounts for a $30 difference in rooms at the same B&B? (And at the same time, you will still find B&Bs at $35 a night for two.) What time is breakfast served? And whose home-away-from-home are you going to? (Can you top the experience of the guest who was reunited—after fifty years—with a high school classmate, a host, because of the profile in the last edition of this book?)

B&B can be a money saver, particularly in big cities and resort areas. In some locations a few have opened with lavish and expensive accommodations. B&B is also chosen for a getaway; for company; for pampering; for food; for a convenient or an off-the-beaten-path location; for an opportunity to meet new people; and for a home away from home. B&B hosts can be a great resource for information about an area's attractions, restaurants, back roads, history, housing, jobs, people.

Whatever, the "best" place is the place that is a good match for *you*. I can recall being at a lovely hilltop B&B, surrounded by peace and quiet, and woods and blue sky, watching the ferry round the bend, all the while listening to another guest rave about a B&B "right in town where all the shops are." On the following pages, check under "Location" for a description of the setting.

Although the popularization of B&B has reached the point where B&B package rates are now offered by some hotels and motels as well as by smaller facilities that are managed but not owner occupied, I still like the traditional interpretation: a home setting with an owner in residence; a maximum of about 10 guest rooms; a common room; breakfast included in the rate, but no public restaurant or bar on the premises.

In *Bed & Breakfast in the Mid-Atlantic States* and its companion volume, *Bed & Breakfast in New England*, you will find hundreds of sharing and caring people who have chosen to be part- or full-time hosts. Whether they have one or two extra rooms or whether they live in an inn, surely they have one of the most envied jobs in this country. One out of five guests leaves with the dream of opening his own B&B. And after eight years of full-time B&B research, six B&B books, thousands of interviews, and hundreds of stays, I see that a good number of guests follow through. Announcements of new B&Bs arrive daily.

And what about you, the traveler? "Adventuresome and flexible, interesting and appreciative—a very special breed," hosts say. The feeling is mutual. The art of letter writing is alive! Excerpts from some of the thousands of letters guests have written to me are included in this book. Those letters, often filled with anecdotes, indicate that conversations are remembered at least as much as the color of the wallpaper. Still, with current interest in interior design, architecture, food, and innkeeping, it turns out that many creative hosts become casual or formal consultants to guests. Hence the symbols with each writeup.

B&Bs confirmed every detail just before press time. This book even tells you if a bath has a shower *and* tub. All the pets, important members of the family, are accounted for. (There must be a link between loving households and long-lived animals.) Please keep in mind that successful hosts sometimes add a room or change the bed size, the menu, the decor, and, yes, the rates, too.

My thanks go to Lourdes Alvarez, who has maintained her strong sense of organization (and humor) while sorting through close to 20,000 mostly-handwritten pieces of paper. It is also a pleasure to work with Jay Howland, my editor. This book has benefited from her knowledge, her sensitivity to the spirit of bed and breakfast, and her eagle eye for such ambiguous phrases as "outdoor lovers." And again it is true that without David, my husband, there wouldn't be any books. He plans all our trips by plane, car, and bicycle. He listens to the extraordinary letter of the day, offers judgment when I solicit objectivity, keeps the household going, and acts as my computer expert in residence.

Suggestions about people and places are welcome for consideration in the next edition. Please address them to me at The Globe Pequot Press, 138 West Main Street, Chester, CT 06412.

Bernice Chester

"Do you believe that a B&B host and hostess can also become friend, confidant, counselor, listener, parent, grandparent, aunt/uncle and babysitter—and still love every minute of it? Our guests have touched our lives also."

—Joan and Jack Grimes, hosts,
The Inn at Brook Willow Farm, Cooperstown, NY

Answers to frequently asked questions

What is bed and breakfast?

It is a package arrangement that includes overnight accommodations and breakfast. Although there are many embellishments (amenities) offered at some American B&Bs, the keynote is hospitality. Think of it as a people-to-people program.

B&Bs range from simple to elegant. A B&B may be a private home with an extra room or a business—"home on a larger scale"—sometimes called a B&B inn. As at home, nothing is standardized. Every room is different. Many are freshly and imaginatively decorated. Some are suites, or they might be in a private wing or a converted carriage house. Most are not just clean; they are immaculate.

Are baths shared?

Some are. But depending on the number of guests, a shared bath could be private for you. It may adjoin the room or be down the hall; sometimes it is up or down the stairs. Trend: Americans, even those who are used to European shared bath arrangements, are requesting—and willing to pay extra for—a private bath as well as the newest luxury, a Jacuzzi. Yet there are hosts in older homes who have no interest in adding baths or who find no problem with shared baths.

Do you have to get up for breakfast?

Again, no one rule. Check each description in this book for the various arrangements. More than one guest has been enticed by the aroma of fresh muffins. More than one guest has helped himself to breakfast after the host has left for work. If you are on business or want to catch the morning ferry, eat-and-run is just fine. If, however, cuisine is a feature, plan on appearing at the specified time!

Vacationers (not skiers) find breakfast a very social time. One hostess says that even when guests say they want to be on the road early, they often linger over breakfast for hours. If hosts join you, please understand when they leave the table after a while.

Is B&B like a hotel?

Not at all! It's not intended to be. You are greeted by a member of the family, an assistant, or a neighbor, or occasionally by a note. Perhaps one Connecticut host put it best: "We seem to live in an era when the human touch is becoming a lost pleasure. We will never threaten Hilton, Marriott, or Holiday Inns. How many times have you written a thank-you note to (or hugged) them?"

Depending on the size and layout of the B&B, it may not provide the privacy—or the loneliness—of a hotel. There's no elevator service and rarely is there an ice machine down the hall. Television is not an important feature. Neither is a phone in the room. Now that business travelers have discovered B&Bs, there may be a phone jack in the room. Very few hosts provide a private line.

How much do they cost?

As little as $25 for a single person. Many are in the $45–$55 range (including breakfast) for two people. Rural regions tend to be less expensive. With soaring real estate prices and the public's desire for more amenities, a few have topped the $100 mark. The season and location can affect the rate. Some hosts who have lived in the B&B for years are happy to charge less, believing that the traveler should be able to find reasonably priced accommodations. Because of all these variables the rate may or may not be indicative of facilities. A B&B is almost always less—often much less—expensive than a hotel in the same area; and for just economic comparison, breakfast should be taken into account.

Other money thoughts:

. . . To tip—or not? Not usually in a private home, but if there are helpful children in the family, they appreciate being remembered. In a B&B inn, treat staff as you would in a hotel. *Some inns, particularly those in resort areas, add gratuities to the tab.*

. . . Unless credit cards are in the B&B description, please do not expect hosts to accept them. Ask if personal checks are acceptable. Most small places prefer cash or travelers' checks. And it's a good idea to check on deposit requirements; refund policies differ. Required local and/or state taxes vary from place to place, and are seldom in the listed rates.

. . . Consider paying upon arrival rather than waiting until departure time. The good-byes can be that much smoother, and you really do feel as if you have visited friends.

How do B&Bs on this side of the Atlantic differ from those in the British Isles or other European countries?

The idea of B&B and away-you-go is not necessarily the norm in North America. Although there are B&Bs with just one room and many where you are expected to leave for the day following breakfast, guests are often invited to spend more time "at home"—by the pool or fireplace, on the hiking trails or borrowed bicycles. Even hosts are amazed at what they do when they get involved in others' lives! They worry about late arrivals. They have been known to drive someone to a job appointment or do laundry for a businessman whose schedule changed or prevail upon the local auto mechanic when the garage was closed.

Another major difference is the concept of a reservation-service, which is responsible for the enormous numbers of part-time hosts here. (Please see page xv.)

Who are the hosts?

Singles, couples, maybe three friends in business together, or families. Parents and even grandparents of grown children. Retirees. Natives and transplants. People who know how to help and when to leave you alone. People who are sensitive to the wishes of nonsmokers. Sharers all. They represent hundreds of occupations—politicians, lawyers, doctors, business people, mid-life career changers, farmers, artists, housewives, hotel executives too. A sociologist or an architect could probably make quite a study with the variety of people and their backgrounds and settings.

Who goes to B&Bs?

The endless list includes travelers who are alone or in small groups; travelers who are with or without children, with or without pets; travelers on business or in an area for professional reasons. Vacationers. College shoppers. Parents of college students and summer campers. International visitors. Conventiongoers. Honeymooners. Retirees. Relatives of hospitalized patients. Transferees. House hunters. Most are people who are looking for a touch of home. Some want to be pampered. Some are looking for a bargain. Budgets aside, most guests intentionally choose B&B—preferring the guest book to the registration desk.

Are all B&Bs "palaces"?

The Virginian who asked me that question had the idea that every place is antique-filled, magazine-picture-perfect with canopied beds. There *are* plenty of those. And there are *some* (not thousands, maybe not even hundreds) with a working fireplace in guest rooms or a hot tub. Many B&Bs are on the National Register of Historic Places. A B&B may be a collector's or decorator's dream. It may be a penthouse or surrounded by rolling acreage. Others that lack lounging space in "cozy rooms" can be counted on for a warm welcome, perhaps a porch, yard, or wood stove. It is the variety and personalized touches that make each B&B so different. This book is written so that you know whether to expect pure luxury, "just plain home" that is sparkling clean and maybe freshly decorated, fine antiques, or "Mother's attic."

Is B&B for everyone?

"What do you mean, a private home? I just want a bed!" That's exactly how some travelers have been introduced to B&B; now they opt for personalized travel everywhere. As you can see by the writeups in this book, many B&Bs are perfect getaway spots—just right for unwinding and a change of pace. However, if you seek total anonymity, B&B probably isn't for you.

One Vermont host said, "Guests who come to B&Bs screen themselves: They are outgoing, want to be sociable and learn about you and the area; are easy to please and most grateful for anything you go out of your way to do for them. They are willing to risk the unknown."

Recommendation: Tell the host if this is your first time at a B&B. When making the reservation, if privacy is a real concern, say that too. Hosts' listening skills are usually well tuned.

Among all the wonderful guests, a few hosts can recall the occasional "memorable" demanding guest; sometimes I think that it is the same person going from B&B to B&B. And I have heard of a first-timer who appeared with considerable luggage—cumbersome, indeed, on the narrow steep stairs to the third floor of the historic house.

Charm. "Tell me," said the older guest, "what's so charming about a tub on legs? I was so glad when built-ins finally became the fashion." Tastes and interpretations differ. Conclusion: *If you must have things exactly as they are in the hotel you usually go to, go to the hotel!*

Because B&Bs are private residences, can we be more casual about cancellations?

Sorry, on the contrary. Hosts plan their lives around your arrival and stay. They may pick (or buy) flowers for your room, prepare certain foods, and schedule appointments according to your reservation. Remember, too, that they may have turned away others. It may or may not be possible to fill the vacancy that a cancellation creates. As a result, many B&Bs have deposit requirements and specific cancellation policies.

Why don't some B&Bs answer the phone during normal business hours?

If they are solo or if they are without paid help, they may be doing an errand. Please remember that most hosts wear many hats—from cleaning person to desk clerk, from chef to fire tender. Some have other jobs. Some have been known to put out a "No Vacancy" sign when they need time for themselves or have visiting family. Much may depend on whether the B&B is a full-fledged business or an avocation. If you do call in the evening, heed the words of a city host: "It's our home. B&B guests know not to call late at night."

If you like people, and enjoy company and cooking, isn't that enough experience to host?

It helps. But experienced hosts have all commented on the time and work involved. Guests who ask, "Is this all you do?" would be surprised to realize that there *is* more to hosting than serving tea and meeting interesting people. Even I have fallen into the trap of multiplying a full house by the nightly rate, only to hear my husband say, "Never mind, that's 600 sheets!"

Why do all these people choose to host "strangers"?

Many of the descriptions in this book will satisfy your curiosity. Lifestyle. That's the word that crops up over and over again. B&B provides an avenue for meeting people whom the hosts wouldn't meet in any other way. Few in private homes host to make a living. Some do it to be able to buy the old place. Other hosts use it to defray expenses. A few contribute B&B fees to their favorite charity. Now that B&B is so popular, there are B&B inns that have opened as a business. (In this book, B&B inns are limited to small, owner-occupied places.)

Compared to Europe, rates seem high. Is B&B a big money maker?

If we could shape the calendar so that it had a week of Saturdays or a year of Northeast Octobers, then B&B might be considered a lucrative undertaking. Experienced hosts will tell you that business can be quite seasonal and uneven. They also quickly learn that, depending on the number of rooms they have and the occupancy rate, it helps to have another source of income. "I have to have another job to support my innkeeping habit," replied one exuberant hostess. The casual traveler does not see the long list of hidden expenses. If there are more than a couple of rooms, local ordinances can go as far as requiring a restaurant stove or other expensive equipment. One-nighters are not necessarily profitable if you consider what it takes to ready a room on a daily basis. It can take three to five years to get established. Many a restorer hangs out the welcome sign only to find that the hideaway has to be marketed.

Help! Our town fathers don't know what a B&B is.

Across the country they are learning. Bed and breakfast doesn't fit into any category on the books of most lawmakers; zoning can be an issue. More than one lawyer has used my B&B books to illustrate the concept. The most convincing argument, of course, is a B&B stay. As each community and each state defines B&B, they hear about the economic benefits and the public relations for an area. Continent-wide, many larger and historic properties are being restored and maintained, thanks to bed and breakfast.

Even when B&B is established, there are concerns: In a few communities where the idea was slow in starting, some think that too many private homes have been converted to inns. (Pockets of the country where B&B has not taken hold can't imagine having such a problem.) When cooked breakfasts were an issue at a Nantucket town meeting, one hostess who had hosted for 13 years declared that she had not yet lost a guest who had eaten her homemade muffins (baked in an impeccable kitchen).

What do you recommend to people who dream about having their own B&B?

Attend a workshop or seminar given by adult education centers, state extension departments, innkeepers, or B&B reservation services. Find some way to try hosting: Apprentice, even for a weekend, or sign up with a reservation service and host in your own home.

Every host in this book enjoys what they call "the great emotional rewards of a stimulating occupation." Some remind couples who wish to make hosting a vocation that it helps to have a strong marriage. One who encourages prospective innkeepers to "Just do it!" adds, "But be aware that you have to be more gregarious than private. You have to learn to carve time out for yourself. Hosting requires a broad range of talents (knowledge of plumbing helps), a lot of flexibility, an incredible amount of stamina, and perseverance. Did I mention you might need some capital?"

Author's note: The mail indicates that this book has a fringe benefit. From Mississippi, from Michigan and from Massachusetts too have come notes from hosts who were inspired by the profiles. And hosts report that guests stay up reading about all these wonderful people. Category: "You never know."

What do you do with all the letters you receive?

Hosts who wish to be included receive a response. Because it isn't possible for any one person to sleep in all these beds, the (thousands of) guests' letters—even the handful of complaints—are a big help.

Every host in this book has subscribed to more than the standards of cleanliness, comfort, and congeniality. There's another c: commitment. And a popular (and enthusiastic) New York host suggested that we could add "confinement" and "confusion" to the list!

Can a host or reservation service pay to be in this book?

No. All selections are made by the author. There are no application fees. And all descriptions are written by the author; no host or service proprietor can write his or her own description.

A processing fee is paid after each *selected* B&B and reservation service reviews its writeup. The fee offsets the extensive research that results in highly detailed writeups reflecting the individual spirit of each B&B.

The processing fee for an individual B&B and fully described reservation service is $100; for a reservation service host, $25. The author pays for all her stays at B&Bs.

What are some of your favorite B&Bs?

Even when you stay in hundreds, you tend to remember the hosts more than the place. It is true that each one is special in its own way. We have enjoyed rather luxurious settings and some casual places too. There's the antique dealer in Virginia who slept in the barn with her horse that was due to deliver; the hostess came in each morning to whip up a wonderful farm breakfast for us. The horticulturist, a septuagenarian, whom we could hardly keep up with as she toured us through her spectacular gardens. We have arrived on bicycles and been greeted with the offer of a car to go to dinner. There's the couple who built their own solar house. Multifaceted retirees. The history buffs who filled us in on the area and recommended back roads. The literary buffs who suggested good books. Hosts in a lovely residential section just minutes off the highway. Hosts we have laughed with. Yes, even some we have cried with too. Great chefs. People who are involved in their communities and trying to make this a better world. People whose home has been a labor of love, love sharing it with others.

Where do you see B&B going from here? Is it a fad?

The hottest trend in United States travel is here to stay! In parts of the country where B&B is just being discovered, the growth rate will be high indeed. In some areas, it seems that real estate values have slowed the number of brand new B&Bs or there are "enough" to feel friendly competition. Always there will be a turnover of hosts, but the appeal is producing some seasoned B&B owners (in business for 5–10 years) who are quite content to stay right where they are—ready to welcome you.

All together, the list of thankful guests numbers well into the millions. The place to stay can be the reason to go. It's wonderful.

B&B Reservation Services:
What They Are and How to Use Them

A reservation service is in the business of matching screened hosts and guests. Although it is considered to be part of a rapidly growing cottage industry that can be seasonal, in some areas the service is a full-time job for an individual, a couple, partners, or a small group. The service could be very small—and almost waiting to be discovered. Others have become quite professional and even computerized.

For hosts, it's a private way of going public because the host remains anonymous until the service (agency) matches host and guest. No signs are on the house or building. This unique system also allows hosts in private homes to have an irregular hosting schedule.

Listings may be in communities where there are no overnight lodging facilities, or they may provide an alternative to hotels or motels. Although most services feature private homes, others include B&B inns, small public lodging places that are usually owner-occupied with 10 or 12 guest rooms.

Beyond homes with a host in residence, some services now offer stays in unhosted homes. Other expanded services might include car rentals, sightseeing tours, and theater tickets.

Each service determines its own area. They may cover just one community, or a metropolitan area, or an entire region. Because some services network with others, in some cases you can make one call and the service will book you into its own area, into another region, or even into another country.

Write for printed information or maybe, better yet, call. The printed information is usually a brochure together with application form that asks about your needs, preferences, purpose of trip, and perhaps special interests. It may also ask about your driver's license and/or place of employment. If you choose to write, please include a self-addressed, stamped business-sized envelope.

A directory, when published by a service, rarely has addresses and phone numbers of hosts. The directory may have a few sample listings on a single sheet or complete listings in a booklet or occasionally in a spiral-bound book. Directory prices are usually in the $2–$5 range. You can use a service and its judgment without obtaining the directory.

A call can save a tremendous amount of time even if you reach an answering service or machine. (Return long-distance calls are usually made collect.) When you speak to the service, you can get a sense of the kind of personalized service offered while conveying your thoughts about price range, location, amenities, ambiance, and just how much hospitality you would like. Before placing the call think about bed and bath arrangements, parking, smoking, pets, children, air conditioning—whatever is important to you. And if you tell the service a little about yourself, it could help toward making a more appropriate match.

Advance notice is preferred and, with many services, required. If you can provide enough information and references, and if a host is available that very night or "tomorrow," some services will flex and accommodate you on the spot.

Length-of-stay requirements vary. One night may be fine. If so, there may be a one-night surcharge. Two nights may be the minimum. Short-term (interim) lodging for weeks or months may also be available.

Rates are usually much less than at area hotels and motels. Depending on the area, rates may average $50–$60 a night for two—including breakfast. The range may cover everything from "budget" to "luxury"—from homes that are "clean, neat, and reasonably priced" to antique-filled mansions that are more expensive. *Deposits are usually required.* Refund policies differ; inquire.

Fee arrangements vary. Autonomy reigns. Many services include their commission in the quoted nightly rate—period. For public inns (in contrast to private homes with one-three rooms), the quoted rate may be the same as what the inn charges or it could be a total of the inn's rate plus a booking fee. Some services have a standard booking fee, perhaps $5, $10, or $15, for any reservation. A few services now have a membership fee, perhaps $25, that entitles you to book through the service for a year.

Guests receive name and address of host only after being booked. Only a handful of services distribute printed lists of hosts' names, addresses, and telephone numbers to allow you to book your own B&B.

Generally, reservation service hosts are screened and homes are inspected. Most services are concerned with quality and high standards. Prospective guests' questions about screening procedures should be welcomed. And if a service requests an evaluation from you as guest, give it! (Even if they don't ask you, think about giving one.) Guests' comments can be helpful to everyone. The (predominantly) complimentary ones are often treasured by hosts.

A reservation service acts as a clearinghouse and frequently provides an opportunity to stay at a B&B that would not be available any other way.

BED AND BREAKFAST
IN MID-ATLANTIC STATES

KEY

Recipes shared, often for house specialties.

Inquiries welcomed about restoration and/or decorating. Symbol indicates that host is willing to share experiences with guests. Tips range from a before-and-after album to rebuilding advice, from furniture refinishing to curtain making. Expertise of hosts ranges from learn-by-doing to professional.

How-to B&B workshop, seminar, or apprentice program offered.

HANDICAPPED ACCESSIBILITY: "Bed and bath" information with each description includes the floor of the rooms and if there are facilities for handicapped persons.

SMOKING: "Restrictions" indicates if smoking is permitted as well as specific rooms where it is allowed. In addition, any smokers-in-residence are accounted for under "In residence."

CHILDREN AND PETS: Check "Restrictions" with each B&B description and "In residence" will tell you about any pets in the B&B.

Delaware

1. Camden, Jonathan Wallace House, 5
2. Dover, The Noble Guest House B&B, 6
3. Laurel, Spring Garden Bed & Breakfast Inn, 7
4. Milford, The Towers B&B, 8
5. Rehoboth Beach, Tembo Guest House, 9
6. Wilmington, Small Wonder Bed & Breakfast, 10

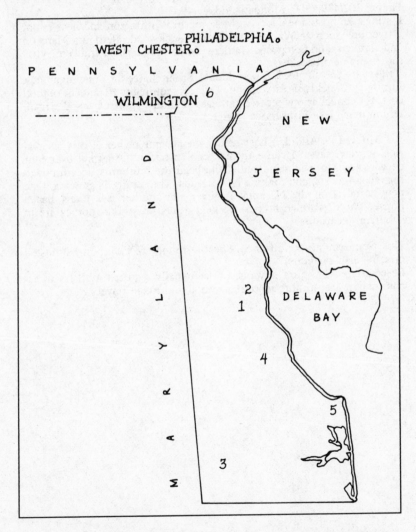

The numbers of this map indicate the locations of B&Bs described in detail in this chapter.

Delaware Reservation Service

Bed and Breakfast of Delaware

Box 177, 3650 Silverside Road, Wilmington, DE 19810
Phone: 302/479-9500. Monday–Friday 9–9.
Listings: 25 hosted residences. Most are in Wilmington and near major attractions such as Winterthur, Hagley, Rockwood, Nemours Mansion and Gardens, and Longwood Gardens. Some in Maryland and Pennsylvania. Some near beaches.
Rates: $45–$50 single. $55–$85 double. $5 surcharge for a one-night stay. Family and weekly rates available. Deposit required is 20 percent of total cost. For cancellations received at least 72 hours before expected arrival, refund made less $10 service charge.

Mildred D. Alford, a host before she became owner of this reservation service, says, "I came to our small wonder (Delaware) over four decades ago. I love being near all of our beautiful museums, accommodating repeat guests, and making new friends. The service is growing. One new home is on the National Register and another is a lovely beach house. The downtown homes are near a bus line; other homes are in suburban locations."

Plus: Some are air conditioned. Short-term (one to two months) hosted housing also available.
Reservations: 24 hours' advance notice usually required. Will try to accommodate last-minute requests. Available through travel agents.

Jonathan Wallace House

7 and 9 South Main Street, Camden, DE 19934
Phone: 302/697-2921
Location: In historic district of town, one-half mile from U.S. Route 13. Three miles south of Dover, four west of U.S. Air Force Base. Near Bombay Hook Wildlife Refuge, Amish and Mennonite farms, Dickinson Plantation.
Hosts: Sally and Chester Hollingsworth
Open: Year round. Advance reservations appreciated.
Rates: $45 single. $55 double.

> From New York: "They have taken great care and pride in selecting the furnishings and antiques. An afternoon could be well spent just 'discovering' in the house ... Fresh flowers everywhere, rich potpourri scents, carefully chosen linens, and personal amenities.... And then there's the food! ... Sally and Chet, the true gems of this B&B, share the gift of knowing when to care, and when to be discreet.... We were also treated to the Hollingsworths' knowledge of the area."

Business travelers, honeymooners, and Colonial Williamsburg craftspeople are among the guests who are delighted that the hosts have opened their restored 1785 brick three-story house as a B&B. Chet, a major in the U.S. Air Force Reserves, is personnel director at the Dover Air Force Base. Sally has many years of antiques shop experience. Inspired by four years of living in England, they are responsible for the restoration and all the stenciling, including a very unusual house pattern that decorates the country kitchen.

In residence: Merlin, an 11-year-old blue roan English cocker spaniel. Windsor, a one-year-old old red English cocker spaniel. A cat named Z.
Restrictions: Infants and children over 12 welcome. Smoking in public rooms only.
Bed and bath: Three second-floor air-conditioned rooms, each with queen bed. One with working fireplace, private full bath, dressing room. Front room with canopied bed and back room with screened porch share a tub bath and sitting room with TV (plus a fireplaced TV room adjacent to master suite).
Breakfast: Flexible hours on weekdays. Usually 8–10 weekends. Fruit, juices, eggs prepared to order, bacon, sausage, cereal. Homemade coffee cakes, rolls, breads. Freshly ground coffee, breakfast or herbal tea. Prepared by Sally, dubbed "Julia Child" by one guest. Served in dining room on white linen. Option of continental served in guest's room.

Plus: Beverages. Thick all-cotton towels. Turn-down service. Tour of house and area. Separate guest entrance. Sometimes, option of dinner ($5–$15). Kitchen and laundry privileges. Historic Camden walking tour information.

The Noble Guest House B&B

33 South Bradford Street, Dover, DE 19901
Phone: 302/674-4084
Location: In historic downtown Dover. On a quiet tree-lined street just off Route 13. Within walking distance of historic buildings, restaurants, shops. Forty miles south of Wilmington and north of Rehoboth Beach.
Hosts: Lisa and Michael Noble
Open: Year round. Two-night minimum for Dover Downs' Delaware 500 weekends (one in June and one in September).
Rates: $45 per room. $10 per child with adult.

"Often I take guests to auctions and flea markets. Sometimes we tour other B&Bs too. Hosting is even more fun than I expected," says Lisa, a lover of old houses who has stenciled walls, refinished furniture, and collected Delaware memorabilia. Each room is different—with lace gloves on a bureau in one, music boxes on a night stand in another.

Since 1986, the three-story Victorian duplex has been home to these two area natives—Lisa, a former police dispatcher, and Mike, a police officer. After they both worked on the house, which had been restored a little by each of the several previous owners, Lisa decided to combine all her interests in a new career. Mike, too, enjoys the lifestyle that brings antiquers, bird-watchers (at nearby Bombay Hook Refuge), and cyclists (from B&B to B&B). "And just about everyone asks for the best place to eat."

In residence: "Ollie is a shy, red mini-dachshund; Emma, an outgoing, black mini-dachshund."
Restrictions: Children 12 and over welcome. Smoking allowed outside. Please inquire about guests' pets.
Bed and bath: Three air-conditioned rooms share a second-floor full bath and a first-floor shower bath. Two second-floor double-bedded rooms; room with two twin beds on third.
Breakfast: "So pretty that I feel I should look instead of eat," said one guest. Served at hour chosen by guests. Homemade muffins (specialty is chocolate chip) and breads. Omelets, pancakes, sausage, or scrapple. Juices and fruit. Special diets accommodated.
Plus: Welcoming beverage and snack. Fireplaced front parlor. Fresh flowers. Mints. Kitchen and laundry facilities. Barbecue, patio table and chairs. Bikes available.

Spring Garden Bed & Breakfast Inn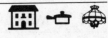

Route 1, Box 283A, Laurel, DE 19956
Phone: 302/875-7015
Location: Hidden from road by pine trees. Bordered by forest, stream, nature trails, fields. Minutes from Route 13. Within walking or biking distance of "our friendly unspoiled rural town" on the National Register of Historic Places. Near antiquing. Four miles to state park; 30 minutes to Atlantic beaches and Chesapeake Bay.
Host: Gwen North
Open: Year round. Reservations preferred.
Rates: Double $50 shared bath, $60 private bath. Suite $70. $12 cot. $5 one-night surcharge. Discounts for stays of five or more days.

"A step back in time" in the land of crabbing and clamming, swimming, fishing and boating. It's a National Register home consisting of a 1786 brick building and an 1800s clapboard Victorian addition. Most of the major restoration was done by Gwen's parents when they bought the house 30 years ago. She has completed the restoration, keeping all the 18th-century furnishings—and adding charming touches. The original wainscoting, dentil ceiling moldings, and latch-style locks, even heart pine paneling are still in place.

Gwen, a counselor, has also been associated with art galleries in New York and Denver. A hit in Philadelphia's Bloomingdale's Meet-The-Hosts program and in Manhattan's Bloomingdale's B&B photo essay (both based on this book), she greets guests with wine and cheese, answers lots of questions about the house, and heads a highly successful group that arranges inn-to-inn biking tours on the Eastern Shore of Delaware and Maryland.

In residence: The hostess smokes. One dog, "Boo Too, a mixed breed, enthusiastic welcomer, bilingual (English and Spanish)."
Restrictions: Children over eight are welcome. Sorry, no guests' pets. Smoking allowed in designated areas unless objected to by other guests.
Bed and bath: Five rooms. A handicapped-accessible suite, next to garden, with double four-poster bed, private shower bath, TV, sitting room. Twin-bedded room and three double-bedded rooms (one with canopy bed and sitting area, one with working fireplace) share two baths. Cot available.
Breakfast: 8–9:30. Juice, seasonal fruits, cereals, yogurt, home-baked muffins, biscuits or buns, Scotch eggs; coffee, tea, or milk. Served in country kitchen with wood stove or on porch overlooking garden. Gwen usually joins guests.
Plus: Bedroom air conditioners. Fresh flowers. Fruit bowls. Tour of house. TV. Library. Bicycles ($10 a day), badminton, croquet, horseshoes. Picnic lunches ($5 per person) by request. Kitchen and laundry privileges (extra charge). Will meet guests at Salisbury airport (15 miles south). Chartered crab or cruise boats (into Chesapeake). Suggestions for "the best oysters" and a place where wild ponies roam free.

The Towers B&B

101 Northwest Front Street, Milford, DE 19963
Phone: 302/422-3814
Location: In an historic river town, minutes from the Atlantic Ocean and beach resorts, Delaware and Rehoboth bays, and River Walk on the banks of the Mispillion River.
Host: Michael E. Real
Open: Year round. Advance reservations preferred. Two-night minimum May–September; three nights on holiday weekends.
Rates: $85 per room. MC, VISA.

Hardly just another mansion, this Victorian, often called "the most unique dwelling in Delaware," is a photographer's delight. The care taken with the outside painting of the intricate architectural detail (in several shades of mauve and plum) was all part of a three-year challenge, well met by the interior decorator/antiques dealer (with shop three doors from the B&B)/former Washington, D.C. floral designer. "We were fussy!" says Michael when talking about his fourth restoration, which was built in 1783 and remodeled in 1891 in "Steamboat Gothic" style. Now it is fully air conditioned, has six working fireplaces, and is filled with his French Second Empire collection and other formal European antiques. One room with a 7-foot window bench overlooking the rose garden also has a 16-foot-ceilinged bath with skylight. There's a walnut-paneled stairway, cherry woodwork in the front parlor and dining room, and a coffered sycamore ceiling in the music room, which is complete with a grand piano. A gazebo, fountain, and swimming pool are on the grounds, a yard with a parklike setting.

Restrictions: Children 12 and over welcome. Smoking allowed in music room and one parlor. No pets.
Foreign language spoken: Spanish.
Bed and bath: Five second-floor double-bedded and air-conditioned rooms. A private full first-floor bath (reached via a spiral staircase) for one room with private balcony. Four rooms (two with working fireplaces) share two full baths with marble and pedestal sinks, footed tubs with showers.
Breakfast: Usually 8–10. Special requests or eggs Benedict, Spanish omelet, homemade breads with jams, French toast, eggs cooked to order, souffles or crepes. On Sunday, brunch with mimosas, quiches, cakes. Served in dining room with silver, crystal, and china; in cathedral-ceilinged kitchen; or in the gazebo. Michael joins guests.
Plus: Sherry is served in the wicker-furnished courtyard or in the music room. Fresh flowers in all rooms. Tour of house. Bedroom ceiling fans. Kitchen and laundry facilities. Murder mystery weekend. Biking inn-to-inn arrangements. Available for special occasions.

Tembo Guest House

100 Laurel Street, Rehoboth Beach, DE 19971
Phone: 302/227-3360
Location: In residential area, one block from beach and five streets south of Rehoboth Avenue in Rehoboth Heights.
Hosts: Don and Gerry Cooper
Open: Year round. Advance reservations required. Two-night minimum May 15–September 30 weekends; three nights on Memorial Day, Fourth of July, and Labor Day weekends.
Rates: Double occupancy. $80 private bath. $60 first-floor double. $55 second-floor double or twins. $10 rollaway. $5 air mattress.

From Pennsylvania: "A highlight for our family. . . . Ideal hosts, immaculate accommodations, congenial atmosphere. . . . (Thankfully) devoid of glitz. . . . We meet other returnees and new faces, low-key people who enjoy the simple pleasures of family and beach. . . . The Coopers share many helpful tips from restaurants to locations for crabbing."

The two-story white frame beach cottage, named after Gerry's elephant collection, has been home to the Coopers since they moved from West Chester, Pennsylvania 14 years ago. (Donald was a life insurance consultant and financial advisor and Gerry an executive secretary.) They made—and continue to make—many renovations. The house is furnished with comfortable pieces, hand-braided rugs, and paintings by Delaware artists. The Coopers "love this people-oriented business."

In residence: During college vacations, Christian and Leslie. "Patches is our elderly loving cat. Amos is a fearless and entertaining box turtle who delights children of all ages."
Restrictions: No smoking inside. Pets allowed November–February only. Children should be at least six.
Foreign language spoken: Christian speaks fluent French.
Bed and bath: Six rooms. Two first-floor rooms. One with private shower bath, king bed. One with double bed, shared hall bath. Four second-floor carpeted rooms (each with four windows)—with two twins, king, or double bed—share a second-floor half bath and first-floor full bath. Rollaway available.
Breakfast: 8–11. Juice, fruit, Danish, scones, homemade muffins, cereals, beverage. Buffet style in country kitchen, on porch, or in fireplaced living room.
Plus: No TV. Bedroom air conditioners. Ironed bed linens. Electric mattress pads. Mints. Fruit. Cookies. Hot pot for help-yourself beverages. Kitchen and laundry privileges. Picnic table. Enclosed outside shower and dressing area. Two beach chairs per room. Pickup service from Salisbury, Maryland, airport and Rehoboth Beach bus.

Small Wonder Bed & Breakfast

213 West Crest Road, P.O. Box 25254, Wilmington, DE 19899
Phone: 302/764-0789
Location: In a suburban neighborhood, five minutes north of downtown Wilmington, 27 miles south of center city Philadelphia. Minutes to Brandywine Valley museums, colleges, and industry.
Hosts: Dot and Art Brill
Open: Year round. Advance reservations preferred.
Rates: $45 single, $55 double, $75 triple. Private bath $5 extra. $5 one-night surcharge. Weekly rates available. AMEX, 4 percent surcharge. MC, VISA, 8 percent surcharge.

Although most guests come for the many world-famous area attractions, such as Longwood Gardens and Winterthur, business travelers, too, express appreciation for the pluses at this B&B.

Larger than it looks—hence the name—from the outside, the beautifully maintained property has been home to Dot, a music teacher and organist, and Art, a counselor and psychologist, for 27 years. The house was built in 1946 with dormered bedrooms. Surrounding it are Art's award-winning grounds, which are filled with blossoms from 1,000 annuals (germinated here under lights) as well as perennials. In the winter, the mature hedges and unusual shrubs are decorated for the holidays.

Restrictions: Children should be at least nine. No pets allowed. Smoking permitted outside only.
Foreign languages spoken: None, but the Brills still hear from the non-English-speaking, German guest with whom they "had a great time." She is learning English and planning a return visit.
Bed and bath: Maximum of two guest rooms at a time. Vary in size from cozy to large. Double, twin, or king beds. Shared or private full bath. Cot available.
Breakfast: 7–9:30. Guest's choice. Perhaps cereal, quiche, French toast, pancakes or waffles. Fruit, local scrapple, meat, juice, beverage, pastry. Special diets accommodated. In formal dining room with china, silver, and crystal, or on pool deck "if the dew is gone."
Plus: Central air conditioning. In-ground pool (five feet deep) May–September. Robes and extra-large towels for year-round outdoor hot tub. Beverages. Fireplaced living room, den, recreation and music rooms, library, piano, organ, VCR, shuffleboard. Laundry. Dinner and concierge services by prior arrangement. They'll even set your alarm clock for you.

From Massachusetts: "A full breakfast was waiting at an early hour. Although I had but ten minutes to enjoy it, that hot tub at the end of the day was absolutely marvelous. The Brills, too, are wonderful."

DISTRICT OF COLUMBIA

1. Capitol Hill
      The Bed & Breakfast League/Sweet Dreams & Toast Host #5, 14
      Bed 'n' Breakfast Ltd. Host #145, 14
2. Dupont Circle
      The Bed & Breakfast League/Sweet Dreams & Toast Host #2, 15
      Bed 'n' Breakfast Ltd. Host #135D, 16
3. Logan Circle
      Bed 'n' Breakfast Ltd. Host #100, 17
4. Northwest
      Kalorama Guest House at Woodley Park, 18

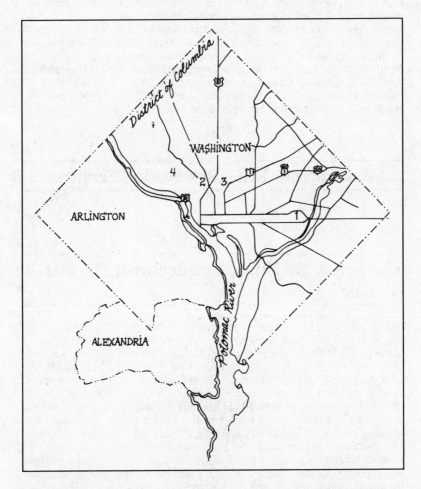

The numbers of this map indicate the locations of B&Bs described in detail in this chapter.

Washington, D.C.

Where do you want to be?

The following descriptions of Washington's B&B locations are provided by Bed 'n' Breakfast Ltd, a reservation service described on page 13:

Dupont Circle: Located on Connecticut Avenue in the hub of activities. Dupont Circle runs a close second to Georgetown as the city's most popular in-town residential area.

Georgetown: Considered Washington's most pretigious residential and tourist area. Georgetown is a blend of richly restored Georgian and colonial town houses with smart boutiques and restaurants.

Logan Circle: Once home to the gentry, Logan Circle fell into neglect during the 1950s; but the renovation of the Victorian town houses is now in full swing, and a renaissance is (well) under way.

Northwest: Lovely homes on broad lawns away from the hustle-bustle of downtown, but still close in.

Nearby suburbs: Both Virginia and Maryland offer charming accommodations with access to good transportation.

Washington, D.C., Reservation Services

The Bed & Breakfast League/Sweet Dreams & Toast

P.O. Box 9490, Washington, DC 20016

Phone: 202/363-7767. Monday–Thursday 9–5; Friday 9–1. Closed the last two weeks of July, December 19–January 7, and all federal holidays.

Listings: 70. Mostly hosted private residences. Ten unhosted apartments. Most are in Washington, D.C., but some are in Chevy Chase and Rockville, Maryland, and in Arlington and Alexandria, Virginia. Many are in historic districts; all are within walking distance of public transportation. All are air conditioned. Many have private baths. All serve at least a continental breakfast. Short-term (over three weeks) hosted and unhosted housing available. Sample list available if you send a business-size, self-addressed stamped envelope. (SASE required.)

Rates: $30–$55 single, $45–$65 double. $10 booking fee per reservation. $25 deposit per room. Deposit is not refundable; balance paid is refunded if cancellation is telephoned to the office more than seven days in advance of arrival; if later, rate for one night charged. MC, VISA, AMEX; 5 percent service charge.

Founded in 1976 and now directed by Millie Groobey, this is one of the oldest B&B reservation services in the country. The philosophy behind host selection is location (must be in a safe and convenient area, within walking distance of public transportation); all hosts are gracious and welcoming to travelers. (It is true! I have used the service several times.)

Reservations: Two-day minimum stay. At least 24 hours' notice required; two weeks preferred. Also available through travel agents.

Bed 'n' Breakfast Ltd. of Washington, D.C.

P.O. Box 12011, Washington, DC 20005
Phone: 202/328-3510. Monday–Friday 10–5, Saturday 10–1.
Listings: 65. Mostly hosted private residences. Some inns. Several unhosted apartments available for long stays (up to several months). Most are located in Washington, D.C., but some are in Bethesda, Rockville, Gaithersburg, and Beltsville, Maryland; and in Old Town Alexandria and Crystal City, Virginia. There are some with swimming pools. Several are large Victorians. Many are convenient to public transportation. All are air conditioned. Free brochure available.
Rates: $35–$80 single, $45–$90 double. $5 surcharge for a one-night stay. Seasonal weekly rates. Apartments recommended for families; $10 for each additional person. $40 deposit required; balance due two weeks prior to stay. If cancellation is received with more than 72 hours' notice, there is a $15 charge; less than 72 hours' notice, one-night charge. AMEX, MC, VISA.

Jackie Reed has considerable B&B experience, both as a reservation service owner and as a host. She and her staff match travelers with hosts whose accommodations range from modest to luxurious. This is a well-established and well-run service.

Reservations: Two weeks' advance notice requested. Last-minute reservations based on availability. Two-day minimum on holidays and peak season. Available through travel agents.

Some Virginia B&Bs in Arlington (page 308) and Alexandria (page 305) are very close to rapid transportation into Washington.

The Bed & Breakfast League/Sweet Dreams & Toast Host #5

Washington, DC

Location: Five-minute walk to the Capitol, the Supreme Court, House and Senate buildings, Library of Congress. Ten minutes to Smithsonian museums. One and a half blocks from subway. Minutes to restaurants, shops, and tennis courts.

Reservations: Year round through The Bed & Breakfast League/ Sweet Dreams & Toast, page 12. Two-day minimum stay.

Rates: $45 single. $55 double.

Restored by many, including a congressman and his wife in 1961, this gracious Victorian Federal, built in 1855, has 11-foot ceilings and interesting architectural details. Its location is superb for both business travelers and sightseers.

The host, an international economist, and his wife, a real estate agent, have lived in Spain and traveled B&B in England. Among their favorite suggestions: a free tour of the State Department diplomatic reception rooms and the Marjorie Post House (advance booking required; $7 per person).

Restrictions: Well-behaved children only. Sorry, no pets or smoking. No food in bedrooms, please. No alcoholic beverages.

Foreign languages spoken: Spanish, French, and Portuguese.

Bed and bath: In the oldest part of the house, two third-floor queen-bedded rooms share one full bath.

Breakfast: 7:30–8:30. Bran muffins, bacon and eggs, cereal, croissants, cappucino. Served in the spacious kitchen, overlooking garden.

Plus: Central air conditioning. Bedroom ceiling fans. Tea. Tour of house.

Bed 'n' Breakfast Ltd. Host #145

Washington, DC

Location: A tree-lined street of historic homes on Capitol Hill. Ten blocks east of the Capitol. One-half block from bus. Five-minute walk to subway.

Reservations: Year round through Bed 'n' Breakfast Ltd., page 13.

Rates: $50 single. $60 double. $25 twin rollaway. One-bedroom apartment, $55 single, $65 double, $10 third person. $5 surcharge for one-night stay.

Whenever this hostess entertains, B&B guests—often from all over the world—are invited. Two, a saleswoman from Milwaukee and a forester from Oregon, were married a year after they met here!

Only owners, including the contractor who built the elegant house in 1891, have lived here. The hostess is responsible for decorating the 13-foot-ceilinged rooms with period furniture and artworks. Since "growing up in Montana and living in all major areas of the country including Alaska," she has restored other properties in Washington, has become a management consultant, and also has started a catering business.

In residence: Two cats, "super intelligent" Merlin and Suki, age 19.
Restrictions: No guests' pets. No food in guest rooms. No parking.
Bed and bath: Four rooms share one half bath and two full baths. King, double, or twin beds. Rollaway available. Plus one-bedroom apartment with a double bed and a sofa bed.
Breakfast: 7:30–9:30. Fresh fruit, juice, milk, hot or cold cereal. Muffins, croissants, scones or bagels. Gourmet coffees and teas (regular or decaf). Served in formal chandeliered dining room with silver, crystal, and china; on patio in good weather.
Plus: Central air conditioning. Bedroom fans. Library with several thousand volumes and current periodicals. Tour of house. Beverages.

The Bed & Breakast League/Sweet Dreams & Toast Host #2

Washington, DC
Location: In a residential neighborhood of turn-of-the-century Victorian town houses. Between Dupont Circle and Adams Morgan. Two miles north of the White House. Near public transportation, convention centers, and hotels.
Reservations: Year round through The Bed & Breakfast League/ Sweet Dreams & Toast, page 12.
Rates: $50–$55 single. $60–$65 double.

"We moved from Oklahoma four years ago. . . . After reading one too many stories about people who left anonymous unfulfilling jobs to open an inn, we decided to host *now*! . . . . Our restoration—of an unusual house that has the Victorian bay windows in back, thus catching the light and sun, and a Mediterranean-style front—was a family effort. When we grew tired of stripping paint, we would hunt for antiques. Our own travels have taken us to B&Bs from New Orleans to England. Now we reap the abundant rewards of sharing with others."

The hostess owns a shop, located in Washington's remodeled (and heralded) Union Station, which features folk art of several Latin American countries. Her husband is a television executive. Their appreciation for their "old and fascinating area" is expressed in their restaurant recommendations: "A combination cafe/bookstore with the most interesting titles, great music (live on weekends) and marvelous desserts; and a small shirtsleeve-style neighborhood restaurant with refreshingly good South American dishes prepared by its Salvadorean owners at incredible prices."

In residence: "Our nineteen-year-old daughter who helped with the house renovation." One affectionate Burmese cat, Pasha, "which loosely translates to 'Head Cat' in Turkish."
Restrictions: Well-behaved children over 12 are welcome. No guests' pets. Nonsmokers please.
Bed and bath: Six rooms, some with bay window, fireplace, English country decor. Four second-floor queen-bedded rooms share two baths—one modern full bath and one with a claw-footed tub, hand-held shower, bath salts, bubble bath, and a decanter of sherry "for a relaxing afternoon soak." Two third-floor rooms, one with a queen bed and one with two twin beds, share a full bath.
Breakfast: Usually 7:30–9. Fresh fruit, homemade muffins, eggs—scrambled, baked, or souffled—freshly ground coffee. Maybe French toast with fresh berries or pancakes with cinnamoned and brandied bananas. In formal dining room with fresh flowers and classical music.
Plus: Central air conditioning. Bedroom ceiling fans. Tea, soft drinks, or sherry. Parking ($6) in nearby hotel garage. Yard. Deck.

Bed 'n' Breakfast Ltd. Host #135 D

Washington, DC
Location: Several blocks north of the White House. Midway between the Capitol and Washington Cathedral. Close to the Metro, shopping, art galleries, and fine restaurants.
Reservations: Available year round, except two weeks at Christmas, through Bed 'n' Breakfast Ltd., page 13.
Rates: $60/$70 single with shared/private bath. $75/$85 double with shared/private bath. $5 surcharge for a one-night stay.

All guests rave about this B&B hosted by a consultant with the navy and a bank office technology coordinator. Once used by a real estate firm as part of an advertising campaign, the exterior of the Victorian house resembles a castle with its stone facade and circular tower. Until the hosts moved here six years ago, the house had been in the same family since it was built in 1895. The woodwork and many fireplaces are original. For their efforts in restoration, the new owners acted as their own contractors and are willing to share what they learned from working with the National Historic Preservation agency. They have also assembled an interesting before-and-after photo album.

In residence: One host smokes but is trying to quit.
Restrictions: Sorry, no children or guests' pets.
Bed and bath: Two second-floor rooms with private baths; one with queen bed and one with twin beds. Two third-floor double-bedded rooms share a full bath.

Breakfast: Coffee from 6 a.m. Breakfast 7–9:30 weekdays, 8–10:30 weekends and holidays. Juices, coffees, cereals, and croissants, muffins, or pastry. Served in the kitchen or the dining room.
Plus: Central air conditioning. Tea available in late afternoon or evening. Suggestions include the hosts' favorite restaurant and art gallery. Limited parking ($7.50 per day).

Guests wrote: "A beautiful home. Exceptional accommodations and a very friendly environment."

Bed 'n' Breakfast Ltd. Host #100

Washington, DC
Location: About 10 blocks northeast of the White House, 14 blocks north of the Smithsonian's American history building. One block from bus stop. Seven blocks from subway.
Reservations: Available year round through Bed 'n' Breakfast Ltd., page 13.
Rates: $50–$65 single, $60–$75 double. $5 crib. $5 surcharge for a one-night stay.

Twice on a Logan Circle House Tour, this restored 18-room Victorian town house has extensive oak woodwork that was stripped of its paint by the hostess and repaired and refinished by the host. Furnished with many antiques, the house has been a wonderful setting for several weddings and large local theater group cast parties.

The host, a lawyer who is now a real estate developer, enjoys sailing and woodworking and is an amateur magician. The hostess is very involved with the bed and breakfast movement in Washington.

In residence: Host occasionally smokes a cigar.
Restrictions: No guests' pets.
Foreign languages spoken: French. A Spanish-speaking maid is here during the day.
Bed and bath: Five rooms share three baths. Second-floor room with queen canopied bed, fireplace. On third floor, two double-bedded rooms; one with queen bed and queen sleep sofa, fireplace; one with a double and a twin bed. Crib available.
Breakfast: At 8 on weekdays, 9 on weekends. Juice, coffee or tea, and a choice of two items—muffins, croissants, raisin toast, bagels. Served in dining room. Hostess usually joins guests.
Plus: Central air conditioning. Color TV in all rooms. Player piano. Use of latticed porch and garden in summer. Limited parking ($3 per day, if available) must be arranged in advance.

Kalorama Guest House at Woodley Park

2700 Cathedral Avenue, NW, Washington, DC 20008
Phone: 202/328-0860
Location: Residential. Downtown in embassy district. A few blocks from the National Zoo and Woodley Park Metro Station. One block off Connecticut Avenue at the corner of Cathedral and 27th Street.
Host: Richard L. Fenstemaker
Open: Year round. Two-night minimum on most weekends March–June, September, and October.
Rates: $40–$60 single with shared bath, $45–$65 double with shared bath. $50–$80 single with private bath, $55–$85 double with private bath. Suite $75 single, $10 each additional person. MC, VISA, AMEX.

Personalized hospitality (and a noncorporate life) was the main attraction of B&B for Richard, a former assistant manager of a 500-room Sheraton Hotel. Guests often comment on the relaxing and warm environment filled with period furnishings and brass beds, Oriental rugs, artwork, and live potted palms. Refinished pedal sewing machines are used as desks. Many rooms have original mantels.

"The area was developed in 1912 for government workers' single-family homes. As a corner house, my house, one of the largest, was valued at $12,000 when the others cost $9,000. It was a rooming house when I took it over and put a lot of myself into it. Among the many many wonderful guests—the Philadelphia String Quartet, who, just after returning from a tour of India, rehearsed for their Dumbarton Oaks concerts in my living room!"

In residence: Freckles, "a friendly cocker spaniel whom guests love."
Restrictions: Sorry, no guests' pets.
Bed and bath: Eleven rooms. Seven with private baths. "Each room is different in size and shape, although the furnishings are consistently antique." One two-room suite has a double bed and a sofa bed. Other rooms have double, twins, or queen beds.
Breakfast: 7:30–10:30 weekdays. 8–11 weekends. Freshly baked croissants (delivered daily by a local baker), English muffins, toast, coffee, tea, butter and jam. In the lower-level breakfast room or on small porch. Richard joins guests.
Plus: Sherry (5–9 p.m.) by the fireplace. Air conditioning in bedrooms and parlor. Coffee is on throughout the day. Candy and flowers in each room. Thick towels. Laundry facilities. Parking ($4 per night). Free use of phone for local calls. Suggestions for favorite restaurants and relatively unknown walking tours of historic buildings.

Maryland

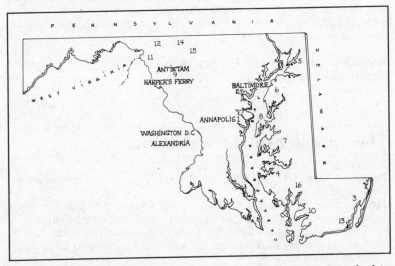

The numbers of this map indicate the locations of B&Bs described in detail in this chapter.

Amanda's Bed & Breakfast Reservation Service

1428 Park Avenue, Baltimore, MD 21217
Phone: 301/225-0001. Monday–Friday 8:30–5:30. Answering machine at all other times.
Listings: Private homes, small inns, and yachts located throughout Maryland. On the Chesapeake Bay, in the northeast corner of the state, there's an antiques-furnished old mill. In downtown Baltimore, there's an air-conditioned turn-of-the-century town house filled with art treasures from here and abroad. Other Baltimore B&Bs are in the Inner Harbor and Fell's Point, and beyond in Towson and Lutherville. Some are on the Eastern Shore of Maryland, Virginia, and Delaware. A few are in Washington, D.C.; Arlington and Mount Jackson, Virginia; Churchtown, Gettysburg, and Loganville, Pennsylvania; Summit Point and Greenbrier, West Virginia.
Rates: $40–$60 singles, $45–$100 doubles. One night's deposit required. Some hosts require a minimum stay of two nights. Weekly rates available. Cancellations with one week's notice receive refund less $25 service charge. AMEX, MC, VISA; 5 percent surcharge.

Betsy Grater is an experienced host as well as reservation service owner. Her listings, visited annually, vary in size, style, and location; some feature fireplaces, pools, and/or Jacuzzis. All are hosted by "wonderful and helpful people" who live near public transportation. Most have air conditioning and private baths.

Reservations: Minimum of 2–3 days' advance notice required. Available through travel agents.

The Traveller In Maryland, Inc.

P.O. Box 2277, Annapolis, MD 21404
Phone: 301/269-6232 (261-2233, local from D.C. metro area). Monday–Thursday 9–5, Friday 9–1.
Listings: Over 150. Mostly hosted private residences plus some inns and unhosted private homes. Located primarily in Annapolis, Baltimore, on the Eastern Shore, and in Civil War battlefield areas. Other communities represented include Beaver Creek, Taneytown, Uniontown, Lutherville, Havre de Grace.
Rates: $50–$70 single, $60–$80 double. Some higher. Deposit of one night's stay plus $5 handling fee per location. If cancellation is received at

least 10 days before arrival date, deposit less $15 refunded. Inquire about bad weather/emergency contingency. AMEX, MC, VISA.

The well-established (seven-year-old) service, led by Cecily Sharp-Whitehill, Greg Page, and Rob Zuchel, offers accommodations that vary from "the practical and central to the historic and pastoral." Hosts are "kind, concerned, well-travelled and locally knowledgable."

Reservations: At least 24 hours' advance notice required. Some hosts require a minimum stay of two nights.
Plus: Entire itineraries can be arranged with B&B reservations. Short-term (a week or more) hosted and unhosted housing available. Membership (optional for reservations) in Traveller Society is a one-time fee of $10; benefits include Maryland travel information (guidebook and maps), national listing of B&B services, special mailings.

KEY

Recipes shared, often for house specialties.

Inquiries welcomed about restoration and/or decorating. Symbol indicates that host is willing to share experiences with guests. Tips range from a before-and-after album to rebuilding advice, from furniture refinishing to curtain making. Expertise of hosts ranges from learn-by-doing to professional.

How-to B&B workshop, seminar, or apprentice program offered.

Dean Street Accommodations

Annapolis, MD
Location: In the historic district. Within walking distance of shops and city dock area. Shuttle bus available to all Annapolitan areas.
Reservations: Available year round through The Traveller In Maryland, page 20. Two-night minimum stay.
Rates: $65 single, $70 double. $15 per futon.

"It's almost like taking a trip around the world," say some guests about this lovely 80-year-old detached town house, which was restored and modernized in the early 1970s. The arts-oriented hosts are particularly knowledgeable about preservation, restoration, and architecture. In addition to helping with the "must-sees," they have some favorite places that they prefer to keep as hidden secrets for the reader of this book, but which they will gladly share with guests. Their off-street parking and swimming pool, too, are special bonuses in this charming part of the city.

Restrictions: Sorry, no guests' pets. No smoking in bedrooms.
Bed and bath: Two second-floor rooms share a full bath. One with two twin beds and TV; a smaller room has bunk beds. Two futons available.
Breakfast: At guest's request; can accommodate early risers for sailing school. Continental plus means extras such as crab omelets in season. Served in dining room or on the patio. Hosts often join guests for coffee.
Plus: Central air conditioning. Mints. Wine. Use of refrigerator, laundry facilities. Guided tours of area and Naval Academy.

Prince George Inn B&B

232 Prince George Street, Annapolis, MD 21401
Phone: 301/263-6418
Location: In historic district with brick sidewalks. Within minutes of shops, restaurants, U.S. Naval Academy, harbor.
Hosts: Bill and Norma Grovermann
Open: Year round. Advance reservations suggested on weekends.
Rates: $65 double. $50 single, available Sunday–Thursday. MC.

The perfect location. Inn ambiance. A private home. A feeling of living history. All provided in a three-story 1884 brick town house that has high ceilings, antiques and art collections everywhere, and Norma's keen sense of display and decorating. (Painting, papering, and color selection are among her many specialties.)

In addition to personally restoring 20 houses, Bill has worked on many state of Maryland restoration projects, including the nearby Governor William Paca House. He also has considerable experience in economic development, historic preservation, and community development. Before becoming full-time innkeeper, Norma—a California native who has lived in New Zealand, Hawaii, and many cities in the United States—established an Annapolis sightseeing tour company (a model of its genre). There's plenty of information here—including, if you'd like, tips for "local flavor" places. In the six years since they established the first licensed B&B in Annapolis, the Grovermanns have hosted dignitaries, boat buyers, parents of Academy midshipmen, many business people, and Annapolis devotees—along with guests who are inspired to open their own B&B! For my own first visit to Annapolis, the stay here was pure pleasure!

Restrictions: Children 12 and over welcome. Smoking allowed on first floor only. Sorry, no pets.
Bed and bath: Four rooms on two floors. Two second-floor rooms—one with high-headboard queen bed and one with antique double brass bed—share a full bath. Two third-floor rooms—one with antique twin brass beds and one with double bed—share a full bath.
Breakfast: 7:30–10, self-serve buffet with juices, cereal, homemade muffins, croissants, jams (some homemade), cheese, fruit; baked apples in winter. On breakfast porch or in garden courtyard. Daily newspaper provided.
Plus: Central air conditioning. Spiced cider in winter. Refrigerator for drinks. Garden chairs. Fireplaced parlor with TV and lots of reading material. Area tours can be arranged.

The Traveller In Maryland Host #1A

Annapolis, MD
Location: One block from U.S. Naval Academy entrance. And minutes to St. John's College too. Within view of College Creek, the Severn River, and the Academy's parade grounds. Five blocks to City Dock and restaurants. Within two blocks of historic sites.
Reservations: Year round through The Traveller In Maryland, page 20.
Rates: $65 per room. $125 apartment.

So many people suggested that this brick town house was perfect for a B&B, the hosts began to agree! The world travelers—he is a computer systems analyst with the U.S. Department of Justice, and she has considerable experience as an accountant/budget and financial analyst—have collected Oriental rugs that are now on the mirror-finished 180-year-old wood floors and on solid white walls. Antique clocks date back to 1770. There's Belgian lace, Japanese silk screens, African masks, art deco, contemporary sofas, and much more—all blended with flair and imagination. And for the piece de resistance—a large, unique, two-tiered roof terrace with vine-covered lattice, built-in planters, and canopied arbor.

When you do leave here, depending on the hosts' schedules, you might have a custom tour of the Academy, go with the hosts to the Naval Chapel, to dinner theater, or to jazz clubs. Or take the hosts' suggestions for off-the-beaten path places. Or relax in the elegant but comfortable living room.

Restrictions: No smoking or guests' pets.
Bed and bath: Three rooms. Two third-floor double-bedded rooms, private full bath. Private entrance and courtyard to apartment with twin beds, sofa bed in living room, private shower bath, kitchen.
Breakfast: Arrange time night before. Fruit, croissants, freshly squeezed juice, homemade muffins, fresh fig bars. Sometimes, quiche. Gourmet coffees and jams. At beautifully set table in dining room or on terrace.
Plus: Air conditioning throughout, except one room with ceiling fan. Tea or coffee. Fruit, flowers, chocolates. Tours of house and area. Study room with TV, stereo, VCR, desk. Use of refrigerator.

Amanda's Bed & Breakfast Host AC

Baltimore, MD
Location: Located in a quiet residential neighborhood, four miles northeast of Inner Harbor. Bordered by two parks, a lake, tennis courts, biking and jogging trails, and a public golf course. Public transportation within one block.
Reservations: Year round through Amanda's Bed & Breakfast, page 20.
Rates: $50 single. $55 double. Weekly rates available.

Both ardent sailors and classical music lovers, the hosts, parents of a grown family, enjoy hosting in their English Tudor-style house "filled with an all-around good feeling known in German as 'gemütlichkeit.'" The hostess teaches German and also is a tour leader for German visitors. The host, a chemist, plays clarinet in a concert band.
In residence: Aja, a beautiful fat cat, "likes to be outdoors and is very shy."
Restrictions: No guests' pets. No smoking.
Foreign languages spoken: German and some French.
Bed and bath: Two second-floor rooms share a modern full hall bath. One room has twin beds. The other has queen bed, ceiling fan, and air conditioning.
Breakfast: Flexible hours. "Full, gourmet style. With the best coffee in town." In breakfast room or on secluded patio.
Plus: Fresh fruit. Flowers. Free parking.

Guests wrote: "We had many nice conversations with the wonderful hostess and her husband. They were very helpful in getting us around Baltimore. The breakfasts were incredible, delicious and extremely generous."

Celie's Waterfront Bed & Breakfast

1714 Thames Street, P.O. Box 38241, Baltimore, MD 21231
Phone: 301/522-2323
Location: In Fell's Point Historic District on an active port with tugboats. Near fine restaurants, shops, nightlife. Twelve blocks to Johns Hopkins Medical Center; short trolley ride to National Aquarium, Science Center at Harborplace, museums, antiques row. Ferry service (in season) to Inner Harbor, Fort McHenry, Little Italy.
Host: Celie Ives
Open: Year round. Advance reservations required. Two- or three-night minimum for major trade shows, on holidays, and Preakness weekend.
Rates: Double occupancy. $85 third-floor suite. New B&B: $85 first-floor handicapped-accessible unit. Upstairs, $90 with private balcony overlooking garden. $95 waterfront view. Singles $5 less. Long-term rates available. Deposit required. AMEX, MC, VISA; 5 percent handling charge.

It is "urban living at its best," whether you stay in the new/old house or around the corner in the newly built waterfront B&B, both created by a Baltimore native who returned home after 30 years' absence in 1981. Starting with an abandoned three-story 1870s town house, Celie developed not only a new home but a new career. She renovated the structure completely, saving only the staircase, and furnished with beautiful antiques, all complemented by the imaginative use of color, light, and textures. There's a brick-paved garden and a roof deck with a 360-degree view of the Baltimore harbor and skyline.

The seven-room B&B (opening fall of 1989) on bustling Thames Street commands a view of the harbor. Furnished in the same style—with antiques and wonderful fabrics—that made Celie's first B&B so popular, its rooms face either the harbor, an interior courtyard, or the garden. Here, too, there's a rooftop deck facing downriver. And then there's Celie, an enthusiastic Baltimore booster who enjoys sharing her historic neighborhood with a wide range of interesting guests.

Restrictions: Children 10 and over welcome. No smoking inside. Sorry, no pets.
Bed and bath: In original B&B, two adults at most in third-floor suite with two twins/king option, wood-burning fireplace/stove, extra-long foldout foam bed in sitting room, kitchenette. In new B&B, seven rooms, all with access to roof deck, all with private baths. First-floor handicapped-accessible unit with king/twin option, private courtyard. Four queen-bedded rooms with small refrigerators. King/twin option in waterfront rooms, each with working fireplace, whirlpool bath, kitchenette. Some rooms can combine into suites.
Breakfast: 7:30–9. Freshly squeezed orange juice, fresh fruit in season, cakes and pastries, jams and jellies, brewed coffees and teas. Serve yourself. Eat in dining room, on private balcony or rooftop deck, in garden, or in your room.

Plus: Central air conditioning. Ceiling fans. Flannel sheets. Bath sheets. Terry robes. Down comforters. Fresh flowers. Fireplaced living rooms. Ironing facilities. TV and telephones available. Free off-street parking.

Harborview

112 East Montgomery Street, Baltimore, MD 21230
Phone: 301/528-8692
Location: On the inner harbor, in historic Federal Hill district. Two-minute walk along promenade to Aquarium.
Host: (Mr.) Marty Mulligan
Open: Year round. Reservations required.
Rates: $85 per room. Single $10 less. $120 for second-floor suite. $10 cot.

"You really should include my mentor, Marty Mulligan, who has an exquisite place that overlooks Baltimore harbor," said the Chester County, Pennsylvania, hostess (page 208).

"I had no intention of doing B&B when I came to Baltimore as an Eastman Kodak technical representative," said Marty. "After two months of living in a hotel when I was transferred from Chicago and looking for a home, I knew there had to be a more personalized kind of lodging for travelers. After buying this Federal period brick house, I completed the interior design, chose the colors, and furnished it traditionally with Oriental rugs. I am delighted when people ask about the decor [Harborview has been on house tours], particularly since I had never done anything like this before. Sometimes we hardly get a chance to talk, but when we do, guests often ask about neighborhood restaurants or 'must-sees.' Meeting all these people has been such a wonderful experience that now, with help, I am able to be on the New Jersey shore on weekends at a B&B inn (page 47) I made from an historic mansion. I bought it in one day after staying at a nearby inn. Even with all my years of marketing training, I marvel at the people who are in this business. They are a giving breed, something most unusual. It's a good feeling for everyone."

In residence: Roberta Hutchinson, assistant.
Restrictions: Well-mannered children are welcome. Sorry, no pets. No smoking, please.
Bed and bath: Three rooms. Two on second floor can be separate or a suite; each room has a queen bed and working fireplace, adjoining full bath (plus a half bath for one room). Entire third floor consists of room with king bed, private full bath, sitting room, and breakfast nook overlooking harbor and a spacious deck. Cot available.
Breakfast: Continental. Coffee is ready. Help yourself to juice, cereal, muffins, coffee.
Plus: Central air conditioning. Afternoon wine. Mints. Fresh flowers. Thirsty towels. Rear brick garden courtyard overlooking harbor. Fireplaced living room and kitchen (which also has a sofa). Laundry facilities. Parking.

Twin Gates

308 Morris Avenue, Baltimore, MD 21093
Phone: 301/252-3131 or 1-800/635-0370
Location: On an acre of land with mature pine trees and circular drive-way framed by twin gates. In Lutherville, a northern suburb; 20 minutes by expressway to Harborplace in Baltimore center.
Hosts: Gwen and Bob Vaughan
Open: Year round. Reservations required.
Rates: $70–$90 double occupancy.

After their twin daughters grew up, Gwen, formerly a corporate medical secretary, and Bob, a hospital management consultant, restored this mid-19th-century house with 12-foot ceilings, built by one of the ministers who founded the village. Soft colors, antiques, and beautiful wallcoverings—"casual elegance"—set the backdrop for their newest career, one filled with exuberance. Hosting for the Vaughans is just as they imagined it would be (wonderful) when they traveled B&B to California, New England, and Cape May, New Jersey, picking up ideas everywhere they went.

The native Baltimorians have sightseeing hints. (They're just 15 minutes from a vineyard tour and the Ladew Topiary Gardens.) They direct guests to universities and hospitals. They share decorating ideas. They provide peace by the fireplace—and are happy to show you "the secret room."

Restrictions: Children should be at least 12. No pets and no smoking allowed.
Bed and bath: Five second-floor rooms, each with a queen bed. Three have private baths—one full, two with showers, no tubs. Two rooms share a full bath. Each room is decorated with a geographical theme such as Maryland Hunt, Sanibel Shores, or California.
Breakfast: 7:30–9:30. Fresh fruit, homemade "muffins of the season," freshly brewed coffee, herbal teas, and, occasionally, an egg dish. Served in the dining room or greeting room, on the front porch, or in a basket delivered to your room.
Plus: Wine and cheese, usually 6–7. Room air conditioners. Bedroom ceiling fans. Tour of the house. Fireplaces in both living room and greeting room. Front porch. Sometimes, bedtime surprises.

Holland House

5 Bay Street, Berlin, MD 21811
Phone: 301/641-1956
Location: In historic downtown district. Seven miles from ocean beaches, Assateague Island, and Ocean City.
Hosts: Jim and Jan Quick

Open: Year round. Closed January 12–February 12. Reservations recommended.
Rates: Double occupancy. May 25–October 1, private bath, $55 single, $60 double. Shared bath, $45 single, $50 double. Rest of year, $10 less. $10 cot or crib. CHOICE, MC, VISA. Personal checks welcome.

"Since moving to Berlin nine years ago and purchasing this house three years ago, we have met the remaining Holland family members. It makes us feel good to know that this was a happy home. Everyone in town knew Doc Holland, as he was called in the 1920s and 30s. He was well-loved and appreciated. There's been a lot of service to the community through this house. When we were doing it all over, saving it as a residence, the townspeople would look in on our progress. . . . Now I do all the baking and serving. Jim, an Eastern Shore native, is a hotel chef with the Marriott Corporation and responsible for our kitchen. Hattie is chairman of the entertainment committee and sometimes clears the tables. We often make dinner reservations for our guests at lovely intimate restaurants in the area. And we also recommend casual crab houses. . . . Some guests want privacy and our house lends itself to that. Others become part of the family."

The Quicks' immaculately kept turn-of-the-century frame house is freshly decorated with comfortable chairs and restored treasures. Jan works part time as a dental hygienist. Among the patients who encouraged her—"a perfect match"—to become an innkeeper: the Holland family!

In residence: Henrietta, "Hattie," age five. One cat, Crystal.
Restrictions: Children over a year old are welcome. Smoking allowed in living room and on porch. Sorry, no guests' pets.
Bed and bath: Five rooms. Private shower baths with first-floor rooms, which have a queen or two double beds. Two second-floor rooms, each with a pineapple-post double bed, share a first-floor tub bath. Rollaway and crib available.
Breakfast: At 9. In summer, locally grown fruit, freshly squeezed orange juice, homemade rolls, muffins and breads, jams. Full breakfast in winter.
Plus: Central air conditioning. Tea, wine, soda. TV lounge room. Front porch. Babysitting available upon request. Sometimes in the winter, popcorn and VCR movies.

Glasgow Inn and Reservation Service

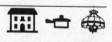

1500 Hambrooks Boulevard, Cambridge, MD 21613
Phone: 301/228-0575. For reservations only, 1-800/225-0575 (nationwide).
Location: A parklike riverside setting with seven acres of lawn and century-old trees. Near summer river cruises, Blackwater National Wildlife Refuge (magnificent), antiquing, outlet shopping, bird-watching, canoeing, country auctions, tennis, sailing, and hunting.

Hosts: Louise Lee Roche and Martha Ann Rayne
Open: Year round.
Rates: Per room. $90 semi-private bath, $100 private bath. Special discounts Monday–Thursday. $15 surcharge for one-night stay on weekends, holidays, or dates of special events.

> From Maryland: "What a delight to enjoy the peaceful elegance of this colonial mansion! . . . Beautifully decorated rooms. . . . Everything was immaculately clean. And our full country breakfast was a delicious experience."

After 25 years of hosting friends and relatives at their beach home in Ocean City, Louise Lee and Martha Ann, college friends, former teachers and quilt-shop owners (who made a quilt that is hanging in the state house), decided to pursue their dream of restoring an historic house and establishing a new career. In 1987 they purchased this National Register "breathtaking 18th-century brick and clapboard Georgian plantation manor," which has spacious rooms with high ceilings, Palladian windows, and deep window seats. Both women scraped and scrubbed Glasgow and then furnished it with 18th-century family heirlooms and reproductions. Soon they hosted innkeeping seminars and established an Eastern Shore inn association. They have a reservation service; and they plan for wedding receptions, programs with artists-in-residence, and Christian renewal retreats.

In residence: Occasionally, visiting grandchildren.
Restrictions: Infants plus children over 12 welcomed. No smoking or pets allowed.
Bed and bath: Eight rooms, five with fireplaces. Private full bath for room with king bed and working fireplace. Six large queen-bedded rooms share four full baths. One living/bedroom has queen-sized sleep sofa, fireplace, screened porch. Rollaways and crib available.
Breakfast: 8:30 Monday–Saturday, 9:30 Sunday. Country style, with juice, cider, fruit, French toast or Amish omelet with scrapple and bacon.
Plus: Central air conditioning. Lemonade and iced tea served on warm afternoons. Saturday high tea at 4:30 p.m. Wine and cheese on Fridays. Videos of musicals by the living room fire. Huge screened porch. Use of bicycles. Nanny service on weekdays. Saturday winter weekend dinners. Holiday dinners with hosts' families. Inn-to-inn biking arrangements. Apprentice program.

Inn at the Canal

104 Bohemia Avenue, Chesapeake City, MD 21915
Phone: 301/885-5995
Location: On the world's busiest canal, the (lockless) Chesapeake and Delaware Canal. In historic district of village that has an annual Maypole Dance, artists' workshops, canal museum. Near horse farm country. Within two hours of Washington, Baltimore, and Philadelphia. Ten miles from I-95.

Hosts: Al and Mary Ioppolo
Open: Year round. Two-night minimum stay on Memorial Day, July Fourth, and Labor Day weekends.
Rates: Double occupancy. $65 small room, $80 large, $85 or $95 water view. Singles $5 less. $15 extra person. Midweek corporate rates available. AMEX, MC, VISA.

The world of antiques helped the Ioppolos discover this rediscovered waterside town. Al is a Philadelphia native who worked as office automation manager with the U.S. Department of Energy. Mary, an Alabama-born occupational therapist, is about to retire from her decade-long job with the Delaware County, Pennsylvania, school district. They had spent two years looking for a country site to redo themselves when a fellow antique dealer—the Ioppolos feature primitives, country pieces, and oil lamps—told them about this inn, an 1870 house built by a tugboat owner. It was restored in 1987 with a new kitchen, the "gather-round" kind with an island and the old fireplace. The Ioppolos report, "We have more collections than we have room for! When we took over in February of 1989, we put antique baskets on top of all the cabinets. Our lamps—some bracket, some oil, some electrified—fit in nicely. Ever since the first day we arrived (along with unexpected guests) we have been meeting terrific people who come for the village and its restaurants. Some go to a beautiful spot where a point of land is surrounded by three rivers."

The living/dining room has the original painted and stenciled ceiling, a parquet floor with rug insert, tall windows with imaginative curtains, and an interesting corner cupboard. By the time you arrive perhaps the brick-floored antiques shop will be open. The enthusiastic innkeepers have plans for landscaping and a gazebo, and for becoming involved in this small community.

In residence: Tekir tends to be a shy cat.
Restrictions: Children ten and over welcome. Smoking allowed in parlor according to other guests' wishes.
Bed and bath: Six second-floor rooms, many with four-posters. Private full baths with antique washstands. Queen, double, or twin beds. Two doubles can be a suite; one room also has a trundle, the other a daybed.
Breakfast: 7–9 weekdays, 8–10 weekends and holidays. Freshly squeezed orange juice, breakfast meats, maybe poached pears with raspberry sauce or French toast stuffed with cream cheese and fresh peaches; hot beverages.
Plus: Central air conditioning with individual control in guest rooms. Refreshments on arrival. TV in most guest rooms. Wicker-furnished side porch overlooking water. Small meeting facility.

Brampton Bed and Breakfast

RR 2, Box 107, Chestertown, MD 21620
Phone: 301/778-1860
Location: One mile south of Chestertown. On 15 landscaped acres sur-

rounded by old trees and cornfields. Within two-hour drive of Baltimore, Philadelphia, Washington, D.C.
Hosts: Michael and Danielle Hanscom
Open: Year round. Advance reservations recommended.
Rates: Double occupancy. $75 and $85. $15 additional person. MC, VISA.

From Massachusetts: "A stately beauty that exudes peace and tranquility. . . . Our room was beautifully decorated and very, very comfortable. We could not hear another sound in the house despite the fact that the B&B was fully booked. Breakfast was delicious, imaginative, sustained us through the day. . . . Warm hospitality. Everything was perfect."

"Everything"—the fireplaces, Michael's craftsmanship, the amenities, and the hosts—was extolled in great detail in other letters written by historians, young professionals, and retirees.

Michael renovated houses in San Francisco before coming to the Eastern Shore in 1987. Danielle, a former Swissair flight attendant, always wanted to own a small hotel. Since opening their 1860 Greek Revival brick plantation house, listed on the National Register of Historic Places, they, too, have warm memories of sharing, "drinking sherry or tea, rearranging the world."

In residence: In private hosts' quarters, Lucas, 17, and Sophie, age 3.
Restrictions: Please inquire about children as guests. Smoking in TV room only. No guests' pets.
Foreign languages spoken: Fluent German and French. Some Spanish.
Bed and bath: Four exceptionally large rooms, plus one suite, on second and third floors. All private baths; some shower, one tub without shower. Four rooms have queen bed (four-poster or canopied), working fireplace or Franklin stove, and sitting area. Suite has antique twin beds, sitting room, writing room with antique desk. Trundle beds and crib available.
Breakfast: Weekdays 8–9:30, weekends 8:30–10. Guests' choice. Eggs "any style except poached!," French toast, or pancakes with sausage and bacon from nearby Amish market. Homemade muffins, breads, and jams. Served at individual tables in formal dining room.
Plus: Afternoon or evening beverages. Fireplaced living and dining rooms. Bedroom air conditioners. Fruit in room. English soaps. Thick towels. Down comforters. Antiques and reproductions throughout, except in TV/smoking room, which has modern leather sofas. Mudroom for wildfowl hunters.

Radcliffe Cross

Route 3, Box 360, Quaker Neck Road, Chestertown, MD 21620
Phone: 301/778-5540
Location: Rural and convenient. A half mile south of Chestertown in Quaker Neck. Ninety minutes from Baltimore and Washington. Two hours from Philadelphia.

Hosts: Dan and Marge Brook
Open: Year round. Reservations preferred.
Rates: $65 per room. $10 for cot or crib.

As you ascend the dramatic hanging spiral staircase in the center entrance hall, the window at the first landing gives you a view of a magnificent 260-year-old Chinese elm that shades a patio (available to guests). The gracious white-painted brick colonial manor house, built between 1700 and 1724 and restored to its present condition in the late 1940s, is surrounded by four acres of manicured lawns and centuries-old plantings. Fine antiques and original pine floors add to the charm. Whip-poorwills, owls, and Canada geese add to night sounds.

Marge, a former registered nurse who likes to cook and bake, grew up in this area. She and Dan, semiretired from the beverage industry, moved from New Jersey in 1985 to the house that they "fell in love with at first sight." Dan is "good at doing everything from building walls to gardening." Marge had a wonderful time with the Christmas house tour that required all-natural decorations designed to represent the period of the house. The parents of three grown sons find they have an extended family, with former guests who have sent poems, with others who stop by when passing through, and with people from all over the world who come to Chestertown for history and festivities.

In residence: Muffy, a fluffy cat; Pepper, "a 'Benjy' type dog."
Restrictions: Children under 2 and over 10 are welcome. Pets sometimes allowed. No smoking in bedrooms.
Bed and bath: Two spacious second-floor rooms, each with an antique double bed, private full bath, working fireplace, views of grounds. Cot and crib available.
Breakfast: Usually 8–9. Fruit, juice, an egg entree, homemade muffins and specialty of puff pastries, hot beverages. Served in "old world charm" dining room at beautifully set table.
Plus: Bedroom air conditioners and ceiling fans. Beverages. Shaded patio. Mints. Flowers. Thick soft towels. Many publications. Logs for fireplace. Cards, card table.

The John S. McDaniel House

14 North Aurora Street, Easton, MD 21601
Phone: 301/822-3704
Location: Three blocks from downtown. In a residential area, surrounded by trees.
Hosts: Bill and Genie Kramedas
Open: Year round. Advance reservations preferred.
Rates: Sunday–Thursday, $55 double, $60 king. Friday and Saturday $5 more, May–November. AMEX, MC, VISA.

"We love old houses, enjoy people, and used to be in the restaurant business," says Bill, a former school administrator. Since he and Genie moved from Newark, Delaware, in 1987, Genie has continued teaching, and they both have restored this large, simply furnished 1890s house with its many-angled roof and peaked turret. The bedrooms are spacious, the stairways wide, and there's a wicker-furnished wraparound porch. One hallway features artwork of Andrew Wyeth, others done by the Kramedases' son, and local scenes.

Restrictions: Sorry, no guests' pets. Children ages 5–9 are booked when third-floor room is available; over age 10 are placed in all rooms.
Foreign language spoken: Greek.
Bed and bath: Five rooms, all private baths. Second-floor rooms have king bed with shower bath, queen bed with full bath, or double bed with tub bath. (Second-floor hall phone reaches into rooms.) On third floor, room with double bed, tub bath with hand-held shower, and TV. Rollaway available.
Breakfast: 8–10. Continental with home-baked breads, juices, coffee, tea, fresh fruit, house specials.
Plus: Central air conditioning. Before-dinner or late-evening wine. Fireplaces in dining and living rooms. Pickup service arranged at Easton airport or Oxford and St. Michaels boat wharfs. Barn for bicycle storage.

From Maryland: "Highly recommended. Lovely and clean. The food is delicious and the hospitality delightful."

Wades Point Inn on the Bay

Wades Point Road, McDaniel, MD 21647
Mailing address: P.O. Box 130, McDaniel, MD 21647
Phone: 301/745-2500
Location: Secluded. Surrounded by farmland, woods, and water. Five miles south of St. Michaels.
Hosts: Betsy and John Feiler
Open: March–December. Advance reservation preferred. Two-day minimum for Saturday reservations.
Rates: Double occupancy. $60–$95 depending on size and location of room. $10 third person. Children under 10 free with accompanying adults. Ten percent less for three days or longer. Senior citizen discount, Sunday–Thursday.

"Pass fields of corn and soybean, then some with gladioli, and come straight ahead to our 120-acre waterfront farm complete with 100-foot dock. Welcome—to an area where there's plenty to do—or to our home with a fabulous view where you can enjoy both the serenity of the country and the splendor of the Bay!"

Featured on the cover of *Mid-Atlantic Country* magazine, the main house was built in 1819 by shipwright Thomas Kemp, builder of the original clipper ship *Pride of Baltimore*. In 1890 the Kemp family added a wing for friends and guests and ran it as a guest house until 1984, the year that Betsy, a Maryland native, and John, a Manhattan corporate executive, were looking for a farm. "We decided to carry on the tradition, updating plumbing and electricity, but keeping the casual atmosphere with comfortable and traditional furnishings, lots of wicker, a grandfather's clock and other antiques, and, of course, rockers on the screened porches. Thanks to our wonderful guests, our surprise vocation is a delight."

Restrictions: Smoking on porches and outdoors only. Sorry, no guests' pets. Children welcome.
Bed and bath: Fourteen rooms, all with water views; 10 in main house and wing, 4 in adjoining guest house. Private full bath for third-floor main house room and first-floor guest house room, each with a double bed and a twin bed. Other rooms share baths (at least one for every two rooms) and have a double bed (one is canopied), a double and a twin, or two twin beds. Rollaway and crib available.
Breakfast: Usually 8:30–10. Fresh fruit, cheese, homemade rolls and muffins, coffee. Buffet style in fireplaced and wicker-furnished room with panoramic view of the Bay.
Plus: Fresh flowers. Library. Fishing and crabbing in season from dock. Extensive lawns for games and sitting. Old-fashioned club house for late-night parties. A perfect setting for weddings and receptions.

New Market

With its 45 antiques shops—many in well-restored houses—New Market is known as "the antiques capital of Maryland." Just steps from the two B&Bs on Main Street is Mealey's, established as a tavern and hotel in the early 1800s, and now open for dinner Tuesday–Sunday. Behind Main Street is dairy country with cows and pastureland. New Market, all of one-half mile from one end of town to the other, is within 60 minutes of Washington, D.C.; Baltimore, Maryland; Gettysburg, Pennsylvania; and Harper's Ferry, West Virginia, and within 15 minutes of historic Frederick. The scenic Catoctin Mountains, site of presidential retreat, are 25 miles away with swimming, boating, hiking. Tennis courts are here in New Market.

National Pike Inn

9–11 Main Street, P.O. Box 299, New Market, MD 21774
Phone: 301/865-5055
Location: In historic district. Just off I-70, exit 62.
Hosts: Tom and Terry Rimel
Open: Year round. Reservations required. Two-night minimum stay on holiday, May, and October weekends and during New Market Days (last September weekend) and Christmas in New Market (first December weekend).

Rates: $60–$65 weekdays. $70–$95 Saturday only. $50–$55 weekly. $65–$80 Friday and Saturday.

Fronted by a herringbone brick sidewalk and topped by a widow's walk, this is "a beautiful old house which deserves to be shared. There are eight fireplaces, each an architect's delight from the Federal period. We've researched it back to 1806, and are hopeful that it goes back further than that. During the 15 years that we lived a half mile from here, I often thought about B&B and consulted the Rossigs at Strawberry Inn. When we bought the house in 1986, it had already been restored (25 years ago) and most of our work was cosmetic. All of our furnishings are wonderful new reproductions mixed with antiques, with room decor ranging from elegant to very country."

Terry, "a homemaker who is interested in baking, church and family," occasionally appears in period costume on Saturday evenings. Tom, a roofing mechanic foreman, joins her in hosting every evening. "Our very first guests were delightful newlyweds; everyone since has been wonderful too."

In residence: Sons Thomas Jr., age 17, and Douglas, age 16.
Restrictions: Children over five preferred. Sorry, no guests' pets. Smoking is not encouraged.
Bed and bath: Five second-floor rooms; two have private full baths. Queen beds (one high canopied with step provided). One room with two twin beds. Suite has two bedrooms, each with a private entrance, one full bath; one room has a queen brass bed, the other has two pencil-post twin beds.
Breakfast: 8–10. Coffee, tea, juice, fresh fruit. Muffins, breads (white, wheat, or chocolate dot pumpkin), shoofly coffee cake, apple pastry; served in the colonial dining room or on tray (bud vase in season) in guest rooms.
Plus: Bedroom air conditioners. Large living room with organ. Dining room. Complimentary Sunday paper. Brick courtyard. Screened porch. Golfing privileges at Eaglehead Country Club, 10 minutes away, at prearranged tee-off time.

The Strawberry Inn

17 Main Street, P.O. Box 237, New Market, MD 21774
Phone: 301/865-3318
Location: In historic district. Just off I-70, exit 60.
Hosts: Jane and Ed Rossig
Open: Year round. Reservations required.
Rates: Large rooms, $50 single, $65 double. Small room, $50 single, $55 double. $10 additional person in room.

A feature of a full *New York Times* travel section page, this B&B was meticulously restored (just about rebuilt) by the Rossigs when Ed retired from 30 years as an electrical engineer with Westinghouse. Often, he is asked about (and shares) his Count Rumford restoration of the common room fireplace. Named after the adjoining Strawberry Alley, the cozy Victorian house with dentil ceiling moldings, wide pine board floors, and reproduction papers is furnished with many period antiques.

In their 17 years at the inn, Ed and Jane, parents of three grown children, have continued their interest in historic preservation and are active in town government. Ed also has a shop, makes picture frames, and is an antique car and radio buff. The Rossigs' pampering of guests is appreciated by returnees and by first-time B&B guests who are "converted."

Restrictions: Children should be at least eight. Sorry, no guests' pets.
Bed and bath: Five rooms—four are large, two have sleep sofas—on two floors. All modern private baths. A first-floor room has four-poster twin beds, full bath, private entrance, porch. On second floor, one room with two double beds, full bath; two with queen beds, full bath. One smaller room with double bed, shower bath.
Breakfast: At time requested by guests. Seasonal fruit, freshly baked breads, and brewed coffee and tea. Served either in the dining room or on a butler's tray left outside the guests' room at their chosen time.
Plus: Bedroom air conditioners. "Touches" include candy in rooms; sometimes flowers, postcards of town. A restored log building on the grounds has a large first-floor room with fireplace, an art gallery with well-known Maryland artists' work, and facilities for a small business conference.

Elmwood c. 1770 B&B

Locust Point Road, P.O. Box 220, Princess Anne, MD 21853
Phone: 301/651-1066
Location: Peaceful. On 200 acres of mile-long waterfront property. Seven miles west of Princess Anne; 45 minutes from beaches. Near Maryland Wildlife Management areas, restaurants, shops, historic sites.
Hosts: Mr. Stephen F. and Mrs. Helen Monick
Open: Mid-January–mid-December. Advance reservations preferred. Two-night minimum on holidays, Memorial Day–Labor Day.
Rates: Double occupancy. $70 shared bath; $75 private bath and fireplace; $80 private bath, fireplace, private porch. Cottage $95 for two; $10 each additional person over 12, weekly rate available. MC, VISA.

Returnees come for the commanding view of the Manokin River, for the tranquility, and for the hosts. Writers have been inspired here. History and architecture buffs, too, are delighted with the Federal brick residence built by John Elzey, whose grandson, Arnold Elzey Jones, became a prominent Confederate Army general.

The Monicks' extensive restoration was a 1984 retirement project on Steve's retirement after 35 years with United Airlines. Helen, a home economist and former teacher, once had a television cooking program. They painted the spacious high-ceilinged rooms in authentic colonial colors and furnished with period antiques and reproductions, wing chairs, and mahogany four-posters. Helen's collection of needlework includes some of her own work. This lovely B&B, *seemingly* in the middle of nowhere, has been hailed as a "best B&B of the year" by the *Pittsburgh Press*. Others call it a showcase.

In residence: "Twenty-five mallards and a few wood ducks come from the river to be fed at least once a day."
Restrictions: Children 12 and over welcome. Younger children welcome in cottage. Smoking allowed on porches only. Sorry, no pets.
Bed and bath: Four rooms, two with private baths, plus a cottage. Three second-floor queen- or double-bedded rooms with working fireplaces. One room shares a bath with third-floor room that has two twin beds. Cottage—room with two double beds, full bath, kitchen, dining and living room, double sofa bed, working fireplace.
Breakfast: 8:30–9:30. Perhaps pecan waffles or stuffed crepes with apples or mushrooms, filled puff pastries, Smithfield sausages or bacon. In dining room by fireplace or on screened porch. Continental breakfast brought to cottage residents who are staying one or a few nights.
Plus: Central air conditioning. Tea or wine. Library with fireplace. Upper and lower screened porches.

The Inn at Antietam

220 East Main Street, P.O. Box 119, Sharpsburg, MD 21782
Phone: 301/432-6601
Location: Rural. The perfect setting for walking. At the hilltop of a long Main Street driveway. Surrounded by lawns. On eight acres overlooking Sharpsburg and the Antietam National Battlefield. Near Harper's Ferry; the C&O Canal; Shepherdstown, West Virginia; Crystal Grottoes Cavern; and hiking, canoeing, antique shops, cottage industry craft shops, and restaurants.
Hosts: Betty and Cal Fairbourn
Open: Year round except two weeks at Christmas. Reservations required.
Rates: $55 double or twins. First-floor suite $85 double, $100 triple. $85 smokehouse, $100 two-bedroom second-floor suite. $5 less for three or more days. $42.50 single rate, weekdays. AMEX.

Here's "homegrown hospitality with a sophisticated touch." It's a relaxed style that works both for guests, who write about "a beautifully restored inn run by a charming couple," and for the enthusiastic hosts, who say "people are fabulous." It has been that way ever since Cal, a former General Motors (Detroit) executive, and Betty, a former hospice counselor, worked three months (day and night) in 1984 in restoring the rambling Victorian. "It just looked like an inn and we liked the inn concept." They were so good at doing their own woodwork—including new moldings and kitchen cabinets—that they now restore other properties. They are so good at "touches" that they selected elegant period antiques with an emphasis on comfort. The inn's wraparound porch is festooned with garlands in the winter, and Cal's flower gardens flourish in the summer. He also enjoys wood carving. Betty has many opportunities to bake and a few moments to quilt and golf.

In residence: Outdoor (only) pets—a dog named Annie and Mary, a calico cat allowed to sit with guests on the porch.
Restrictions: Well-mannered children over six may be weekday (only) visitors. No guests' pets. Smoking restricted to common areas.
Bed and bath: Five rooms, each with private bath. The first-floor suite has an 1800 queen-sized four-poster bed, sitting room, private bath. Second-floor suite has one room with brass double bed and one with spindle twin beds. One room with queen bed, dressing room. Adjoining "Smokehouse" has loft with double bed, fireplace, private bath, wet bar.
Breakfast: 7:30–10. Freshly squeezed orange juice, fruit, freshly ground whole wheat toast, muffins, coffee cakes, and croissants. Served in the dining room, by fireplace in smokehouse, or in guests' rooms.
Plus: Air conditioning. Afternoon tea or complimentary wine. Solarium, parlor. Beautifully landscaped large lawn. Porch swing and rockers. Brick patio overlooking Blue Ridge Mountains. Box lunches with advance notice.

Blue Bear Bed & Breakfast

Route 2, Box 378, Holiday Drive, Smithsburg, MD 21783
Phone: 301/824-2292
Location: In a quiet residential neighborhood with a view of South Mountain. In apple and peach orchard country. Within 30 minutes' drive southwest to Antietam Battlefield or northeast to Gettysburg. Ten miles from Appalachian Trail. Six miles to Hagerstown restaurants. A little over an hour from Washington, D.C.
Host: Ellen Panchula
Open: Year round; two-night maximum stay. September–June, available weekends only. Advance reservations required.
Rates: $30 single, $40 double. $8 child up to age 18.

From South Carolina: "Her warm welcome was especially appreciated after an 11-hour drive. Ellen is a gracious hostess who makes you feel at home—with touches such as a plate of homebaked goodies in your room."

Ellen, an elementary school teacher, lives in a comfortable 25-year-old Cape Cod–style house that has many country crafts, some purchased from guests who have come to Smithburg's Steam & Craft Show in September. Every room has stenciling. On the handmade quilts in the guest rooms are many stuffed bears—and yes, some are blue!

In residence: Maggie is a 50-pound border collie/husky/German shepherd.
Restrictions: Children should be at least 12. Nonsmokers preferred. Sorry, no pets please.

Bed and bath: Two second-floor double-bedded rooms share a full bath. Rollaway available.
Breakfast: 7–9. Juice; fruit; quiche, baked French toast, or egg casserole; homemade rolls and breads; coffee. Served in the kitchen. Ellen joins guests.
Plus: Central air conditioning. Evening snack. Mints. Laundry facilities available.

Chanceford Hall Bed & Breakfast Inn

209 West Federal Street, Snow Hill, MD 21863
Phone: 301/632-2231
Location: On landscaped grounds with English boxwood and 200-year-old walnut trees. In historic district of residential area. Near the Pocomoke River and canoeing. Three hours from Washington, D.C., and Baltimore. Half an hour to ocean, to Crisfield and boats for Smith and Tangier Islands.
Hosts: Michael and Thelma C. Driscoll
Open: Year round. Advance reservations preferred.
Rates: Per room. $105 first floor. Upstairs, $95 queen, $85 double bed. $105 queen and single bed with fireplace. Less off season, midweek, and for more than two nights.

Such detailed and enthusiastic guests' letters! They comment on the personal attention, the friendliness, the too-brief stay, the craftsmanship, the food—at this restored 1759 brick Greek/Georgian, declared "a gem" by the Maryland Historic Trust. Dan Rodricks of the Baltimore *Evening Sun* and WBAL-TV wrote, "Chanceford Hall has finally been brought back to greatness. . . . One wonders if George Washington slept there."

The Driscolls, parents of two grown daughters, had experience in graphics, real estate, market research, and sales in various parts of the country when, in 1986, they started to work on "the hulk" that, although lived in, "had never been cared for." They added heat and new bathrooms, scraped and sanded original crown moldings and 10 fireplace mantels, installed a kitchen in the former ballroom, and much more. Now Oriental rugs are on all the refinished floors. Throughout there are handsome Queen Anne reproduction furnishings—some are for sale and some are made by Michael. Decor, done by Thelma, is Williamsburg. The walls are 18 inches thick. In 1988 Chanceford Hall was on the Maryland House and Garden Tour.

In residence: Both hosts smoke, but not in presence of guests.
Restrictions: "Sorry, our inn does not meet the needs of small children." Please, no guests' pets.
Bed and bath: Five rooms, three with working fireplaces; all private (two full, three shower) baths. First-floor room, wheelchair accessible, has queen canopy bed, working fireplace, exceptional woodwork. Four second-floor rooms, all canopied beds. Most are queen-sized; one is double.
Breakfast: 7–11. Juice, eggs, bacon and sausage, potatoes O'Brian, home-

made apple-cinnamon-raisin sticky ring (one for each couple). Served in crystal-chandeliered dining room with silver, cloth napkins, china.
Plus: Central air conditioning. Beverages and snacks. Fruit basket. Down comforters. Tour of house. Dinner option ($75 for two, served with sterling, antique china, and Waterford crystal). Bicycles. Lap pool. Formal living room. Informal solarium with puzzles, games, TV.

Glenburn

3515 Runnymede Road, Taneytown, MD 21787
Phone: 301/751-1187
Location: In the country, on a 575-acre farm on Route 140 between Westminster and Taneytown. Surrounded by spacious lawns and towering trees. Thirteen miles from Gettysburg. Within 15 minutes of Catoctin Mountain State Park, Carroll County Farm Museum. Antiques shops, a winery, and a golf course nearby. Sixty miles from Washington, D.C., 38 from Baltimore.
Hosts: Robert and Elizabeth Neal
Open: Year round. Reservations required.
Rates: Main house—$50–$75 single, $55–$80 double. Guest house—$55–$85 single, $60–$90 double; 15 percent less Monday–Wednesday.

The unique setting arouses expectations that are fulfilled at this B&B—one that is reminiscent of British B&Bs in historic homes. Cross the iron bridge that stretches over a vigorous creek and proceed along the winding drive to the 1840 house, which served as a 19th-century boys' private school. The imposing country Georgian home with Victorian addition has been in Robert's family for more than 50 years; it is elegantly furnished with heirlooms and American and European antiques. Several times on a Maryland House and Garden Tour, it has also served as a backdrop for a Quaker Oats commercial!

Now that all five Neal children are grown, Elizabeth, a seventh-generation area resident who is active in real estate sales, and Robert, a former history professor who has always been involved with this 575-acre farm, are continuing the tradition of hospitality by sharing their home with travelers. Many guests rise early to see the deer by the creek, jog, bird-watch, or cycle, and then return for breakfast.

Restrictions: Arrival time is 4–6 P.M. unless notified otherwise; departure by 10:30 A.M. No guests' pets. No smoking in bedrooms. "Because of the farm machinery and cattle, please ask us about walking in the fields."
Bed and bath: Private guests' wing with three second-floor double-bedded rooms (each with air conditioner or ceiling fan). Private bath for room with screened porch. Air-conditioned guest house with two large bedrooms—one with queen, the other with two twins—one and a half baths, living room, kitchen/dining area.
Breakfast: 7–9:30. Orange juice, fresh country eggs, country bacon or

sausage, sweet rolls, toast, coffee and tea graciously served in dining room that has grandmother's china displayed on wall plate racks.
Plus: Swimming pool. Fireplaced living room. Tea and coffee always available. Tour of house. Guests' refrigerator.

Guests wrote: "The busy world comes to a gentle stop as you approach the serene lawns of Glenburn, a haven for the weary world."

The Newel Post

3428 Uniontown Road, Uniontown, MD 21157
Phone: 301/775-2655
Location: Rural. In historic town with pastures, meadows, country roads for jogging. Five miles northwest of Westminster. Near antiques shops (closed Mondays), hiking trails, wineries, working gristmills. Ten miles to Ski Liberty downhill ski area. Fifty-minute drive from Baltimore and Washington, D.C.
Hosts: Roger and Janet Michael
Open: Year round. Advance reservations preferred.
Rates: $45 single. $65 private bath, $50 shared bath.

When the Michaels left city life for "a more rural uncomplicated area," they found a town with a tiny general store, a post office, and a street with maple trees that form an archway. Their home, built in 1908 by a country doctor, has the original lighting fixtures, woodwork (from the first owner's nearby family farm), handmade interior chestnut shutters, and stained glass. The reproduction wallpaper is hand-printed. Everything from the lamps to the rugs is Victorian and there is an extensive library on Victoriana.

Hosting fulfills a long-held ambition for Janet, who has fond memories of her grandparents' boardinghouse in Maine. While sharing this home and the peace and quiet of the country, she meets many who "are intrigued with the elaborate decor of an earlier era."

Restrictions: Children 16 and over welcome. Smoking on porches only. Sorry, no guests' pets.
Foreign language spoken: French.
Bed and bath: Four cozy rooms with antique beds. Private full bath with double-bedded first-floor room. On second floor, two double-bedded rooms and one with two double beds share a full bath.
Breakfast: 7–10. Large fresh fruit platters and freshly baked muffins, breads, and scones. Served in formal dining room with china, crystal, lace tablecloth, cloth napkins.
Plus: Tea, sherry, or lemonade. Tour of house. Fresh summer flowers; dried arrangements in winter. Down pillows. Formal garden with fountain and picnic tables.

Tavern House

111 Water Street, P.O. Box 98, Vienna, MD 21869
Phone: 301/376-3347
Location: On the Nanticoke River (much wildlife) in historic Eastern Shore town between Salisbury and Cambridge. At the intersection of Routes 50 and 301. Few blocks from public tennis courts and boat ramp; 100 miles from Washington, D.C.
Hosts: Harvey and Elise Altergott
Open: Year round. Advance reservations required.
Rates: Double occupancy. $55–$60. CHOICE, MC, VISA.

Tradition lives on! One owner of the clapboarded tavern built in the early 1700s was a postmaster—as well as ferry operator and bridge builder. Before moving to this "quiet little town" in 1985, Harvey was a manager at the postal services headquarters in Washington, D.C. Now he is a postal consultant and a pilot (building his own plane) who sometimes tells sea stories about navy life. He and Elise, a former Girl Scouts field executive, have restored everything here "to elegant simplicity"—including the staircase carvings, three massive chimneys, and many window sills. The woodwork painted in authentic colors frames white lime-sand-and-hair plaster. Colonial antiques and reproductions fit just perfectly. And so does their hosting style, one that provides for privacy—or company, just as in the pensions of Italy during the Altergotts' trip there in the 1950s.

In residence: Phineas Calhoon is "a not very talkative parrot." A neighbor's cat, Cricket, drops in routinely.
Restrictions: Children should be at least 12. No smoking in bedrooms. Sorry, no guests' pets.
Foreign languages spoken: "Basic" German and Spanish.
Bed and bath: Three second-floor rooms, two with working fireplaces, share two full baths. Double or twin beds. One double-bedded room "beyond the steps has rum barrel stains on the floor—or what we like to think are rum stains."
Breakfast: Social; 8–noon. Fruit, melons, cheeses, muffins, rolls, French toast. Served in room with two fireplaces, one at each end.
Plus: Afternoon tea or wine with cheeses. Dinner option with advance arrangements. Air conditioners and ceiling fans in bedrooms.

New Jersey

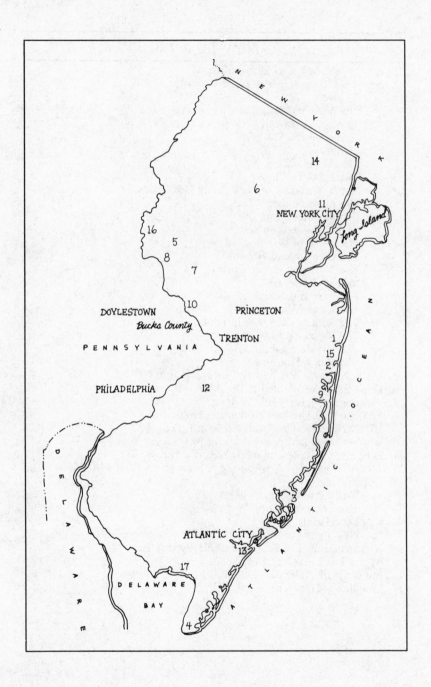

The numbers of this map indicate the locations of B&Bs described in detail in this chapter.

Bed & Breakfast of New Jersey, Inc.

103 Godwin Avenue, Suite 132, Midland Park, NJ 07432
Phone: 201/444-7409. Monday–Friday, 9–4.
Listings: More than 90 hosts, including 45 private homes, 26 inns, and at least 20 unhosted private residences, are located throughout the state of New Jersey. Directory ($5).
Rates: $35–$70 single, $40–$140 double. $5 surcharge for a one-night stay with some hosts. Some family rates. Five percent discount for senior citizens. Monthly rates and off-season specials. Deposit of 25 percent of total cost or one-night rate (whichever is larger) required.

Booking fee of $10–$15 or $25 annual membership fee for reservations anywhere in United States or Canada. If cancellation notice is received one week in advance, deposit less a service charge of $25 will be refunded. AMEX, MC, VISA.

Aster Mould represents accommodations that range from modest to luxurious, all with hosts who "maintain high standards." They all are hosting because they enjoy people and have a desire to share their home and community. Many hosts are bilingual.

Ms. Mould's Bed & Breakfast Adventures offers package tours (accommodations and discounts for restaurants and area attractions) in many parts of the country, as well as consulting services. Ms. Mould is also president of Bed & Breakfast Reservation Services World-Wide Inc., a trade organization that certifies some reservation service homes.

Reservations: Two weeks' advance notice preferred but will make every effort to accommodate requests with a minimum of six hours' notice. Some hosts take one-nighters, sometimes with a small surcharge. Most resort areas require two nights on weekends in season and three on holidays. Also available through travel agents.
Plus: Airport pickup services. Some hosts offer tours. Short-term housing (up to six months) available.

Northern New Jersey Bed & Breakfast/Temporary Lodgings for Transferees

11 Sunset Trail, Denville, NJ 07834
Phone: 201/625-5129. Year round Monday–Friday, 9 A.M.–12 noon and 4–6 P.M.
Listings: 150. Mostly hosted private residences, some inns.
Rates: $35–$65 single, $44–$70 double. Weekly rates available. Deposit

for B&B equivalent to one night's lodging; for transferees, one week's stay. If cancellation is made at least a week in advance, deposit less a $15 service charge is returned.

All of the hosts listed with Annette and Al Bergins are within 50 miles of New York City, in about 50 different northern New Jersey communities. Some are available for the traditional style of B&B, which includes breakfast. Most hosts accommodate corporate transferees and consultants for long-term (up to six months) stays, offering hospitality without the morning meal. Send self-addressed stamped envelope for listings.

Reservations: Enough advance notice needed to allow for receipt of deposit by mail.

KEY

Recipes shared, often for house specialties.

Inquiries welcomed about restoration and/or decorating. Symbol indicates that host is willing to share experiences with guests. Tips range from a before-and-after album to rebuilding advice, from furniture refinishing to curtain making. Expertise of hosts ranges from learn-by-doing to professional.

How-to B&B workshop, seminar, or apprentice program offered.

Cashelmara Inn

22 Lakeside Avenue, Avon-by-the-Sea, NJ 07717
Phone: 201/776-8727
Location: Facing the ocean, which is 100 yards away. To the side is a lake with swans and ducks. In a noncommercial one-square-mile town. Near seafood restaurants; 50 miles from New York City; 60 miles from Philadelphia.
Host: (Mr.) Marty Mulligan
Open: Year round. Advance summer reservations recommended. Three-night minimum stay, July–Labor Day.
Rates: Double occupancy. July–Labor Day, $60–$100. Off season, $50–$75. Rate depends on view (some are panoramic) and size of room. $10 less for singles.

"When I stood on the veranda that blustery January afternoon and saw the sunset over the lake and heard the ocean waves breaking on the beach, I knew that this was the perfect location for a bed and breakfast inn. It took me about five seconds to make an offer after a Realtor led me through this Colonial Revival home that was built in 1901 by the U.S. Postmaster General with an open center hall staircase and many fireplaces. I gave it a Gaelic name that means "house by the sea" and furnished it with wicker, Oriental rugs and period (sittable) antiques to give an English country feeling. Each guest room has a water view. Many have sleigh or high-back Victorian beds and marble-top bureaus."

And thus started—in 1986—a complete career change for Marty, an Eastman Kodak technical representative for 15 years. Now the corporate world comes to him midweek, off season, when they book the inn for seminars or small meetings. ("They love it!") Innkeeping is a perfect fit for Marty these days—right along with auctiongoing. "It is gratifying to see so many guests enjoy this historic, rather awesome yet warm, sunny seaside mansion."

In residence: During summer months and some off-season weekends, Marty's children, Amy, an art student, and Marty, Jr., age 14.
Restrictions: Well-mannered children (booked into first-floor guest rooms) are welcome. Sorry, no guests' pets. Smoking allowed in parlors.
Bed and bath: 14 rooms, each with a water view, on three floors. All private (new) baths; most are tubless. First-floor suite has working fireplace. King, queen, or double beds. A few rooms with two doubles. Cots available.
Breakfast: 8–10:30. Orange juice, homemade baked goods, imported coffees, teas. Entree might be omelets; French toast made with challah; or house specialty of tomatoes, poached egg, bacon, and cheese on English muffin. Served on veranda or on glass-enclosed, heated sun porch.

Plus: Tea or wine, crackers and cheese, 4–5. Fresh flowers in rooms year round. Three parlors, one with working fireplace. Mints. Thirsty towels. Bedroom ceiling fans. Badminton. Croquet. Special weekends, e.g., chili cookoff and New England–style clambakes. Will meet guests at train or bus station. No parking problem. Bicycles provided. Lifeguarded ocean beach right here.

Conover's Bay Head Inn

646 Main Avenue, Bay Head, NJ 08742
Phone: 201/892-4664
Location: One block from the beach. Sixty miles from New York City; 65 miles east of Philadelphia. One hour north of Atlantic City.
Hosts: Carl and Beverly Conover
Open: Year round. Weekends only December–February. Reservations recommended. "In off-season we enjoy our area; please call to make sure we are here." Two-night minimum weekend stay. Three or four nights on holiday weekends.
Rates: Second floor $95 or $105; $130 private porch, all private baths. Third floor $70–$85, shared bath. Single $5–$10 less. Extra person in room $20. Seventh night free. Off season, much less.

The almost-legendary innkeepers live in a quiet one-square-mile town that is still without parking meters and billboards. It has year-round antiquing, shopping, and (most years) golf. Guests play tennis and go swimming, fishing, crabbing—and come "home" to more peace and quiet.

It's 20 years since the Conovers were looking for their very own home in the area where they had spent childhood summers—only to find this 1912 residence with a still-valid 1916 hotel license. Now, many bedrooms are stenciled. The new Palladian window has created everyone's favorite place, a light-filled living room with chintz-covered love seats by the fireplace. Furnishings include turn-of-the-century pieces, plants, ruffles and needlework.

Carl has continued as a structural steel erector and avocational steam engine restorer. Currently he is restoring a 32-foot 1936 Elco wood boat. Beverly has acquired a real estate license.

In residence: Son Tim, age 25. In summer, Beverly's parents, aunt, and uncle.
Restrictions: Children at least age 12 are welcome in the summer months. Sorry, no guests' pets. No smoking inside.
Bed and bath: Twelve rooms in summer, six off season. Six second-floor year-round rooms (one with private porch) have private baths. One third-floor room with private bath. Five "summer" third-floor rooms, all with ocean or bay views, share one full bath. Rooms have double bed, queen, or a double and a twin.
Breakfast: Continental plus with fresh fruit and muffins daily, Aunt Julie's Florida mango jam. Egg casserole Sunday and one midweek day, May

1–September 30. Full breakfast October–May. Eat in dining room or take tray outdoors.
Plus: Air-conditioned bedrooms. Afternoon tea November–April. Outdoor hot/cold showers. Garden sitting area. Porch rockers. Beach passes.

The Bayberry Barque Bed & Breakfast Inn

117 Centre Street, Beach Haven, NJ 08008
Phone: 609/492-5216
Location: In historic section. One block to ocean beach. Within walking distance of summer band concerts, Long Beach Island Museum, restaurants, shops. One hour from Philadelphia, ¾ hour from Atlantic City, 2½ hours from New York City, 20 minutes to historic Barnegat Lighthouse.
Hosts: Pat and Glenn Miller, Gladys Ponterio
Open: Year round. Two-night minimum July and August weekends.
Rates: Double occupancy. Vary according to room. Summer $75–$110, midweek packages available. After Labor Day $50–$60. $15 third person. Special weekend rates for Thanksgiving, Christmas (with dinner), and New Year's. AMEX, MC, VISA.

The staircase stained glass window provides dramatic lighting in the 19th-century Victorian cottage that became a B&B in the early 1980s. "It has a wonderful layout," says Pat, who always wanted to be an innkeeper. Her mother, Gladys, is retired from the New York City traffic department. Glenn is a New Jersey state employee.

"Guests relax, go to the beach, sit on the porch where they have a view of the summer theater and everyone strolling and of the ice cream parlor too. They mingle with each other at our wine and cheese parties, and ask for restaurant recommendations (we know the best!). We have been coming to this area all our lives. Now we enjoy the winter, too, a time when it feels like you're living on a private island. It's really fun to see so many paying guests leave as friends."

In residence: In hosts' quarters, Michael, 13; Christine, 9; Stacy 6; two friendly dogs.
Restrictions: Children five and over welcome. Sorry, no pets.
Bed and bath: Nine rooms. Two with private baths; one of these has ocean view. Four second-floor rooms share one full bath. Three third-floor rooms share one full bath. Most have king/twin or queen beds. Rollaway available.
Breakfast: 8:30–10. Plenty of locally baked muffins, bagels, and Danish. Juices, fruit, cereals, beverages. Sometimes, "Glenn's surprises," hot entrees. Buffet style. Eat in dining room or on front porch.
Plus: Afternoon coffee or iced tea. Saturday evening wine and cheese. Bedroom ceiling fans. Picnic table. Beach passes and outside shower. Babysitting.

Bed & Breakfast of New Jersey Host #475

Beach Haven, NJ
Location: On a side street, A block and a half from ocean. One block from boulevard with shops and restaurants. Within walking distance of summer stock, movies, churches, library, historical museum, cruise boat to Atlantic City—everything!
Reservations: Available May–September through Bed & Breakfast of New Jersey, page 45. Three-day minimum, July and August weekends. Four days on Memorial Day, Fourth of July, and Labor Day weekends.
Rates: Per room. $65–$70 double, shared bath. $75 large double or twin beds, shared bath. $80–$85 double or queen, private bath, air conditioning. $95 king or queen, private bath, air conditioning. $95 suite. No charge for rollaway.

The hosts, northern New Jersey residents, knew the area from years of summer trips. They knew hosting from the vantage point of guests next door, so when this century-old house that "always offered some type of lodging" came on the market, the timing seemed just right. The hostess, a collector of early American antiques who is a talented seamstress, had experience leading tours to Manhattan. Here in Beach Haven, she redecorated with a country theme and wicker on the front porch. Her husband, too, finds that meeting "professionals and students and people with many different interests" is a fascinating lifestyle. Both hosts were involved in organizing a Victorian Weekend in Beach Haven. Many guests return and/or send their relatives and friends here where "the coffeepot is on automatic."

In residence: Two teenagers.
Restrictions: Children 10 and over welcome. Sorry, no pets or smoking please.
Foreign language spoken: German.
Bed and bath: Twelve rooms plus one first-floor queen-bedded suite with private entrance. Private baths with most rooms. Four share two baths. King/twin, queen, double beds, and rollaway available.
Breakfast: 8:30–10:30. Home-baked goods. Homemade butter, jams, and jellies. Juice, coffee, decaf. Served buffet style in enclosed porch.
Plus: Four rooms are air conditioned. Two outside hot/cold showers. Beach badges. "No phones, radios, or clocks." Plenty of street parking.

Pierrot by the Sea

101 Centre Street, Beach Haven, NJ 08008
Winter address: 1611 Haworth Street, Philadelphia, PA 19124
Phone: 609/492-4424
Location: "Thirty seconds from the ocean." On a beach corner. One block from Surflight Theater. Close to shops and restaurants. Five min-

utes east of the Garden State Parkway. Seven miles south of Long Beach Island Causeway.

Hosts: Catherine Forrestal and Richard Burdo
Open: May–October. Advance reservations required. Two-night minimum July–Labor Day. Three-day minimum holiday weekends.
Rates: July 4–Labor Day, $85 shared bath, $100 private bath. May 1–July 4 and Labor Day–October 31, $65 shared bath, $75 private bath. MC, VISA.

"Completely Victorian down to the doorknobs!" Stained glass (much of it made by Catherine and Richard), gates, lamps, tall bedsteads, linens, cast iron urns.... It's all here in the authentically restored summer cottage built as The Tea Cup Inn in 1876.

For Catherine, a former Saks Fifth Avenue fashion coordinator, and Richard, a professional house restorer, opening a B&B was a natural progression from their most recent enterprises, an antiques business and a five-star restaurant in Philadelphia. If you'd like to follow the restoration done here in 1984, there's a before-and-after album. Flowers are everywhere. Candy is on the pillow at night. Guests are served tea on the wraparound porch. The five-course breakfast is a feature. A gazebo in the garden completes the Victorian environment.

In residence: College-age daughter, Megan. "Cassidy is our 15-year-old orange cat with green eyes."
Restrictions: Well-behaved children seven or older welcome. Smoking on front porch only. Sorry, no pets.
Bed and bath: Eight rooms (most with ocean views) with king/twin, queen, or double bed. Two first-floor rooms with private baths and separate entrance. Four second-floor rooms share one full bath. Two third-floor rooms share a full bath. Rollaway available.
Breakfast: 8:30–10. Homemade breads and muffins. Entree possibilities include eggs Benedict and French toast. Served in dining room at candlelit tables for two or four people.
Plus: Fireplaced living room. Afternoon tea with home-baked goodies. Saturdays, wine and cheese. Dinner option ($25). Tour of house. Bedroom ceiling fans. Outdoor showers. Beach tags. Bicycles. Local paper delivered to your room.

Cape May

Known as the oldest seaside resort in America, Cape May might well be called the largest B&B community of today. Homes, guest houses, and hotels, all with Victorian architectural detail, were built by the hundreds in the 19th century. Other resorts closer to home by way of "the machine" became more fashionable after the turn of the century. But early in the 1970s, Cape May, now a National Historic Landmark city, began to experience a renaissance.

The profiles of B&B owners on the following pages indicate how one has inspired another. Several hosts don appropriate hats and conduct walking tours of the historic district or of their own restored and refurbished B&Bs. There are trolley tours in town, a boardwalk, and the main summer attraction, the beach. Some B&Bs provide bicycles, direct you to the restored Physick Estate, and tout their proximity to the Washington Street Mall with its many art galleries, crafts shops, and antiques emporiums. Hiking and bird-watching opportunities are here too. Daffodils, tulips, and Victorian balls have become the theme for so-called off-season weekends. Christmas is celebrated in glorious Victorian style with many special events and decorations. And in 1988, over 60,000 people climbed to the top of the Cape May Point Lighthouse, providing funds for continued restoration.

The Abbey

Columbia Avenue and Gurney Street, Cape May, NJ 08024
Phone: 609/884-4506
Location: One block from the ocean. Two blocks from the main shopping area. Within walking distance of most restaurants.
Hosts: Marianne and Jay Schatz
Open: April–November. Reservations suggested. June 15–September 30, three-night minimum weekday stay, four nights for weekends. Longer minimum for some rooms.
Rates: Double occupancy. $60–$115 depending on size of room. Single $10 less. Ten percent discount for Sunday-to-Sunday stay.

> Guests wrote: "A picture of graciousness. Attentive hosts who make a vacation a memorable occasion. A home filled with love and laughter. Guest rooms filled with beautiful Victorian furniture, lace curtains, flowers, lavender soaps, lace-trimmed pillows and sheets."

When Manhattan's Bloomingdale's had a photo essay based on *Bed & Breakfast in the Mid-Atlantic States*, a million people viewed the gorgeous picture of the harp in The Abbey's opulent living room. Throughout this Gothic Revival home, built in 1869 as a summer retreat for coal baron John B. McCreary, there are exquisite antiques, chandeliers, and window treatments. In 1977 it was the fourth Schatz house restoration. That's the year that Marianne left her 14-year job as a chemist to run the B&B. Soon after, Jay, a chemist with an MBA, took his last train ride in a three-piece suit, donned one of his many period hats (he still collects them), conducted his first croquet game on the lawn, and became full-time innkeeper. Ten years and many delicious breakfasts later, the house next door, originally built by Mr. McCreary for his son, came back "into the family" with the Schatz touch.

In residence: "Long-haired, beautiful red cat named Fergie, a calico named Hillary, and an adorable, husky gray cat named Bubba."
Restrictions: Children should be least 12. Sorry, no pets. Smoking limited to verandas.
Bed and bath: In two adjacent houses—14 rooms on three floors. Baths—11 are private—include a unique one in the turret and another with a fern that covers the entire ceiling of what may be Cape May's smallest bath. King, queen (one canopied), or double beds.
Breakfast: 8:30 and 9:30. Spring and fall—entree (perhaps casserole or quiches with fettucine or fritters), muffins, fresh fruit, juice, coffee and tea. Marianne is chef; Jay serves in dining room. In summer—continental on veranda with freshly baked breads and cakes, fresh fruit, juice, cereals, coffee and tea. Hosts join guests. "It's the best time of our day."
Plus: Air conditioning in six rooms; ceiling or portable fans in others. Late-afternoon refreshments. Tour of house (free for guests, charge for public tours). Morning croquet while noncompetitors cheer from the veranda. Off-street parking for some rooms. Beach passes.

Barnard-Good House

238 Perry Street, Cape May, NJ 08204
Phone: 609/884-5381
Location: Two blocks from the main beach. Ten minutes' walk from the center of town.
Hosts: Nan and Tom Hawkins
Open: April–November. June 15–September 15, three-day minimum in all rooms, four days in suites.
Rates: Double occupancy. $75 or $78 private half bath, shared shower. $85 private full bath, $95 suite with sitting room, private bath. Singles 10 percent less. Ten percent discount for seven-day stay. MC, VISA accepted to guarantee last-minute reservation (one-night charge only).

From New Jersey: "Nan and Tom become representatives of that gracious period of time. . . . Casual atmosphere . . . fantastic culinary experience . . . addicting!"

We found that, indeed, the hosts love life and guests love the hosts— and their extraordinary breakfasts. It was early in the season when we visited, but it was a full house with many in the 25–35 age range and others young at heart.

"I really do love Victorian," said Tom as he scraped the shutters scheduled to go on the formerly white, now lavender house.

Before coming here in 1980, the Hawkinses had lived in central New

Jersey with early American "complete with hanging baskets in the kitchen." About the time of their 30th wedding anniversary, when Tom was a purchasing director for a plastics manufacturing firm and Nan was marketing director for a shopping center, they were searching for a career change and found this Second Empire mansard-roofed house—empty. They did (and continue to do) all the restoration themselves. The dining room has a gasolier made of iron, pewter, and brass. The 100-year-old organ in the living room really works if you pump hard. Each guest room is quite different, with the flamboyant pink, white, and green Hawkins Suite a popular honeymooners' room. One of the bathrooms has a copper tub and pull-chain john.

Restrictions: Children should be at least 14. No guests' pets. Smoking on verandas only.
Bed and bath: Five rooms or suites on second and third floors. One with private full bath. Two with private shower. King or double beds available.
Breakfast: Their hallmark. Starts at 8:30. In dining room with lace tablecloth. Menu never repeated regardless of your length of stay. (Special diets accommodated.) Maybe freshly extracted and blended juices, muffins, crepes, fruit soup, cheese bread, exotic chicken dish, chocolate chip banana cake. Can last two hours "depending on how much fun we are having."
Plus: Living room with gas fireplace. Rockers and wicker furniture on wraparound porch. Bedroom ceiling fans. Off-street parking right here. Beach tags.

Bed & Breakfast of New Jersey Host #495

Cape May, NJ
Location: Centrally located in the historic district. Half a block from the beach, two blocks from shopping mall.
Reservations: Year round through Bed & Breakfast of New Jersey, page 45. Three-night minimum stay summer weekends.
Rates: Double occupancy. $70 shared bath. $80–$100 private bath. Singles $10 less. $10 rollaway. (Plus reservation service booking or membership fee. Please see page 45.)

Once again the outside of this house built in 1869 as a part of a hotel for railroad executives and their families has dainty gingerbread trim along the dormers, roof, and balcony. All the inside woodwork has been stripped and refinished. Lace curtains are on the windows. Decor is a combination of country Victorian and French Renaissance with Oriental rugs and stained glass.

After the hosts purchased the Carpenter Gothic house in 1983 for a summer retreat, they spent three years restoring just about everything, reversing the "modernization" that had taken place in 1915 when all the trim was removed. The host, captain of a charter boat, is the millwork expert. (The house was featured in *Mid-Atlantic Woodshop News*.) His wife is the interior designer. Hosting fulfills a long-time dream.

In residence: One daughter in her twenties.
Restrictions: Children 10 and over welcome. Sorry, no pets or smoking allowed.
Bed and bath: Six double-bedded rooms, three with canopied beds (one with double Murphy bed also). Four with private bath. One second-floor room also has a private porch. Two third-floor rooms share a full bath. Rollaway available.
Breakfast: 8:30–10:45. Fresh fruit, pastry, orange juice, coffee, tea. Served in formal dining room or sun room. "At times, it lasts until noon."
Plus: Bedroom ceiling fans. Wicker-furnished front veranda. Flower-filled third-floor sun room; chess. Piano in parlor. Off-street parking. Tour of house.

The Brass Bed

719 Columbia Avenue, Cape May, NJ 08204
Phone: 609/884-8075
Location: In the historic district, two blocks from the ocean.
Hosts: John and Donna Dunwoody
Open: Year round. Reservations required. Two- or three-night minimum stay (depending on accommodations) on all weekends plus July and August.
Rates: Double occupancy. January 1–March 31, $65–$70 shared bath, $75–$79 private half bath, $83–$87 private bath. April 1–June 15, $70–$75/$80–$85/$90–$95. June 16–September 15, $80–$85/$92–$98/$112. September 16–December 31, $75–$80/$85–$90/$90–$95.

Personal touches are everywhere—family heirlooms, old photos of relatives, the 1895 upright piano that may be a gathering spot for singing, and daughter Mary's dollhouse in the foyer. "It's like grandma's where everything is touchable and guests are treated like family." And at Christmas time, during house tour time, you have a full-dress picture of an era gone by.

The Dunwoodys came for a retreat, "fell in love with Cape May, sold everything in Voorhees, New Jersey, borrowed as much as we could and jumped in (in 1980) to a new lifestyle." They moved in the month of January and John continued all that winter to commute at dawn to Philadelphia for his graphic design position.

Now, in addition to period brass beds in every room, there are lace curtains, period wallcoverings, and patterned Oriental carpets. Many restored furnishings in the 116-year-old house are original—armoires, marble-topped tables, washstands, and dressers. There's also a 19th-century Graphonola (purchased in 1962) that John restored. Frequently early recordings can be heard. As the guest from Maryland wrote, "Magical."

In residence: Clouseau, the cat, is not allowed in guest rooms.
Restrictions: No smoking indoors. "Children under 12 are best left with grandma."
Foreign languages spoken: Some French and Spanish.
Bed and bath: Eight rooms on second and third floors. Two with private baths. Two with private half baths. Four share two full baths. King, double, and twin beds.
Breakfast: Fresh fruit, cereal, homemade baked goods, beverages. Eggs, pancakes, or other hot entrees in fall and winter. Served by the Victorian hearth.
Plus: Afternoon tea, lemonade, or cider and refreshments. Front porch rockers. Bedroom ceiling fans. Outside hot/cold shower, dressing room. Bicycle rack. Beach passes.

Captain Mey's Inn

202 Ocean Street, Cape May, NJ 08204
Phone: 609/884-7793 or 884-9637
Location: Two blocks from the beach. A half block from the Victorian shopping mall. Within walking distance of all restaurants.
Hosts: Carin Fedderman and Milly LaCanfora
Open: Year round. Two-night minimum weekend stay, off season. Three-night minimum in season.
Rates: Vary according to room location and bath arrangement. Double occupancy, $65–$125 July–Labor Day. $20 additional guest in room. Less off season. Singles $5 less.

For a national television feature on Dutch Christmas, the cameras came here, where there's a delightful mix of Dutch and Victorian—with lots of brass, copper, and pewter; a Delft Blue collection; Tiffany glass; and Victorian furniture. The fastidiously maintained and comfortable inn—where guests awake to the strains of classical music—is hosted by the creators of Cape May's Tulip Fest, Carin and Milly, both from Holland. Their own grounds have a show of 400 bulbs as well as an herb garden with 15 varieties.

Once a doctor's residence, then a tearoom and later a rooming house, Captain Mey's, named after the Dutch founder of Cape May, was converted to a B&B 10 years ago. That was when Carin, a travel coordinator, and Millie, a computer programmer, stripped and refinished all that woodwork—all the way to the third floor. The authentic exterior colors were custom-mixed. Milly's mother made the afghans and quilts. Fresh flowers, mostly from the garden, are in the rooms.

In residence: Two cats, Wetzel and Co-Co.
Restrictions: Children should be at least 10. Sorry, no guests' pets. No smoking indoors.
Foreign languages spoken: Dutch and Italian.
Bed and bath: Eight rooms on first, second, and third floors. Two with private baths, six with semiprivate baths. Double and twin beds available.

Breakfast: 8:30–9:30. Fresh fruit, homemade breads and cakes, yogurt, assorted Dutch cheeses. Hot entree such as cheese strata, quiche, or almost-famous French toast. Enjoyed buffet style in the dramatic foyer, in the candlelit dining room, or on the wraparound veranda with privacy afforded by Victorian wind curtains.

Plus: Iced tea (with mint from the garden) and cookies on the veranda in summer, sherry by the fire in winter. Bedroom ceiling fans. Beach passes, chairs, and towels. Turn-down service with pillow mints. Garden area for picnic lunch. Off-street parking.

From New Jersey: "It's like a dream. . . . We have watched the inn become more authentic and beautiful each year. . . . A step back to a period when gracious living was a way of life."

COLVMNS by the Sea

1513 Beach Drive, Cape May, NJ 08204
Phone: 609/884-2228
Location: On the ocean. Across the street from fishing. One block from a not-so-crowded protected swimming beach. A short bike ride to mall, restaurants.
Hosts: Barry and Cathy Rein
Open: May–October. Reservations required. Two-day minimum stay at all times.
Rates: July–Labor Day $95–$105 twin beds, ocean view, and private bath. $105–$125 private bath, ocean front. $25 extra person in room. Singles $10 less. Ten percent discount for weekly bookings, Penn State graduates, Audubon Society members. MC, VISA.

"Fall asleep to the sound of the ocean. Wake up to a breathtaking view." That's exactly what attracted the couple who went from being tourists to summer house owners to innkeepers in just four years. When Barry decided to make a career change from managing new business development, the Reins (and help) brought this turn-of-the-century "great cottage" complete with oversized windows from its then apartment status "back to the original splendor, as they say." They restored coffered ceilings, the three-storied staircase, and wainscoting—and furnished with Victorian antiques, "the kind you can sit on," and reproduction beds. Recently they bought, after exhibition at the Smithsonian, a three-piece bedroom suite built for the 1878 Centennial; it had been in the Blair House in Washington, D.C. For a personal touch, Cathy has written notes about the history of wicker or the fashion of the times.

The hosts still spend winters in New York City. Six months of the year, Barry is in Cape May while Cathy, a lawyer who is senior vice-president of Metropolitan Life, flies in for weekends.

Restrictions: Children should be at least 12. Sorry, no guests' pets. No smoking indoors.
Foreign language spoken: German.

Bed and bath: Eleven rooms on second and third floors. All with private full baths. Five are ocean front. King, queen, or twin beds. Three rooms with trundles sleep up to four.

Breakfast: A feature at 9:30. (Coffee is ready at 8.) Fruit, juice, homemade breads and coffee cakes, blintz souffle, Barry's scrambled eggs with country smoked bacon, caramelized French toast, cheese bread, and "any other great recipe we come across." Served in bay-windowed dining room with marble tiled fireplace.

Plus: Tea at 5. Evening sherry. An L-shaped porch that Barry has learned to call "a wraparound veranda" overlooking the ocean. Living room with fireplace, nickelodeon. Upstairs parlor and large foyer for reading or writing. Downstairs parlor with TV. Tour of house. Bedroom ceiling fans. Ice. Parking. Bicycles. Beach badges. Spontaneous clambakes and barbecues. Victorian Holmes weekend.

The Duke of Windsor

817 Washington Street, Cape May, NJ 08204
Phone: 609/884-1355
Location: In historic area. Four blocks from beach, "close enough, but quiet too."
Hosts: Bruce and Fran Prichard
Open: Year round. Three-night minimum stay, July–September. Other months, two-night minimum. Reservations suggested.
Rates: Double occupancy. $63–$68 shared bath, $65–$90 private bath. Off season, $55–$60 shared bath, $60–$70 private bath. $10 extra person. Ten percent discount for a seven-night stay.

Although the Prichards instantly took to Cape May and its pace ("People greet strangers in a friendly way on the street") in 1980, they weren't quite sure about the abrupt change in lifestyle made by their friends from home (Voorhees, New Jersey); "but when we came to help them open The Brass Bed, it was neat to see the restoration progress. We soon bought this grand (in every way) 1896 house and extended our entertaining style to new friends. Hosting is wonderful. We love our guests!"

The classic Queen Anne detailing includes Tiffany stained glass; a restored dining room with replica wallpaper of Queen Victoria's throne room, ornate plaster ceiling, and 1871 chandelier; original natural oak woodwork; and a three-story cantilevered stairway. Research and restoration are ongoing; there are plans for restoring the exterior too. Furnishings are antiques and period pieces.

Fran is a library/media specialist, and Bruce is a teacher of chemistry and physics. Occasionally, when they are not able to be in Cape May, daughter Barbara, granddaughter Maria Frances, or Fran's mother, Helen, hosts.

Restrictions: Children should be at least 12. Please leave pets with friends. No cigar smoking indoors.
Bed and bath: Nine rooms (two in turret) on second and third floors with

a double or a double and a twin bed. Private baths except for two rooms that share one.

Breakfast: 8:30–10, but late sleepers won't go hungry. June 15–September 30, fresh fruits, juices, cereals, and a home-baked specialty. Plus, in off season, hot entree such as eggs and bacon, pancakes, or French toast.

Plus: Afternoon tea. Beach passes. Hot and cold outside showers. Parlor with corner fireplace. Bedroom fans. Dining room and "family" parlor. First-floor tower game room for cards, chess, and checkers. Off-street parking.

A guest wrote: "Personal touches everywhere, from the sheets hung in the sunshine to the candies by the door. I arrived tense and tired and drove home singing."

The Gingerbread House

28 Gurney Street, Cape May, NJ 08204

Phone: 609/884-0211

Location: In the historic district, half a block from the beach. Within walking distance of restaurants, shops, and homes open for tours.

Hosts: Joan and Fred Echevarria

Open: Year round. Four-night minimum weekend stay during summer months and holidays. Two- or three-night minimum weekend stay at other times.

Rates: Double occupancy. $70–$75 shared bath, $98–$120 private bath. $15 additional person. Six percent discount for week-long stays. Midweek discounts October–May.

First you notice the tricolored gingerbread trim on the outside of the beige 1869 house, which is listed on the National Register of Historic Places. Then you are given a warm welcome by Fred, a clinical psychologist turned B&B manager, photographer, and woodworker. Ever since the Echevarrias bought the house in 1979, Joan has been an evening-and-weekend hostess because of her daily commute to a Philadelphia investment advisory firm where she is manager of data processing. She arrives back in Cape May with renewed energy but over the years has added staff so that planting pansies by flashlight is no longer a routine spring task. On weekends she enjoys a bike ride to Cape May Point beach "where you can tuck yourself in between the dunes, listen to the ocean and read your favorite book."

Many family members helped in this restoration, creating a bright, warm, and airy feeling. All the wonderful watercolors—with the exception of the one of the house done by the first paying guest—were painted by Fred's mother, Jane Echevarria, an artist featured in her own book, *Victorian Interiors.* (When a guest buys a painting, Jane creates a replacement!) Furnishings are walnut, rosewood, wicker, and oak. And always, there's some new accessory such as a silver tray or a Limoges piece acquired "right in this area which is great for antiquing."

In residence: Moby the cat. One host (Fred) smokes.
Restrictions: Children should be at least seven and well-behaved. Sorry, no guests' pets.
Bed and bath: Six double-bedded rooms. Three second-floor rooms (one with two double beds and private porch) with private baths. Three third-floor rooms (one with skylight, one with cathedral ceiling) share one tub bath.
Breakfast: 8:30–10. Buffet includes fresh fruit and homemade coffee cake or muffins.
Plus: Fireplace in living room. Bedroom ceiling fans. Outside enclosed shower. Front porch. Garden. Beach tags.

From New Jersey: "Beautiful rooms, delicious continental breakfast and friendly people—all the ingredients for a wonderful stay. Highly recommended!"

The Mainstay Inn & Cottage

635 Columbia Avenue, Cape May, NJ 08204
Phone: 609/884-8690
Location: On a side street, within walking distance of everything.
Hosts: Tom and Sue Carroll
Open: March–November. Three-day minimum weekend stay in spring and fall and mid-June to mid-September. Advance reservations strongly recommended. First-time guests, in particular, should call so that the rooms and amenities can be described.
Rates: Spring/fall $80–$110. Weekends/summer $90–$125.

Elegance. Attention to detail. A visual feast that is enjoyed by "both those who want to be alone and others who seek friendship." But hardly a hidden treasure. Many major publications have pictured the long walnut dining room table, gas chandeliers, and ceiling-high mirrors in addition to the beautiful exterior of what was built in 1872 as an exclusive clubhouse for gamblers.

The Carrolls loved old houses, even when Tom was a Coast Guardsman in Cape May. For postservice living, they bought their first Mainstay, which had a few rooms for summer guests. Tom worked with the planning board. Sue taught. In 1977 they acquired the current Mainstay with many of the original furnishings and fixtures. Ahead of the renewed interest in Victoriana, Sue created swag patterns and wallpaper borders. Now Oriental rugs are in the 14-foot-high parlors that feature Bradbury and Bradbury screened papers. The cottage next door, where we stayed, is also furnished with choice Victorian antiques. Other questions are answered during the public tours (no charge for guests).

In many ways this is considered a model of the evolution of a B&B business, beginning with the hosts' struggle to overcome local opposition to the dramatic (positive) impact of B&Bs on an entire community—and continuing to the innkeepers' community involvement (Mid-Atlantic Center for the Arts, Shakespeare Weekend, Cape May Point Lighthouse restoration). Sue still answers mail with handwritten notes. This is a business run with joy, style, and personalization.

In residence: Othello, a 21-year-old cat who is "very important and he'll let you know it." Pandora, a young cat.
Restrictions: Children should be over 12. "Young children generally find us tiresome." No smoking inside. No guests' pets.
Bed and bath: Twelve large rooms with private baths on three floors (one with steep staircase). One first-floor room. Two with private porches. King, queen, double, or twin beds available.
Breakfast: 8:15–9:45. In season, light meal with homemade breads. Off season, a full meal could include corn quiche, chicken pie, or bacon and fish rolls. Served on the veranda or in the dining room.
Plus: Afternoon tea. Drawing room with coal stove. Three parlors. Veranda with rockers and swing; private porches with some guest rooms. Garden. Ladder to climb to cupola for ocean view. Beach passes. Outside shower.

Manor House

612 Hughes Street, Cape May, NJ 08204
Phone: 609/884-4710
Location: On a quiet side street in historic district, 1½ blocks from the ocean. One block from shops, restaurants, and pedestrian street mall.
Hosts: Mary and Tom Snyder
Open: Year round. Two-night weekend reservations preferred; three nights on holiday weekends.
Rates: Double occupancy. July and August—king or queen with private bath $120, shared bath $85. Less rest of year, according to season. Winter weekends—king or queen with private bath $90, shared bath $70.

Barbershop quartet singing is the newest interest of the host, who serves breakfast in bow tie, starched shirt, and colored suspenders. Between both hosts, there's experience in college administration, potato chip manufacturing (their own), and (for a short time) the corporate world. The quilts are Mary's (and her mother's) creations. Furnishings are of the period, with each room being quite different in size and decor. Information about doings, past and present, is spiced with facts and humor.
    When the mid-life career changers bought this 1906 house, they acquired a homey place that had been completely redone in 1983 by a wood carver who had a special appreciation for the chestnut and oak staircase, the floors and moldings. Originally a summer home, the house without gingerbread has bay windows, ornate radiators, a great fireplace, and some original as well as new stained glass.

In residence: Apple Butter, "our 16-year-old long-haired dachshund, the gentle lady of the house."

Restrictions: Children should be at least 12. Sorry, no guests' pets. No smoking.
Foreign language spoken: Pennsylvania Dutch.
Bed and bath: Ten rooms on the second and third floors, four rooms with private baths, three with half baths, and three with sinks and shared baths. Rooms have king (canopied), queen, or double beds.
Breakfast: 8:30 and 9:30 seatings. Two entrees prepared from a repertoire of more than 30. Guests choose one of two. Possibilities include asparagus on homemade English muffin toast, poached eggs and sauce Mornay, apple-cheese pancakes, Mexican quiche, strawberry crepes, and Manor House French toast.
Plus: Punch, cider, tea, or wine. Theme weekends include one for runners in May, a December Dickens program, and a cooking seminar. Living room with fireplace. Some bedrooms with air conditioners; ceiling fans in others. Off-premises valet parking. Beach tags. Hot/cold outdoor shower.

A guest wrote: "Warm and beautiful home. Out-of-this-world food. The perfect atmosphere for total relaxation."

The Mason Cottage

625 Columbia Avenue, Cape May, NJ 08204
Phone: 609/884-3358
Location: On a quiet tree-lined street in historic district.
Hosts: Dave and Joan Mason
Open: May–October. Three-night minimum on holiday weekends. Other weekends, two-night minimum stay.
Rates: Double occupancy. $65–$75 shared bath, $80–$105 private bath. (Vary according to room size and location.) Ten percent discount for four or more nights excluding holiday weekends. Five percent AARP discount. MC, VISA.

Honeymooners receive special attention. Others come for their anniversary. Everyone remembers the hospitality in this B&B, which has been in the Mason family since 1946. Returnees of the 1980s have seen the constant changes made by Joan, a registered nurse and clinical editor, and husband Dave, an electrical engineer and licensed contractor, who took over in 1981. For an almost-final project, they did a floor-to-ceiling restoration of the parlor (already the scene of a wedding). It now has an Oriental rug, blue plaster medallion, chandelier and sconces, rose-colored swags, lace curtains, and authentic bordered Victorian wallpaper. Furnishings include family heirlooms and some pieces that were original to the mansard-roofed house, built in 1871 as a summer residence by the Warne family of Philadelphia.

In residence: Dave is here on all weekends; Joan, May–October weekends. Patty and Clyde Hoar are May–October weekday hosts.
Restrictions: Sorry, no guests' pets. No children under 12. Smoking only on veranda.

Bed and bath: Five double-bedded rooms on two floors. Four with private baths; one with semiprivate bath. Beds are Victorian wood or brass and painted.
Breakfast: 9–10. Juice, fresh fruit, pastries, and cereals; brewed coffee, tea. Buffet at snack tables set up in parlor or on veranda. Hosts join guests for the leisurely meal.
Plus: Saturday afternoon tea. Bedroom ceiling fans. Private outside showers with hot/cold water, dressing areas. (Also available to guests after checkout.) Beach passes. Bike rack.

A guest wrote: "The rooms and the surrounding neighborhood are almost like a scene out of a movie. A prime example of the charm and hospitality this historic town has to offer."

The Queen Victoria

102 Ocean Street, Cape May, NJ 08204
Phone: 609/884-8702
Location: In the historic district, one block from the beach and 1½ blocks from Washington Street shopping.
Hosts: Joan and Dane Wells
Open: Year round. Phone reservations recommended. Holidays and weekends may require much advance notice. Two-night minimum stay on weekends. May–October, three- or four-night minimum.
Rates: Vary according to season. Double occupancy. $69–$120 (weekends mid-June–mid-September $99–$120). $128–$178 suites for two. Single $10 less. $10 extra person or crib. MC, VISA.

The two-year transformation of the century-old summer cottage was featured with 23 photographs in *Victorian Homes* magazine. That was after the Wellses had researched, demolished, caned chairs, and located antiques—and opened the comfortable and elegant country inn in 1981. The most recent addition—beyond two luxurious suites and additional private baths—is a player piano, located through a guest. Some former guests have become year-round Cape May residents. And some arrive with pictures of their own restoration. "We love to see them," says Joan, the former executive director (now she's on the national board) of the Victorian Society in America. She was also curator of the "Unsinkable" Molly Brown House museum in Denver, where she was responsible for the beginning of its restoration. Dane's latest claim to fame is his certification as a beer judge by the American Home Brewers' Association. Before becoming an innkeeper, he was in neighborhood commercial revitalization and economic development in Philadelphia, "but most important, as a boy he worked in a hardware store!"

In residence: Elizabeth, age six. Two cats, Mumbles, named for a Welsh town, and Shoes (short for snowshoes because of his extra thumbs).
Restrictions: Nonsmokers preferred. Smoking in library and on porches

only. Infants welcomed. No pets, please. $3 parking fee (free parking in lot four blocks away).

Foreign languages spoken: Dane is fluent in French. Joan struggles with some Spanish.

Bed and bath: Eleven rooms (on three floors); all private baths, some shower only. All antique beds and handmade quilts. Two air-conditioned family suites; each sleeps two to four and has 1½ baths, TV. Carriage House suite has a Jacuzzi; a full kitchen is in Cottage House suite.

Breakfast: Usually 8–10. Buffet style. Always includes homemade raisin bran, breads, granola, baked apple. A different egg dish each day. Eat at dining room table (seats 12), in bay window of the parlor, or on side porch.

Plus: Afternoon tea with homemade cookies, pâtés, and cheese spreads. Bedroom ceiling fans. Refrigerator in some rooms. Porches. Fireplaced parlor. Bicycles (free). Beach tags. Bathhouse with changing room and showers. Family-style Thanksgiving, Christmas decorations, caroling, or Dickens weekends.

The Summer Cottage Inn

613 Columbia Street, P.O. Box 27, Cape May, NJ 08204
Phone: 609/884-4948
Location: On a quiet tree-lined street in the historic district. One block from the beach.
Host: Nancy Rishforth
Open: Year round; weekends only in January and February. Advance reservations usually required. Three-day minimum on holidays and June–September weekends; two nights other weekends.
Rates: Vary according to size of room, location, bath arrangement, amenities (such as private entrance or porch). Double occupancy. $65–$105 all weekends and June 15–September 30. Rest of year, weekdays 20–25 percent off. Singles $5 less. $20 extra person. MC, VISA.

> Guests wrote: "Memorable in the summer . . . superb in windy and cold weather . . . delicious all year round." Others wrote to me about Nancy; her cuisine of "invented recipes"; the family heirlooms; the decor; personal touches; the cleanliness; the total ambiance; their "favorite B&B in the whole world"; even their initial call of inquiry.

First-timers go home and tell their friends and relatives about this Italianate "cottage" built complete with a cupola in 1867. The mutual love affair began after Nancy, a former caterer, "fell in love with the town," restored (in 1982) one of its oldest buildings, and filled it with Victorian antiques and collectibles. Now she's a landmark tour guide who finds joy in sending guests to the prettiest gardens or the most newly painted house. She'll pack a picnic basket, share snippets of past and present Cape May gossip, suggest sources for quality Victorian wallpapers, and maybe send you on your way with fresh herbs or flowers.

Restrictions: Children over 12 welcome. Smoking allowed on veranda only. No pets, please.
Bed and bath: Nine rooms, each named for style of furniture, such as Eastlake, Renaissance, or Empire. Three second-floor double-bedded rooms, each with a sink, share two full baths. Private baths with each third-floor room; one double bed, two doubles, or one double and a twin available. Garden suite with private entrance, double bed, full bath, a sitting room, and a dressing room.
Breakfast: Renowned. Summers, two-hour buffet. Winters, with crystal, china, and linen, at 8:45 or 9:45. Perhaps melon with lime-blueberry mousse, a torte of layered crepes with a seasoned spinach-sausage-cheese filling, rum raisin creme buns and chocolate nut bread with imported teas and coffee.
Plus: "Sweet and savory teatime delights." Tour of house and garden. Window and ceiling fans. Fireplaced sitting room. Baby grand piano. Game table. Antique music boxes. Mints. Flowers. Wicker- and plant-filled wraparound porches; one with swing. Enclosed outside shower and dressing room. Bike storage. Restaurant and sunset recommendations. Yes, a cookbook too!

The Victorian Rose

715 Columbia Avenue, Cape May, NJ 08204
Phone: 609/884-2497
Location: In historic district, 2½ blocks from ocean. Five blocks to the Victorian Mall. Within walking distance of most restaurants. Golfing and tennis nearby.
Hosts: Bob and Linda Mullock
Open: March–December 25. Three-night minimum stay on weekends June–September.
Rates: $62–$115. Off season about $10 less.

From Pennsylvania: "A rose among roses."

It was a private home, a tearoom, a school for girls, and an inn. For the last nine years it has been a B&B, owned and run by a couple who feel they got into the business "by luck." Their "before" life was in Philadelphia, where he was in marketing and she was a Realtor and nursery-school teacher. Here Bob has an insurance office just three blocks away. On Saturday mornings he wears a straw hat when he leads historic district walking tours. (Ask about the trees and he'll tell you what he learned from a 97-year-old botanist/guest.)
The parlor is the "comfortable 30s." The dining and bedrooms are Victorian. The "romantic" rose theme is everywhere—on teapots, wallpapers, fabrics, linens. Some of the 150 rosebushes and the arched porch are pictured on a Cape May greeting card. Evening taped music is from the big band era. At breakfast it's Mozart.

In residence: Cynthia, age 12, and Zachary, age 4.
Restrictions: No guests' pets. In the main inn, children should be over 12. (Children of all ages allowed in the cottage.)
Bed and bath: Eight rooms. Five with private baths. One with half bath. Two third-floor rooms share a bath. Single, double, or king-sized bed. Cots available.
Breakfast: At 9. Could be fruit cup, eggs in puffed pastry, and cheese with sausage. Served at a long table that seats 18. Linda cooks, serves, and joins guests. "It's my favorite part of the day." Can last up to three hours.
Plus: Bedroom ceiling fans. Front porch rockers. Beach tags.

The Wooden Rabbit

609 Hughes Street, Cape May, NJ 08204
Phone: 609/884-7293
Location: In historic district "on what we consider the prettiest gaslit street in town." Two blocks from beaches. One block from shops. Within easy walking distance of restaurants.
Hosts: Greg and Debby Burow
Open: Year round. Usually, three-night minimum in July and August, two nights rest of year.
Rates: Double occupancy. $95–$115 late May–September. $80–$105 April–late May and October–January 2. $65–$85 January 3–March. $15 extra person. Ten percent less, seven-night stays. MC, VISA for deposit only.

The country decor follows the lead taken from the original cooking hook still in the fireplace of the house built in 1838. The rabbit theme is from Beatrix Potter's storybook characters. And for a unusual twist in this area, children of all ages are welcome.

"We stayed in B&Bs for seven years before moving in 1988 to this wonderful lifestyle. I commute two days a week to Philadelphia for my job as an art director/graphic designer. Greg, a former salesman and carpenter, enjoys photography, sports, and baking sticky buns. We painted and papered, hung baskets, and arranged crafts. The country touch is without breakables or no-touch furnishings. Our instant expanded family fulfills our expectations. For guests, this is a home away from home, a base for exploring our town of architectural wonders, a place to read by the fire or even do nothing."

In residence: Ben, age six; Adam, age two. "Our cat, Oscar, who is not supposed to visit guest rooms, loves the fireplaces and guests' laps."
Restrictions: No smoking allowed. Sorry, no guests' pets.
Bed and bath: Three second-floor rooms; all with private baths, TV, and air conditioning. One with king/twins bed option, sitting room, shower bath en suite. One king/twins, shower bath. One queen bed, full bath. Cots (but no crib) available. Please bring your own portacrib.
Breakfast: 8–9:30. Fruit or fruit dish. Quiche or egg casserole. Homemade

cinnamon buns, bread and muffins. Greg's "famous homemade granola." Teas and coffee. Buffet style in dining room.

Plus: Home-baked goodies at 4 P.M. tea. Chocolate on pillows. Outside hot/cold shower. Beach tags, chairs, towels. Clothesline for bathing suits. Enclosed backyard with flower garden. Wicker-furnished sun porch. Off-street parking.

Woodleigh House

808 Washington Street, Cape May, NJ 08204
Phone: 609/884-7123
Location: Centrally located in the quiet historic district.
Hosts: Buddy and Jan Wood
Open: Year round. Advance reservations required. Three-night minimum stay on June–October weekends.
Rates: Double occupancy. $50–$65 shared bath. $80 private bath. Winter, $45 shared bath, $75 private bath.

> From New Jersey, Pennsylvania, and New York City: "The decor is authentic without being cloying. . . . An atmosphere of warm friend-liness . . . splendid accommodations, exceptional housekeeping, good breakfasts. . . . Whether it is the charm of the house, the unob-trusive care of the innkeepers and their family, or the spell that was cast by Mabel Wood which never left 808 Washington, I cannot tell you. . . . There are other B&Bs in Cape May which are fancier, but none can match the Woodleigh House when it comes to hominess and hospitality . . . A house for all seasons!"

That's it, folks, a home away from home offered by the consummate hosts, who were "in and out" as assistants through all the years that Buddy's mother ran the guest house until she died in 1983. Since taking over, they have added their own touches by renovating and redecorating completely. From the moment you call for a reservation, you can tell that they enjoy their role—a real balance to their other positions, where they work with "other wonderful people." In neighboring communities, Buddy is an elementary school principal and Jan is a kindergarten teacher.

Restrictions: Smoking permitted on porches only. No pets, please. Chil-dren five and over are welcome.
Bed and bath: Eight double-bedded rooms (plus a single bed in some) on first and second floors. Four rooms have private baths; four share two full baths.
Breakfast: 8:30–10. Homemade pastries, fruit, cheese, juice, coffee, tea. Self-serve in dining room during winter, on porch in summer. Hosts join guests.
Plus: Bedroom ceiling fans. Comfortable porches. Use of refrigerator. Picnic table in garden. Courtyard lounge area. Bicycles. Beach tags. Out-side shower. Off-street parking.

Leigh Way Bed and Breakfast Inn

66 Leigh Street, Clinton, NJ 08809
Phone: 201/735-4311
Location: In an old residential neighborhood. Minutes to shops, restaurants, art center, mill with working waterwheel, summer concerts in quarry-turned-park. Trout fishing in Raritan River, 600 feet away. "Close to countryside with early farmhouses, orchards and wineries where you can enjoy getting lost." About an hour from Manhattan and Philadelphia.
Hosts: Peg and Bob Haake
Open: February–December. Advance reservations recommended.
Rates: Weeknights, $50 single, $60 double. Weekends and holidays, $10 more. Weekly rate available. AMEX, MC, VISA.

Guests wrote: "We were fortunate to find Leigh Way when being transferred from California. A charming Victorian house where you are transported back in time. . . . Beautiful decor. High ceilings. Immaculate, even in nooks and crannies. I'm a neatnik and checked. . . . Caring and sharing hosts who welcome you as a friend. . . . A refreshing alternative to the Park Avenue hotel we had just stayed at. . . . I had great trepidations about B&Bs. I don't see how the facilities at Leigh Way can be beaten or even matched. . . . Interesting books . . . knowledge of historic sites, restaurants, community, outlet shopping . . . a quiet retreat."

Hosting comes naturally to these community activists. Peg grew up as a minister's daughter in a family of eight children. Bob, a Cornell School of Hotel Management graduate and now owner of a Mr. Fix-It business, was an AT&T manager when he and Peg thought about their visits to Cape May and an early-retirement occupation that would allow them to stay in this restored village. The slate mansard-roofed 1862 house was two years in the restoration stage. Authentic colors were researched for the exterior. Inside, it has a light and airy feeling, with auction finds displayed against a backdrop of cheerful color schemes and bright chintzes.

In residence: Sisaket, a Siamese cat who adores being stroked.
Restrictions: Children 13 and over welcome. Smoking on porch only. Sorry, no guests' pets (good kennel nearby).
Foreign language spoken: Some French.
Bed and bath: Five rooms, all with semiprivate baths, on second and third floors. Twin beds with private half bath, queen, and doubles available. Some four-posters.
Breakfast: Weekdays 7–9, freshly squeezed orange juice, fresh fruit, homemade baked goods, bagels with "special" cream cheese, freshly ground coffee. Weekends until 10 with entree such as quiche or baked egg platter. In dining room with family china, crystal, linens. Option of breakfast in bed.
Plus: Welcoming coffee or tea. Bedroom ceiling fans and air conditioners. Fireplaced living room. Wicker-furnished porch with swing. Mints. Flow-

ers. Fluffy towels. Clothes storage for relocators. Picnic lunches and balloon rides arranged. Off-street parking.

Lakeside Bed & Breakfast

Denville, NJ
Location: One mile from I-80, midway between Pennsylvania and New York City, on the bay leading to Indian Lake. Within walking distance of the (one-hour ride) train or bus to New York City.
Reservations: Available year round through Northern New Jersey Bed & Breakfast, page 45. One week's advance notice required.
Rates: $40 single. $50 double. $10 cot.

"After seven years of hosting, we find that it is still a wonderful way to meet people from all over the world. Our setup allows for privacy and socializing too. In addition to the facilities here at our comfortable lakeside house, we offer suggestions for antiquing or small interesting towns to explore. B&B really is fun. How otherwise might we have met the young Swedish couple whom we then visited during our own travels? In a way, the spirit is contagious. A few years ago we started to book other area hosts with our overflow, and that has continued."

The host is a high school teacher/administrator. His wife is a landscape designer.

In residence: A cat named Pewter, and Leo, a Lhasa apso.
Restrictions: No guests' pets. Moderate smoking allowed. Midnight curfew (because Leo likes to bark).
Bed and bath: First-floor room with double bed, bath with shower, private entrance. Cot available.
Breakfast: 7–9. Juice or fruit, cold cereal, choice of pancakes, French toast, or omelet, all with bacon or sausage, coffee or tea. Hosts usually join guests for breakfast in the dining room overlooking bay.
Plus: Central air conditioning. Late-afternoon wine and cheese. Will meet guests at train or bus. For guests, a family room with color TV. Deck overlooking bay. Rowboat. Beach passes.

From Rhode Island: "Comfortable and pleasant. Just what I was looking for."

Jerica Hill

96 Broad Street, Flemington, NJ 08822
Phone: 201/782-8234
Location: In historic district, a residential area two blocks from Main Street, near shops, outlets, restaurants, tennis. Sixty miles west of Manhattan and northeast of Philadelphia; 14 miles from New Hope, Pennsylvania.

Host: Judith S. Studer
Open: Year round. Reservations recommended. Two-night minimum on weekends.
Rates: Double occupancy. $55–$80. $15 additional guest. AMEX, MC, VISA.

"My childhood memories of this house are special. Often, I came here to visit the grandfather of a best friend. My parents ran the local hotel and I would dream of opening my own place. After buying this in 1984, I supervised the work done by a restoration firm and did all of the decor."

Judy's creative ideas are everywhere in the antiques-filled 1901 Victorian, which features a graceful center hall staircase and individually decorated guest rooms. (Many guests request decorating advice.) As you tour the house, you can tell that she enjoys books, auctions, theater, gardening, and hot air ballooning.

"Corporate and business travelers love this style of travel. Some guests come to shop at the factory outlets, for antiquing or the Delaware River sports. They discover the architecture in this beautiful, historic town, the area wineries—and the joy of hot air ballooning."

In residence: Jessica and Eric during college vacations. Two cats—Sam, a 19-year-old, and Binky, age 3.
Restrictions: Children over 12 are welcome. Sorry, no pets; "ours would love your attention." No smoking, please.
Bed and bath: Five rooms. One first-floor room with queen canopied four-poster, private bath. Upstairs—one room with double bed, private bath. Two double-bedded rooms and one with two twin beds share a full bath. All antique beds—pineapple, pine, iron-and-brass. Rollaway available.
Breakfast: 8:30–10 weekends, at guests' convenience on weekdays. Juice, assorted teas and coffees, fresh fruit, homemade breads (pear a specialty), local jams, cereal, yogurt, warm pastry. Served in dining room or on screened wicker- and plant-filled porch.
Plus: Air conditioners in four rooms. Flowers and fruit in rooms. Sherry (or hot cider in winter); iced tea in summer. *The New York Times*. Baskets of local information. Cable TV. Fireplaced living room. Bedroom ceiling fans. Limited kitchen privileges. Yard. Off-street parking. B&B&B (and ballooning) packages. Winery tour with picnic arranged.

A guest wrote: "It's like being in the home of a friend."

The Old Hunterdon House

12 Bridge Street, Frenchtown, NJ 08825
Phone: 201/996-3632
Location: Just off the main street of a small renaissance village. Within walking distance of shops, galleries, restaurants. One block from the Delaware River. A 15-mile hike (for some) to New Hope, Pennsylvania. In antiquing and cycling country.
Host: Rick Carson

Open: Year round. Advance reservations recommended. Two-night minimum for Saturday bookings, three nights on some holidays.
Rates: $68 double. $80 double/twin. $90 queen with fireplace. $95 double canopy, queen, or twins with sitting room. $42–$50 single, available Monday–Thursday only. MC, VISA.

"Now being discovered," reported the *Philadelphia Inquirer* about Frenchtown in 1987, barely a year after Rick had opened this Italianate-style Victorian. The intricate cast iron front fence, "a puzzle to assemble," was found in pieces in the basement. The interior had been "frozen in time" since the 1940s.

A favorite place for many New Yorkers and Philadelphians, the antiques-filled inn is an elegant 19th-century residence with a crystal chandelier and a nine-foot mirror in the foyer and a carved faux marble fireplace in the breakfast room, the former parlor. The tall-windowed library has deep green walls. Fresh flowers are in the rooms. Bathrooms "fit" where none existed. Hospitality is combined with attention to detail. Guests climb to the cupola for a view of the town, for reading, even for photography. For Rick, formerly a Washington political consultant, it's a new lifestyle—all because he was intrigued with the idea of renovating an old house.

In residence: The cat, Oven, is in host's quarters or outside "unless she sneaks in with a house guest."
Restrictions: Children, welcome on weekdays, should be at least 14. Smoking in guest rooms or common rooms. No pets, please.
Bed and bath: Seven rooms on three floors; all private baths. First-floor room has "Gothic" queen bed, shower bath, working black marble fireplace. On second floor, one room with canopied double bed, full bath; one with two twins and a sitting room. On third floor, one room with separate sitting room. Shower baths for all other rooms; each has a queen or a double bed.
Breakfast: Presented 8:30–10 after juice and morning paper are left outside guest rooms. Fresh fruit. Coffee, tea. Muffins, breads, and croissants—all made by Rick.
Plus: Afternoon tea, sherry, or juice with homemade cookies. Air-conditioned bedrooms. Front porch. Rear patio under huge chestnut tree. Assistance with planning activities and dining arrangements.

The Studio of John F. Peto

102 Cedar Avenue, Island Heights
Mailing address: Box 306, Island Heights, NJ 08732
Phone: 201/270-6058
Location: Surrounded by 150-year-old oak trees. "We're so quiet we look out to see whose dog goes by." Three miles from Toms River, one hour from Philadelphia or Atlantic City, two hours from New York City.
Host: Joy Peto Smiley
Open: Year round. Reservations necessary.
Rates: $45 single, $75 double. AMEX.

Still-life artist John F. Peto designed his spacious studio in 1889 and then had the rest of the house built around it. The unique home, now on the National Register of Historic Places, was opened as a museum in 1980. Two years later, Joy, the artist's granddaughter, who gives lectures and museum tours here, turned it into a B&B. Her guests come to enjoy the town located where the river (three swimming beaches) meets the bay (one beach). Island Heights, a "dry" town with no commercial traffic, is an ideal spot for joggers. The local Artists' Guild has year-round exhibits.

The Studio, located in a community with 375 historic houses, still has many of the objects Peto used as models in his paintings. Guests tend to gather in the interesting oak-ceilinged room with the white stucco fireplace, multipaned windows, baby grand piano, and paintings. The cheery large country kitchen is another welcoming room. As unusual as the B&B is, the warmth of the hostess is often the highlight for guests.

In residence: Yuri, "official greeter," a lovable silver-haired husky.
Restrictions: Children five and over welcome. No guests' pets, please.
Bed and bath: Seven rooms, all with original furnishings, with a double, single, or two twin beds. Three shared full baths. Cot available.
Breakfast: Fruit plate, hot popovers, "ethereal" eggs. Full and attractively served in the kitchen. Quick for "birders" or "beachers"; quite leisurely for others.
Plus: Library. Sun room. Screened porch with view of sailboats on the river. Bicycles. Spontaneous music sessions, even before breakfast sometimes. Complimentary motorboat rides on the river. Rental sailboats and bird sanctuary nearby.

From Vermont: "Marvelous memorable breakfast that we took a picture of. A beautiful home filled with warmth and love."

Bed & Breakfast of New Jersey Host #444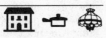

Lambertville, NJ
Location: High on a 10-acre estate with a formal sunken garden, boxwood, magnolia, mature plantings, lawns, river view. One mile from New Hope, Pennsylvania; a half mile from Lambertville.
Reservations: Year round through Bed & Breakfast of New Jersey, page 45. Two-day minimum stay on weekends.
Rates: $75 double. $95–$125 queen. $135 king. (Plus reservation service membership or booking fee. Please see page 45.)

What started out in 1820 as a low-ceilinged farmhouse with 18-inch-thick walls grew with the addition of three wings in 1927. It had been in one family for 50 years when the present owners, designers (faux finishing) in the furniture field who had renovated nine houses, grew weary of the three-hour commute from Pennsylvania to Manhattan. One of them designed the elegant master bedroom here for a Designers' Showhouse, held before the hosts received their first B&B guests. Now the 15-room house with raised paneling and wide plank floors, nooks and crannies, verandas, gables, and wide-silled windows is filled with original works of art, antiques, and reproductions. Flowers are from the heated greenhouse. The beamed solarium has a large stone fireplace, flagstone floor, French windows, hand-crafted wrought iron chandelier, and comfortable sofas. Breakfast features nationally acclaimed raspberry jam made from berries grown on the property.

In residence: Nicholas, a small poodle mix.
Restrictions: Children should be at least 12. Sorry, no smoking or pets allowed.
Bed and bath: Six rooms, private baths. One on first floor, five on second. King, queen four-poster, or double bed available. Features vary: private stairwell, fireplace, feather mattress. All rooms are carpeted and individually decorated with designer fabrics.
Breakfast: 8–10. Fresh-squeezed orange juice, gourmet coffee. Omelets with asparagus, pancakes with cooked apples and raspberry sauce, or French toast with Grand Marnier. Apple pecan muffins. Cooked and served by hosts in garden or at large table or candlelit tables for two in 1820 fireplaced dining room.
Plus: Late-afternoon sherry. Pantry with setups and ice. Tours of house and farm. Living room. Gardens with Adirondack chairs. Pure cotton sheets. Thirsty robes and towels. Freshly brewed coffee and tea always available.

The Jeremiah H. Yereance House

410 Riverside Avenue, Lyndhurst, NJ 07071
Phone: 201/438-9457
Location: Across from a riverside park with walking and jogging path, bicycle trails, picnic areas, tennis. Twelve miles from New York City. From airports—10 miles to Newark, 25 to LaGuardia, 35 to JFK. Five minutes from Giants' football stadium in Meadowlands sports complex. Three miles from New Jersey Turnpike. One mile from Fairleigh Dickinson University.
Hosts: Evelyn and Frank Pezzolla
Open: Year round except holiday weekends, Easter, first two weeks in August, Thanksgiving, Christmas. Advance reservations required.
Rates: $70 single. $75 double. $15 each additional child over age 12. Weekly rates available.

The friendly hosts are enthusiastic and energetic. As Evelyn says, "We just love old buildings and hands-on experiences. Having been born and raised in this community, where I was an elected official for six years, I had a special interest in what was a very dilapidated house in 1984. It's now on the state and national registers, has a new cedar roof, and is completely restored with original floors, moldings, and doors. The older wing was built by a ship joiner in the late 1700s, the later one in 1840. We have furnished it simply, with some antiques. It's 'home' and most of all, private. Now we are restoring the next-door one-room schoolhouse, an 1893 Queen Anne–style building with bell tower; it is currently a local museum. We are also involved in an area vaudeville theater; the official restorers of that project stayed in our B&B and made us feel proud of the work we did on our little house. Our primary business is a family truck dealership, but our labor of love results in historic preservation and restoration along with meeting wonderful people."

Restrictions: Children should be at least 12. No smoking. Sorry, no pets.
Bed and bath: One first-floor two-room suite with its own exterior entrance. An air-conditioned double-bedded room, a parlor with wood-burning stove and double sofa bed, private shower bath, breakfast area. Rollaway available.
Breakfast: Homemade muffins or breads or cakes, jellies, fresh fruits, juices, dry cereals. Coffee, tea, or cocoa. Self-serve buffet.
Plus: Italian dessert and wine upon arrival. Fresh flowers. Lots of towels. Wisteria-covered outside sitting area. Tour of house. Champagne for special celebrations.

From New Jersey: "The charm of yesterday with the convenience of today."

Bed & Breakfast of New Jersey Host #463

Mount Holly, NJ
Location: One mile from Route 206 on a country road surrounded by corn and soybean fields. Across the road from a wooded hill. Within one hour's drive of Philadelphia and New Hope in Pennsylvania, Atlantic City and Princeton in New Jersey.
Reservations: Available year round through Bed & Breakfast of New Jersey, page 45. Two-day minimum stay preferred.
Rates: Double occupancy. $74 twin beds. $80 double bed. $87 queen bed with fireplace. Single $66.

"Pretty as a picture." That's just what *Country Living* magazine thought when they featured the restoration that took four years. Formerly a dairy farm on 250 acres, it is once again—"with the help of a contractor and much of our own labor"—a gracious Federal brick farmstead set among mature trees.

The 1840 house with fan-windowed entrance, three-storied open circular staircase, and hundreds of touches of whimsy and country has the ambiance of an historic era. Baskets hang from the kitchen beams. A spinning wheel is in one guest room. Hooked rugs are in the entrance hall. Collections—quilts, grapevine wreaths, potpourri, hooked rugs—are everywhere.

The hostess is a family counselor. Her husband ("he treats everyone like family") is retired from the Air Force. In addition to tips about the nearby historic sites, canoeing, and hiking and nature trails, the hosts remind visitors about the monthly antiques flea markets and craft shows held in a neighboring village.

In residence: Two "mostly outdoor" cats. On the farm—sheep, pony, mules, horses.
Restrictions: Children should be in their teens. No guests' pets. Prefer to host one family or traveling party at a time.
Bed and bath: Entire third floor for guests has three guest rooms and one shared full bath. One room with queen bed and working fireplace. One with double bed. One with two twin beds.
Breakfast: Until 10. Choice of eggs, waffles, scrapple, bacon, chipped beef, ham, muffins, biscuits, assorted juices, homemade jams and preserves, seasonal fruits, coffee, tea, milk. Served in front of living room or dining room fireplace, in the center hall, or, if preferred, in the kitchen. Prepared and served by both hosts, who will join you for coffee.
Plus: Central first-floor air conditioning. Separate guest room air conditioners. Beverages. Formal fireplaced living room. Third-floor sitting room with books and antique puzzles. Tour of house and farm.

BarnaGate Bed & Breakfast

637 Wesley Avenue, Ocean City, NJ 08226
Phone: 609/391-9366
Location: On a corner, 3½ blocks from beach and boardwalk, two blocks to shopping. Seven minutes from the Garden State Parkway. Ten miles south of Atlantic City, 40 minutes north of Cape May. One hour from Philadelphia.
Hosts: Frank and Lois Barna, Donna Barna
Open: Year round. Two-night minimum in summer; three nights on holiday weekends.
Rates: Double occupancy. July 1–Labor Day $60 private bath, $55 with powder room, $50 shared bath. Memorial Day–June, $5 less. Fall–spring $10 less. Singles, $10 less. $10 extra person. MC, VISA.

B&B has made the hosts local history buffs and antiques collectors. It's all part of the fun for Lois, who often planned social functions and business seminars while assistant to a bank president, and Frank, an avid sports fan who had his own TV repair shop. Now he creates stained glass lamps. (The one in the front hall is his.)
When looking for a career change, the Barnas took a B&B seminar, stayed at B&Bs, and then bought this 1895 Victorian, which was a guest house. In time to redecorate the guest rooms completely for the 1988 season, they moved from Somerville, New Jersey, to "America's greatest family resort, a town with a friendly atmosphere." All the beds have quilts. The furnishings are country Victorian. For special treats on holidays, the hosts make their own ice cream. "And much to our surprise and delight, people from all over the world stay with us."

In residence: Donna, a daughter, is in her twenties.
Restrictions: Children 10 and over welcome. Sorry, no facilities for pets. Smoking on front porch only.
Bed and bath: Five rooms. On second floor, private full bath for one double-bedded room. One twin-bedded room with powder room shares a tub bath with a double-bedded room. Two third-floor corner double-bedded dormer rooms share a tub bath and a private sitting room. Rollaway available.
Breakfast: 8–10. Juice; fruit; sweet rolls, muffins and breakfast cakes; coffees and teas. Buffet style in dining room with ceiling fan and period antiques.
Plus: Bedroom ceiling fans. Enclosed outside shower, available after checkout time too. Refrigerator privileges. Backyard with table and chairs. Clothesline for wet beach clothing. Free beach tags provided.

From New York: "Immaculate, comfortable, attractively furnished. Frank and Lois made our stay a pleasant one. I recommend this B&B!"

The Enterprise Inn

1020 Central Avenue, Ocean City, NJ 08226
Phone: 609/398-1698
Location: Two blocks from beach and boardwalk. Ten miles south of Atlantic City, 40 minutes north of Cape May.
Hosts: Stephen and Patty Hydock
Open: May–September. Two-night minimum stay on weekends, three nights on major holidays.
Rates: Per room. $65 shared bath. $75 private bath. $85 Jacuzzi. $10 less in May and September. $20 for showers and beach towels on checkout day. Three-day midweek package rate. MC, VISA.

Cape May has done it again! After falling in love with the B&B concept there, the Hydocks returned to Ocean City, where Steve is a plumber and Patty has a contractor referral service. They put their interests in meeting new people and renovating old houses together, bought this four-storied small hotel, and, in 1987, "made everything new"— floors, walls, windows, and wallpaper. Steve, of course, knows just how to fit bathrooms into an old place, and Patty prides herself on finding just the right piece, whether it's wicker porch furniture or a lace-covered table. At present, she is president of The Innkeepers Guild of Ocean City.

In residence: Amy, 14, and Jason, 13.
Restrictions: Children over 10 welcome. Smoking allowed in rooms and on porch. Sorry, no pets.
Bed and bath: Eight double-bedded rooms on second and third floors. All but two have private baths. One has a Jacuzzi.
Breakfast: 8:30–9:30. Pancakes or waffles with fruit topping, omelets or

French toast with sausage. Juice. Coffee. Served on porch at tables for four.

Plus: Bedroom air conditioners and fans. Outside grill. Ice machine in lobby. Beach tags. Package plans for murder mystery weekend, day trips, casinos, boat trips.

Laurel Hall

48 Wesley Road, Ocean City, NJ 08226
Phone: 609/399-0800
Location: In a quiet residential section of family resort area. Four blocks from boardwalk, beach, boating, and fishing. Ten minutes south of Atlantic City; 40 minutes north of Cape May.
Hosts: Pat and Dick Harris
Open: Year round. Reservations required. Two- and three-day minimum stays, Memorial Day–September.
Rates: Per room. Memorial Day–Labor Day $42 shared bath, $52 private bath. Off season $35 shared bath, $40 private bath. $8 extra person.

> From Virginia: "A gem! The rooms are charming and white-glove clean. Breakfast is delicious and delightful. Pat and Dick are gracious hosts; helpful, considerate and accommodating. There is a gentle warmness about Laurel Hall."

The three-decker house with covered front porches (now each with an awning) was built in the 1920s. About 10 years later, it was raised on pilings, creating a fourth (bottom) floor. The Harrises have decorated country style with some antiques and white wicker, giving a comfortable and homey feeling. Thoughtful touches include fresh flowers, plenty of current magazines, and "forgotten" toiletries.

"It's just something we wanted to do," says Pat, a former stockbroker who teaches in the winter. "Guests from all over are memorable." Since the hosts came here in 1983, Dick has continued as a sales engineer. During the summer, Pat runs craft shows on the boardwalk. Their community activities include the Guest House and Civic Associations, the Art Center, the Humane Society, and the local school board.

In residence: Brian, age 16, and Jo, age 14. Moose and Mandy, "mostly outside cats." Dogs Debbie and Molly "enjoy sharing the porch with guests."
Restrictions: Children should be at least 10. Sorry, no guests' pets. Smoking allowed only on the balconies.
Bed and bath: Six rooms on three floors. Two with private baths. Four share two full baths. Rooms have a double bed or two twins. Top-floor room has a double bed and a sofa bed, private balcony. Cot available.
Breakfast: 8:30–10. "Good time for visiting." Hot breads (muffins, hot cross buns, or nut bread), Danish pastries, several seasonal fruits, juice, coffee, tea, toast. Served buffet style in the dining room.

Plus: Iced tea after beach time, when awaiting use of enclosed outside showers. Ceiling fans in living room, kitchen, bedrooms. Wood stove in living room. Candies in room. Thick towels. Bicycles. Rockers on front porches. Grill and picnic table.

New Brighton Inn

519 Fifth Street, Ocean City, NJ 08226
Phone: 609/399-2829
Location: Overlooking a church and a quiet park. Three blocks from beach and boardwalk.
Host: Dan and Donna Hand
Open: Year round. Advance reservations required. Two-night minimum on weekends.
Rates: Double occupancy. $55 shared bath, $65 private bath. $5 additional guest. AMEX, MC, VISA.

> From Philadelphia: "We will never stay in a hotel or motel again! Donna and Dan made us feel very welcome. They have redone their entire home in a charming antique and country decor. It is very clean and well-kept. . . . We were treated to a healthy homemade breakfast and after the beach, a glass of tea or wine on the porch swing. . . . We loved it!"

With memories of childhood vacations in Ocean City and adult vacations at B&Bs, cabinetmaker Dan, who studied art, and quilt maker Donna, former computer programmer, transformed the turreted Queen Anne into a B&B in 1988. Along the way they made a video of the major project, which included stripping of hall woodwork (all three floors) and adding baths. Oriental rugs, brass beds, lots of rockers, and light colors give a warm ambiance. Now, during summer sunsets, the hosts often join guests on the porch. And a nearby state park that has dunes is among the hosts' favorite suggestions. In December, the inn is included on the Historical Society's house tour.

Restrictions: Children 10 and over welcome. Smoking allowed on front veranda only. Sorry, no pets.
Foreign language spoken: Limited French.
Bed and bath: Four second-floor rooms with queen or double bed. Two private shower baths. Two rooms share one full bath (claw-footed tub). Rollaway available.
Breakfast: 8–10:30. Homemade breads, muffins, and coffee cakes. Juices. Fresh fruit. French toast. On sun porch by the windows. Newspaper provided.
Plus: Iced or hot tea. Ceiling fans in bedrooms and on sun porch. Airport (10 minutes away) pickup. Babysitting. Outside hot shower, changing stalls. Bicycles. Beach tags.

From Georgia: "The first time we had ever stayed at a B&B. A delightful experience. Beautiful. Well-kept. Delicious breakfast. The hospitality made our stay complete."

Bed & Breakfast of New Jersey Host #411

Ridgewood, NJ
Location: On a through street in village, but in a quiet neighborhood.
Walking distance to bus and train (about a 45-minute ride to New York
City); 45-minute drive to Atlantic Ocean beaches.
Reservations: Available year round through Bed & Breakfast of New Jer-
sey, page 45.
Rates: $35 single. $45 double. $55 suite. (Plus reservation service booking
or membership fee. Please see page 45.)

"My home is the stopover for friends and relatives from around the
country on their way to New York City or the Jersey shore, but because I
love to entertain, B&B allows me to do it more often.

"When we moved here from a very different lifestyle, I found this
area at times very frightening, especially because of the fast New York
metro area pace. That was one of the reasons why I eventually started a
business to assist transferees in their move to New Jersey. I accumulated
a great deal of information and a completely different feeling about this
state and its warm, friendly people. You can do anything and everything
here or you can do nothing! This is the New Jersey feeling I want my
guests to remember."

The hostess is very involved with the B&B movement, and her husband is associated with a large chemical company. Their two-story colonial home is within either a half hour or one hour of a very long list of
attractions and possibilities.

In residence: "A lovable and gentle 15-year-old collie, loves children."
Restrictions: No guests' pets, please. Nonsmokers are welcome.
Bed and bath: Two double-bedded second-floor rooms that can be closed
off from rest of house. Together the rooms can be a suite with a full bath.
Breakfast: Might include cranberry pecan muffins from host's prizewinning "best breakfast in the world" recipe. Weekdays, continental. Served
with china and crystal in dining room. Weekends, option of joining hosts
for full meal in dining room or in attractive kitchen filled with plants and
copper pots.
Plus: Air-conditioning units. Screened porch or den with music, wine,
cable color TV, and VCR. Beverage and munchies. Kitchen and laundry
privileges. Babysitting. Fresh flowers, turn-down service with warm cookies or candy on pillow.

Ashling Cottage

106 Sussex Avenue, Spring Lake, NJ 07762
Phone: 201/449-3553
Location: On a sycamore-shaded residential street one block from ocean, two-mile-long boardwalk, and lake. Two blocks from downtown shops. One hour from Philadelphia or New York, 1½ hours to Atlantic City.
Hosts: Goodi and Jack Stewart
Open: March-December. Three-day minimum weekend stay in July and August, two nights on other weekends.
Rates: Double occupancy. Weekdays $75 shared bath, $85–$95 private bath. Weekends $80 shared bath, $94–$105 private bath. $25 cot. Fifteen percent less late September–mid-May. Singles $4 less.

"We wanted to live in Spring Lake, a noncommercial New Jersey shore resort that goes back to 1877. Ashling Cottage fell right in line with our desire to work together and enjoy people. (Jack was a sales executive in Los Angeles and New York; Goodi was in the barter business in New York.) We have seen neighbors meet here. We have hosted a fashion film crew, and have seen guests who have been our inn-sitters become innkeepers.

"Our house was built in 1877 with lumber from the Philadelphia Bicentennial agricultural exhibit. We have blended tasteful antiques with comfort, leaning toward the 'genteel mood of yesterday,' rather than formal Victorian and total authenticity. White wicker fills out our screened solarium which overlooks the ocean to the east and the spring-fed lake (with surrounding park) to the west."

In residence: Lady Latimer, the cat, "the real mistress of Ashling Cottage."
Restrictions: "Children's visits are discouraged." Sorry, no guests' pets. Smoking allowed in the common areas only.
Foreign language spoken: A little German.
Bed and bath: Ten rooms, each with a queen bed and cross-ventilation, on three floors. Eight rooms with private baths. Two with sinks in the room share a bath with tub, hand-held shower. One of the guest rooms has a private porch, another a sunken bathroom. Cot available.
Breakfast: 8:30–10. Freshly ground coffee or brewed tea, two fruit juices, cold cereals, seasonal fruits, eggs (maybe in a casserole). At least two home-baked goods, which might be muffins (about a dozen varieties in repertoire), Irish soda bread, sour cream pound cake, nut braid, or brioche. Served buffet style in the parlor or solarium, on porches, or in living room.
Plus: Year round, fresh flowers. Living room with TV and VCR. Board games. Gas grill and picnic table on the patio. Impromptu wine gatherings. St. Patrick's Day Open House. Labor Day Creative Black Tie Weenie Roast. Will meet guests at Spring Lake train or bus station.

The Stewart Inn

Box 571, RD #1, South Main Street, Stewartsville, NJ 08886
Phone: 201/479-6060
Location: Pastoral. On 16 wooded acres with trout stream. Minutes from
I-78. Five miles from Easton, Pennsylvania; 10 from Bethlehem. Near
many corporate headquarters, Bucks County, historic and agricultural
Warren and Hunterdon counties in New Jersey, wineries, shopping, fine
restaurants. One hour from New York City.
Hosts: Brian and Lynne McGarry
Open: Year round.
Rates: Double occupancy. $65 shared bath. $75 private bath. MC, VISA.

Although many of the McGarrys' guests are relocators and business
travelers from all over the world, weekend romantics, too, appreciate this
gracious 1770s fieldstone manor house. It is hosted by a couple who met
during a Sierra Club trail cleanup—a former small town mayor/tax col-
lector/kennel owner (Lynne) and the equally welcoming (and fun-loving)
Brian, a lawyer.

With B&B in mind, they opted for rural living in 1986, choosing a
historic estate that needed "decorating only." It is complete with Palladian window and working fireplaces. Oriental rugs, early American antiques, and arranged flowers are throughout. The landscaped grounds
include a free-form swimming pool, horseshoes, and badminton, and
then there are all those animals.

In residence: One dog, 5 cats, 10 sheep, 2 goats, 2 peacocks, geese, chick-
ens, ducks, raccoons, rabbits, a parrot, doves, and parakeets.
Restrictions: Smoking in guest rooms only. Sorry, no guests' pets.
Bed and bath: Eight rooms, all with four-posters, TV, private phone. Six
with private baths. First-floor poolside room has double bed, private bath.
On second floor, queens or double beds.
Breakfast: 7–9:30. Farm-fresh eggs, country smoked bacon, pancakes,
French toast, fruits, granolas. Served in dining room with a corner fire-
place. Hosts join guests.
Plus: Bedroom air conditioners and oscillating fans. Game room. Fire-
placed living room and library. Tour of house and farm. Fishing equipment, 10-speed bikes, barbecue.

The Henry Ludlam Inn

Cape May County, RD #3, Box 298, Woodbine, NJ 08270
Phone: 609/861-5847
Location: In a rural area on Route 47, overlooking a 55-acre lake. Ten
miles from Garden State Parkway; 20 minutes northwest of Cape May; 25
miles to Atlantic City.
Hosts: Ann and Marty Thurlow

Open: Year round. Two-night minimum on holiday weekends.
Rates: Single—$45 shared bath, $50 private. Double—$65 shared bath, $75 private. $20 extra person. $10 surcharge for single weekend night. $160 winter weekend, two nights with Saturday dinner and wine. MC, VISA (with service charge).

"A New England house by the water is what my wife wanted. We bought this in five minutes. It is furnished with many of the antiques from a shop my wife had and from auctions. She takes care of all the 'scissors jobs' such as draperies or wallpaper. I design and install kitchens when I'm not experimenting around here." (Marty duplicated an old stairway, and from a picture Ann found, he plans to make the "right" front door.)

The Thurlows had traveled B&B but had never thought of hosting until they moved here five years ago. Now the inn is often selected for historic house tours and has been photographed for a *Mid-Atlantic Country* feature. "Guests examine every nook and cranny of this 1760 (with 1804 addition) house. They tell us that it's a romantic place. One gentleman from California booked on a night with a full moon to propose on our lake in our canoe. (She accepted.) Hosting is really fun."

Restrictions: Children should be at least 12. No guests' pets. Smoking in restricted areas.
Bed and bath: Six rooms, all with feather beds in winter, on three floors. Two with private baths. First-floor room with double bed, fireplace, private bath with shower only. Second-floor room with working fireplace and both a single and a double bed shares a bath with shower with a double-bedded fireplaced room. One room (circa 1760) with beamed ceiling has a double bed, couch, and private full bath. Two third-floor double-bedded rooms share a shower bath.
Breakfast: 7–9:30. Really a brunch. "The most enjoyable time of the day." Freshly squeezed orange juice. Entree could be French toast with bananas and walnuts, pear or mushroom omelets, Eggs Ludlam with asparagus, or gingerbread pancakes. Homemade breads, popovers, or corn bread; freshly ground coffee. Served by dining room fireplace or on enclosed porch overlooking the lake.
Plus: Afternoon wine or tea. Fruit basket. Mints on pillow. Bedroom fans. Player piano. Kitchen privileges. Fishing equipment. Swing near lake. Beach tags. Option of dinner ($30 per person) on winter Saturdays with advance reservations.

New York

Eastern New York
(South to north, from Long Island to the Adirondacks)

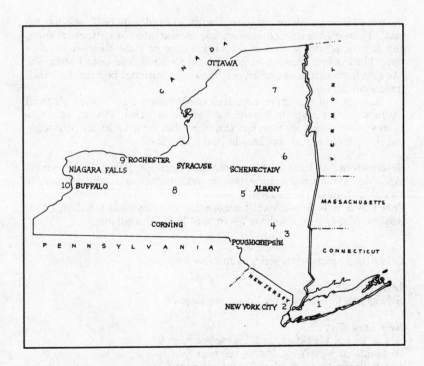

The numbers on this map indicate the regions for which there are detailed maps in this chapter.

New York Reservation Services

Most areas of the state have some B&Bs represented by:

Bed & Breakfast U.S.A., Ltd.

P.O. Box 606, Croton-on-Hudson, NY 10520
Phone: 914/271-6228 or 800/255-7213. Monday–Friday 9 A.M.–3 P.M. For
Albany area reservations: 518/273-1851.
Listings: 300. Mostly hosted private residences; a few inns and some
unhosted homes. Directory $4.
Rates: $30–$100 single, $35–$225 double. Family and weekly rates available. Booking fee for nonmembers is $15. Members ($35 annual fee) book
reservations without a fee and receive a quarterly publication. Deposit
required is one-half of total cost. Cancellations made with less than
seven days' notice receive refund less one night's charge (and, for nonmembers, the $15 booking fee). MC, VISA; 3 percent surcharge.

Since Barbara Notarius started with 20 homes in 1983, she has expanded beyond her immediate area, has moved into a storefront location,
and is now servicing almost the entire state of New York—as well as
some Florida locations, in Miami Beach, Orlando, and Boca Raton. She
has also been instrumental in establishing a national bed and breakfast
trade association.

Barbara and her representatives book guests into a wide range of
listings, from budget to luxurious. Bed & Breakfast U.S.A., Ltd. also
makes reservations for travelers through other services located throughout the United States, in Canada, and in England.

Reservations: At least 24 hours' advance notice required. Single nights
available; some hosts require two or more nights as a minimum. Also
available through travel agents.
Plus: Car rentals. Some hosts have special offerings such as fishing or ski
lessons. Short-term (two months or less) housing available.

Other B&B reservation services in New York state:

Long Island
A Reasonable Alternative. Please see page 89.

New York City
Abode Bed & Breakfast, Ltd. Please see page 97.
At Home in New York. Please see page 97.
Bed & Breakfast (& Books). Please see page 98.
Hosts & Guests Inc. Please see page 98.

New World Bed & Breakfast. Please see page 99.
Urban Ventures. Please see page 99.

Leatherstocking/Central New York
Bed & Breakfast—Leatherstocking/Central New York
Reservation Service. Please see page 117.

Albany Area to Lake George
The American Country Collection. Please see page 137.

Syracuse/Finger Lakes Area
The Blue Heron Bed and Breakfast Reservation Service.
Please see page 156.
Bed & Breakfast of the Greater Syracuse Area. Please see page 156.

Rochester Area
Bed & Breakfast of Rochester. Please see page 179.

Niagara/Buffalo/Chautauqua Area
Rainbow Hospitality. Please see page 185.

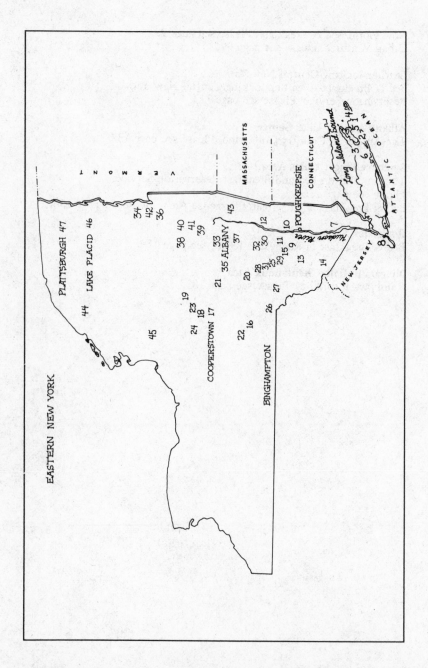

The numbers on this map indicate the locations of eastern New York B&Bs described in this chapter. The map for western New York is on page 154.

EASTERN NEW YORK

(Regions are arranged from south to north.)

A Reasonable Alternative, Inc.

117 Spring Street, Port Jefferson, NY 11777
Phone: 516/928-4034. Monday–Thursday, 10–4.
Listings: 50–70 (number varies according to season) hosted private residences in Nassau and Suffolk counties, including many in Garden City, Long Beach, and Glen Cove, all 30–45 minutes from Manhattan. Among the communities represented in Suffolk County are all the Hamptons, Stony Brook, and the North Fork (winery country), Port Jefferson. B&Bs are colonials, Victorians, and contemporaries; they are on or near the water, close to universities and Route 110 corridor.
Rates: $32–$60 singles, $40–$68 double. In July and August, $40–$100 singles, $52–$125 doubles. Some weekly rates. Deposit required: at least one night's lodging. If cancellation received three days before scheduled arrival, all but a $10 service charge returned; no refund if received later. MC, VISA.

Kathleen Dexter started her reservation service in February 1981 and to this day has many of her original hosts, friendly people who enjoy sharing their homes with others. "The only reason they stop hosting is if their kids come home from school or they sell their house. As our guests say, 'They are wonderful people.' We take pride in running a quality service."

Reservations: Three-day minimum advance notice. In Hamptons during summer months, two-night minimum, three nights on holidays.
Plus: Very accommodating hosts; many provide pickup service at the train station or drive carless guests to restaurants.

Centennial House

13 Woods Lane, East Hampton, NY 11937
Phone: 516/324-9414
Location: In historic district of early farmhouses (one next door has expansive lawn) and country/summer estates. Within walking distance of village and beach. Along the main road; 100 yards from "Currier and Ives pond" just as you enter village.
Host: Harry Chancey and David Oxford
Open: Year round. Advance reservations required. Three-night minimum May–September. Two nights rest of year.
Rates: $185 per room. Cottage $350 per night (for minimum stay of one week). MC, VISA.

Restoration number four is, for the hosts, "a passion that has become a venture."

Built in 1876 as a family residence, the shingled Victorian had changed hands once before David, a lawyer, and Harry, a television executive, bought it in 1987. During restoration, they uncovered the signature of the noted builder, Thomas E. Babcock. For English and American country decor, they added swags and balloon shades, antiques and traditional furnishings, and in the double parlor, crystal chandeliers. Requests for house tours are cheerfully filled. Most guests come for the sense of peace and quiet, privacy and contentment.

In residence: Two dogs. Earl, a fawn-colored Lhasa apso. Buda(pest), a black puli.
Restrictions: "Sorry, the inn is not appropriate for children." No smoking inside. No guests' pets.
Foreign language spoken: French.
Bed and bath: Three second-floor air-conditioned rooms. One double, one queen canopied bed, and one queen four-poster bed. Each with sitting area and desk. All adjoining private full marble baths with wainscoting. "Fairytale cottage" also available.
Breakfast: 8:30–9:30. Guest's choice. Variety of fruit, juice, eggs, homemade muffins or scones, oatmeal, maybe ham and grits, breads, cakes, coffees. Served in Georgian dining room "with authentic Williamsburg style."
Plus: Liqueurs in each room. Sherry. Chocolates. Parlor with Italian marble fireplace. Front porch seating. Tour of house. The Sunday *New York Times*. Terry robes. Chocolate truffles. Potpourri. Thick towels.

Guests wrote: "Charming . . . luxurious . . .friendly . . . attention to the smallest detail."

Mill House Inn

33 North Main Street, East Hampton, NY 11937
Phone: 516/324-9766
Location: Seven houses from the shopping district, on a fork off Main Street. Opposite the village green and Old Hook Windmill. "One mile to New York's most pristine beaches." Short drive to North and South Fork wineries and to whale watch excursions.
Hosts: Barbara and Kevin Flynn
Open: Year round. Three-night minimum on summer weekends; four nights on holiday weekends; two nights on fall weekends.
Rates: Mid-June to mid-September, $95 weekdays, $115–$125 weekends. Rest of year, $65–$75 weekdays, $75–$90 weekends.

Original hand-hewn ceiling beams are in the living and dining rooms of the 1790 colonial house, which was expanded in 1898. When the Flynns bought the then guest house in 1987, they redecorated using chintzes and designer fabrics, coordinating wallpaper or stenciling, some country pieces, antiques, Orientals, and botanical prints. Thus began the fulfillment of their decade-old New England college days' dream of becoming innkeepers.

"Before"—Barbara was a software engineer and Kevin a steamship executive. They had at least one stint at inn-sitting and spent months "looking" in the mountains. A *New York Times* ad brought the Nassau County natives back to Long Island. Guests who come for the beach, for a getaway, or for the arts comment about the decor, the cleanliness, and the hospitality offered by hosts who are also "having a lot of fun."

In residence: Daughter Caitlin is almost two years old. Beamer is a playful cat.
Restrictions: Kevin, too, abides by the 'no smoking inside' rule. No guests' pets.
Bed and bath: Eight rooms, most with sloping ceilings. Private baths (most with shower and without tub) for first- and second-floor rooms. Two on third floor have semiprivate bath. Queen, doubles, twins, and a pair of three-quarter beds.
Breakfast: 8:30–10. Entree might be French toast stuffed with cream cheese and apricot preserves. Juice, fruit, homemade muffins, coffee. Served at dining room table or on sun porch with lace tablecloth, Depression glass, and china teacups.
Plus: Lemonade, hot tea, or apple cider. Bedroom fans. Fireplaced living room. Porch. Back yard with lawn furniture. Two hammocks. Parking. Will meet guests at train or bus. Bicycles with baskets. On some off-season weekends, complimentary theater tickets with two-night reservation.

House on the Water

Box 106, Hampton Bays, NY 11946
Phone: 516/728-3560
Location: On Shinnecock Bay. On two acres in a friendly neighborhood good for jogging. One mile from the village center and train. Two miles from bus and to ocean beaches. Seven miles from Southampton.
Host: Ute
Open: May through December. Two-night minimum stay except July and August (three nights); four nights for July Fourth and Labor Day weekends.
Rates: Memorial Day–October 1, $60–$80 single, $65–$85 double. $25 extra (folding) bed. Off season, 20 percent less.

"One weekend we represented people of five different nations. My home seems to appeal both to those who want to rest, relax, and hardly leave the premises, and to those who try to take in everything from discos to restaurants."

The large ranch house has a part shade/part sun 50-foot terrace where you can lounge and watch the boats go by. You are welcome to borrow a bicycle (there are four), the pedal boat, the windsurfers, or the small sailboat, all without charge. (A small fee is charged for the small motorboat sometimes used for fishing or clamming.) Transportation can be provided from bus or train stations and to ocean beaches.

After 20 years of owning a boutique in Acapulco for custom-made resort wear (for all ages), Ute sails, plays tennis and golf, and pursues her interests in health foods, diet, and exercise. She continues hosting from January 15 through April in her Acapulco condominium, which is on a lovely beach, has two pools, and is within walking distance of restaurants.

Restrictions: Sorry, no children. No pets. Smoking in restricted areas.
Foreign languages spoken: German, Spanish, and French.
Bed and bath: Three first-floor rooms; two twin beds in each. One room with private entrance and private bath can connect with another room (available only with first room) with which it then shares the full bath. One cozy room with full bath, water view. Two folding beds.
Breakfast: Generally 8–12. Fried, boiled, poached, scrambled, or Mexican eggs, French toast, Spanish tortilla, various breads, hot and cold cereals. Special diets accommodated. Served in kitchen, living room, or on the terrace.
Plus: Coffee, tea, hot chocolate always available. Beach lounge chairs and umbrellas. Kitchen privileges. Laundry facilities.

Guests wrote: "Custom breakfasts, lovely gardens, interesting conversations. A oneness with nature. A memorable visit."

Mattituck Bed & Breakfast

795 Pike Street, Mattituck, NY 11952
Phone: 516/298-8785
Location: In the North Fork village, within walking distance of everything, including business district, restaurants, theaters, bay beach, bicycle rental, Long Island Railroad, Sunrise Bus Line, Matamar Marina.
Host: Michael Herbert
Open: Year round. Advance reservations required.
Rates: Single—$55 shared bath, $60 private bath. For two—$60–$70 shared bath; $75 or $85 private bath. $10 extra person. MC, VISA.

> From New York: "We are confirmed inngoers. Michael Herbert is by far the most hospitable and personable host we have met. . . . Very accommodating, even making reservations for a particular table at a local restaurant. . . . Lovely antiques . . . beautiful grounds. . . . Geography is what brought us to the B&B initially, but a lot more than that caused us to return."

Plans changed on many levels. Before Michael moved from New York City in 1983, he was running the family ladies' handbag business. He became a Realtor and bought this 1907 house with the thought of converting it to an apartment house. As Michael tells the story, "I realized how gracious the interior was and didn't want to make major alterations. And that's how I became an innkeeper!"

All the moldings are intact. Period furnishings include many family pieces. Papers are from the Laura Ashley collection. The artistic landscaping was done by the previous owner, a horticultural society chairman. And guests are delighted.

Restrictions: Children 10 and over welcome. Smoking allowed on first floor only. Sorry, no guests' pets.
Bed and bath: Six rooms. First-floor queen-bedded room, private shower bath. On second floor, private full bath for queen-bedded room. Four rooms—with twin beds, a double, or a double and two twins—share two baths plus a half bath.
Breakfast: 8:30–10. Freshly squeezed juice, fruit salad, croissants with homemade jams, cereals, homemade muffins, coffee, tea. Buffet style with cafe tables set up in parlor. Michael is chef and social director.
Plus: Tea or wine. Air conditioners on first and second level (outside of bedrooms). Wraparound porch. All sorts of suggestions, including wine-tasting tours and yard sales too.

Greenhedges Oceanside Villa

P.O. Box 122, Essex Street, Montauk, NY 11954
Phone: 516/668-5013
Location: Secluded. On an acre of land. Two blocks from "a magnificent

public beach." One block from Montauk Village. Tennis across the street. Five-minute drive to 18-hole municipal golf course designed by Robert Trent Jones.

Hosts: Ellie and Warren Adams
Open: Mid-March–mid-November. Reservations required. Two-night minimum stay on weekends in June, July, and August. Three-night minimum on holiday weekends in season.
Rates: Memorial Day–Labor Day weekday/weekend $70/$80 queen, $80/ $90 king. Weekly and off-season rates. $10 additional person (one at most) in king- or queen-bedded rooms.

"We had three extra rooms and a good location, so decided to try B&B. What great fun! Each guest brings special experiences. Most come here for the beach, to fish, to rest and relax, and to eat at good seafood places. For something different, we suggest a nearby health spa that has massages and a heated pool."

Ellie enjoys quilting and gardening and designs jewelry. She was personnel director at the Cornell University Medical Center before she joined Warren in their management consulting firm. Their brick and stucco Tudor home, surrounded by 20-foot-high green hedges, was built as one of the original Carl Fisher mini-estates in 1926. A recent *Newsday* spread included a photo of the huge sunken living room with beamed ceiling, the place to enjoy a crackling fire on cool evenings. On cool mornings, the Adamses light a fire in the dining/breakfast room.

In residence: Miss Molly, "a calico kitchen cat."
Restrictions: Sorry, no pets allowed and no accommodations for children under seven.
Foreign language spoken: Polish.
Bed and bath: Three rooms, each with private bath. Two with queen beds; one also has a single bed and a couch. One with a king-sized bed and a single bed/couch. Color TV with HBO in each room.
Breakfast: 8:30–11. Juice, seasonal fruits, assorted breads, rolls, cereals; coffee, tea, and decaf. In dining room or sun room or on the patio.
Plus: Beach towels and mats provided. Guests' refrigerator. Hot and cold outdoor shower. Solarium/patio and the latest addition, a gazebo. Garden barbecue. Bedroom window fans. Fresh flowers. Will meet guests at Long Island Railroad or the Hampton or Montauk jitney stops.

Guests wrote: "Our room was tastefully furnished and immaculate. Warren and Ellie are interesting people who provide a welcoming atmosphere. You feel that you are at a manor house at the beach— from days gone by. One of the most delightful places we have ever stayed."

The Old Post House Inn

136 Main Street, Southampton, NY 11968
Phone: 516/283-1717
Location: In the village. One block from Jobs Lane boutiques, the Parrish

Art Museum, and the Southampton Cultural Center. Two doors from
Saks Fifth Avenue. Less than a mile to ocean beaches.
Hosts: Cecile and Ed Courville
Open: Year round. In season, two-day weekend minimum; three days on
summer holiday weekends.
Rates: Per room. May, $80 weekday, $95 weekend. June, $90 weekday,
$115 weekend. July–August, $115 weekday, $150 weekend (two-day mini-
mum), $160 summer holiday weekends. September, $80 weekday, $110
weekend (two-night minimum). $80 October–April. $50 late checkout
(between 11 a.m and 4 p.m.). All major credit cards accepted.

Antiques, floral prints, fireplaces and charm, together with private
baths and air conditioning. All wrapped up in the fantasy life of an innkeeper surrounded by history in this seaside resort just two hours from
Manhattan. The ceiling beams of the common room date back to the
17th century. English soldiers were quartered here during the Revolutionary War. An archaeological dig (Ed's idea) in the basement indicated that
the oldest privately owned and occupied English wood frame house in
New York state was part of the Underground Railroad.
    When Ed retired early, in 1984, from his AT&T executive position,
he and Cecile, a former department store buyer, searched for a New
England–type inn where they could work together. What they found was
a run-down boardinghouse for summer help. The added-on-to 1684 farmhouse was a guest house when the railroad came to town in 1870. "As you
can well imagine, a house at this age did not have a straight wall or a level
floor in it. We left them that way, of course," says Ed, a frequent visitor to
the local library and historical society. No longer a newcomer, he is now
president of the Southampton Chamber of Commerce. In addition to
hostessing, Cecile has found a new career in interior design. Their "oldest bed and breakfast country inn in Long Island" is listed on the National Register of Historic Places. In three years, the Courvilles have
hosted guests from 34 states and 32 countries.

Restrictions: Children over 12 welcome. No pets, please. Check-in after
2:30 p.m., checkout by 11 a.m.
Bed and bath: On three floors, seven rooms named for "our country's
founders and famous local residents." All private shower baths. Double
or twin beds available.
Breakfast: 9–10:30. Juice, croissant, coffee, tea, decaf. Buffet style in fireplaced common room. Hosts join guests.
Plus: Wicker-furnished and lattice-enclosed porch. Courtesy van to and
from beach every two hours in season. Courtesy service to and from train
or bus station.

Seafield House

2 Seafield Lane, P.O. Box 648, Westhampton Beach, NY 11978
Phone: 516/288-1559 or 1-800/346-3290
Location: "In a small village atmosphere" on a quiet lane, two blocks

from Main Street shops; 15-minute brisk walk to ocean beach; 90 minutes' ride from Manhattan.
Host: Elsie Collins
Open: Year round. Reservations recommended. Two-day minimum on weekends. Three-day minimum on holiday weekends.
Rates: Per suite. Double occupancy. $175 daily Memorial Day–Labor Day. $90 daily September–May. (Hi-rise is one-half suite rate.) $600 for Monday–Thursday for two; $1,150 for seven days. Seasonal rates upon request.

From Vermont: "I have spent most of my life on the road travelling in every state except Alaska. I've been to England, Europe and Japan and I can say that the accommodations and food that Elsie offers are Number One on my list. Her warm personality only adds to the charm of the house."

From Michigan: "All the warm fuzzies she sent our way made our visit memorable . . . electric blankets turned on for us after a chilly evening walk on the beach, flower arrangements, apples and mints, the thirsty towels, the special shampoo and soap and the *New York Times* outside our door on Sunday morning."

Elsie's low-keyed approach is appreciated by guests who come to her comfortable century-old estate. The dining room features a 1907 Modern Glenwood potbellied stove, "the hero during Hurricane Gloria." Victorian, primitive, English, and Chinese antiques all blend into the ambiance of a country retreat that is complete with a swimming pool and a tennis court. And all year round, Elsie, an early-childhood educator who retired early, comes up with interesting ideas—a Saturday tea/sherry hour; a series of senior citizens' luncheons; local bird-watching places; and last February, a bird-watching trip of her own—to Iceland! A B&B since 1982, Seafield House is considered a "hidden treasure" by many.

Restrictions: Sorry, no guests' pets. No smoking, please.
Bed and bath: Three suites. Two upstairs suites; one with two double brass beds, sitting room, shower bath; the other with double bed, sitting room, claw-foot tub. Third suite in a rustic converted 100-year-old barn with a floor-to-ceiling window has a double brass bed, a hi-rise that can be two twins, shower bath, microwave oven, refrigerator, and, for decoration, handmade quilts on rafters.
Breakfast: 9:30–10:30. Freshly squeezed juice. Homemade breads, rolls, and jams. Bacon and eggs, pancakes, or French toast. Teas, freshly brewed coffee. Barn suite has option of breakfast there or in main house.
Plus: Beverage on arrival. Piano. Parlor with fireplace. Complimentary homemade "goodies" upon departure. Off-street parking.

New York City Area Reservation Services

Abode Bed & Breakfast, Ltd.

P.O. Box 20022, New York, NY 10028
Phone: 212/472-2000. Year round, Monday–Friday 9–5, Saturdays 10–2. Answering machine at other times.
Listings: 100 hosted and unhosted private residences in New York City area. Almost all accommodations have air conditioning and most have private baths. All are within a $5 cab ride of the center of Manhattan and have good access to public transportation.
Rates: $50–$80 single. $60–$100 double. $80–$250 unhosted studios to three-bedroom apartments. Discounts for extended stays. $20 one-night surcharge. Deposit required is 25 percent of total stay. Deposit minus a $15 booking fee is refundable if cancellation notice is received at least 10 days prior to scheduled arrival date. AMEX.

Shelli Leifer knows B&B from the inside out. After being a host herself for several years, she opened a personalized service, selecting hosts who "put out the welcome mat," meet guests (in both hosted and unhosted arrangements), and maintain clean residences with a warm ambiance.

Reservations: Two-night minimum for most hosts. Advance reservations advisable. Last-minute reservations accepted, according to availability.
Plus: Short term (one to three months) hosted and unhosted housing available at monthly rates. Occasionally, airport pickup can be arranged.

At Home in New York

P.O. Box 407, New York, NY 10185
Phone: 212/956-3125. Year round, seven days a week. Weekdays 10–noon and 2–5:30. Weekends until noon.
Listings: 100+. Mostly hosted private residences, some unhosted. Most are in Manhattan; a few are in Brooklyn, including Brooklyn Heights. For a sample listing of accommodations, send a self-addressed stamped envelope.
Rates: $45–$80 single. $60–$100 double. $75–$250 unhosted apartments. Family rates. Some weekly rates. One-night surcharge of $10 for single, $15 for double. Deposit required—25 percent on four-night (or more) stay, or one night's rate on up to three-night stay. $15 cancellation fee applied to deposit refund if notified 10 days prior to arrival date, otherwise deposit is forfeited.

Lois Rooks is happy to book guests with hosts who have similar interests or careers. "They have all been screened for cleanliness, convenience, security and comfort." When she knows you are coming for theater, concerts, or museums she will often send listings and/or reviews along with your reservation confirmation. And, if you'd like, this ex-professional singer/actress will offer her personal critique of current theater she has seen! Her accommodations range from modest with a shared bath to luxury with private bath, maid service, and breakfast in bed. They are all in Manhattan—from the South Street Seaport to the Upper West Side (Columbia University) and Mount Sinai Hospital in the East 90s.

Reservations: At least two-week notice suggested for best availability. Minimum two-night stay required by most hosts. Available through travel agents.
Plus: Discount (up to half price on some) museum passes. Free concert tickets when available.

Bed & Breakfast (& Books)

35 West 92nd Street, New York, NY 10025
Phone: 212/865-8740. Year round, Monday–Friday 9–5.
Listings: 25. Mostly hosted private residences, some unhosted. All in Manhattan. Send business-sized self-addressed stamped envelope for directory.
Rates: $57.50–$70 single. $67.50–$80 double. $75–$125 for unhosted residences. $15 one-night surcharge. Some weekly rates. Deposit of one night's stay required. With five days' notice of cancellation, deposit minus $15 service fee refunded.

"Your hosts become your guides," is the way Judith Goldberg Lewis describes her B&Bs. The range includes residents of the Upper West Side who overlook Central Park, a renovated Victorian brownstone near the Museum of Natural History, and an artist's loft in Soho (described below).
The service began when Judith's husband, a former bookseller who was also in the travel business, saw the need to offer Manhattan visitors a more personalized style of traveling. Now the list includes many arts-oriented hosts, several of whom have libraries in their homes.

Reservations: Two-night minimum stay. Also available through travel agents.
Plus: Most have air conditioning and are near public transportation. Short-term (up to a year) hosted and unhosted housing available.

Hosts & Guests Inc.

P.O. Box 6798, New York, NY 10150
Phone: 212/874-4308. Monday–Friday 9–11 and 4–7.

Listings: 150+. Most are hosted private residences; some are unhosted. All are in Manhattan.
Rates: $50–$65 single. $65–$75 double. Deposit of first night's lodging required. Deposit less $15 processing fee refundable if cancellation is received 72 hours prior to arrival. MC, VISA.

David Gottlieb's listings are "only the highest quality obtainable in New York City. We reject many more apartments than we accept! They are in prime residential areas including Lincoln Center, the Upper East Side, Murray Hill, Sutton Place, Gramercy Park, Greenwich Village, the financial district, and Battery Park. Most have air conditioning, private baths, and a 24-hour doorman. With enough notice, we accommodate single-night weekday reservations."

Reservations: Two weeks' advance notice required. Two-night minimum stay on weekends and holidays.
Plus: Short-term (two to four weeks) hosted and unhosted housing available.

New World Bed & Breakfast

150 5th Avenue, Suite 711, New York, NY 10011
Phone: 212/675-5600 (New York state) or 1-800/443-3800 (out of state). Monday–Friday 9–5.
Listings: 150. Mostly hosted private Manhattan residences. Some unhosted apartments also available.
Rates: $40–$80 single, $50–$90 double. Deposit of 25 percent of total booking required. Full refund made if notice received at least five days before arrival date. Monthly rates available for unhosted housing. AMEX, MC, VISA.

Laura Tilden and her staff (including a licensed New York City tour guide) feature their toll-free number for placements with hosts who live in settings that represent the varied lifestyles of Manhattanites. B&Bs are in brownstones, lofts, and luxury high-rise buildings. Along with all the tourists, a tremendous number of business travelers have contributed to the growth of this service. Many of its hosts have been welcoming travelers for over five years.

Reservations: Two-night minimum stay at all times.
Plus: Tour packets (weight: one-half pound) include maps, bargains, free events, recommended restaurants, and tour information.

Urban Ventures

P.O. Box 426, New York, NY 10024
Phone: 212/594-5650. Monday–Friday 9–5; Saturday 9–3.

Listings: At least 700. About 450 are hosted private residences; others are unhosted. Residences are located in Manhattan, Brooklyn, and Queens. Free sample listing (SASE appreciated).
Rates: $45–$75 single, $58–$85 double. Special rates available for children under 12. For two-night reservations, $5 per night booking charge. Deposit equal to cost of one night's stay is required. Cancellations with three days' notice get deposit less $15 booking fee; with less notice, one night's fee is charged. AMEX, MC, VISA.

This well-established service keeps growing! The many different accommodations range from quite simple to luxurious; all are inspected. Mary McAulay's staff books you with "achieving New Yorkers, our main stock in trade. They chat and give advice. And for those visitors who feel at home in New York, the apartments with no host offer the privacy of a hotel room combined with the comforts of home. Our apartments, throughout the city, range from studios to three-bedroom, two-bath homes."

Reservations: Two to three weeks' advance notice preferred. Will try to accommodate last-minute requests. Two-night minimum stay for hosted listings; three-night minimum for unhosted. Available through travel agents.
Plus: Short-term housing available for up to three months.

KEY

  Recipes shared, often for house specialties.

Inquiries welcomed about restoration and/or decorating. Symbol indicates that host is willing to share experiences with guests. Tips range from a before-and-after album to rebuilding advice, from furniture refinishing to curtain making. Expertise of hosts ranges from learn-by-doing to professional.

How-to B&B workshop, seminar, or apprentice program offered.

New York City Area

B&Bs are located just about everywhere, near any place you want to be. They are in town houses, brownstones, apartments, penthouses, lofts, and other possible city spaces. Among the hosts are legal secretaries, lawyers, interior designers, social workers, executives, craftspeople, actors, teachers, writers, caterers, antiques shop owners, and scientists. And some places are hostless, entirely for you. Here, as in all major cities, depending on location, parking can be an added expense.

Not always, of course, but often B&B in New York City can be quite different from any other large city in the country. It is a place where guests may be looking for particular location at a particular rate and personal interaction may not be the top priority. Some hosts arrange for you to have the key, your own access to continental breakfast, and very little face-to-face exchange. But among the hundreds of Manhattan hosts there are many interesting, busy, and caring people who have comfortable to luxurious residences that they are happy to share. B&B in New York can be a home-away-from-home arrangement; and when the chemistry is right, some find that they have made new friendships and/or become repeat guests.

New York City Area B&Bs

Please see p. 90 for nearby Long Island B&Bs.
Please see p. 73 for the Jeremiah H. Yereance House in Lyndhurst, New Jersey, just 15 minutes from Manhattan.

Alexander Hamilton House

Croton-on-Hudson, NY
Location: In a friendly neighborhood, on a cliff with view of Hudson River. A 10-minute walk to the center of town, $2.50 cab ride to 50-minute train to New York City.
Reservations: Available year round through Bed & Breakfast U.S.A., page 84.
Rates: $35–$50 single. $50–$55 double. $75 for three in one room. Suite $125 for two, $25 each additional person. (All rates plus booking or membership fee, see page 84.) One-bedroom apartment is $60 daily; $250 weekly for one, $300 for two. Weekly rates available.

English B&B experiences were the inspiration for this family's hosting activities. The hostess, a psychologist now involved in B&B full time, enjoys meeting guests from all over the world. The large Victorian residence is furnished with Oriental rugs and antiques. Guests take walks in nearby woodlands and bird sanctuaries; bicycle (it's hilly); attend town meetings; visit an historical restoration (Van Cortlandt Manor); swim (here); and sometimes use the home as a base for touring New York City.

In residence: An assistant. A nine-year-old daughter.
Foreign language spoken: A little French.
Bed and bath: Five rooms. A first-floor suite with double bed and fire-placed sitting room with queen sofa, private shower bath. Four second-floor rooms with a double or two twins share two full baths. Plus one-bedroom apartment. Cot available.
Breakfast: Full. Could include raspberries from host's garden or apples from mini-orchard here. Served on patio beside pool or in 35-foot sun room.
Plus: Air conditioning. Thirty-five-foot in-ground pool. Free loan of bicycles. Fireplaced living room. Piano. TV in two double-bedded rooms and the suite.

Abode Bed & Breakfast Host #2

New York, NY
Location: In Gramercy Park, on Manhattan's East Side. Not far from Wall Street and Greenwich Village.
Reservations: Year round through Abode Bed & Breakfast, page 97. Two-night minimum stay.
Rates: $67 single. $80 double. $150 triple. Available unhosted during holiday periods—$120 for two, $150 for three.

Every day fresh flowers are placed in the lobby of this building. And from the host's apartment, furnished with antiques and traditional pieces, you have a lovely view of New York City's only private park. The host, a financial writer and outdoor enthusiast, shares his key to the park, a pleasant place to relax in this big city.

In residence: One small dog.
Restrictions: Children should be at least 12. Sorry, no smoking. No guests' pets.
Bed and bath: One large double-bedded room shares host's full bath. Three-quarter sofa bed in living room.
Breakfast: Flexible hours. Juice, freshly brewed coffee, muffin, cereal.
Plus: In bedroom, air conditioner, large TV, stereo, telephone. Elevator; 24-hour doorman.

From Florida: "Perfect neighborhood. Stunning apartment. Consummate host."

Abode Bed & Breakfast Host #4

New York, NY
Location: Three blocks from Lincoln Center. One-half block from Central Park (west) and buses. Two blocks from subway.
Reservations: Year round through Abode Bed & Breakfast, page 97. Advance reservations required. Two-night minimum stay.
Rates: $120 for two, $150 three, $180 four.

The hosts had such a good time decorating this well-located brownstone that there are days when they think about moving into one of the B&B areas themselves! Quite comfortable and contemporary, each unit features large windows, French doors between the living room and bedroom, one mirrored wall, and wall-to-wall carpeting. You're "at home" with a microwave, a refrigerator, and even an answering machine. The hosts work in the real estate field. Here, in their high-demand location, they welcome guests and help to orient you during your stay.

Restrictions: Children welcome. Sorry, no pets.
Foreign language spoken: Some Spanish.
Bed and bath: Two one-bedroom apartments, each with built-in queen-sized bed plus living room double sofa bed. First-floor apartment has dishwasher and marble bath with whirlpool.
Breakfast: Self-serve. Juice, muffins, jams, coffee.
Plus: Air conditioning. Nearby parking garage.

Abode Bed & Breakfast Host #6

New York, NY
Location: On a tree-lined street of Upper East Side, near Lexington Avenue. Close to all major museums and art galleries. One block from subway and uptown/downtown/crosstown buses.
Reservations: Year round through Abode Bed & Breakfast, page 97. Two-night minimum stay.
Rates: $67 single. $80 double.

Delight. That's the reaction of most guests who have sought "location" and found a traditionally furnished residence hosted by an art dealer who gives directions, knows about museums and how to get theater tickets—and has many suggestions for restaurants. ("We have it all right here.") The spacious crystal-chandeliered living room in the beautifully maintained prewar building has a high ceiling, French windows, and a wood-burning fireplace.

Restrictions: Sorry, no children and no pets. Light smoking permitted.
Bed and bath: One second-floor air-conditioned room with two twin beds (placed together) shares bath with host.

Breakfast: Fruit, toast, butter and jams, coffee, tea.
Plus: Afternoon or evening tea. The *New York Times*. VCR. Color TV and telephone in room. Laundry room. Doorman and elevator.

Abode Bed & Breakfast Host #8

New York, NY
Location: High in a midtown building. Five minutes to Lincoln Center and Carnegie Hall.
Reservations: Year round through Abode Bed & Breakfast, page 97. Two-night minimum stay.
Rates: $115 single or double.

The view of the Hudson River is so spectacular that many guests from near (this country) and far (abroad) have suggested an apartment swap. "Tempting," says the host, a banker, who offers "the works" in his contemporary L-shaped studio abode—stereo, television, fresh flowers, mints, use of dishwasher—"all the accoutrements of home" together with plenty of privacy. (The apartment is yours.) And for those who ask (and many do), he has restaurant and entertainment suggestions.

Restrictions: No smoking, please. No pets.
Bed and bath: One air-conditioned studio with king bed, plenty of guest closet space, full bath, kitchen.
Breakfast: Self-serve. Continental provided. (You're on your own here.)
Plus: Twenty-four-hour doorman. Elevator. View from high floor.

Abode Bed & Breakfast Host #10

New York, NY
Location: "On Manhattan's fashionable Upper West Side." Within walking distance of Lincoln Center, Museum of Natural History and Columbus Avenue's shops and restaurants. Bus stop directly outside building. Five-minute walk to subway on Broadway.
Reservations: Year round through Abode Bed & Breakfast, page 97. Two-night minimum stay.
Rates: $100 double bed. $115 queen bed.

This landmark building has been in the family for several generations. Through the years, as it was converted to apartments, the architectural detail was kept intact. As a B&B, the spacious studios have been furnished by the hostess with antiques and treasures from "hunting trips" all over New York and New England. As part of her days at home "raising an active toddler," she finds that B&B provides the opportunity to share her knowledge of the city while meeting interesting travelers. Her husband is a photographer and computer consultant.

Restrictions: Children welcome. Sorry, no pets.
Bed and bath: Two separate fourth-floor studios. One with a double bed, marbled tub bath. One with a queen bed, double sofa bed, tiled tub bath. Third-floor studio has queen bed, ornately carved mantel, private bath.
Breakfast: Self-serve from refrigerator stocked with juice, muffins, bagels, cereal, coffee.
Plus: Air conditioning. Private kitchens. Pure cotton linens. Terry robes.

Guests wrote: "Loved it! Perfect. Unique."

Bed & Breakfast (& Books) Host #1

New York, NY
Location: In Soho, lower Manhattan, within walking distance of Chinatown, Little Italy, and Greenwich Village. Convenient to subway. Near major galleries and boutiques.
Reservations: Year round through Bed & Breakfast (& Books), page 98. Two-night minimum stay.
Rates: $50 single, shared bath. $75 single, private bath. $90 double, private bath; $130 four people.

The cast iron building was a warehouse before being renovated for residential use. The 4,000-square-foot "comfortable and arty" loft is the home and studio of an accessory designer and a retired judge who enjoy "good conversation and the chance to tell guests about nontouristy restaurants, tours, and sights."

In residence: One cat.
Restrictions: Children welcome. Sorry, no guests' pets.
Bed and bath: Three rooms. Large first-floor double-bedded air-conditioned room with semiprivate shower bath. On second floor, one very large air-conditioned room with two double beds, full bath en suite; and one small room with one twin bed, shared bath.
Breakfast: Flexible hours. Fruit juice, fruit, bread, jams and jellies, cereals, coffee, tea.
Plus: Tea. Wine. Flowers. Option of holding party here (fee charged).

From Ohio: "A tremendous host. And what a great apartment! Everything about our stay was perfect, perfect, perfect."

Bed & Breakfast (& Books) Host #2

New York, NY
Location: Upper West Side. Near Lincoln Center, Central Park, midtown theaters, Carnegie Hall. Convenient to City Center, Rockefeller Center, department stores and East Side museums.

Reservations: Available year round through Bed & Breakfast (& Books), page 98.
Rates: $70 single, $80 double.

The combination of a great location, a wonderful place, and a sociable host (except in tax season) brings many returnees to this sunny, plant-filled, comfortable, and immaculate apartment. The host is an accountant/magazine editor/music lover who enjoys his guests.

Restrictions: Children 12 and older are welcome. No smoking. No guests' pets.
Foreign languages spoken: German and French.
Bed and bath: One twin-bedded room with adjacent private shower bath.
Breakfast: Flexible hours. Juice, fresh muffins or croissants, cereals, eggs, freshly brewed coffee. Host often joins guests.
Plus: Fully air conditioned. TV in living room. Telephone extension in room. Twenty-four-hour doorman and elevator service.

From California: "Our accommodations were excellent. Our charming host made us feel quite at home."

Urban Ventures Host #3015

New York, NY
Location: Within walking distance of Central Park, Lincoln Center, the theater district, hotels.
Reservations: Year round through Urban Ventures, page 99.
Rates: $52 single.

"One charming Japanese gentleman who spoke very little English, heard opera on my record player. He understood all opera. Immediately we could understand one another through music."
From all parts of the United States, France, Scotland, England, Russia, and Austria—"just to name a few"—have come guests who "stay with a friend," an executive for a shirt manufacturing company, in his comfortable and "pristine clean" apartment. He is a "people person" who also enjoys baking. (Cakes and pies are his specialties.) In addition, he puts in many hours each week as a volunteer for the elderly. *New York* magazine featured him as one of the city's treasures.

Foreign languages spoken: French, Italian, and Yiddish.
Bed and bath: One room with one twin bed shares the host's full bath.
Breakfast: Flexible hours. Juice, cereal, fresh fruit cup, toast, Danish, beverage. Occasionally, eggs and bacon. Self-serve on weekdays.
Plus: Central air conditioning. Tea. Wine. Fresh flowers. Candy on pillow. New York City maps. Events information. Doormanned building.

Urban Ventures Host #4002

New York, NY
Location: High. Facing the East River. Near exit for 23d Street off FDR Drive. Good bus transportation.
Reservations: Year round through Urban Ventures, page 99. Two-night minimum stay.
Rates: $50 single. $60 double.

The hospital administrator and children's wear production manager, both native New Yorkers, score high marks for accommodations, hospitality, and exuberance. "A friend who is a host thought we might like B&B and it might like us. Our location is a most unusual apartment living experience. It's relaxing! And we are very informal. People seem to feel at home here. We face up the East River with a phenomenal view. On a clear day you can see five bridges. Boats travel back and forth and toot their horns. Sea planes land in front of one bedroom. . . . We are antique collectors and have collected many items through the years. . . . We have made friends with guests from around the world. One couple got engaged here!"

Many United Nations delegates appreciate the international flavor and convenience of this B&B.

Restrictions: Children of all ages and pets are welcome.
Foreign languages spoken: French, Italian, Yiddish.
Bed and bath: Two queen-bedded rooms share full bath with hosts.
Breakfast: 8:30. Orange juice, muffins, butter and jam, coffee, tea, milk. Bowl of fruit. Very informal.
Plus: Central air conditioning. Sweets. Babysitting. Washer and dryer. Parking $10 per day. Airport pickup available for a fee. Stores on building's promenade level.

Hudson Valley Reservation Service

Some B&Bs in Hudson Valley are represented by Bed & Breakfast U.S.A., page 84.

Hudson Valley B&Bs

Captain Schoonmaker's Bed and Breakfast

Box 37, High Falls, NY 12440
Phone: 914/687-7946
Location: On Route 213, a state highway but a country-style road. On sloping land with grass and gardens by a trout stream, waterfall, woodlands. Half a mile from tiny High Falls village. Ten miles south of Kingston; 20 minutes to Woodstock.
Hosts: Sam and Julia Krieg
Open: Year round.
Rates: $45 single. $75 double. $85 double with private bath. October–March, double with fireplace $85.

When the Poughkeepsie Mall held its grand opening, there was Julia, merrily cooking while introducing the B&B concept to hundreds who stopped to taste her specialties. Such joie! You don't forget this effervescent grandmother and elementary school teacher who co-hosts with friendly Sam, a biology professor. One visit to their B&B is hardly enough for a huge number of guests; many return several times a year.

Both *Woman's Day* and *Seventeen* magazines have used the setting for photographs. Weddings have taken place here. One guest sent note paper with a sketch of the inn. The grounds, quilts, antique toys, stenciling, and Americana give the illusion of many years' residence. However, all the "magic without fussiness" was created by the Kriegs, starting in 1981 with their college-age children, when they bought "renovation project #8," the 1760 historically registered stone cottage with its 1800 eyebrow colonial Greek Revival addition, then without plumbing, electricity, water, heat or cosmetics. Within 10 months they opened as a B&B. Soon after, the 1810 barn/carriage house was renovated to accommodate more guests, and then came the lock-tender's house on the Delaware-Hudson Canal, a pleasant half-mile jog or cycle to the sumptuous "expanded family" breakfast table.

In residence: Schooner, a golden retriever. Babo, a Maine coon cat.
Restrictions: Children welcomed Sunday through Thursday; over the age of five on weekends.
Bed and bath: Three guest houses, each with four rooms that have twin, double, or single beds. Some with private bath, canopied bed, working fireplace, private veranda overlooking stream. Cots available; a cradle too.
Breakfast: At 9. A seven-course feast. Home-baked bread, juices, poached honey apple, souffles or crepes, sausage, blueberry-walnut strudel with filo, rocky road fudge cake. Almond mocha coffee. Served in front of original working fireplace with candlelight, fine china, crystal, and fresh flowers.
Plus: Late afternoon tea, sherry, or wine in solarium furnished with wicker. Living room with Hudson Valley Dutch fireplace. Option of sailing on the Hudson River on the Krieg's 1939 30-foot Hinckley.

From New York: "Nicer than we could have imagined."

House on the Hill

P.O. Box 86, Old Route 213, High Falls, NY 12440
Phone: 914/687-9627
Location: On a hill just off country Route 213. Minutes' walk to the village, gourmet dining.
Hosts: Shelly and Sharon Glassman
Open: Year round. Two-night minimum on holiday, summer, and fall weekends.
Rates: $65 single, $85 double. $10 child age six and older, $20 additional adult.

"What makes this personalized business such fun is the variety of human beings," according to Sharon. She was a teacher and Shelly a Manhattan business executive before they moved in 1981 to this charming big old house and the worlds of professional flower arranging, real estate, and shared parenthood. "Because so many of our guests have come to look at property, we now have another career. Shelly has his real estate office in the B&B and I have joined him as associate. We have real estate weekends with the Realtor/chef talking with you about your needs!" Getaway guests find innkeepers who know when to be available for conversation, information, and suggestions "for hidden spots that wouldn't be hidden if in this book!"

Their 1825 eyebrow colonial house with graceful stone and hand-forged iron fence (1856) across the front was in the same family until the Glassmans bought it. A strong personal touch in the decor is a collection of quilts made by southern Illinois women (mostly Sharon's family members) and displayed at the huge landing at the top of the center hall and on every bed in the house.

In residence: Gregory, age 11. Two dogs, Bill and Speedy. Four cats, Kiddo, Oddik, Panda Cat, and Cuddles.
Restrictions: Sorry, no guests' pets. Smoking in common rooms only.
Bed and bath: Three suites, each with antique beds and private bath. One with double bed, sitting room, dressing room and adjoining shower bath. One family suite with double bed in large room and a twin bed in the sitting room (which has room for a cot). The third suite has a room with double bed and a sitting room with skylight. Cot available.
Breakfast: Served 8:30–10. Fresh fruit dishes, home-baked pastries, bread, omelets, crepes and country meats. Served in front of the fire in the keeping room, on the glassed-in porch, or in the eat-in kitchen with its view of pond, woods, and old pink brick smokehouse.
Plus: Wine, cheese, and crackers or chowder at just the right moment. Fruit, flowers, candies, nuts, and even a bottle of seltzer. Piano. Bedroom fans. Lawn games. Barbecue facilities. Rubber raft for use on pond in summer. Skating in winter. One-and-a-half-mile canal walk runs along the property. Beach and waterfalls a five-minute walk away.

Guests wrote: "Not only better than a hotel, but better than home!"

Fala

East Market Street, Hyde Park, NY 12538
Phone: 914/229-5937
Location: On a wooded lot, minutes off Route 9 north. One mile from Franklin Delano Roosevelt's home and library and Vanderbilt Mansion. Three miles to Culinary Institute of America or Vall-Kill, Eleanor Roosevelt's cottage. Fifteen-minute drive to Vassar or Marist colleges.
Hosts: Ish and Maryann Martinez
Open: Late March through early November. Reservations preferred. Two-night minimum stay on holiday weekends.
Rates: $50 single. $60 double. $5 cot if under age 18; $10 over 18. Ten percent discount for week's stay.

Surprises await guests who drive up to this house; it looks contemporary but actually has a part that was built in the 1850s. Weave through to the dramatic solarium that looks like it could have been a greenhouse. Leave by the rear door and walk 15 feet to the guest house, a small building converted by previous owners for visiting family. Because it is the only guest room, you are visiting family!

The Martinezes started B&B in 1982 as a way for Maryann to exchange ideas with other adults (and help them enjoy the area) while being a full-time mother and herb gardener. It has worked—for the whole family and for hundreds of guests. Through the years Maryann has also worked in public relations. Currently she is studying for her master's degree in psychology and counseling. Ish is a computer software programmer, a gracious host "and super wallpaperer." Adam and Ryan will tell you about their own local favorite spots. Other Martinez suggestions might be secluded places on the Vanderbilt Mansion site, a waterfall in the park right next to Fala, or restaurants in the Culinary Institute.

In residence: Adam, age 10. Ryan, age 6. Jesse is their black cat.
Restrictions: Nonsmokers preferred.
Foreign language spoken: Spanish.
Bed and bath: One-room guest house with double bed, private shower bath, wicker and antique furniture. Heater and fan unit built into wall. Cot available.
Breakfast: 8:30. Fresh fruit. Coffee and herbal teas. Homemade coffee cakes or muffins. Locally produced jams, jellies, teas, and coffees. Attractively served in solarium overlooking the pool.
Plus: In-ground swimming pool flanked by greenery. Samples of today's baking. Fresh flowers in season. Babysitting.

> From New York: "They made us feel Hyde Park as well as see it. The privacy, too, was something dear to two people-weary, noise-weary and crowd-weary Manhattanites."

Rondout Bed & Breakfast

88 West Chester Street, Kingston, NY 12401
Phone: 914/331-2369
Location: On two acres in an old residential neighborhood. On a hill with views of Catskills. Near Hudson River, antiquing, historic sites, hiking; 25 minutes to Bard College, Vassar, Woodstock, and New Paltz; 40 minutes to Hunter and Bellayre mountains. Ten minutes from New York State Thruway.
Hosts: Adele and Ralph Calcavecchio
Open: Year round.
Rates: $40 single. $55 double. $10 child under 12 sharing room with adults.

> Guests wrote: "The rooms are fresh, airy and pretty—and big; the breakfasts are delicious—and big! The house itself is wonderfully pleasant to sit about in, as are the porches and grounds . . . heard crickets at night . . . welcoming yet unobtrusive hosts who were very helpful with arts and sightseeing information."

When theater friends asked the Calcavecchios, both thespians, to accommodate actors in 1985, they started a whole new "pleasurable life-style" for the hosts, whose five older children were working or in college. And after recent travels to Australia, India, Europe, Japan, and Brazil, Adele and Ralph enjoy the opportunity to meet other travelers here at home.

Built on a grand scale with a 33-foot living room and 20-foot dining room, their 1905 Federal Revival house had seen many uses when the Calcavecchios bought it in 1980. Now "loved" once again, it is furnished eclectically, with paintings and prints "everywhere." Lately, daughter

Donna has added her artistic touches. Adele, a writer and teacher, and Ralph, an engineer and pilot, share many area suggestions. One of their favorites is a "magnificent-in-any-weather" place that they compare to Lake Como in Italy.

In residence: Son Daniel, age 14. Sherlock the dog and Pierre the cat are not allowed in guest rooms.
Restrictions: No smoking inside.
Foreign languages spoken: None, but some French and Italian understood.
Bed and bath: Full bath shared by two double-bedded carpeted third-floor rooms with a view of the Catskills.
Breakfast: Usually at 9. Lots of fresh fruit, waffles, French toast with Ralph's and Daniel's own maple syrup. Endless coffee or tea. Served with crystal and silver in dining room or on porch.
Plus: Living room with fireplace. Sitting room. Evening tea, wine, cheese and crackers. Piano. TV. Phonograph. Books. Large porches. Lawn furniture. Outdoor and indoor games. Refrigerator space. Will meet guests at Kingston airport, or Skypark (Red Hook), Rhinecliff train, or Kingston bus.

The American Country Collection Host ᗄ #066

Philmont, NY
Location: On eight wooded acres on a quiet country road in the Hudson Valley. One mile from Taconic State Parkway, 30 from Tanglewood in Massachusetts, 38 from Albany. Near orchards, historic homes, antiquing, museums.
Reservations: Available year round through The American Country Collection, page 137.
Rates: $50–$55 single. $55–$70 double. Playpen, no charge.

"Guests have written for Dick's recipes for sour cream biscuits and popovers. One M.D. had to be practically dragged away from the computer after he learned how to play 'Jet.' Others had the experience of being almost snowbound in a surprise October storm. We really enjoy hosting!"

The mid-life career changers (in their early forties) were, until 1987, a music teacher and the acting chairman of Scarsdale (N.Y.) High School's science department. That's when they decided that their Columbia County weekend retreat would be "a temporary country home for guests." Built in 1972 as a ski lodge–style ranch home (the kitchen has a real pantry) and added on to in 1986, it has been theirs for five years. With two living rooms, each with a large stone fireplace; a sun room overlooking the woods; and outdoor decks and a patio, there's plenty of room for their "adopted family members who come for one or two days."

In residence: Kit, a large cat "fond of joining guests' parties, but can be isolated in our suite, if necessary."
Restrictions: Children are welcome. Smoking allowed in common areas only. Sorry, no guests' pets.
Bed and bath: Four rooms. On upper level, two king-bedded rooms, each with private bath. On ground level, one with double bed and one with king/twins option share a bath. As a unit, lower-level rooms can include a living room, refrigerator, sink alcove, bath. Playpen available.
Breakfast: Usually 7:30–9:30. Juice and fresh fruit. Maybe pancakes, sausage, sauteed apples; eggs Benedict; chili/cheese omelets; or French toast. Eat in kitchen, sun room, or fireplaced living room or on patio.
Plus: Electric blankets in winter. Individually controlled air conditioning. Clock radios. Horseshoes, volleyball court, yard games. Hammock and tire swing. Picnic tables. Guests' refrigerator. Piano. TV, stereo, VCR. Plenty of books. All those woods for hiking.

> From Colorado: "Warm and gracious hosts. The place is comfortable. Delicious full breakfast."

Sunrise Farm

RD 1, Box 433A, Pine Bush, NY 12566
Phone: 914/361-3629
Location: A thirty-acre farm on a quiet country road. Three miles south of the hamlet of Pine Bush. Half an hour west of New York State Thruway. Close to good restaurants, hiking, canoeing, skiing, horseback riding, golf, wineries, museums, historic houses, antiquing.
Hosts: Janet and Fred Schmelzer
Open: Year round. Reservations preferred.
Rates: $30 single, $45 double. $20 third adult in room. Half rate for children under 15.

> "When guests stroll around the farm or in the adjoining woods, bluebirds are likely to be in evidence. Sharp-eyed folk sometimes spot a pair of pileated woodpeckers. Most people love our beautiful Scotch Highland cattle with their shaggy coats and horns. If you're a beginning cross-country skier, here only the docile cattle (raised as breeders) will see you fall down! The living room woodstove and the attached solar greenhouse keep this Cape Cod–style energy-efficient house cozy. We had it built in 1979 and once the second floor was finished, I, with my British background, realized that it was just right for B&B. Fred was an office supply salesman before 'retiring' as a farmer. Instead of office work (former job), I much prefer farming our organic vegetable garden and hostessing."

In residence: Spooky, a black cat, never in guest rooms.
Restrictions: Children of all ages welcome. Smoking allowed outside only. Sorry, no guests' pets.
Bed and bath: One second-floor paneled room with twins/king bed option, double sofa bed, skylight, adjoining private shower bath.

Breakfast: Flexible; preferably before 9:30. Bacon or sausage and eggs, cereals, toast, English muffins, juice, fruit. If available, homegrown berries, homemade bread, preserves, and "their own" honey.
Plus: Shared living room. Evening tea and cookies or wine. Bedroom fan. All-cotton bath sheets. Flowers. Magazines. Lawn chairs in garden.

From Florida: "A unique and satisfying experience . . . more like a visit with friends than overnight lodging for a price."
From New York: "A refreshing delight. Interesting people, hearty farm fresh breakfast, spacious room, a country treasure."

The American Country Collection
Host #064

Slate Hill, NY
Location: High in scenic countryside on a 90-acre horse farm. Ten minutes to Delaware River; 20 to Hudson River; 2½ miles from Routes 6 and 84; 75 minutes from Manhattan. Near antiquing, wineries, crafts shops, hot air balloon rides, canoeing, historic homes, apple orchards, museums.
Reservations: Year round through The American Country Collection, page 137.
Rates: $45 single. $60–$75 double. Suite $90 triple, $120 with four. $10 rollaway.

Rise early on a hunt day and you might see the gathering and start of the horses and hounds. Walk to the other side of the pond and sit under the trees, listen to the trickling water and the peepers, and enjoy the country view. Cross-country ski, fish, and hike right here. Relax in the whirpool and sauna of the newly built health spa at this spacious hunt club decorated with an English country flavor. What started out as one room in 1843 later became a dairy farm, part of the Underground Railroad during the Civil War, and a summer resort.

The hostess, an artist and skilled seamstress, breeds thoroughbred horses and Jack Russell terriers and has a tack shop on the premises. Her husband, a retired engineer, works with her here on the farm they bought in 1986 "for its beauty, size, and location." Guests are happy that they did.

In residence: Three Jack Russell terriers "are a big hit with guests." Four horses: one stallion and three mares.
Restrictions: Well-behaved children welcome. Smoking in common areas only. Sorry, no guests' pets.
Foreign languages spoken: Some German and French.
Bed and bath: Five second-floor rooms share two baths. Rooms have double or twin beds. One two-room suite with a queen and a twin bed and another suite with a double bed and sink in one room, two twins in the other. Rollaway available.

Breakfast: 7–9:30. Fresh fruit. Eggs Benedict, blueberry pancakes, or pecan waffles. Croissants with homemade jams. Homemade sausage. Served in English Morning Room or The English Pub.
Plus: Bedroom air conditioners and window fans. Tea or wine, cheese and crackers. Fresh flowers. Designer sheets and comforters. Pickup at Stewart airport, train, or bus station for a fee. Tour of house and farm.

From New York: "Beautiful and romantic. Homey, classy, immaculate. The perfect getaway. Excellent hosts."

Baker's Bed and Breakfast

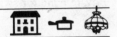

RD #2, P.O. Box 80, Stone Ridge, NY 12484
Phone: 914/687-9795
Location: Quiet. On 16 acres overlooking fields and mountains. Close to a four-star restaurant, craft shops, antiques centers, sailing on the Hudson or tubing the Esopus.
Hosts: Doug Baker and Linda Delgado
Open: Year round. Reservations recommended. Two-night minimum stay for Saturdays.
Rates: Double occupancy. $68 shared bath. $73 private half bath. $78 private full bath. $85 suite with private bath, sitting room, and fireplace. $20 cot.

From New York: "A comfortable place to wind down and warm up, to enjoy the outdoors and each other. Nothing fussy. Food is a highlight."

Restaurant owners have brought their staff for a midweek rest. *Travel & Leisure* has raved about Baker's too. It is definitely relaxed in tone, pace, and decor. The restored 1780 stone house with hand-hewn beams and 18th-century furnishings has wood stoves in the living room and kitchen and a Rumford fireplace in the dining room. There's a plant-filled solarium and, in the greenhouse, a hot tub. And all of this is in an area that is much as it was in the 1700s.

Biology professor Doug is beekeeper, farmer, maple sugarer (using a pan), and energy system builder. (A heat pump is used for the hot water and hot tub. Wood with oil backup is used for winter heat.) Linda, formerly with Shearson Lehman in New York City, has counseled minority women in higher education. Currently she is an adjunct professor of history. With all their experience of preparing memorable breakfasts, Linda and Doug recently opened the nearby 1820 House, a restaurant featuring American regional cuisine and Doug's smoked foods.

In residence: In another building, Danielle, age 10; Chrisopher, age 17. Two outdoor Siamese cats, Lilac and Meese.
Restrictions: No guests' pets. Nonsmokers preferred.
Foreign language spoken: Spanish.

Bed and bath: Six double-bedded rooms on second and third floors. Two (one is a suite) with private bath; two with private half bath and shared full bath; two share a full bath. Cot available.

Breakfast: 9:30. Juices, fruit (most from garden) dishes, homemade strudels, chocolate bread, jams, jellies, granola, house-blended coffee, herbal teas. Maybe poached eggs with tarragon butter sauce laced with fresh-squeezed lemon juice, broccoli and caviar served with tomato eggs, or native Puerto Rican dishes. Home-cured meat, smoked salmon and trout, venison.

Plus: Beverages. Popcorn, apples, nuts. Chocolates. Bedroom window fans. Down comforters. Hammock for two under an old apple tree. The gardens, chicken, geese, ducks. Cross-country skiing from front door. Private pond for swimming or skating.

KEY

 Recipes shared, often for house specialties.

 Inquiries welcomed about restoration and/or decorating. Symbol indicates that host is willing to share experiences with guests. Tips range from a before-and-after album to rebuilding advice, from furniture refinishing to curtain making. Expertise of hosts ranges from learn-by-doing to professional.

🏠 How-to B&B workshop, seminar, or apprentice program offered.

Leatherstocking/Central New York Reservation Service

Bed & Breakfast—Leatherstocking/Central New York Reservation Service

389 Brockway Road, Frankfort, NY 13340
Phone: 315/733-0040. Year round 7 A.M.–10 P.M.
Listings: 35. All hosted private residences. Three country inns. Directory ($2).
Rates: $20–$50 single, $30–$75 double. Weekly rate is 10 percent less. Family rates and senior citizen discount available. $3 service charge for each booking. Deposit of 50 percent of one night's stay required. On cancellations received 10 days prior to arrival, deposit is refunded. MC, VISA.

Floranne McCraith lives in an area that is "relaxing and unhurried." She has hosts, "beautiful people with generous, warm hearts, who feel B&B is a special adventure in our magnificent part of the country." They live on small family farms, in Victorian mansions, near antiques shops or college campuses. Many (and still more are pending) are on the National Register of Historic Places. This service is an association of independent B&B entrepreneurs whose names and addresses (without phone numbers) appear in the directory for direct booking, if you wish. The nightly rate is the same, whether you go through the service or book directly.

"Leatherstocking" includes Afton, Alder Creek, Bainbridge, Boonville, Brookfield, Clinton, Cobleskill, Cooperstown, Dolgeville, Durhamville, Fly Creek, Fort Plain, Frankfort, Forest Port, Hamilton, Herkimer, Howes Cave, Ilion, Little Falls, Mohawk, Morrisville, Nelliston, Newport, Old Forge, Oneida, Oneonta, Oxford, Pallintine, Poland, Remsen, Richfield Springs, Rome, Saint Johnsville, Speculator, Turin, Utica, Vernon, Waterville.

Reservations: Accepted by phone and secured either with MC or VISA or when deposit is received (must be within five days of your call). No minimum stay requirement at most B&Bs. Two weeks' advance notice preferred. Available through travel agents.
Plus: Car rentals. Tours. Special (ski, golf, bicycle tour) packages, restaurant reservations, pickup at transportation points. Laundry privileges, babysitting, and pets allowed in some homes. Short-term (up to three to five months) hosted housing available.

Berry Hill Farm B&B

RD 1, Box 128, Bainbridge, NY 13733
Phone: 607/967-8745
Location: On a winding country road overlooking miles of rural scenery. On 180 acres of woods and meadows. Thirty-five minutes to Deer Run and Greek Peak ski areas. Seven miles from I-88, Bainbridge, and Afton.
Hosts: Jean Fowler and Cecilio Rios
Open: Year round. Advance reservations required.
Rates: $35 single. $50 double.

Away from it all. A treat. A friendly informal atmosphere. Sunrises. Sunsets. Stargazing. Fresh air. Views. Peace and quiet. Everywhere—space! All offered by ex-Brooklynites who came for all those good things eight years ago. They restored an 1820s farmhouse and filled it with primitive and European antiques. Outside they established extensive vegetable and flower gardens. In 1986 they started to share this large comfortable house with B&B guests.

Now Cis, an ex-teacher, and Jean, a former textile designer, sell antiques, braid rugs, and quilt. (And Jean is a Realtor.) Their guests unwind, cross-country ski, or go sledding right here. During warmer months, they hike, pick berries, swim in the pond, and go to auctions; year round they enjoy warm hospitality.

In residence: Patrick is 14. Cis smokes. One Labrador mix, Sam.
Restrictions: Children age five and over welcome. Smoking in main living room only. Sorry, no guests' pets.
Foreign languages spoken: Spanish, French, Italian, German, Latin.
Bed and bath: Three second-floor double-bedded rooms share two full baths, one with antique brass shower.
Breakfast: Until 10. Juice, cereals, fresh fruit, eggs/pancakes/French toast with ham, sausage, or bacon; homemade muffins, jellies, jams, cheese, yogurt, freshly brewed coffee, tea. Served in the front room overlooking the valley.
Plus: Tea, coffee, juice always available. Flannel sheets. Down comforters. Extra pillows. Porch. Grill, picnic table. Some ice skating and ski equipment (no charge) available.

Creekside Bed & Breakfast

RD #1, Box 206, Forkshop Road, Cooperstown, NY 13326
Phone: 607/547-8203
Location: On an old stagecoach route. Surrounded by huge manicured

lawns. Bordered by creek (for swimming and fishing). Three miles from Cooperstown center, off County Route 26.
Hosts: Fred and Gwen Ermlich
Open: Year round. Minimum two-night stay on major holiday and summer weekends; three nights on Baseball Hall of Fame weekend.
Rates: Double occupancy. $55–$65 double. $65 suite. $95 cottage. $10 additional person, cot or crib.

The atrium lights twinkle all year round in the colonial house that has grown from 9 to 16 rooms. "Last year we converted the goat's house into a honeymoon cottage," said the hosts, as they brought all of us gathered around the elegant dining room table up to date on all sorts of changes. Weddings have taken place in the huge living room and on the grounds since the Ermlichs started hosting in 1983. Gwen gets just as excited about house decor as she did for all the opera costumes she used to make. The company she and Fred founded 14 years ago no longer performs in the high school; during the summer you might see the multi-faceted hosts perform at the acclaimed Glimmerglass Opera theater built on Otsego Lake in 1987.

Before coming to Cooperstown in 1970, Gwen was an actress and singer in Manhattan. Fred, a former Roman Catholic priest and arts consultant, is assistant to the president at SUNY Oneonta. As hosts they offer privacy and company, warmth and joy to "Buddhists, Christians, Jews, Bahai, Moslems, actors, artists, baseball luminaries, international travelers, balloonists, cyclists, and all-American families."

In residence: Paul, age 15, and Patrick, age 13.
Restrictions: Well-behaved children welcome. No smoking inside. Sorry, no guests' pets.
Foreign languages spoken: French and German.
Bed and bath: Four rooms; all private baths, some skylit. One with queen canopied bed, ceiling fan, private entrance and deck. One double-bedded room. Suite with queen bed, huge sitting area. Cottage with queen bed, bath, living room, wet bar, cable TV, HBO, deck. Rollaway bed and crib available.
Breakfast: 7:30–9. Maybe scrambled eggs with dill, cinnamon French toast, or pancakes. Juice, bacon or ham or sausage, fruit, coffee, tea, hot chocolate. Option of "scrumptious low-cholesterol meal." Cooked by Fred. Beautifully served in dining room or on deck at umbrella tables.
Plus: Beverages. Refrigerator space. At Christmastime, five decorated trees in the house. Restaurant suggestions and reservations. Opera and theater tickets. Babysitting.

The Inn at Brook Willow Farm

RD 2, Box 514, Cooperstown, NY 13326
Phone: 607/547-9700
Location: Quiet. Up a tree-shaded drive, over a creek, onto 14 acres with views of meadows, cows, deer, and mountains. Five minutes to Glim-

merglass Opera theater and to swimming and boating at Otsego Lake.
Hosts: Joan and Jack Grimes
Open: Year round. Reservations required. Two-night minimum stay on weekends Memorial Day–Columbus Day.
Rates: Double occupancy. $50–$60. $10 cot. Crib free.

> From Connecticut: "Tops. Beautiful location. Lovely decor. Great food. Super clean. Provided restaurant menus and suggestions and made theater reservations for us. Joan even ironed our son's shirt for church! A fantastic experience. Please include them in your book."

Guests have arrived on Thursday and announced that they would like to be married this Saturday, right here. (It happened.) Some young parents have had their "first night out since baby arrived" with Joan and Jack, grandparents of two, as babysitters. The Grimeses declare, "We still consider this all a dream come true. After moving to this former hops farm from Long Island twelve years ago, we redid the 1900s Victorian cottage house and our 1880s barn—the last of the big barns—keeping the exposed beams in one room and decorating with antiques, wicker, collectibles and lots of plants. Each spring the creek—on what we call our pastoral retreat—is stocked. Visitors who come for the Baseball Hall of Fame (five minutes away) are surprised to find other museums, the theater, Victorian homes, and antiquing possibilities. Thanks to our thousands of guests from all over the world, we have warm memories of travelers who share hopes, dreams and experiences."

Joan is a former nurse/teacher who currently runs a Cooperstown gift shop. Jack is an educator.

Restrictions: Sorry, no guests' pets. No smoking in bedrooms.
Bed and bath: Four rooms. Three, each with private bath, in reborn barn. Suite in main house has a large bath with twin sinks, tub, and shower. Queen, double, or twin beds; cot and crib available.
Breakfast: 7:30–9. Juices, fresh fruit, homemade muffins, eggs, cereal, toast, jam. French toast, pancakes, or waffles, coffee, tea, milk. Served by candlelight on china in the dining room. "We judge breakfast success by how far down the candles burn."
Plus: A Great Room with fireplace, books, puzzles. Fireplaced parlor. Beverages. Fresh flowers, fruit and candy. Thick towels. Bedroom ceiling fans. French toiletries in each guest room. Decks. Paths through woods. A glen to climb. Kitchen privileges. Barbecue. Badminton. Discount at gift shop in town.

Litco Farms Bed & Breakfast

Fly Creek, NY
Mailing address: P.O. Box 1048, Cooperstown, NY 13326
Phone: 607/547-2501
Location: On 70 acres with plenty to do right here. On New York Route 28, three miles north of Cooperstown. Restaurants within walking distance.

Hosts: Margaret and Jim Wolff
Open: Year round. Reservations preferred. Two-night minimum weekend stay from Memorial Day through Columbus Day.
Rates: $50–$65 double. $75 triple. $85–$95 quad in suite. Ten percent less, November–March.

Two guests, an Italian sculptor and an English art critic, fell in love with the area, "bought a home around the corner and were married by Jim in our living room!" Some guests accompany Margaret and Jim and Ruby, their dog, at sunset to the eight-acre beaver pond, which also has ducks and geese. Some just relax, tour the area, or even get tips about refinishing floors or rearranging furniture every time a new auction treasure is acquired. By the time you arrive at this added-on-to 1820s house, there may be a greenhouse and sauna. For sure, you'll receive a warm welcome.

Before Jim became Otsego town justice, he had his own imported lumber and plywood business and helped to organize the local natural food co-op. Margaret, a former home economics teacher and co-owner of a restaurant, is placement director for vocational/technical students and operates the county teen job bank. "And my dream has come true with Heartworks right here at the B&B; it's a unique shop which features handmade quilts, dolls, and creative stitchery."

In residence: Gregory, age 18. During college vacations, James and Christopher. Miss P., a pussycat, and Ruby, "the wonder dog who is very tricky."
Restrictions: All ages welcome. "We enjoy families." Sorry, no guests' pets. Non-smokers preferred, no smoking in bedrooms.
Bed and bath: Two first-floor rooms (one with a double bed, one with two double beds, nonworking fireplace, and cable TV) share a bath. Upstairs suite has one room with a double bed and a double sofa bed, adjoining room with two twin beds, private full bath. Very private carriage house with double bed, bunk beds, shower bath, kitchenette, cable TV.
Breakfast: Usually 8:30 or 9. Whole-grain freshly baked breads, homemade fruit preserves and granola, farm-fresh eggs, bacon, French toast or hotcakes with pure maple syrup, freshly brewed coffee.
Plus: In-ground 20-by-40-foot pool. Hiking, nature, and cross-country ski trails. Deck overlooking meadows. Canoe (at your own risk). Trout fishing. Common room with books, magazines, and board games. Bedroom window fans. Picnic baskets by advance arrangement.

From New York: "I consider Litco Farms the hospitality capital of central New York. Guest rooms are very pleasant. Breakfast is among the best I've had at a country inn."

Adrianna Bed & Breakfast

44 Stewart Street, Dolgeville, NY 13329
Phone: 315/429-3249
Location: Five minutes from the village center, with panoramic views of

Adirondacks. Six miles from New York State Thruway, exit 29A; 28 miles northeast of Utica.
Host: Adrianna Naizby
Open: Year round. Advance reservations preferred.
Rates: $40 single, $45 double. $10 extra person. MC.

One guest liked the town so much he moved here. A couple found the B&B so appealing that they were inspired to open their own.

The contemporary house, which "looks smaller from the outside than it is," is the immaculate and comfortable home of a Dolgeville sixth-grade teacher who has "the beginnings" of a very large wildflower garden. Through her own travels in the British Isles, Adrianna realized the benefits of staying with local residents. Her long list of recommendations here "in my quiet, clean and inviting village" includes African violet greenhouses, the Beaver Sprite Wildlife Sanctuary, Daniel Green Slipper outlet, and unusual restaurants and shops.

In residence: Son John, a college student. Barney, a friendly cat. Goliath, the dog.
Restrictions: Children five and over welcome. Smoking in living and dining rooms only.
Foreign language spoken: Limited Italian.
Bed and bath: Three second-floor rooms share a shower bath. Downstairs tub available. Double bed, high queen bed, or two twins.
Breakfast: 8–10. Fresh fruit. Juices. Pancakes, French toast, or egg casseroles; ham or sausage, coffee, tea, hot chocolate. Served by candlelight with crystal and china in dining area.
Plus: Bedroom air conditioners and ceiling fans. Wine. Champagne for newlyweds. Welcome with tea and cookies. Toiletries. Candy. Babysitting by prior arrangement. Kitchen privileges. Laundry. Picnic table.

From New York: "A beautiful house with a woman who is very loving and caring and will make you feel like you are staying at some fancy resort."

Breezy Acres Farm Bed & Breakfast

RD 1, Box 191, Hobart, NY 13788
Phone: 607/538-9338, 9 A.M.–9 P.M.
Location: On a dairy farm, surrounded by grazing cows and 300 acres of rolling hills. Five minutes from Deer Run ski resort. Half hour to Plattekill, Windham, and Hunter ski areas. Two miles south of Stamford (and hang gliding).
Hosts: Joyce and David Barber
Open: Year round. Two-night minimum on holiday and special weekends.
Rates: $45 shared bath, $55 private bath. $5 less for singles or for one small room with two twin beds. Family rate, $75, two adjoining twin-bedded rooms. $10 additional child. $5 single weekend night surcharge. MC, VISA.

Guests wrote: "You feel as if you're visiting friends. . . . Joyce creates breakfasts that are a feast for the eyes as well as the palate. . . . So close to country fairs, antiquing, and hiking. Fresh air and scenic views are right there and through the woods . . . cozy country style, but it's the warm hospitality that makes the difference . . . a wealth of knowledge about everyone and everything happening in Delaware County. I plan to stay there regularly until I find a house in the area."

Talk about unwinding! As Joyce noticed one Sunday afternoon, "Some guests who have been watching TV or playing pool just asked about muffins left from breakfast. Other guests are in the Jacuzzi after snowmobiling."

A blend of antiques (some local pieces), crafts, and contemporary furnishings are in this impeccably kept 18-room added-on farmhouse. (There's a very funny story about a family who arrived separately, didn't realize the house had two wings, and didn't meet until the morning.) Often, guests "hang out" in the kitchen. Or they settle in on the wide curved leather sofa by the fieldstone fireplace flanked by mounted deer heads and a collection of commemorative rifles. In March and April there are opportunities to watch the production of 1,000 gallons of maple syrup. As for the popular hosts: Joyce, a former teacher, is a professional home economist who attended Cornell's School of Hotel Administration. She and Dave, a dairy farmer and avid hunter, enjoy antiques auctions held at a nearby former creamery.

Restrictions: Children over six are welcome. Smoking in sitting room only. Sorry, no guests' pets.
Bed and bath: Four second-floor rooms. Private full bath for one double-bedded room. Two twin-bedded rooms and one with a double bed share one full and one downstairs half bath. In three rooms, foldout chair with sleeping bag for a child.
Breakfast: 8–10. Juice. Maybe baked stuffed pears or melon balls with fresh mint sauce, French toast made with homemade bread, or pumpkin pancakes with "our own" maple products. Homemade muffins. Milk, coffee, tea.
Plus: Joyce bakes often. Treats in each room. Garden flowers. Wicker-furnished porches with rockers.

The American Country Collection
Host #058

Howes Cave, NY
Location: On a hill, "overlooking a tiny New Englandish village in the Catskills foothills." Off I-80; 1½ miles from Howe Caverns; near Cobleskill; about 30 miles east of Cooperstown. Near The Barn Carp, "a junk shop to end all."
Reservations: Year round through The American Country Collection, page 137.

Rates: $35 single, $45 double. Suite—$50 single, $60 double. Additional person, $5 under age 10; $10 over 10. $5 cot or crib.

"People seem to feel at home surrounded by all the old things we have here: *Life* magazines from the '40s, early calendars, and canning jars that now contain pastas and beans. Herbs hang on towel racks. Antique cooking utensils hang from the beamed ceiling. A spinning wheel and child's ironing board grace our living room. The original part of this structure was built in 1790. During the five years that we have been married, we have made several renovations. In what is now a guest room, the first editor of our local weekly paper did his first printing. My husband is a manager for a farm equipment company (hence the interest in farm antiques). I have an herb garden; enjoy art and painting; have made all the curtains, pillows and quilts; and have experience working with severely handicapped children. We're not elegant, but we're happy that our house turned into a B&B. We've had a bubbly college student who gave new arrivals a tour while I was on the phone. A very fussy guest who had us checked out beforehand has returned many times. And some have asked us to share a silent blessing at breakfast."

In residence: Two teenagers. One beagle "who snores loudly" (and lives outside) and a springer spaniel who "does not realize she is a dog and has been known to try to room with guests."
Restrictions: No pets please. ("Enjoy ours!") No smoking in bedrooms.
Bed and bath: Three rooms, all private baths. On first floor, one queen-bedded room. One suite with double bed and sitting room with daybed, nonworking potbelly stove. Upstairs, a double-bedded room. Rollaway and crib available.
Breakfast: Usually at 8:30. Menu varies. Maybe bananas and coconut in heavy cream. Ham/cheese strata, corn oysters/ fritters dipped in syrup, or cheese-filled cherry blintzes. Homemade muffins. (And still, "some ask for just toast!") Hosts join guests.
Plus: Tea or wine, cheese, crackers, soda. Homemade potpourri. Tour of house. Bedroom window fans. Picnic tables. Grill.

From New York: "Great attention to detail. Warm and friendly hosts. The area is tranquil. It was a joy to stay there."

Cavern View

Howes Cave, NY
Location: On a hilltop surrounded by 47 acres with a view of the Schoharie Valley. One mile from lodge at Howe Caverns. Near Bramanville Grist Mill, Old Stone Fort, SUNY Cobleskill. Forty-five minutes to Cooperstown; 2½ miles from I-88, exit 22.
Reservations: Year round through Bed & Breakfast—Leatherstocking, page 117.
Rates: $35 single. $45 double, shared bath; $50 private bath. $10 rollaway. $5 crib.

Each of the 14 beef cattle has a name. They are part of the scene on the rolling farmlands that surround this 1872 Italianate house, which was owned by one family before becoming a guest house in 1970. Antiques, however, are the real focus of this B&B. The hosts were museum curators in the Oswego area for 10 years before moving here in 1987 to have an antique shop in their own home. (They can lead you to 40 shops in the county.) Two guest rooms have Laura Ashley wallpaper. One has an 1880s cottage-style painted bedroom set. Furnishings are Empire and Victorian. The shop, four rooms of the house, are filled with 19th-century furniture and decorative items (lots of white ironstone, chairs, small tables, linens, and framed prints). The hosts cane chairs, collect teddy bears, and have an interest in genealogy—and, of course, auctions too.

In residence: Tippy, the dog, and Carmel, the cat, live outdoors.
Restrictions: Well-mannered children welcome. No smoking. Sorry, no guests' pets.
Bed and bath: Four second-floor rooms, two shared baths. Rooms have double, twin, or a double plus a twin bed. Rollaway and crib available.
Breakfast: 7:30–9. Continental plus. Homemade muffins, breads, or coffee cakes. Fruit, sausage or bacon, cereal, juices, coffee, tea, milk. Entree might be homemade kuchen, waffles, egg casserole, or French toast. Served in dining room overlooking scenery. Hosts join guests.
Plus: Hot or cold beverages. Tour of house and farm. Ceiling fans in some bedrooms. Large living room and front porch. Suggestions for winding back roads to explore.

From New York City: "Yummy breakfast. Interesting hosts."

Whitegate

Oxford, NY
Location: On 196 acres bordering Bowman State Park. Six miles west of Oxford. Near Gilbertsville Polo Grounds.
Reservations: Available year round through Bed & Breakfast—Leatherstocking, page 117.
Rates: Double occupancy. $45 shared bath, $50 private bath. $10 third person in room.

Against "big sky" and miles and miles of land far from the madding crowd is this Greek Revival farmhouse built in the early 1800s and added on to, in the same style, in the 1970s. Shortly after the retired engineer and watercolor artist bought (and redecorated) the property in 1986, they began welcoming B&B guests in the same way that they have entertained relatives and friends through the years. A full-wall fireplace is in the family room. Bedrooms are furnished with a period theme. Family heirlooms, European antiques, and traditional pieces blend. The Finger Lakes Hiking Trail, from Buffalo to Binghamton, crosses the property, which has two trout ponds. The hospitality here is appreciated by antiquers, wedding guests, property buyers, hunters, and snowshoers too.

In residence: Colleen and Timmy, 13-inch beagles "who love attention but are kept away from guests who don't enjoy dogs."
Restrictions: Children 13 and over welcome. No smoking. Sorry, no guests' pets.
Bed and bath: Three rooms. On first floor, Williamsburg Room with queen bed, private full bath. On second, Country Room with two twins and a daybed shares a shower bath with 1930s Room, which has a double bed and love seat twin bed.
Breakfast: As early as 4 for hunters; as late as 10 for late risers. All prepared by hostess, a gourmet cook. Possibilities include juices, fresh and spiced fruits, homemade breads, muffins, sausage/cheese strata, creamed chipped beef, eggs, bacon, pancakes, and cereals. Served in country kitchen or dining room. Hosts join guests.
Plus: Beverages. Pedestal fans in second-floor bedrooms.

From Washington, D.C.: "Made our first B&B experience a very positive one. Very helpful with directions to museums and antique shops."

Jonathan House

39 East Main Street, P.O. Box 9, Richfield Springs, NY 13439
Phone: 315/858-2870
Location: In the center of an historic village on U.S. Route 20. Amid rolling countryside of farms, fields, woods, and streams. Twenty minutes north of Cooperstown. Near Erie Canal Village, Howe Caverns, Madison/Bouckville antiques center. Convenient to I-90 and Colgate University.
Hosts: John and Peter Parker
Open: Year round. Advance reservations preferred.
Rates: $45 single. $50 double. Suite $65 single, $70 double. $10 per rollaway. $10 less November 1–April 30. MC, VISA.

More than a place to stay, Jonathan House is an experience. Full of English, French, and American antiques, it is authentically furnished in mid-19th-century style with paintings, crystal chandeliers, Oriental rugs, and gilt mirrors. The grand 17-room house built at the height of Richfield Springs' fashionable spa days is the restored home of two brothers, both artists, who drove by in 1984 and saw a "for sale" sign. When a neighboring B&B asked them to accommodate overflow, their hosting days started.

And so did the questions about why a retired attorney and a stage/film actor/director from Los Angeles settled here. With memories of Pennsylvania childhood days among green fields and rolling hills, and both recent widowers and retirees, they moved with their mother to this residence with its cherry moldings and paneling, three full floors and a tower room, and plenty of room for everyone. Both community activists, John and Peter have become experts on local history. They suggest unique as well as traditional places to visit. "In turn, we enjoy having our guests tell us about themselves and their part of the world."

In residence: "Our 13-year-old dog Lucky is a family member but we keep him out of the path of guests."

Restrictions: Children of all ages welcome. Smoking allowed outside only.

Bed and bath: Three second-floor queen-bedded rooms. One suite has a large bedroom with half-canopy bed, sitting room with cable TV, private adjoining full bath. One full bath shared by room with full-canopied bed and another with a half-canopied bed. Rollaways available.

Breakfast: 8–10. Varies daily. Juice; eggs and sausage or ham with fruit garnish; coffee, tea, or milk; toast of specialty breads. Served with damask linens, English silver, and bone china in a very elegant dining room.

Plus: Sherry. Coffee available an hour before breakfast. Ice and setups at 5 P.M. Fireplaced parlor with baby grand piano. Garden.

Summerwood

P.O. Box 388, 72 East Main Street, Richfield Springs, NY 13439
Phone: 315/858-2024

Location: On three acres surrounded by lawns and trees. On Route 20, midway between Albany and Syracuse; 12 miles from New York State Thruway, I-90; 15 miles from Cooperstown; seven miles from Cooperstown Theater Festival, Glimmerglass Opera, and dairy farms.

Hosts: Lona and George Smith

Open: May–November; other times by advance reservation only.

Rates: Double occupancy. $45 shared bath. $55 private. $10 rollaway. Singles $10 less. Ten percent less for stays of more than three days. Family rates available.

Drive up to the portico, alight from your motor-driven "carriage," and enter the Queen Anne Victorian that is on the National Register of Historic Places. There are fireplaces in the parlor and dining room, and as Lona says, "there's always a chair at the kitchen table when I'm cooking." Many gables and stained glass windows command your attention, but the real hit—particularly with children—is the authentic turn-of-the-century carousel horse in the dining room.

When the Smiths lived on the West Coast, Lona was a microbiologist and George was in computer sales and management. They came east several years ago to take over George's family dairy farms. In 1984 they bought (and redecorated) this big 1890 house "with 86 windows, acres of lawn, and a barn with wainscoting that fascinates many guests. There are also acres of woods for hiking and high hills with magnificent views." George is happy to tour guests through the farms. And now the Smiths host weddings, play readings, and opera and theater benefits—with Lona as the caterer. "Bernice, one guest came just for the pancakes described in your book!"

In residence: A black Lab named Joe. Two cats, Tuffie and Misty.

Restrictions: Sorry, no accommodations for infants or pets. Smoking allowed in sitting rooms.

Bed and bath: Four guest rooms. One second-floor double-bedded room with private full bath. Entire third floor is for guests; two rooms with queen beds and one with twin beds share a full bath plus a sitting room and game table. Rollaway bed available.

Breakfast: 7:30–10. Seasonal fruits; assorted quiches; eggs from local farms; bacon, sausage, and ham (also local); homemade coffee cakes, rolls, and muffins; sourdough pancakes with local maple syrup and homemade jams. Served in formal dining roon, in kitchen, or on the sun porch.

Plus: Wine or soft drinks. Sitting room with TV. Wicker-furnished porches. Yard games. Refrigerator and ice. Tour of house. Assistance to guests who are seeking ancestors. Laundry facilities. Picnic lunches ($5–$10); some with wine. By advance arrangement, theater and opera tickets purchased and dinner ($8–$12) here.

Bed & Breakfast of Waterville

Waterville, NY

Location: In historic district, one block from N.Y. Route 12. Just over a mile from U.S. Route 20 and antiques shops. Twenty minutes from Colgate University and Hamilton College. Near SUNY Morrisville, Oneonta, Cazenovia, Bouckville, and music museum in Deansboro.

Reservations: Available year round through Bed & Breakfast—Leatherstocking, page 117.

Rates: Shared bath, $30 single, $40 double. Private bath, $45 per room. $10 rollaway. $5 crib.

Inspired by their own B&B stays while visiting their college daughters, the hosts, who have also traveled B&B in England and Scotland, now meet many parents who are visiting college students. The quilt maker/teacher and her husband, a utility company manager, both community activists, are the second owners of this 1871 Victorian, which has all original woodwork. Collectibles and antiques form a backdrop for the hostess's quilts (many are original designs) and needlework. For guests who have time to explore, the friendly hosts suggest Root Glen, "wonderful to wander through in all seasons."

Restrictions: Children and very well-behaved pets welcome. Smoking in common areas only.

Bed and bath: Three rooms. Private full bath for first-floor room with two twin beds. On second floor, one room with double bed and one with two twin beds share a full bath. Rollaway and crib available.

Breakfast: Flexible hours. Fruit in season. "Eggs in many guises," homemade bread, muffins and jam. Served in dining room, where there's another hand-stitched quilt. Hosts join guests.

Plus: Bedroom fans. Fireplaced living rooms. Second-floor porch. Fresh flowers. TV.

From New York: "We have traveled in many B&Bs and this is certainly one of the finest. . . . Everything one could ask for. . . . Delicious breakfasts. Great dinner suggestion."

Catskills Reservation Services

Some B&Bs in the Catskills are represented by:

Bed & Breakfast U.S.A. Please see page 84.
The Blue Heron Bed and Breakfast Reservation Service. Please see page 156.

Catskills B&Bs

Maplewood Bed & Breakfast

P.O. Box 40, Chichester, NY 12416
Phone: 914/688-5433 (same-day return calls for reservations left on answering machine)
Location: On a quiet country lane in a beautiful valley. On more than an acre of grass, trees, and gardens. Two miles north of Phoenicia; 12 miles northwest of Woodstock; 28 miles northwest of Kingston; 12 miles from four ski slopes. Near major hiking trails.
Hosts: Nancy and Albert Parsons
Open: Year round. Reservations required.
Rates: $40 single, $55 double.

From New Jersey: "A magnificent piece of property complete with towering pine trees, a backyard mountain and an in-ground swimming pool. Nancy and Albert are gracious and friendly, unobtrusive when privacy is wanted. They went out of their way to make our visit interesting and relaxed. . . . Delicious breakfasts. Welcoming, well-appointed, and clean. Our five-year-old daughter thinks it is charmed. A back staircase, an under-the-stairs bathroom, a secret passageway leading to the bedroom, a laundry chute, two lounging cats—what more could a city kid ask for!"

Many guests are surprised at the size. Built in 1923, this was formerly the manor home of Beryl Swartzwalder, owner of Chichester Wood Products, who owned the entire village. Although this spacious colonial has been the Parsonses' for over 30 years, it is only within the last 5—since their family has grown—that they have satisfied their desire to be innkeepers. Skiers, tourists, fishermen, and getaway weekend travelers appreciate the hospitality here. One family that gathered from all over the country found it a perfect reunion spot.

Nancy, an accountant, and Albert, a sales manager, are active with civic organizations and politics, sports, and gardening.

In residence: Whippett, "our large, male, affectionate cat."

Restrictions: Sorry, no guests' pets. No smoking please.

Bed and bath: Four second-floor rooms with semiprivate full baths plus a half bath downstairs. One king bed, one canopied double, one queen bed, and one single.

Breakfast: 8:30–9:30. (At 7 for skiers.) Freshly squeezed juices, grapefruit or fruit salad, freshly ground coffee, omelets or crepes, bacon or sausage, French toast, pancakes, home-baked breads. Albert is chef. Served in dining room or on porch overlooking gardens. Leisurely (except for skiers) with hosts often joining guests.

Plus: Beverages, cheese and crackers. Family room with fireplace, color TV. Library with piano. Samples of toiletries. Thick towels. Croquet, badminton. Sun porch. In-ground pool. Hiking trails right here.

The White Pillars Inn

82 Second Street, Deposit, NY 13754

Phone: 607/467-4191

Location: Quiet. Among 18th-century Federal and Greek Revival homes in a lumbering and farming community (with well-known Americana antiques shop) on old Route 17. Surrounded by roads with farms and fields, streams and Cannonsville Reservoir. In foothills of the Catskill Mountains; 25 minutes east of Binghamton; three hours from Manhattan.

Host: Najla R. Aswad

Open: Year round. Two-night minimum stay on holiday weekends.

Rates: May–October—$55 single. Double, $65 shared bath, $70 private bath. $110 two-room suite. Rest of year, $45 single; $55 double/shared bath; $65 private bath; $85 suite. AMEX, CB, Diners, MC, VISA.

From New York: "A delightful experience. . . . Run by an energetic gracious proprietor whose inn is in a sleepy, rural, quaint town. . . . Elegant but comfortable. The rooms should be featured in *Better Homes and Gardens.* Guests are pampered . . . beds with piles of down pillows . . . all sorts of magazines, candy, even shoe polish! . . . Yet, it's the hospitality that I would put at the top of the list."

Talk about timing. At age 22, after college, Najla decided, after much experience in the food and hotel industries, and after managing a hometown (Binghamton) restaurant, that the nonstandardized world of innkeeping would allow her "to make a huge impact on a small scale." That's when she opened here, in April 1987, in the 1820 Federal Greek Revival house that had been built by the founder of the town. Najla knows how to cook (meals are created and presented) and how to bake (wedding cakes, fruit pies, and chocolate chip cookies marketed in the area) and has established an inn apprenticeship program for dreamers. ("There's a time for hosting and a time to let go.") At least half a dozen couples have sought her consultation on their own home decor. Still, the inn kitchen seems to be a popular gathering place. And now local Realtors will tell you that Deposit has been discovered by residents of New York City and other "downstate" areas.

Restrictions: Children over 12 welcome. No smoking inside. No pets.
Bed and bath: Five rooms. Three and a half baths; some private. Two double-bedded rooms. One with a double and a twin daybed. Suite has canopied (with century-old hand-crocheted tablecloth) double bed, private bath, TV ("hidden" in armoire), sitting room with double bed, phone jack, small refrigerator, private staircase to kitchen, and option of breakfast in bed! Rollaway available.
Breakfast: 8–10. Grand Marnier French toast with blueberries and steaming local maple syrup, blueberry-banana buttermilk Belgian waffles, three-inch-high omelets, quiches. Blended juices, fresh fruit. Homemade breads and muffins. Specialty coffees. Served in dining room with heirloom Haviland Limoges, gold flatware, Waterford crystal, fresh flowers, "and the sounds of Windham Hill artists."
Plus: Central air conditioning. Evening refreshments by the fire. Coffees and teas always available. Fine toiletries. Pima cotton bath sheets. Dinner by reservation ($17.95–$22.95). Directions (in spring) to a spectacular waterfall "where the mist can be seen for half a mile," plus local hiking, bicycling, swimming, fishing, canoeing, cross-country skiing, sledding.

Adams' Farm House Inn

Main Street, P.O. Box 18, Downsville, NY 13755
Phone: 607/363-2757
Location: Two blocks to town. With sidewalk in front and babbling brook ("to dab your toes in") in back. In the Catskill Mountains on Route 206, "the scenic route to Niagara Falls and the New England states"; 15 miles west of Roscoe.
Hosts: Nancy and Harry Adams
Open: April–December.
Rates: $35 single. $50 double; $55 holidays and in summer. $15 extra person. $7.50 child.

It's the house with the old horse-drawn carriage on the front lawn, an 1898 farmhouse that was "too big for two people" when the Adamses came here two years ago from the New York City area, where Nancy was a high school teacher and Harry a policeman.

"We rebuilt most of it, staying as close to the original plans as possible. Many of our furnishings, especially those in the dining room, are antique oak. Attached to the inn is our antiques and thrift shop. This village, settled in 1792, has 500 people, all friendly. Over 60 of them have their works for sale in a local arts and crafts shop! Holidays and festivals are really fun here. At the B&B we meet fishermen (if you'd like, we'll cook your catch), hunters, lots of antiquers, and many interesting people who are glad to have such a nice place to stay while they are passing through."

In residence: Gizmo, a two-year-old toy poodle, "loves people!"
Restrictions: Well-behaved children welcome. Smoking allowed in dining room only. Sorry, no guests' pets.
Bed and bath: Three second-floor rooms share one large shower bath. Two double beds, two twin beds, and one room with one double and one twin bed.
Breakfast: 6:30–9:30. Juice, homemade muffins, cereal, eggs, meat, potatoes, toast, coffee, tea, milk. Sometimes crepes with fresh fruit and cream. In dining room at table set with linen, silver, and china.
Plus: Coffee, tea, cider, cookies; wine, cheese. "Our famous brownies to take with you." Computer bridge. Dinner ($10) during fishing and hunting season. Wicker-furnished front porch (good for people watching). Back deck. Yard with huge maple trees. Guest pickup at Roscoe bus station. Nearby new state park, Bear Spring, for walking and swimming.

Blue Heron Bed and Breakfast Host #35

Fleischmanns, NY
Location: On main street of a small village. In central Catskills near Esopus and Delaware rivers. Two miles from Belleayre and Highmount ski centers. Adjacent to acres of state game lands. Near antiquing, tennis, and softball area.
Reservations: Year round through Blue Heron Bed and Breakfast Reservation Service, page 156. Two-night minimum stay on holiday weekends.
Rates: $40–$45 single, $55 double, $55–$70 queen, $75 king. (Plus reservation service booking or membership fee, see page 156.)

Their three daughters and three sons grew up in New Jersey, where the host was an oral surgeon. In 1987 the empty nesters bought a late Victorian inn "in these beautiful Catskills" where the host could spend more time fly-fishing and upland bird hunting. In winter, their inn is a haven for skiers. During other seasons, the host and guest instructors conduct hands-on sessions in the fly-fishing school; hikers enjoy the trails in Forest Preserve; cyclists pedal the country roads. Area attractions include chamber music concerts, country fairs, and Saturday night auctions.

The interior design skills of the hostess are evident in the decor—an English country theme with hunting prints, decoys, deer hides, and deer head. A baby grand piano is in the fireplaced parlor. Videos on fishing and hunting are in the book-lined library. And now that inside is all restored, the hosts are working on the gardens "and perhaps a gazebo by the rushing stream in the rear of the yard."

In residence: Two cats, a lively border terrier, and a young Gordon setter to be trained for upland game hunting.
Restrictions: Children are welcome. Smoking in parlor only. No guests' pets in B&B (but okay in efficiency apartment).

Bed and bath: Eight rooms named after area fly-fishing streams. Four second-floor rooms with private baths; king, queen, double, or twin beds. Four third-floor rooms with queen or twin beds share two full baths. Two efficiency apartments.
Breakfast: Usually 8–10. Juice, fresh fruit, hot breads and muffins, jams, honey, butter, hot cereal, tea, and coffee. Buffet style in breakfast room at tables for four by stained glass window.
Plus: Flannel sheets. Tour of house. Fishing equipment for guest use. Adirondack chairs on the wraparound porch. Off-street parking.

Mount Tremper Inn

Route 212 and Wittenberg Road, P.O. Box 51, Mount Tremper, NY 12457
Phone: 914/688-5329
Location: In the Catskill Mountain Forest Preserve; 20 miles west of Kingston; 10 miles west of Woodstock. Across from one well-known French restaurant and near others.
Hosts: Lou Caselli and Peter LaScala
Open: Year round. Reservations required. Two-night minimum on weekends, three nights on holiday weekends.
Rates: $55 shared bath. $70 private bath. $85 suite. MC, VISA.

Discovered! By dreamers in 1984. By the *New York Times* in 1986. By *Ski* magazine in 1987. And by guests who "love it and keep coming back." Victoriana through and through with velvet walls, French lace curtains, and ornate prismed lamps, it is just what the two New Yorkers, Lou, a former marketing coordinator, and Peter, a fabric importer, envisioned while they collected museum-quality antiques—everything from armoires to bedsteads—for eight years. They found the 23-room 1850 summer guest house, last used as an orphanage, all boarded up and in need of everything. In five and one-half months, the two men did everything all themselves. Ever since, they have been pampering guests—and smiling. The innkeepers, too, love this business.

Restrictions: Children 16 and over welcome. Smoking in game room and parlor only. Sorry, no pets.
Bed and bath: Twelve rooms; every one with a sink. Private tub bath for first-floor suite with two double beds. Private shower bath for first-floor room with two twin beds. Ten second-floor rooms with a double or twin beds share three baths.
Breakfast: 8–10. Juice, cereals (including homemade granola), "their own" breads, baked eggs with cheese and vegetable, coffee and Twinings teas. Buffet style with crystal and silver in elegant dining room with classical music playing. On veranda in summer.
Plus: Sherry by the bluestone parlor fireplace. Full game room and library. An old music box that plays beautifully; an old organ that plays reluctantly. Croquet, badminton, shuffleboard.

Pearl's Place

Route 23A, Palenville, NY
Mailing address: P.O. Box 465, Palenville, NY 12463
Phone: 518/678-5649
Location: In a small residential community on scenic Route 23A. Ten miles east of Hunter Mountain; 15 miles northeast of Woodstock; 150 yards to swimming at Kaaterskill Creek swimming holes.
Hosts: Mark and Melanie Overton
Open: Year round. Two-night minimum stay on weekends.
Rates: Double occupancy. $65 private bath. $55 shared full bath. Singles, $10 less. $125 with living room and private bath (not available as single). $10 rollaway. $5 crib.

It's two years since the New York City Ballet costume maker (Melanie) and the Metropolitan Opera House stagehand and production carpenter (Mark) brought their love of the arts, good food, and country living to this well-cared-for 1901 house—named after the "woman of the house" who lived here for half a century. The comfortable home, redone with joy, has refinished woodwork throughout. Fresh wallpapers are hung, and Melanie has sewn the window treatments. Plenty of pillows are on the twin living room sofas; overhead is Mark's newly installed tin ceiling and a period chandelier. The hosts' longtime goal was inspired by their own "great experiences at B&Bs."

Restrictions: Children welcome. No pets or smoking please.
Bed and bath: Four rooms. First-floor room with private entrance has private bath with whirlpool tub, living room, TV, wood stove, sleeping loft with double bed. On second floor, private tub bath for double-bedded room. Room with twin beds shares full bath with double-bedded room and hosts. Rollaway and crib available.
Breakfast: 8–10; earlier in winter for skiers. Sample menu—juice; orange pecan muffins; grapefruit; tomato cream cheese and basil omelet; sausage and toast; coffee.
Plus: Tea, lemonade, hot chocolate or hot cider. Trailways bus from New York City stops at inn's doorstep. Some bedroom air conditioners. Babysitting with advance notice. Enclosed wraparound porch. Lawn chairs. Towels for swimming.

Guests wrote: "On a getaway (from river rafting business) found the perfect R and R place. It has a special coziness that tempts me to keep it a secret, but that would be too selfish. . . . We felt well taken care of. And Melanie was up to the challenge of our toddler who loved the carpeted stairs and the acres out back where she could run and explore."

Two Brooks for Fly Fishing & X-country Skiing

Route 42, Shandaken, NY 12480
Phone: 914/688-7101
Location: Secluded. Surrounded by woods and meadows. Across two wood bridges "at the confluence of two brooks teeming with trout." Thirty miles west of Kingston, in the heart of the Catskill Mountains. Within 15 minutes of Belleayre and Hunter Mountain ski centers. Two and a half hours from Manhattan.
Hosts: Doris and Jerry Bartlett
Open: Year round. Reservations required. Two-night minimum stay at all times. Three nights on holiday weekends. On nonholiday weekends in May, June, and September, fly-fishing students (and companions) only.
Rates: Double occupancy. $58. Singles $8 less. MC, VISA.

From New York: "Natural-born hosts. Congenial and informal. Breakfast was epicurean. We had one complaint: we had to leave."

Guests fall asleep to the sound of the brooks. They enjoy the wood stove, the fireplace, the country furnishings, and the ambiance of natural wood. Some come specifically for special weekends when Jerry, a New York state licensed fishing guide, conducts fly-fishing schools for beginners and novices on well-known nearby Esopus Creek and leads tours of famous Catskill streams for experienced fly fishers. In the winter he is just as enthusiastic about cross-country ski instruction and tours.

As the host says, "It's our home where the city comes to visit us. When I see everyone relax with a variety of people, I am reminded of the reasons we moved to this old summer lodging house that we have rehabilitated." Jerry was in corporate planning; he has continued as a business development consultant (and become a breakfast chef of some reknown). Doris, a former client relations manager for a software firm, is a tax preparer and official baker.

In residence: Jerry smokes a pipe. Three dogs: two collie/shepherd mixes and a husky/shepherd mix. Three cats.
Restrictions: Children who sleep through the night are welcome. For guests' dogs (only), inquire about compatibility with hosts' pets. Smoking in common rooms only.
Bed and bath: Four upstairs rooms share two hall baths with hosts. Three double-bedded rooms; one with two single beds. Cot available.
Breakfast: 8:30. Perhaps (organic) garden-fresh zucchini and tomatoes with basil sauce in omelets or crepes. Or apple cinnamon pancakes, apricot-stuffed French toast, Roesti potatoes, maple yams. Freshly squeezed orange juice or homemade vegetable juice, fruit, muffins, cereals, eggs, bacon, sausage, trout (with luck). Low-fat and low-salt preparation.

Plus: Big front porch. Three sitting rooms. TV, VCR, books, magazines, piano, guitar, fiddle, games. Sleds. Rent 12-speed bicycles. Fly-fishing and cross-country skiing videotapes. Fly-fishing equipment and tackle for sale.

The Eggery Inn

County Road 16, Tannersville, NY 12485
Phone: 518/589-5363
Location: At 2,200-foot elevation, minutes to Hunter, Cortina Valley, and Windham alpine ski areas; 1 1/2 miles from the village. Forty miles south of Albany; 14 miles northwest of I-87; 18 miles north of Woodstock; 125 miles from Manhattan.
Hosts: Abe and Julie Abramczyk
Open: Year round. Two-night minimum stay during winter, summer, and fall weekends. Three-night minimum on holiday weekends. No meals served in April, early May, or early November.
Rates: Per person. Midweek—$37.50 single, $60 double. Weekend—$60 single, $75 double. Suite—$85 per room midweek, $125 (MAP) weekends. Additional person—$20 weekday; weekend charge depends on age. $220 high-season weekend for two includes two nights, two breakfasts, Saturday dinner. (Wine list available.) AMEX, MC, VISA.

From New Jersey: "They treat guests like family. The inn is charming. The rooms are comfortable, cozy and clean. We enjoy our time in the inn as much as our time on the ski slopes!"

The idea of having a ski slope in their backyard is what attracted two Long Island health care administrators (who are also jazz fans) to the then 23-room summer lodging house 10 years ago. "We found a few projects to do, starting with the landscaping of 13 acres. Inside we have made extensive changes, refinished wainscoting, added baths, and furnished with antique finds. It is the country inn we hoped to have, a place where we meet delightful people. Summer and fall guests have the chance to see breathtaking views from a one-lane road carved into the mountainside of the Catskill Forest Preserve which has many hiking trails. Saturday night dinners (with a French chef) began because of the skiers; with the weekend package plan, everyone becomes quite a group by the time Sunday rolls around."

In residence: David is home during college vacations. Two cats, Tootsie and BoBo. Babe, a black Labrador.
Restrictions: Well-supervised children are welcome. Sorry, no guests' pets. No smoking in dining room.
Foreign language spoken: Spanish.
Bed and bath: Thirteen rooms. All private baths (most are shower baths). Seven rooms are on the second floor. Six rooms are handicapped accessible. New third-floor skylit two-room suite has a queen bed, two double beds, full bath. Cot available.

Breakfast: About a two-hour span. Juice, fruit, hot and cold cereals, muffins, local jams and maple syrup, coffee, herbal teas. Eggs, French toast or pancakes, bacon, sausage, home fries. Served in the plant-filled air-conditioned dining room with picture windows that face mountain range.
Plus: Antique player piano with many rolls. Parlor with wood-burning stove and color cable TV. Cable TV in each guest room. Wraparound porch. Sitting room. Ceiling fans in living and dining rooms. Croquet. Volleyball.

Albany Area to Lake George Reservation Services

The American Country Collection

984 Gloucester Place, Schenectady, NY 12309
Phone: 518/370-4948. Monday–Friday 10–noon, 1–5.
Listings: Over 90. Mostly hosted private residences. Some inns and private unhosted residences. Communities represented in New York state are in the Albany/Saratoga, the Hudson Valley, Catskill, Central Leatherstocking, Northern Adirondack, and Lake George regions. New England listings are throughout the state of Vermont and in the Berkshires in western Massachusetts. Many homes are on the National Register of Historic Places. Range includes budget to luxurious. Directory is $3.
Rates: $30–$70 single, $40–$130 double. Weekly rates. Family rates at some locations. Senior citizen discounts only for multinight weekday stays (excluding foliage season and Saratoga in August). Deposit of one night's lodging or one-half of total stay required, whichever is greater. Deposits are refundable less a $10 service fee if reservation is cancelled no less than 14 days prior to scheduled arrival (30 days August–October). If cancellation is received between 14 days and arrival (between 30 days and arrival August–October), deposit is refunded if room is filled. MC, VISA; 4 percent service charge.

"When a guest walks in and says, 'This is just the way The American Country Collection described it,' we know we have done our job well," says Beverly Walsh, a reservation service owner who lists customer satisfaction as top priority. Her "delightful hosts" are attentive to guests' needs but aware of the need for privacy. They present homemade foods, know their area, and often have attended Beverly's comprehensive workshops about running a B&B. In addition, they are inspected ("mattress testing is included!") before being selected. From all reports, the hosts, too, are content with placements.

Reservations: Two weeks in advance preferred. Last-minute accepted when possible. Some B&Bs have a two- or three-day minimum during busy seasons.
Plus: "Ski 'n' B&B," romance, and theater packages and short-term (up to several months) hosted and unhosted housing available. Pickup at transportation points provided by some hosts. Available through travel agents.

Another service with B&Bs in this area:

   Bed & Breakfast U.S.A., page 84.

Albany Area to Lake George B&Bs

Appel Inn

Route 146, RD #3, Box 18, Altamont, NY 12009
Phone: 518/861-8344
Location: Twelve miles southwest of Albany and Schenectady. Near SUNY and Union College. One-half mile from golf course; 2 miles from Altamont and local performing arts center with free summer Thursday evening presentations; 30 miles to Saratoga. Across the street from old cemetery, Hendrick Appel's burial place.
Hosts: Gerd and Laurie Beckmann
Open: Year round.
Rates: Second floor—$55 per room, $60 when fireplaces are used. Third floor—$40 single, $50 double. $10 third person. $10 child in room with adults. Infants free. MC, VISA.

The pillars give it the feeling of a Southern mansion. When the hosts, not yet 25, bought this property in 1981, it was a private home on both the State and National Registers. Hendrick Appel—hence the name—originally built the generously sized rooms for a tavern in 1765. Those six pillars and the solarium were added in 1900.
The Beckmanns opened in 1983 after furnishing with antiques (some for sale), dust ruffles, and thick towels. The large (15-by-25-foot) rooms are appreciated by getaway guests, business travelers, and returnees who feel like family. Appel descendants have come. And many weddings are held here.
Laurie and Gerd, who have known each other since they were 12, started collecting antiques (pocket watches and silver) in college days. To innkeeping, Laurie brought experience as an Empire State Plaza restaurant manager, she was also cook and steward on Riviera charter boats. Gerd, a metallurgist who is "heavily into computers," is studying for a PhD at RPI. He is comfortable around the kitchen and lots of people.

In residence: In hosts' quarters—David is six years old; Christopher is three; Jason was born June 30, 1988. Attila is "a bear of a Swiss mountain dog."

Restrictions: Sorry, no guests' pets. Smoking on first floor only.

Foreign language spoken: German.

Bed and bath: Four rooms. On second floor, one with canopied double bed and pullout queen sofa shares claw-foot tub bath with room that has queen and a twin; a fireplace with working gas logs in each room. Two third-floor rooms, each with a double bed and a single, share a shower bath. Crib and cot available.

Breakfast: 7:30–9. Fruit, juices, homemade muffins or croissants, eggs, French toast, filo pastries, coffee and assorted teas. Served in an oval solarium with wraparound windows overlooking grounds and flowing stream, swimming pool, and wishing well.

Plus: Third-floor room ceiling fans. Evening beverages. Living room with big fireplace. Games and TV. Guest refrigerator. Tennis court. Volleyball, croquet, badminton. Cross-country skiing (rentals $10 nearby) and ice skating (on creek) on grounds.

Hilltop Cottage

P.O. Box 186, 6883 Lakeshore Drive, Bolton Landing, NY 12814

Phone: 518/644-2492

Location: Quiet. A half mile from village center on Route 9N. On two acres across the road from Lake George. Minutes from beaches, marinas, and the refurbished Sagamore luxury resort hotel. Nine miles from I-87, exit 22.

Hosts: Anita and Charlie Richards

Open: Year round. Reservations preferred.

Rates: $30 single. $40 double. $10 extra person in room.

> From New York: "The hosts themselves are the real charm of the place! A warm, friendly homelike atmosphere. Comfortable, attractive, immaculate, plenty of hot water all the time. And Anita is a great cook who delights in surprising you with new treats every day. We have stayed in many pensions abroad. Hilltop ranks with the best of the European tradition."

The retired educators—Charlie was a guidance counselor and Anita taught German—appreciate the cycling, hiking, and cross-country ski possibilities here. Since they acquired this house in 1985, they have been very involved with complete redecorating and updating, using siding from the old farm outhouse for wainscoting in one bathroom, retaining original hemlock woodwork, and installing a new kitchen and, in the living room fireplace, a ceramic stove. Pictures reflect the estate area as it once was and the hosts' German background.

Anita had lived here with her family from the age of 8 until she was 25; at that time, this was the caretaker's house belonging to one of the estates along Millionaire's Row. (Anita's parents ran this house as a tourist home from 1950 to 1980.) For what to do or see, you couldn't find a better resource than Hilltop, a B&B since 1986. The Richardses' favorite little-known place is the Marcella Sembrich Memorial Studio (open summers) with its memorabilia from the golden age of opera and its parklike grounds bordering the lake.

In residence: Max the dog and cats Toby and Mietze "live mostly outdoors."
Restrictions: Children should be at least four. No smoking in the bedrooms.
Foreign language spoken: Anita is fluent in German.
Bed and bath: Three second-floor rooms with two twin beds or one queen bed share a bath with shower. Cot available.
Breakfast: Usually 8–9:30. Fruits, homemade breads and coffee cakes, jams, jellies, plus standard fare, if requested; but Anita prefers to offer quiches, sausage-egg-cheese bake, German apple and potato pancakes, or French toast with locally produced maple syrup. Served in the dining room or kitchen or on screened porch shaded by lush Dutchman's-pipe vines.
Plus: Piano. Picnic table. Lawn chairs. Ample parking for boat trailers and RVs. Bedroom ceiling fans.

The American Country Collection Host ⟶ #008

Clarksville, NY
Location: On 10 wooded acres in a rural community, 16 miles southwest of Albany. Within half an hour of SUNY Albany, Union and Siena colleges, and RPI. An hour to Saratoga or Tanglewood.
Reservations: April–December through The American Country Collection, page 137.
Rates: $55 ($60 when pool is open) for room with wood stove. $35 for second room. $5 cot or crib.

"We encourage guests to use the refreshing pool and all the common rooms of the house, including the TV room with old fireplace and joyously warm wood stove.

"Built in the 1760s with wide board floors, open beamed ceilings and lines of an old Dutch farmhouse, our house with rural antique decor was owned by members of one family until the 1920s. Then apparently it was lived in by a 'rum-runner' during Prohibition. We came here in 1972 and have been hosting—thanks to our own very first host who suggested we begin—since 1984. The land has two streams which pour down in the spring, and there is a small cemetery with gravestones that date back to 1806."

The host is a retired business school professor. The hostess taught first grade. Now they have time for gardening, sailing, dance and music concerts, theater—and B&B.

In residence: "Our antique (20-year-old) cat, Bob Dylan Thomas."
Restrictions: Children may use pool only with close parental supervision. Smoking allowed in common rooms only.
Bed and bath: Two second-floor double-bedded rooms (available only to the same traveling party). One has a canopied bed, air conditioning, wood stove, and color TV. Each has a cathedral ceiling. Both rooms share a full bath and common library area. Cot and crib available.
Breakfast: Usually available until 11. Juice; fruit; cereal; homemade muffins; omelets, waffles, or pancakes; sausage or bacon. Quite leisurely in the dining room or by the pool.
Plus: Beverages. Fresh fruit. Flowers. Tour of house. Guest pickup at airport, train, or bus station for $5.

From New York: "Delightful on all counts."

The Crislip's Bed & Breakfast

RD 1, Box 57, Ridge Road, Queensbury, NY 12801
Phone: 518/793-6869
Location: On Route 9L, two miles from I-87. Twenty minutes from Saratoga; 15 minutes from Lake George's recreation area. An hour to Albany or Killington, Vermont. Near Glens Falls summer opera performances. Ten minutes to West Mountain; 45 minutes south of Gore Mountain.
Hosts: Ned and Joyce Crislip
Open: Year round. Reservations appreciated.
Rates: $55 single. $65 double; $75 in August. $10 extra per child. MC, VISA.

A hitching post and carriage mount are in front of the early 19th-century Federal-style house. (At one time the surrounding land was the largest working farm in the county.) Williamsburg decor is featured in the guest rooms of this third restoration done by Ned, a vocal music teacher, and his wife, Joyce.

Originally the residence of the town's first doctor, the Quaker-built home was used for many years as a training center for young medical interns. The Crislips bought the property from a family that had owned it for over a century. Since opening as a B&B, the enthusiastic hosts find that their guests are interested in antiques, music, eating, and skiing. Some of them follow the hosts' suggestion and visit the Hyde Collection in Glens Falls.

In residence: Tashi, a 15-year-old dog. Kaija is a 16-year-old cat.
Restrictions: Guests' pets sometimes allowed; arrange in advance. Smoking allowed on porch only.
Foreign language spoken: Some German.
Bed and bath: Four rooms. On first floor, one large efficiency with double four-poster bed, private shower bath. On second floor, a room with king-sized four-poster, private shower bath. One double room with canopied

double bed, private full bath. One room with three-quarter Jenny Lind bed, shared bath, for children or other family member.

Breakfast: Until 10. Juice, sausage, eggs, English muffins, or pancakes and syrup. Prepared by both hosts and served on linens in dining room, which adjoins keeping room with massive stone cooking fireplace and sun room with view of lawn, stone walls, and mountains.

Plus: Living room with grand piano. Tour of the large and interesting house. Bedroom fans. Front porch with view of mountains and, in late September, the balloon festival.

Tibbitts Guest House

100 Columbia Turnpike, Rensselaer, NY 12144
Phone: 518/472-1348
Location: On Routes 9 and 20, opposite Sterling-Winthrop Research Company gates. Two miles east of state capitol in Albany.
Host: Claire Rufleth
Open: Year round.
Rates: $38 single. $40 double. $70 apartment (breakfast included).

"I am an old-fashioned homespun extrovert. The house is cozy. The floors are highly polished. The beds are comfortable."

Sixty years ago Claire's grandfather Tibbitts converted the old farmhouse (now 142 years old) into a tourist house. When it was 100 years old, Claire bought it from her widowed grandmother. She and her husband "changed it to B&B in 1978 after many guests requested breakfast as they had enjoyed it in Europe. And through all these years of hosting, we discovered the universality of man." She enjoys suggesting places and directing guests to shopping; historical sites; the 45-mile jogging, cycling, and hiking path starting in downtown Albany; Saratoga attractions; and restaurants, from gourmet to fast food.

In residence: Angel, "a social-minded cat."
Restrictions: Sorry, no pets or children. No alcoholic beverages.
Bed and bath: Five second-floor rooms share one and one-half baths. Single, double, or twin beds available. Ground level apartment has double bed, keeping room with fireplace and original beams, shower bath, kitchenette.
Breakfast: 7–8:30. Juice, toast, homemade jams and jellies, tea, coffee, milk, or hot chocolate. Eat in dining room or on the 84-foot enclosed porch.
Plus: Shaded patio with wrought iron furniture. Picnic tables. Yard with trees and flowers.

From New York: "Bright, convenient, homey, reasonable. Claire makes instant, warm friends of the assorted strangers at the table."

The Westchester House (at Five Points) 🍳

102 Lincoln Avenue, Saratoga Springs, NY 12866
Phone: 518/587-7613
Location: Within walking distance of downtown. Within five minutes of historic Congress Park, thoroughbred racetrack, Skidmore College, Performing Arts Center, Museum of Dance, walking tours of town, state park with groomed cross-country trails. Across from grocery store and laundromat.
Hosts: Bob and Stephanie Melvin
Open: Year round except January. Advance reservations required in summer. Two-night minimum stay in July; three-night minimum on August weekends.
Rates: Per room. $50 semiprivate bath. $75 private bath. $15 more, Jazz Festival–Labor Day. Racing season, $120 semiprivate bath, $160 private bath.

> From California (and echoed by many): "After many years with (major) hotels, my expectations have been finely tuned. It wasn't the beautiful home, the careful lighting next to the beds for reading and at the wash basin, or the Victorian lace curtains that made me want to return. Bob and Stephanie's personal touch made my stay all the more enjoyable."

Stephanie still finds time to sing opera and classical music. Bob, a former computer analyst, combines innkeeping with making stained glass—all in a carefully selected location that offers rich cultural and recreational opportunities. In 1987 this personable couple transformed a well-built 1880s Queen Anne Victorian house that had been a rooming house run by "an independent, resourceful, loved woman" for 50 years. From Washington, D.C., they brought their antiques and fine furnishings, a collection that ranges from pre–Civil War to contemporary art glass. "We, too, are delighted with the interaction here. One carousel restorer gave a spontaneous seminar; subsequently everyone, even those guests who had not planned on going, went to an auction. Guests discuss a concert or the baths for which Saratoga is known, or they solve the problems of the world."

In residence: Tiger Lily, "a thirty-five pound, mostly Labrador retriever who shares the social responsibilities with us."
Restrictions: Children 12 and over welcome. Smoking allowed on porch only. Sorry, no guest pets.
Bed and bath: Seven air-conditioned rooms. Private bath with first-floor room with a Shaker double bed. On second floor, rooms with double bed, private full bath; three-quarter Louis XVI bed, private bath; a balconied room with ornate brass king bed, private bath. One bath shared by two double-bedded rooms.
Breakfast: 8–9:30. Locally baked goods, tea, coffee, juice. Fresh fruit in summer. In dining room with china and crystal by arched window that looks out on old maple tree.
Plus: Hot and cold beverages. Bedroom fans and air conditioners. Baby grand piano. Stereo system. Porch. Garden.

The Widow Kendall House

10 North Ferry Street, Schenectady, NY 12305
Phone: 518/370-5511. (Guests receive calls on 370-5972.)
Location: On a quiet street in the "stockade" historic district. Near Union College, General Electric, Mohawk River parks and trails, antiquing; 23 miles to Saratoga Springs.
Host: Richard W. Brown
Open: Year round.
Rates: June–October—$90 queen, $80 double with fireplace, $65 double, $45 single. November–May—$75 queen, $65 double with fireplace, $55 double with private bath, $40 single.

> From Washington, D.C., and New York: "The house is very old and wonderfully renovated and decorated. Subtly updated . . . Rich Brown is a warm and gracious fellow. . . . Delicious breakfasts are attractively presented. . . . Very comfortable, relaxing, quaint and romantic. The bathrooms and kitchen are as beautiful as you would see in a magazine."

"One room at a time" is Rich's secret to restoration. After 10 restoring years, friends suggested B&B to the host, an attorney whose partner is in theater arts. "Modernized" in the 1830s, the late colonial/early Greek Revival still has "a charmingly tipsy front door, and in the back, beautiful gardens." When the brick-front saltbox house was built in 1790, Widow Annie Kendall served cakes and ale here. Richard has furnished with antiques and reproductions. He loans bicycles. He directs guests to walking tours, the gardens at Union College, or the historical society. Many write about "the perfect host."

Restrictions: Children are welcome. Smoking permitted "in consideration of other guests' wishes."
Foreign languages spoken: A little French.
Bed and bath: Two ground-floor rooms and three on second floor. Four rooms share a bath with Jacuzzi and walk-in shower plus a half bath. One "deluxe" room has queen bed; another a double bed, fireplace; two small rooms have a single bed. Next door is double-bedded room—"not deluxe"—with private bath.
Breakfast: 6:30–10:30. Fresh muffins, croissants, or bagels. Fresh fruit cup and juice. Hot or cold cereal. Cheese or mushroom omelets; sometimes pancakes or French toast. Bacon, yogurt, low-fat cottage cheese, raisins. Served in large kitchen or in dining room.
Plus: Air conditioning. Tea, wine, or beer. Fresh flowers in rooms. Guest pickup ($10) at Albany airport, Schenectady Amtrak, or bus station. Babysitting arranged. Kitchen and laundry facilities. Often, cuttings from herb garden.

The Inn on Bacon Hill

200 Wall Street, Schuylerville, NY 12871
Phone: 518/695-3693
Location: "In the grove across from the barn." Surrounded by dairy and horse farms. Twelve minutes east of Saratoga's racetracks, Performing Arts Center, restaurants, battlefield. Eight miles from I-87 Northway. Forty-five minutes to Albany, Lake George, and Vermont.
Host: Andrea Collins-Breslin
Open: Year round. Two-day minimum on August racing season weekends only.
Rates: June, July, September, October, double $55 shared bath, $60–$65 private bath. August, $20 more. $5 less November–May. MC, VISA (for balance after deposit).

> From Rhode Island, Virginia, and California: "Down to earth, beautiful folks who make you feel at home from the moment you walk through that door. . . . Excellent accommodations. A peaceful place to come home to and a hard place to leave in the morning. . . . From the bedroom window, the peaceful sight of waving corn stretching down the hill . . . wine before going out to dinner . . . the kind of breakfasts mothers warn about. . . . A perfect experience."

With all her experience in the career counseling field, including the design of General Electric's first Career Development for Women course, Andrea decided, in 1987, to "stay with people" but leave the corporate world. (Her last position was as an engineering project planner.) She and her husband, an engineer, restored the 1865 mid-Victorian country home, which has bay windows, original moldings and border paper, a kerosene chandelier, and marble fireplaces. Victorian furnishings grace the formal parlor; the less-formal living room is decorated in traditional Queen Anne style. "Guests ask all kinds of questions about the house and its history and then the inevitable 'where to eat.' Response is a myriad of fine restaurants in and around Saratoga."

In residence: "Vicki, a gentle golden retriever, and her buddy Muffin, a friendly cock-a-poo, similar to Benji" live with Andrea's mother in the carriage house next door.
Restrictions: Children 16 and over welcome. No smoking inside. Sorry, no guests' pets.
Bed and bath: Four rooms. Private baths for two first-floor double-bedded rooms. On second floor, room with two twin beds shares a full bath with room that has a double four-poster bed.
Breakfast: Usually at 8:30. Juice, fruit, homemade muffins and jams, cold cereals, coffee, tea. French toast and bacon, egg and sausage, blueberry pancakes and sausage, or walnut waffles and bacon. "Can last up to two hours!"

Plus: Hot or cold beverages. Homemade soup for skiers. Two parlors. Baby grand piano. Stereo. Books galore. Wicker-furnished porch. Basket of amenities in each room.

The American Country Collection Host #005

Stillwater, NY

Location: Quiet. In the country on 130 acres with mountain views. Fifteen minutes from Saratoga Springs, one-quarter mile from Saratoga National Historical Park (Revolutionary battlefield). Four miles from Saratoga Lake.

Reservations: Year round through The American Country Collection, page 137. Two-night minimum stay in July and August; three nights in racing season.

Rates: July 1–October 31, $75 suite, $65 room. Rest of year, $60 suite, $50 room, except August racing season, $95 suite, $80 room. $10 one-night surcharge ($15 in August).

Such foresight! It's almost 20 years since the hosts decided to leave the city for the peaceful countryside. That's when they converted a barn built in 1800 to an exquisite home, a blend of old and new with original beams on angled ceilings. Three years ago, when the children were grown, the hosts, both in finance and real estate, opened one room for B&B guests. The match was right. Now more travelers enjoy good food and conversation surrounded by country decor in this quiet retreat.

In residence: One German shepherd.

Restrictions: Children 10 and over welcome. No smoking inside. Sorry, no guests' pets.

Bed and bath: Four rooms, three with private baths. First-floor room with queen bed. On second floor, two suites each with four-poster king bed, sitting room. Adjacent to one suite, a room with one twin bed and sofa bed.

Breakfast: At 9. Menu decided ahead of time, according to guest's choice. Could include fresh fruit, pancakes or eggs. Served in dining room or on back deck.

Plus: Flowers. Candy. Fruit. Tour of house. Bedroom ceiling fans. Brick patio. Countryside for jogging, cycling, walking.

From Connecticut: "Absolutely first class in every way. Warm, caring hosts. Beautiful view. Extra large room. Hardly could believe our luck."

White House Lodge

53 Main Street, Warrensburg, NY 12885
Phone: 518/623-3640
Location: In the center of a quiet village that has 12 antiques shops. Four miles north of Lake George. "Five minutes' drive to Lake George, Bolton Landing, Saratoga Race Course, Gore Mountain, everything!" Within walking distance of restaurants.
Hosts: James and Ruth Gibson
Open: Year round.
Rates: Per room. $65 double bed, $70 extra-large room with double bed. $60 room with single twin bed. MC, VISA.

"What a warm experience to meet such special guests! We are thrilled that we moved to Warrensburg with all its down-to-earth home-town out-of-the-past feeling. Upon retiring (Jim was an electrical inspector and Ruth a customer relations supervisor) we had plans to move to Florida from our home in Long Island. Jim's parents had run this old lodging house for ten years. When they died, we took a second look at it (in 1985), and here we are. Built in 1847, it was once a place where carriages were rented to people who came by stagecoach. Jimmy has done all the plumbing, electrical work, and carpentry, including the halls that are now beamed and paneled. (He has also restored three antique cars.) The freshened neon sign still works. We made one of the rooms into a TV lounge, and find that people often turn off the TV and talk! They seem to enjoy our album that shows how we restored our antique cars. We're hardly retired now, but we love what we're doing."

Warrensburg is also the home of the world's largest garage sale the first weekend in October. From all there is to do in the area, the Gibsons' favorite spot is "a beautiful crystal clear cold water spring with delicious drinking water."

In residence: Free-Way Ling, a Lhasa apso "who is so intelligent hosts have to spell rather than mention her favorite goodies."
Restrictions: Children should be at least seven. No guests' pets. No alcoholic beverages. No cigar smoking.
Bed and bath: Five second-floor rooms share two shower baths. Four double-bedded rooms; one with one twin bed. All have beamed ceilings, window and ceiling fans.
Breakfast: 5:30–11. Juice, rolls, homemade muffins and jelly donuts, coffee or milk.
Plus: Air-conditioned lounge. Beverages and cookies or cake. Fresh flowers. Porch rockers and chairs. Lawn furniture. Restaurant reservations made.

From West Germany: "Only one night there and we felt like family."

Ananas Hus Bed & Breakfast

130 South Road, West Stephentown, NY
Mailing address: Route 3, Box 301, Averill Park, NY 12018
Phone: 518/766-5035
Location: On 30 acres. On a hillside with panoramic view of the Hudson River Valley. Halfway between (within half hour of) Albany, New York, and Berkshire Mountains. Fifteen minutes to Jiminy Peak ski/alpine slide resort; 20 minutes to Brodie Mountain ski area; 30 minutes to Williamstown Theater Festival; 40 minutes to Tanglewood.
Hosts: Clyde and Thelma Olsen Tomlinson
Open: Year round. Advance reservations required. Two-day minimum on holiday weekends.
Rates: $40 single, $50 double.

Hospitality ("Ananas" in Norwegian) is the theme at this ranch home built on family land in 1963. Designed by Thelma, it is sited to take advantage of a view that the local paper calls "unmatched in the area." The focal point of the living room is a large fieldstone fireplace made with stones that Thelma and her father picked off the hay field each spring when she was a child.

Photographers Thelma and Clyde have exhibited locally and competed in national and international contests. Retirement inspired B&B. "Over the years we have hosted folks from Europe and Asia through the People-to-People program. And because our son is the local minister, we have often had singers, ministers and missionaries as overnight guests."

Restrictions: Well-behaved children 13 and over welcome. No smoking. No guests' pets, please.
Foreign language spoken: Norwegian.
Bed and bath: On first floor, two double-bedded rooms and another with two twins share a connecting full bath.
Breakfast: Flexible hours. Possibilities include juice, fruit, egg dishes or Finnish pancakes with sausage, muffins or coffee cake, hot or cold cereal. Tea, coffee, or milk. Special diets accommodated. Clyde is chef. Thelma serves in dining area or on roofed patio.
Plus: Fireplace and TV in living room. Tea or coffee. Bedroom fans. Kitchen and laundry privileges. Badminton, volleyball, horseshoes.

From New York: "A comfortable, warm home away from home . . . wonderful, vital people who have given us much good advice about building in the area. Their breakfast has so many selections that we have yet to try them all . . . heart shaped homemade waffles are unique and delicious."

Stone House Inn

Star Route, Box 187, Canton, NY 13617
Phone: 315/386-2779
Location: On 175 acres, part of a wildlife preserve with three ponds. Near universities—Saint Lawrence and Clarkson—and colleges—Potsdam and Canton. Ten miles to Potsdam Music Theater North. Two miles from Route 11. Eighteen miles from Canadian border; 90 minutes to Ottawa; two and a half hours to Montreal.
Hosts: Becky and Peter Van de Water
Open: Year round. Two-night minimum on major college weekends.
Rates: $55 per room. $35 cabin. $18 additional person.

The only B&B for miles around is a treasure. It's a "real country place," a post-and-beam Cape Cod–style house built 15 years ago with stone from the land and foot-thick walls. Ceilings are beamed. There's a marvelous floor-to-ceiling fieldstone fireplace in a book-lined living room. And the hosts love the idea of meeting people who want to know about this part of the North Country.

As Becky says, "As students, we knew we wanted to settle here. Now our grown children all live in the Adirondacks. Year round there's a full schedule of cultural events. Guests are welcome to watch the spring activity in our new sugarhouse or the fall pressing of apples. We have five kilometers of trails, a big vegetable garden, chickens, sheep and Angora rabbits. If you'd like to fish, canoe (maybe at our camp—located about 35 miles from here—for overnight), or cross-country ski, Peter would be happy to accompany you."

Through the years Becky, a counselor, has collected 300 cookbooks and considerable culinary experience. Peter was director of admissions and vice-president of student affairs at Saint Lawrence and headmaster at Vermont Academy, where Becky assisted in the Admissions Office. Now is the perfect time in their lives for B&B—in the perfect place.

Restrictions: No smoking inside. No guests' pets. (Kennel nearby.)
Bed and bath: Three very private rooms; private baths. On first floor—two twin beds, full bath. On second, one double-bedded room with full bath and one large room with two double beds with shower (no tub) bath. Plus—a cabin that sleeps four has Franklin stove and outhouse; three-quarters of a mile (tractor or wagon ride provided) into the woods near two ponds; cabin guests eat breakfast and have access to full bath in stone house.
Breakfast: 7–9. Very full. Juice, fruit, yogurt, homemade granola, sausage or bacon, eggs, hot breads, muffins or rolls, and an entree such as sourdough waffles.

Plus: Welcoming beverage. Bedroom window fans. Loan of cross-country skis, snow shoes, ice skates, hiking boots. Dinner by arrangement. In the shop here—"simple country antiques we liked at auctions," homemade jams, Indian corn, maple products, and—from a daughter's hand—ceramics and knitted and woven items.

Hinchings Pond B&B

Glenfield, NY
Mailing address: P.O. Box 426, Lowville, NY 13367
Phone: 315/376-8296
Location: Overlooking a private 18-acre, 40-foot-deep glacial pond. In a tall pine forest of Adirondack Park. One and one-half miles east of Chases Lake; 20 minutes east of Lowville; 45 southeast of Watertown/Fort Drum; one hour north of Utica/Rome; under two hours from Syracuse.
Hosts: Skip and Connie Phelps
Open: "By Christmas 1989." Year round. Advance reservations required.
Rates: $45 single. $55 double. $10 rollaway. No charge for crib. Family rates and clergy packages available. MC, VISA.

Very new and very special. An Adirondack-style rustic house designed and built by the Phelps family on wilderness acres, it is surrounded by Adirondack state park lands that adjoin the 50-mile network of state-maintained Otter Creek Horse Trails. Guests can look forward to weekend ice skating, and cross-country skiing on groomed trails. During the summer, you are welcome to swim, snorkel, canoe (provided), and fish on the crystal-clear blue pond from which water was once bottled and sold. A panoramic view of the pond is available from the living room, cathedral-ceilinged dining room, screened porches, and deck.

One of the few B&Bs in the country built from the ground up, this unique structure reflects the Phelpses' desire to raise and educate their children in a backcountry environment, their love for Adirondack Park (where they have lived in a winterized camp for the past five years), and memories of wonderful European pensions. When I met Skip at a bed and breakfast conference, the house was in the planning stage. During the approval process with the Adirondack Park agency, it was declared a model project. As Skip—in the construction business—says, "All three sons show a real potential as construction hands. We are all quite excited about this wilderness lifestyle."

In residence: Hunter, age 12; Austin is 10; Logan, 6.
Restrictions: Children are welcome. Sorry, no pets. Smoking in sitting room only. No snowmobiles or ATVs allowed on property.
Bed and bath: All on second level. Three rooms with double or queen beds and private show baths. One two-bedroom family suite with shared shower bath. Rollaway and crib available.
Breakfast: 8–9:30. Traditional menu including bacon/ham, eggs, local Mennonite breads, pastries. Cereals with fruit or baked apples.

Plus: Huge open fireplace in living room, soapstone wood stove in dining room. Tea or coffee. Dinners ($8–$15 per person) with prior reservation. Airport pickup and babysitting if arranged in advance. Kitchen privileges.

Blackberry Inn

59 Sentinel Road, Lake Placid, NY 12946
Phone: 518/523-3419
Location: On the main road, Route 73, one mile from village center. Two blocks from Olympic Training Center. One mile to ski jump center. Five miles to Olympic cross-country skiing, bobsled, and luge. Nine miles to Whiteface Mountain.
Hosts: Gail and Bill Billerman
Open: Year round. Two-night minimum on winter weekends and major holidays.
Rates: $30 single. $35–$60 double, depending on bed and room size. $10 cot. No charge for crib.

While house hunting three years ago, Bill, a carpenter and maintenance supervisor for the Holiday Inn, and Gail, a bookkeeper and caterer, found an established rooming house. They did everything—carpentry, electrical work and plumbing, wallpapering and painting. They even made thermal shades for the casual and comfortable home decorated with a country theme. Then came the world championships, which brought the Canadian biathlon officials who hosted a social here. (For interesting reading, check out the guest book.)

In residence: In hosts' quarters, Cori, age nine, and Kate, age seven. One independent cat is outside most of the time.
Restrictions: Smoking allowed in common room and on porch only. Children welcome. Sorry, no guests' pets.
Bed and bath: Five second-floor rooms share two full baths. One room with king bed, a trundle bed, and bay window sitting area. Two double-bedded rooms, one with a sitting area. One twin-bedded room. One with one twin bed plus a separate sitting room. Rollaway and crib available.
Breakfast: 8–9. Homemade apple/raisin crepes; souffle made with eggs, cheese, bacon, and croutons; or French toast from homebaked bread. Fruit cup and homemade quick breads.
Plus: Tea. Baked goods. Fresh flowers in rooms, year round. TV in guests' living room. Bedroom window fans. Babysitting may be arranged. Picnic area with gas grill.

From New York: "Very comfortable and clean. Color-coordinated bedrooms . . . a warmer, friendlier atmosphere than the run-of-the-mill hotel or motel in resort areas."

From Florida: "Bright and sunny, nicely furnished. . . . Helpful hosts changed breakfast schedule to accommodate my husband's early golf game."

Stage Coach Inn

Old Military Road, Lake Placid, NY 12946
Phone: 518/523-9474
Location: On a side road in wooded residential neighborhood between Routes 73 and 86. One mile from Lake Placid village.
Host: Lyn Witte
Open: Year round. Two- or three-night minimum stay on weekends and holidays; four-night during Christmas holiday week.
Rates: Double occupancy. $50 shared bath, $60 private bath, $70 working fireplace. Singles $10 less. Triple $10 more. Deposit required.

When you relax in the rustic two-storied Adirondack living room complete with balcony made of birch logs, you know you're in a former stagecoach stop filled with legend and history. Revived as an inn by owners Peter and Sherry Moreau in 1977, the farmhouse-style clapboarded building with a long front porch still has wainscoting throughout, bark on the main support beams, and two fireplace mantels fashioned from half a log. The most recent freshening of decor was carried out by Lyn—innkeeper for the last six years—after she moved from her own home, where she hosted (and established a B&B reservation service). Before that she was executive secretary to the president of the 1980 Olympics Committee, and she had experience in the ski business.

An application has been filed for listing on the National Register of Historic Places.

In residence: Panda Bear, an old English sheepdog, "loved and spoiled by all."
Restrictions: Children 12 and over welcome. No smoking at breakfast table.
Foreign language spoken: A little French.
Bed and bath: Nine rooms, no two alike, on first and second floors. Baths—most are private—are full, some with claw-footed tub and hand-held shower. Twin, double, or three-quarter antique (many brass) beds. Suite possibility. Two rooms with working fireplace; one with cable TV. One room with private entrance for pets. Rollaway bed available.
Breakfast: 8–9:30. Waffles with ham, cream cheese, and pineapple; scrambled eggs, sausage, and bread; Danish pancakes or French toast; or "sammies"—egg/ham/cheese on English muffins. Fruits, juice, coffee, tea, milk. Served in breakfast room with fireplace and garden view.
Plus: Tea and coffee always available. Guest pickup at bus station. Babysitting. Front porch rockers. Picnic table in backyard. Color cable TV in living room. Unfinished *hard* puzzle. Mints. Thick towels. Flowers.

Guests wrote: "A most romantic setting . . . a lovely experience for the entire family . . . fabulous."

Sunny Side Up Bed & Breakfast

RD 1, Box 58, Butler Road, Plattsburgh, NY 12901
Phone: 518/563-5677
Location: On a country road. Across from cows on a dairy farm. On the outskirts of the city. Minutes from the airport. Two miles from I-87 Northway.
Hosts: Ed and Bonnie Lee, Doug Imler, Ingrid Shepard
Open: Memorial Day–Labor Day
Rates: $30 per room. MC, VISA.

The warm welcome here starts when the hostesses greet you in their attractive long skirts, bibbed aprons, and caps. All three generations of this family—Bonnie and her husband, their son, and her mother—spent two years designing, wiring, plumbing, and renovating the traditional house, which began as a log cabin. Throughout, they have displayed their own handmade crafts. For guest room themes they chose European, desert, wildlife, and safari. In the beamed living room, scene of many Sunday afternoon local gatherings, there's an antique pump organ and a player piano. Everything is neat and immaculate in this European-style home away from home.

Ingrid, a former hobby shop owner in New York City, and Bonnie are secretaries. Ed is a civilian supervisor at the Air Force base. You won't forget these friendly folks. They, too, find that B&B is filled with wonderful memories.

Restrictions: Children and pets are welcome. Smoking allowed on main floor. Hosts smoke but will refrain at guest's request.
Foreign languages spoken: Norwegian, some German and French.
Bed and bath: Four second-floor rooms share a shower bath and a half bath. One double-bedded room, three with twin beds.
Breakfast: At guests' selected time, 6–11. Served in the country kitchen. Your choice of Norwegian pancakes, eggs, French toast, hot or cold cereal. Smorgasbord that might include fruit, breads, Dutch cold-cut platter, grits, homemade jellies, potatoes.
Plus: Tea, coffee, or coolers. Tour of house, farm, and area. Fans in all bedrooms. Antique player piano and pump organ. Large deck. Small gift shop with their own crafted items including the aprons and caps.

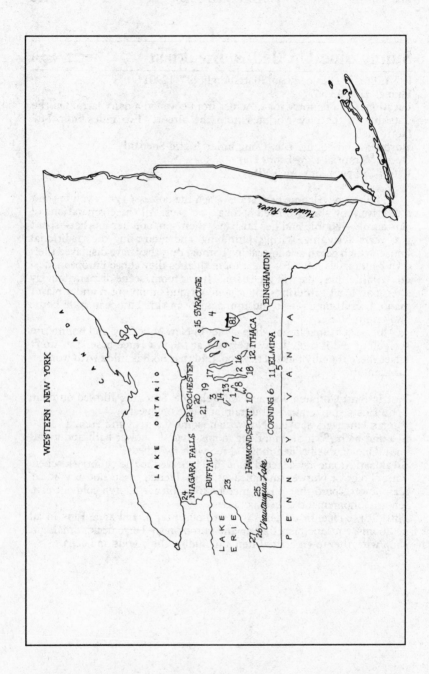

The numbers of this map indicate the locations of western New York B&Bs described in detail in this chapter. The map for eastern New York is on page 86.

WESTERN NEW YORK

Syracuse/Finger Lakes Area Reservation Services

The Blue Heron Bed and Breakfast Reservation Service

384 Pleasant Valley Road, Groton, NY 13073
Phone: 607/898-3814 or 898-4100; 800/255-7213 (for reservations only).
Monday–Friday, 9–1 in winter, 9–3 in summer. Usually closed on holidays.
Listings: 30. Most are hosted private residences. A few are unhosted. A few are inns. Directory $2 plus $.65 postage.
Rates: $30–$75 single. $40–$125 double. Plus $15 booking fee or $25 membership fee (directory, newsletter, and unlimited bookings for a year). $5 one-night surcharge. Weekly and family rates. Off season, senior citizen discounts offered. Full payment required for confirmation. Eighty percent refund allowed on cancellations received at least 10 days prior to arrival date. For graduation period reservations, 80 percent refund allowed if cancellation is received prior to April 1 of graduation year; $10 charged for every change after confirmation.

Susan Camin's hosts live in the Finger Lakes, Catskills, western Adirondack, and Seaway regions—in Ithaca, Naples, Groton, Fleischmanns, Downsville, Hammondsport, Montour Falls, Parish, Homer, and Marathon. The range includes residences on lake shores and mountain tops. One is a log cabin on several acres. One is a restored Victorian with museum-quality antiques. All are inspected and selected.

Reservations: Two- or three-night minimum stay on holiday or college weekends. Also available through travel agents.
Plus: Overnight conferences for groups of up to 20 people. Package tours include bicycling from one bed and breakfast to another. Car rentals and tours arranged. Short-term hosted and unhosted housing available. Corporate retreats planned. Workshops and seminars announced in newsletter.

Bed & Breakfast of the Greater Syracuse Area

143 Didama Street, Syracuse, NY 13224
Phone: 315/446-4199. 10 A.M.–9 P.M.
Listings: Over 25 hosted private residences.
Rates: $32–$55 single. $42–$75 double. Luxury suites are higher. $10 for third person in a room. $8 surcharge for special university weekends. Some weekly rates. One night's deposit required. Deposit minus $5 ser-

vice fee is refunded with two weeks' notice of cancellation. With less notice, refund is made only if the space is filled.

Elaine Samuels's hosts live in Syracuse, DeWitt, Fayetteville, Jamesville, Lafayette, Baldwinsville, Cazenovia, Clay, Saratoga Springs, Seneca Lake, and Skaneateles. Some have resident pets; some take visiting pets. Many prefer nonsmokers. Houses range from a custom-built contemporary in the country to a 1920 mansion in Syracuse. Others include a Queen Anne Revival, an English colonial, ranch styles, and Cape Cods.

Reservations: Two weeks' advance notice preferred.
Plus: Many hosts will pick up guests at transportation points (fee charged). Some short-term (two weeks to two months) housing available in hosted homes.

KEY

Recipes shared, often for house specialties.

Inquiries welcomed about restoration and/or decorating. Symbol indicates that host is willing to share experiences with guests. Tips range from a before-and-after album to rebuilding advice, from furniture refinishing to curtain making. Expertise of hosts ranges from learn-by-doing to professional.

How-to B&B workshop, seminar, or apprentice program offered.

Four Seasons Bed & Breakfast

470 West Lake Road, Route 54A, Branchport, NY 14418
Phone: June–October 607/868-4686, November–May 607/732-5581
Location: On 2.5 acres along on a scenic road that follows Keuka Lake's west shoreline. Nine miles north of Hammondsport. Five miles south of Branchport. Minutes' drive to six wineries, three lakefront restaurants. Short walk to private beach. Half hour to Corning Glass Center.
Hosts: Brent and Martha Olmstead
Open: Daily June–October. Weekends rest of year. Two-night minimum stay on weekends November–May, holidays, and special events.
Rates: $45–$55 twin or double bed, shared bath. $60 double bed, private bath.

> From Buffalo, New York: "Totally delightful experience from the Laura Ashley rooms to the Julia Child breakfasts. Visiting the Olmsteads is like being entertained by long lost friends."

Those Buffalo folks are right. I wanted to move right in to this century-old "jewel" with its vaulted living room ceiling and walls done with old barn siding. Quilts, collectibles, lots of wicker, and treasures from the Olmsteads' world travels are everywhere.

To this setting the Elmira natives bring many interests. Brent, a practicing physician, is an accomplished violinist. Martha, a registered nurse, has served as wine chairman for a regional cookbook. When Martha says, "We go with the flow," she really means it. She has returned from errands to find two priests (who, she thought, had gone to dinner) conducting a service in the "perfect setting" they discovered on the back patio. The hosts have cheered for regatta participants and later greeted them with a warm fire and homemade cookies. Those sailors flew their spinnaker from the flagpole to dry. There's more. Go and experience.

In residence: "Muffin is our non-meowing cat who is not allowed in guest rooms."
Restrictions: Children accepted depending upon available accommodations. No guests' pets. Nonsmokers preferred.
Foreign language spoken: Martha speaks Spanish.
Bed and bath: Four carpeted and wallpapered rooms. A first-floor room with double bed, private shower bath. Full bath shared by three rooms (off living room balcony) with double or twin beds.
Breakfast: 7:30–9. Main course could be puffed apple pancake, eggs Gruyere, dishes with homegrown herbs. Homemade coffee cakes and muffins. Fruits in season. Served in dining room by wall of windows with views of evergreens.

Plus: Air conditioners in two bedrooms; fans in all. Private beach. Beach towels. Chaise longues and chairs. Open front porch. Expansive lawn. Boat trailer parking. Bicycle storage. Den with color TV. Fireplaced living room.

The Red House Country Inn

Finger Lakes National Forest, Picnic Area Road, Burdett, NY 14818
Phone: 607/546-8566
Location: In New York state's only national forest, with 28 miles of maintained (year round) trails at the door. On the east side of Seneca Lake. Short drives to Glen Gorge, Corning Glass Museum, swimming, wineries.
Hosts: Sandy Schmanke and Joan Martin
Open: Year round except Thanksgiving and Christmas Day. Two-day minimum on weekends.
Rates: $32 single. $47 double; $55 with working fireplace, private sitting room, additional twin, or three-quarter beds; $65 with double bed plus queen sofa bed. $10 extra person. AMEX, MC, VISA.

Guests wrote (and wrote): "Absolutely wonderful . . . comfortable country atmosphere with lovely antiques, quilts and crafts. . . . Breakfast is a celebration . . . plenty of hot water, fresh thick towels daily, even a supply of shampoo . . . We walked, talked, played the piano and pump organ, joked, snoozed. . . . Perfect for hiking, birdwatching, fishing, berry picking, cycling, cross-country skiing and peace of mind. . . . Gracious hostesses who share their corner of paradise."

One of a kind. The only private property in the forest. (The only farm not purchased by the federal government during the Great Depression.) Built in 1844, restored by owners in the 1970s, and purchased in 1981 by Sandy and Joan, who opened it as a freshly wallpapered inn in 1983. Since, they have built an addition and landscaped five acres of lawns and gardens. They have been featured in *New York Alive* and been etched in the hearts of their guests and their friends and relatives. Before they became innkeepers (once they discovered the shortage of guest rooms in the area) Sandy owned a media buying service and Joan, also in Rochester, New York, was in TV and radio production and business management.

In residence: In hosts' quarters only, Samoyeds Mishka, Joby, Susie, and Muffin, and Penny, a beagle. The goats—Nellie, Annie, Sarah, Andy, and Tina—have their own quarters. Lots of chickens.
Restrictions: Children 12 and over welcome. No smoking inside. Sorry, no guests' pets.
Bed and bath: Six rooms share four full baths. First-floor room has wicker double bed, French door entrance off living room. On second floor, rooms with a single bed, a double and a single with a private staircase, a double

(one has a working fireplace, one a queen sofa bed too), and a room with two antique three-quarter beds. Rollaway available.
Breakfast: 8–9:30. Fresh fruit, freshly squeezed orange juice or local grape juice. Homemade popovers or scones and jams. Fresh eggs gathered by guests with slab bacon or honey-glazed ham. Homemade pilgrim's bread, apple flaps, or cinnamon crisp French toast. Freshly ground coffees, fine teas. Served in two dining rooms with sterling and crystal.
Plus: Local sherry and port; afternoon tea. Candy. Bedroom fans. Indoor barbecue. Veranda. Horseshoes, darts. Picnic area. With reservations, option of dinner ($15 per person) with wine. Cross-country ski weekends (November–April). Kitchen privileges. Gift shop.

Wilder Tavern

5648 North Bloomfield Road (Country Road 30), Canandaigua, NY 14425
Phone: 716/394-8132
Location: Surrounded by working farms; two miles from historic downtown Canandaigua; 20 minutes from Rochester.
Host: Linda C. Swartout
Open: Year round.
Rates: Single, $45 shared bath, $55 private bath. Double, $50 shared bath, $60 private bath. $16 third person. MC, VISA.

Originally a stagecoach stop built in 1829, Wilder Tavern was a private residence from 1876 until purchased by Linda in 1985. Now it is a country haven hosted by a chef/ architectural historian/tennis player/ quilt maker who has experience with the restoration of four other structures. And during seven years in the food industry, Linda went from "the bottom up" to general manager of a *Mobil* four-star restaurant.

Restored over a period of nine months, this B&B, now once again under its original name, is furnished in comfortable country style with family memorabilia and handmade quilts and samplers. A restored original stencil pattern is in one guest room; an antique pump organ is in the living room. Old fruit trees, berry bushes, and grapevines now thrive beside new peach trees and quince. Sidewalk superintendents are welcome to watch the progress on the walled garden. And, of course, food is a feature.

In residence: Four cats live in a converted chicken house.
Restrictions: Children over 12 are welcome. No smoking. No pets. Seeing eye dogs are permitted.
Bed and bath: Four second-floor rooms. Private full bath with queen-bedded room. Full hall bath shared by two rooms with king/twin option and one room with queen bed.
Breakfast: Until 10. Fruits, juices. Homemade jams and jellies. Many homemade breads and muffins. Breakfast meats. Eggs "any which way"; perhaps cheese/mushroom omelet. Coffee, tea, hot chocolate, mulled cider in season. Served by the fireplace.

Plus: Central air conditioning on second floor. Tea, cookies or cake. Brick barbecue, horseshoes, croquet. Three acres of pine woods. Dinners by prior arrangement.

Bed & Breakfast of Greater Syracuse Host #3

Cazenovia, NY
Location: In a neighborhood of lovely old colonial and Victorian homes close to the college president's home. Two blocks from shops and restaurants.
Reservations: Available year round through Bed & Breakfast of the Greater Syracuse Area, page 156.
Rates: $38 single. $48 double.

The children are grown and gone. The Federal-style house "at least 150 years old" has been an avocation for this couple for about 25 years. It has a beautiful front staircase, Oriental rugs on the wide pine floors, pine and cherry antiques, and an informal ambiance.

The hostess, a cook of local fame, is an art dealer who specializes in antique prints and reproductions of pre–Civil War art. She also has her own private collection of American folk art. The host, a native Cazenovian, is a landscape designer who enjoys canoeing and skiing.

In residence: Nicki, a Samoyed, and Rocky the cat.
Restrictions: No smoking, please. Will take well-behaved dogs.
Bed and bath: A fireplaced room with two singles and another with one twin bed share a full bath.
Breakfast: Flexible hours. Buffet style with fresh fruit, juice, cereals, eggs, sour cream coffee cake or bran raisin muffins.
Plus: Tea. Picnic table. Lawn chairs. "Our beautiful village with a park and swimming at Cazenovia Lake—just a short walk from here."

Notch House Bed & Breakfast

1056 Snell Road, Chemung, NY
Mailing address: RD #1, Box 56, Lowman, NY 14861
Phone: 607/529-3428
Location: Gorgeous. Off the beaten path, among three mountains. Two miles off Route 17C. Ten miles east of Elmira. Half-hour drive to Watkins Glen, Hammondsport wine country, Corning Glass.
Hosts: Robert and Susane Govelitz
Open: Year round. Reservations preferred.
Rates: $25 single. $35 double. Children under three free. $5 for cot. Weekly rate available.

From North Carolina: "The kindest of hosts, warm and friendly. A simple, clean, pleasant private suite. The surroundings were breathtaking, resplendent with mountain wildflowers."

When Sue and Bob moved here nine years ago, they bought a big home "to accommodate visiting family." Now their extended family includes travelers, with whom they are delighted to share "our new casual lifestyle. The dock on the pond gives you the feeling that you are miles and miles away from everyone. You can fish, take out the canoe, just relax. . . . We have raised sheep, goats and chickens. Last year we acquired neighboring land so we now have 300 acres that include an apple orchard and a blueberry farm on top of the mountain. It makes a great hike!"

Sue is a retired registered nurse. Bob was with the New Jersey state police and is now a salesman for a band instrument company. Carrie Lynn is a teenager who loves children.

In residence: Carrie Lynn is 16. Ginger is a Siamese cat. Teddy is a friendly dog. Two guinea hens live in the barn. Four ducks on pond.
Restrictions: Housebroken pets are allowed. No smoking in bedrooms.
Bed and bath: A suite (which can be closed off from rest of house) with king bed, sitting area, and private full bath. Additional bedroom in main house with one full bed available for older children. Cot available.
Breakfast: At guest's convenience. Choice of French toast, homemade pancakes or eggs, bacon, potato patty, cereals; freshly picked fruits, juice; coffee, tea, or milk; homemade jellies. Served by window with a busy bird feeder and a view of the valley.
Plus: Beverages. Bedroom window fans when needed. Pond for fishing, boating, swimming, ice skating. Babysitting. Kitchen privileges. Hunting for small game and deer.

Rosewood Inn

134 East First Street, Corning, NY 14830
Phone: 607/962-3253
Location: On a tree-lined residential street, one block south of Route 17. Within walking distance of Corning Glass Center, museums, downtown historic district.
Hosts: Winnie and Dick Peer
Open: Year round. Reservations recommended.
Rates: $60/$70 single with shared/private bath. $68/$80 double with shared/private bath. Suites $80 single, $95 double. $15 extra person. Crib, free. Diners, MC, VISA.

Guests wrote: "The hosts were exceptional. . . . We received a basket of fruit with our room key. . . . It was our honeymoon and they gave us a champagne toast. . . . Breakfast was incredible. . . . The children were treated to hot chocolate and familiar cereals. I enjoyed reading the period magazines. . . . Charming. Beautifully decorated."

Join Dick when he dons his white apron and serves from a silver tea set on bone china and you'll hear about Corning's past and present. Or listen to his twice-weekly radio broadcasts. Or read the *Rosewood Inn Gazette.* Dick is a retired editor and still popular columnist of the local paper; Winnie is retired from her first-grade teaching position. Together they are considered the (revered) deans of Finger Lakes B&Bs. Ten years ago they sold their house outside the city and started "the most reward-ing business a people-lover could be in."

Appointed with fine Victorian antiques, Oriental rugs, and lace cur-tains, their 1853 Greek Revival was renovated in 1915 into an English Tudor. Now harpoons are in the Herman Melville Room. Glass blowers' tools are in the Fred Carder (originator of Steuben Glass) Room. The George Pullman Room has train memorabilia. Always, there's a marvel-ous blend of guests who appreciate this home environment filled with family portraits and records.

In residence: Sometimes, daughter Amy and Chanel, her dog. Amy smokes.
Restrictions: Well-behaved pets are allowed with advance arrangements. No smoking in guest rooms.
Bed and bath: Six rooms, four with private baths. Double, twin, or queen beds. First floor has two large suites, each with private bath, private entrance, color TV, air conditioning; a working fireplace in one suite, a kitchen in the other. Rollaway and crib available.
Breakfast: Full; usually 8:30–9:30. (Coffee available at 7:30.) Fruit. Home-made (by Dick) breads and muffins and Rosewood brandy butter. Home-made granola. In winter, "there is nothing as good as hot oatmeal." Gourmet blend coffees and teas. Served in the candlelit dining room. "The highlight of our day that can last for hours."
Plus: Fruit basket. In winter, flannel sheets. Postcards (sketches) of Rose-wood rooms. Special winter weekends. Sitting room with TV. Porch. Will meet guests at Trailways bus.

Margaret Thacher's Spruce Haven Bed and Breakfast

9 James Street, P.O. Box 119, Dryden, NY 13053
Phone: 607/844-8052
Location: Surrounded by more than 100 spruce trees. One block from the village center; 25 minutes northeast of Ithaca.
Host: Margaret Thacher Brownell
Open: Year round. Advance reservations required.
Rates: $35 single. $40 double. $50 king. $10 rollaway bed. No charge for crib. Weekly rates available.

Guests wrote: "A superb place. Margaret Brownell welcomed us all so warmly . . . got us a babysitter. . . . She shops at natural food stores

and stocks her shelves with wonderful tea and honey . . . made great
muffins each morning. . . . You get the feeling she really cares about
people who enter her life, even if it's only for one night! . . . An
incredibly beautiful log cabin with spruce trees surrounding it. The
inside is very warm, clean and attractive with a woodburning stove
. . . a place where peace and serenity prevail. . . . The best part, however, is Mrs. Brownell. . . . She was also very helpful in our job and
home search."

After Margaret and her family had the log home built in 1974, they
finished the inside themselves, everything from wiring and plumbing to
wallpapering and cupboards. They had planted the spruce trees as seed-
lings in the 1950s. Today they are over 50 feet high, providing a feeling of
"living in the woods in the village." Guests are mesmerized by the birds,
who like it here too.

Margaret has experience as a nurse and as an activity director at a
nursing facility. Currently, she is a dental assistant and B&B hostess.

Restrictions: Children of all ages welcome. No smoking. Sorry, no pets.
Bed and bath: Two rooms share a full bath with hostess. First-floor room
has a double bed. Second-floor room has a king/twins option. Rollaway
bed and crib available.
Breakfast: 6:45–9. Eggs or hot or cold cereal. Juice, fruit, muffins or toast.
Coffee, teas, milk. Served in dining room, by window with bird feeders.
Plus: Tea, cider, juice. Bedroom fans. Garden flowers.

Lakeside Terrace B&B

RD #1, Box 197, 660 East Waneta Lake Road, Dundee, NY 14837
Phone: 607/292-6606
Location: With 175-foot frontage on Waneta Lake (between Seneca and
Keuka lakes). Fifteen miles south of Penn Yan, nine miles north of Ham-
mondsport.
Hosts: Chris and George Patnoe
Open: Year round. Advance reservations required. Two-night minimum
on weekends May–November 1.
Rates: $45 single. $50 double. (1990, $5 more.) Confirmed reservations
required; full amount forfeited on cancellations made with less than two
weeks' notice. MC, VISA.

The lake. The view. The warm welcome. That's what this rustic B&B
is all about. "It's an old place that we've remodeled a lot. Our home is
your home during your stay." And it's been that way for four years, ever
since Chris, a registered nurse supervisor, and George, a housekeeping
aide foreman, decided to think about retiring (still five years away). Actually, it took just about no time at all for travelers to discover these very
sharing folks, parents of six grown children. If you don't know how to
canoe, George will explain. And for those who know about sailing,
there's a boat for you to use. And if you just want to come for a getaway,

that's fine too. Some guests use this B&B as a base for day trips—to the Corning Glass Museum, Watkins Glen, or wineries. In true B&B style, the hosts are remembered as much as their comfortable home.

In residence: Binky and Satchel, two small dogs that bark but don't bite.
Restrictions: Children 10 and over welcome. Smoking allowed in dining room, living room, and kitchen. Inquire about guests' pets.
Bed and bath: Three rooms, all with queen beds, share two baths. All air conditioned and carpeted.
Breakfast: 8:30–9:30. Juice, cereal, pastries, fruit, coffee. Served in dining room overlooking the lake.
Plus: Self-serve hot and cold beverages. Probably fruit and nuts too. Swimming. Fishing. Use of raft, canoe, and small sailboat.

Blue Heron Bed and Breakfast Host #31

Groton, NY
Location: Along a country road on 185 acres of fields and woods. Five minutes from the village; 15 miles northeast of Ithaca; 20 minutes from SUNY Cortland, Ithaca College, Cornell University.
Reservations: Year round through Blue Heron Bed and Breakfast Reservation Service, page 156.
Rates: $35 single. $50–$55 double. $15 rollaway. $10 crib. (Plus reservation service booking or membership fee, see page 156.)

When this was a successful working farm, the Italianate and Second Empire farmhouse often had as much as a ton of cabbage stored in the basement. Following a two-year restoration, the century-old house was on a 1988 historic society house tour. The high ceilings, hand-milled woodwork, and wide-board floors are still here; but the owners, a contractor who was formerly a landscaper and his wife, gardener/chef/antiques lover, can tell you how they made a parlor into a dining room, a second kitchen (the house is now a two-family) from a storeroom, a bedroom into a rear entry. Plants, wallpapers with traditional prints, and the hostess's handmade quilts all contribute to what many call a "homelike atmosphere."

In residence: Angus, a black Labrador. Kitty, a long-haired cat.
Restrictions: Children welcome (crib, cradle, and high chair provided). Sorry, no guests' pets. ("Plan to enjoy ours.") No smoking inside.
Foreign language spoken: Some Italian.
Bed and bath: Four second-floor rooms. Two double-bedded rooms share a full bath. Tub bath shared by four-poster rooms, one with a three-quarter bed, the other with two twins. Rollaway and crib available.
Breakfast: 7:30–10. Fresh fruit. Pancakes, waffles, egg dishes. Muffins. Beverages. Served in dining room, beside living room bay window, or in kitchen.

Plus: Tea or cold drink. Bedroom fans. Fresh flowers. Thick towels. Baby-sitting may be arranged. Assistance with dinner reservations. Kitchen privileges (fee charged).

Guests wrote: "Superb breakfasts and hospitality."

The Salt Road Tavern

RD #2, 973 Elm Street, Groton, NY 13073
Phone: 607/898-5739 (home); 607/272-2433 (office)
Location: In dairy country. Surrounded by wooded hills. Ten minutes to Cortland; 20 to Cayuga Lake and Cornell University; 30 to Ithaca College.
Hosts: David and Terry Ofner
Open: April–November. Advance reservations required. Two-night minimum stay during special college weekends.
Rates: Double occupancy. Shared bath, $45 small double, $60 large rooms. $70 private bath. $10 rollaway.

As you sit under the crystal chandelier at breakfast, maybe it's fun to think about being in the house that was the first to have a cooking stove in town. The tavern, built in Federal style in 1824, was an overnight stop for stagecoaches and salt wagons before the days of the Erie Canal. Dances, too, were held in the large high-ceilinged rooms. Local residents rescued and restored the building in the 1970s before the Ofners, former Maine residents, opened the B&B in 1987. From area estate sales they acquired Empire, Sheraton, and early American antiques. The house has been on several historic house tours; one was broadcast on radio!

David is a retired Air Force intelligence officer. When Terry completed her PhD at Cornell, the Ofners chose to remain in the area, where Terry is the director of an adult rehabilitation center.

In residence: Spot, a good natured middle-aged Labrador retriever.
Restrictions: Children over 12 welcome. Smoking allowed in family room only. Sorry, no guests' pets.
Foreign languages spoken: Some Spanish. Some sign language (ASL).
Bed and bath: Three second-floor rooms. Depending on bookings, private or shared adjoining full bath for large room with canopied queen bed and large room with canopied double. Smaller double-bedded room shares a full bath. Plus first-floor half bath. Extra twin bed and crib available.
Breakfast: Flexible hours. Fresh fruit, muffins with homemade jam, waffles or pancakes with local syrup, sausage or bacon, scrambled eggs with steamed fresh vegetables, local cider and maple syrup. Served at antique dining room banquet table with antique china and sterling silver.
Plus: Tea or wine by the fire in the Victorian parlor. Mints. Tour of house. Fans available. Picnic table. VCR and color TV in family room. Two pianos.

Guests wrote: "A special experience with caring people. Wonderful home-cooked breakfast. Charming period decor."

The Bowman House, a bed and breakfast

61 Lake Street, P.O. Box 586, Hammondsport, NY 14840
Phone: 607/569-2516
Location: In a picturesque village with free summer jazz concerts. In the land of wineries. Two-block walk to village center, shops, restaurants, museum. Two hours south of Rochester.
Hosts: Manita and Jack Bowman
Open: Year round.
Rates: $55 private bath, $45 shared bath. Single $5 less.

> Guests wrote: "A fantastic experience. . . . From all my travels, one of the most comfortable and appealing B&Bs in the U.S. and Europe. . . . Bowmans seem to sense just how much privacy and how much help the guests need. . . . Wonderful food . . . very clean. . . . Felt so much at home, hated to leave. . . . We first heard about it through friends, very fussy ones. . . . Ideally suited home for B&B. . . . A treasured find. . . . Their personal charm extends to their surroundings."

And the accolades go on and on about the hosts, who moved from a smaller nearby residence in 1988. The Bowmans started hosting in 1983, "just about the time our youngest left the nest." Jack is a personnel manager at Corning Glass. And you can tell that Manita enjoys interior decorating "in a comfortably elegant style, using several shades of blue." They have done over this turn-of-the-century completely. Most furnishings are antique. And there are lots of "touches," but most of all, they enjoy "making people feel at home in a nice setting at a very reasonable price."

Restrictions: Children 12 and over welcome. No smoking indoors. Sorry, no pets.
Bed and bath: Four large second-floor rooms with double or queen bed. Three full baths; two private, one shared.
Breakfast: 7:30–9. Abundant fruit, homemade breads and jellies, butter, coffee, tea, milk, local fruit juice. "Close to two hours sometimes!" In dining room with linen, silver, china, and crystal.
Plus: Fireplaced first-floor sitting room. TV in second-floor sitting room. Wine and cheese. Juice. Flowers. Mints. Bedroom fans. Small guest refrigerator.

The Blushing Rosé B&B Inn

11 William Street, Hammondsport, NY 14840
Phone: 607/569-3402
Location: Within walking distance of historic area, village park bandstand, free beach, Glen Curtis Museum, shops, "all in this friendly place to live." Forty-five minutes northwest of Corning; 10 minutes from Bath;

two hours from Rochester, Syracuse, and Binghamton; four from Toronto. Near wineries, waterfalls, and gorges.
Hosts: Ellen and Bucky Laufersweiler
Open: May–October with two-night minimum holiday weekends, July, August, and October foliage season. January–April, "open by chance."
Rates: Per room. $55 private hall bath. $65 bath en suite. $20 rollaway.

Quite a combination: a host who is a wood floor specialist/refinisher and a hostess who loves decorating, sewing, and cooking.

Three years ago, Ellen and Bucky—skiers, cyclists, and boaters—moved to this Victorian Italianate with widow's walk, which was built in 1843. "We restored and redecorated the whole house and loved every minute of it." The exterior, "painted a blushing rose," is trimmed with a deep burgundy. Inside, ruffled (Priscilla) curtains are on all the windows. The country decor is complete with handmade quilts, a spinning wheel, grapevine wreaths, and a braided rug under the dining room oak table. For Ellen, making all this happen has been a dream come true. In addition, she has designed a brochure on Finger Lakes B&B and small inn accommodations. And in her first year of hosting, she appeared on an ABC-TV "Home Show" bed and breakfast segment.

Restrictions: Children six and over welcome. No smoking. Sorry, no guests' pets.
Bed and bath: Four second-floor rooms with cozy sitting area. All private baths; two en suite, two in hall. Double bed (one four-poster), queen, or king. Rollaway available.
Breakfast: 8:30–9:30. (Early-bird coffee at 7:30.) Juice, fresh fruit, homemade granola and muesli, breakfast casserole, baked specialties. Maybe oatmeal blueberry pancakes or cinammon bread surprise. Homemade jams and jellies. Leisurely indeed.
Plus: Air-conditioned bedrooms. A sitting room with TV, stereo, VCR, much reading material. Traditional music. Wicker-furnished porch. Guest refrigerator. Guest pickup at bus station.

Guests wrote: "Fond memories of friendliness, large breakfasts, country antiques. . . . Charming . . . and clean, clean, clean! . . . Every detail was perfect."

The Muse

5681 Middle Road, Horseheads, NY 14845
Phone: 607/739-1070
Location: Tranquil. Country setting. Within a half hour of Elmira, Ithaca, Watkins Glen, Corning, and 20 wineries. Ten minutes north of Horseheads and Route 17; 10 minutes to the Mark Twain Drama.
Hosts: Dick and Diana Castor
Open: Year round. Advance reservations required. Two-night minimum stay on weekends.
Rates: Shared bath, $55 or $75 double; $85 triple. $110 carriage house. MC, VISA.

Paradise. A retreat. A getaway. Impeccable restorations furnished with period antiques. Seemingly, a growing number of outbuildings on the terraced grounds filled with manicured lawns, drywall stone fences, wild and perennial gardens. Much of the work has been done by Dick, a dentist, and family members. Diana, a nurse, knows how to paint, sew, stencil, and collect early coverlets. Their 14-room 1838 Classic Revival has been home to Dick and Diana and their six children for 25 years. Walls have documentary wallcoverings. There are pine plank floors, family heirlooms, a pewter and glass collection, and Pennsylvania folk art. Salvaged from Horseheads is a charming carriage house, rebuilt by the Castors and decorated in Williamburg colors. The latest project is a Swiss bank barn, constructed (with windowed cupola) from parts of a felled 1850 barn located a mile from The Muse. Then there's the pond, a tennis court, trails, tall trees, pine forests, and Sunset Hill. All shared. All beautiful.

In residence: A dog named Hans and a cat named Tigger.
Restrictions: No smoking allowed. Sorry, no guests' pets. Limited accommodations for children.
Bed and bath: Three rooms. Two second-floor residence rooms—one with double bed, the other with one twin and one double bed—share a full bath. Carriage house has double bed, shower bath, living area, and trellised patio.
Breakfast: 7–9. Baked Alaskan grapefruit, stuffed French toast, fresh fruits and topping. In formal dining room.
Plus: Floor fans in bedrooms. Tour of house and grounds. Wooded walk to pond for swimming and ice skating. Cross-country skiing.

Buttermilk Falls Bed & Breakfast

110 East Buttermilk Falls Road, Ithaca, NY 14850
Phone: 607/272-6767 or 273-3947; 24-hour answering service
Location: Just off Route 13 at the foot of a long series of cascading waterfalls in adjoining Buttermilk Falls State Park; 2½ miles south of Ithaca center; 3½ miles from Cornell University and Ithaca College.
Host: Margie Rumsey
Open: Year round.
Rates: Double occupancy. $60–$95 depending on room, date, and length of stay. MC, VISA (for holding reservations only).

The pool at the base of the waterfalls is more than a magnificent sight. We appreciated the swim when we arrived in 100-degree heat. And in the morning we had the treat of a before-breakfast dip topped by Margie's exotic juice blended from fresh fruits.

Her lovely old painted-brick 1814 house has been restored through five generations. Now the fifth generation is around to help with B&B during school vacations. Although Margie first hosted travelers when she moved in as a newlywed and her husband Ed was a Cornell student, it was the empty nest (three sons are grown) and a 1983 B&B trip to England that inspired B&B in the 1980s.

Margie is a class of 1947 Cornellian, native Ithacan, and private pilot who loves to travel. She is in real estate and sails on Cayuga Lake. Furthermore, she is an expert on waterways (we learned about the canal we were to travel along), on paths that have spectacular waterfalls and gorges, on off-the-beaten-path cross-country ski trails, and on bicycle routes too.

In residence: Margie's "resident genius" is Allen Hayes, "our flight instructor who recently retired from the charter flying business and still writes articles about flying." When deep in thought, Allen occasionally smokes cigarettes.
Restrictions: Sorry, no pets. Smoking allowed in the large kitchen.
Bed and bath: Seven rooms on first and second floors. Four have private shower baths. King-bedded suite, twins, double, or queen beds. Shared bath has tub and shower. Extra beds and "a large antique toy box for babies" available.
Breakfast: 7:30–9:30. Full. Menu changes with the seasons and features fresh fruits and hot whole-grain cereals with a variety of toppings such as raisins, dates, walnuts, maple syrup, honey, yogurt, or cream. Bacon and eggs with toast and apple fritters. Buffet style on busy weekends. In kitchen, in formal dining room, on plant-filled screened porch, or under trees at picnic table at foot of waterfall.
Plus: Fireplaced living room. Dining room with organ. Hi-fi stereo. Screened porch. Yard swing. Badminton. Hot or cold drinks. Swimming and hiking. Air conditioning and wood stove in first-floor room with king bed. Cross-country skiing from the door. Handmade (by son) Windsor chairs for sale.

Glendale Farm Bed & Breakfast

224 Bostwick Road, Ithaca, NY 14850
Phone: 607/272-8756
Location: In the country on 100 acres of corn fields, woods, hills, and meadows. Ten minutes' drive from Cornell University and Ithaca College. Near state parks, Cayuga Lake, ski areas.
Host: Jeanne Marie Tomlinson
Open: Year round. Advance reservations preferred.
Rates: $65 double. $75–$100 cottage. $20 extra person. AMEX, MC, VISA.

From Massachusetts: "Because we loved everything from the floral decorations to the breakfasts, we planned our own fall reunion instead of waiting for another full year. Jeanne is terrific and has a beautiful home."

Several parents (and their student children) have been so delighted with the house and setting that they have subsequently planned weddings here. Cycling groups have discovered this B&B. Single travelers have too.

For an introduction to the completely renovated 1856 farmhouse, you enter by the kitchen (the main gathering spot), which has a blue and yellow antique Dutch porcelain stove and electrified oil lamp with hand-pierced shade set against a brick wall with copper utensils. The living room has a beamed ceiling, a wood stove, a pump organ, and a Steinway. Throughout, there are antiques and Oriental rugs.

Jeanne's family was grown and she was a supervisor at the Statler Inn associated with Cornell's hotel school when she realized (in 1983) that there was a shortage of lodging facilities in town; "but I didn't realize that there would be such a call for a friendlier atmosphere than a hotel can provide." Now she's a full-time innkeeper.

In residence: A large angora rabbit named Alf.
Restrictions: Guests' pets are sometimes allowed.
Bed and bath: Six rooms plus a cottage (which was a milk house). One first-floor room with double bed, private shower bath. On second floor, single, double, or king bed and family accommodations; two shared baths. Cottage with double bed and sleeping loft has a full bath with small antique tub surrounded by ruffles "commented on by most men!"
Breakfast: At guests' convenience. Full country meal with French toast or eggs, ham, bacon, sausage. Fresh fruits, pastries, homemade jams (a specialty). In the fall, grape juice from the local vineyards. Served in fireplaced dining room with china and silver.
Plus: The house is yours. Living room with fireplace. Wood stove. Screened porch overlooking carriage house and valley. Bedroom fans. Guests' refrigerator. Special weekends for singles, wine tasting, and skiing. Will meet guests at transportation points.

> From Florida: "A pleasure. Many touches. Refreshments by the fire. . . . A gourmet breakfast provided us with enough nourishment until dinner."

Wagener Estate Bed and Breakfast　　

351 Elm Street, Penn Yan, NY 14527
Phone: 315/536-4591
Location: "Away from city traffic and hustle and bustle." At the edge of the village on four acres of lawns, apple trees, stone walls. About an hour from Corning, Syracuse, and Rochester. Near many wineries, restaurants, festivals.
Hosts: Evie and Norm Worth
Open: April though December. Reservations strongly advised. Two-night minimum stay on holiday weekends.
Rates: Shared bath—$40 single, $50 double. $10 cot. Private bath—$50 single, $60 double. AMEX, MC, VISA.

"People are a constant wonder to us. One couple flew into Penn Yan Airport, set up their collapsible bikes and found us. A Californian was inspired to sketch the dining room her first morning at breakfast. Then she sketched her room showing the latched door and the grapevine wreath over the bed. . . . After our guests settle in, we usually invite them for wine or tea. Later we sometimes join them in their living room or our family room, the one that has wainscoting done by Norm from attic floorboards. The large pillared porch (with wicker furniture), part of the 1830 addition to the house, is a great gathering spot too. We gladly answer all sorts of questions about the town founder who first owned our property and built the 1790 rooms, one of which still has the fireplace and oven. And guests express amazement that we lived through the upbringing of ten children! (There are now 14 grandchildren, ages 1–24). . . . When Norm retired as director of Keuka College's physical plant and I retired from teaching, we did some traveling and realized we weren't ready for retiring. We love this house that we have lived in for 25 years. It is decorated with the country look, with many crafts and with useable and comfortable antiques."

It's a natural. It's home. A hideaway. It is recommended for a place on the National Register of Historic Places. It is recommended as a B&B.

Restrictions: "Sorry, we are not equipped for very young babies." No guests' pets. Smoking reluctantly permitted in living room.
Bed and bath: Four second-floor rooms—king, double, and twin beds— share two full baths. Also one room for two persons with a four-poster double bed, private bath with shower.
Breakfast: 8:30 and 9:30. Juice (maybe a white grape juice blended from local vineyards), seasonal fruits, homemade sticky buns, toast or muffins. Cheese, tomato, and mushroom omelet with ham or bacon; buckwheat (Penn Yan is the world capital) and corn pancakes; crepes with blueberry sauce and sausages, or French toast.
Plus: Fresh flowers. One bedroom has air conditioning; three have window fans. Living room with TV.

From Massachusetts: "We loved being away from it all and with the Worths in their wonderful home."

Lakeview Farm Bed n' Breakfast

4761 Route 364, Rushville, NY 14544
Phone: 716/554-6973
Location: Rural. On 170 acres on both sides of the road, overlooking the east side of Canandaigua Lake. Between (five miles from) tiny Rushville and (six miles south of) Canandaigua's Sonnenburg Gardens. One mile to restaurants, public beach; 20 minutes to Naples and Widmers Winery; 45 to Rochester.
Hosts: Elizabeth and Howard Freese
Open: Year round. Reservations preferred.
Rates: $35 single. $45–$50 double. Tax included.

"The view. That's what this place is all about. When we first got here twelve years ago, it was the only thing that didn't need fixing! We have a country place with some interesting family antiques from the south, circa 1850s or 60s together with other pieces that blend well. Our latest change is a family/dining room addition that has twenty feet of windows overlooking the lake and the pond and all the birds and wildlife that we seldom saw before. We love it and so do our guests. Sometimes they walk down to the gully, a beautiful spot with a little waterfall and loads of fossils. Or they go fishing, antiquing and wine tasting. Yes, I'm still pickling Jerusalem artichokes with our secret recipe and making jelly. At the moment we have just finished packing 10,000 books into boxes so the library can be painted over the summer."

Before Betty was a high school librarian, she was a newspaper journalist. Howard is a retired engineer working with their son in his machinery business located in the barn. Their home is what some travelers call "a real B&B."

In residence: Outdoor dogs—Melissa, a black Lab with white beard, resident woodchuck catcher; Keesha, a collie shepherd who announces guests; Ginger, a Cairn Terrier; and Tobey, a mostly Gordon setter who chases squirrels.
Restrictions: Children should be at least eight. Sorry, no guests' pets. No smoking indoors.
Bed and bath: Two double-bedded second-floor rooms, both with lake view, share a full bath. Cot available.
Breakfast: Early-morning coffee and tea available in upstairs sitting room. Juice, homegrown fruit, eggs, bacon or sausage. Buns or interesting breads, homemade jellies. French toast or pancakes on request. Cereal available.
Plus: Welcoming beverage. Living room, family room, and sitting room. TV. Bedroom window fans. Horseshoes, badminton, volleyball. Trails through woods and fields for cross-country skiing. The gift of a jar of jelly or Jerusalem artichoke pickle.

From New York: "Everything we could possibly want and then some. We loved it."

The Russell-Farrenkopf House

209 Green Street, Syracuse, NY 13203
Phone: 315/472-8001
Location: Residential. In the Hawley–Green Street historic district. About a half mile from downtown. Five-minute drive to the campus, Carrier Dome, Upstate Medical Center. Within minutes of "the city's most prestigious restaurants."
Hosts: Joan Farrenkopf and Robert MacGregor Gifford
Open: At least April through November.
Rates: $65 private bath. $55 shared bath. Singles, $10 less.

"The entire full house of our 1988 opening weekend—all parents of entering Syracuse University students—made reservations for Parents' Weekend. The solarium has become an attraction in itself. There are spontaneous porch parties. And we are asked many questions about this 1865 French Second Empire/Italianate house."

Often part of benefit house tours, this B&B is the creation of "the urban pioneer," according to local press. "It was boarded up and in need of everything when I bought it in 1976. This house taught me how to restore," says Joan, the fine arts major—and ski instructor—whose interest in historic preservation has resulted in a new career. (Subsequently, she restored several other houses on the block.) The whole fascinating story involves Syracuse's public television station, skilled local craftspeople, and Joan's many talents. The eclectically furnished house has 12-foot ceilings, ornate friezes, many mantels in its large rooms, and various woods. Some floors and doors may look like oak, rosewood, or mahogany, but they are grained through a process that Joan figured out—and photographed in process.

Mac, a tennis coach who thinks that Syracuse's fine and reasonably priced golf courses are one of its best-kept secrets, is also enthusiastic about hosting and the city. "We talk about everything from politics to the terrific local ethnic restaurants."

Restrictions: No smoking. No guests' pets. Children should be at least 14.
Bed and bath: Four rooms. First-floor room has king/twins option, private full bath, and private entrance. On second floor, large full bath shared by one double-bedded room, one with a single bed, and one with king/twins option.
Breakfast: 7:30–9:30. Features "bakery du jour" selected by Mac from many—including Greek, Arabic, whole grain. Juice, fresh fruit, hot beverage, and, in season, locally pressed cider.
Plus: Welcoming beverage. Bedroom ceiling fans. Some off-street parking. Chocolate mints. Fragrant soaps. Down comforters. Electric blankets. Parlor reed organ in the music room. If you'd like, a tour. (Can you find the artist's initials in the graining?) Small second-floor library with rocker. Swing on side porch. Open front piazza. That solarium. And a golf partner.

Conifer Hill Bed and Breakfast

6785 Route 227, Trumansburg, NY 14886
Phone: 607/387-5849
Location: Rural. Two miles west of Trumansburg and Route 96; 12 miles north of Ithaca. Surrounded by tall conifer trees and picturesque barns. Near wineries, and antiques and craft shops.
Hosts: Lee and Cindy LaBuff
Open: Year round. Reservations preferred.
Rates: $50 single. $60 double. $10 extra person. Children under age six free.

Guests wrote (and wrote): "Made us feel as if we were visiting dear friends. . . . All the privacy we wanted but we chose to spend a good deal of time with Lee and Cindy. . . . Delicious breakfasts . . . wonderful pool . . . our favorite B&B because they make our children feel so welcome. . . . Charming . . . clean as a whistle . . . tastefully decorated in country French style."

Thanks to a visitor who came to buy a puppy (and saw the house), the idea of B&B came to the LaBuffs, who opened in 1985. Before hosting, Cindy was with the Cornell University development office. Lee, an Ithaca fire lieutenant, is a skilled builder and chef. In their early 20th-century farmhouse they have combined antiques with plush carpeting, using lots of roses and blues. The sun deck overlooks the pool and grounds (and, sometimes, deer). On the opposite side of the house is the barn with pens for turkeys and two pigs. There's a large vegetable garden. And peach trees. And the highly recommended hosts.

In residence: Kyle, age five. Coal and Kendra, two black Labrador retrievers, "the first to greet you."
Restrictions: Smoking allowed in living room, on deck, and, if there aren't other guests, in dining room.
Foreign languages spoken: A little Spanish and Italian.
Bed and bath: Two second-floor rooms. One with a double bed and one with two twins share a full bath. Cot and crib available.
Breakfast: 7:30–9:30. Hearty continental on weekdays. Full on weekends. Maybe fresh strawberries and cream, croissants, French creamed scrambled eggs with fresh mint, bacon, local grape juice, tea or freshly ground coffee. Served on deck or in dining room. Can last for hours.
Plus: Lemonade or hot mulled cider. Chocolate at bedside. Newspaper. Guests' living room with wood stove. Gas barbecue grill. Free loan of bicycles and cross-country skis.

Sage Cottage

Box 626, 112 East Main Street, Trumansburg, NY 14886
Phone: 607/387-6449
Location: Two blocks from the village center in a town of 1,800 people. Ten miles north of Ithaca on Route 96; 30 miles south of the New York State Thruway. Near Cornell University, Ithaca College, wineries, Taughannock Falls.
Host: Dorry Norris
Open: Year round. Two-day minimum stay for homecoming, parent weekends, college graduation weeks, and three-day holidays.
Rates: $40–$45 single, $43–$48 double. $10 extra person.

From Connecticut: "Pampered and welcomed like an old friend. Luxury and comfort combined with a homey feeling."

And that's exactly how we found Sage Cottage to be—with fresh, wonderful, and uncontrived traditional decor. The "old friend" is an herb enthusiast who has established one garden for kitchen herbs, one for drying and dyeing, one for medicinal herbs, and another for weaving. Schoolchildren come here for field trips. (Ask to see one of their sketches used on a Sage Cottage Christmas card.) Herb and cooking classes are held here. (Inquire about the recipe booklets.) Honeymooners, too, express their appreciation. ("Another great restaurant recommendation," said the couple who had just returned from dinner when we arrived.) Period publications are by the bed. Linens are trimmed with antique lace.

It is five years since Dorry rejuvenated the 1855 Gothic Revival house, which was built by a carpenter and lumberyard owner complete with circular staircase. While researching and planning, she worked with Cornell landscaping and historic preservation students. For "a sympathetic addition to an historic structure" she received a 1988 Historic Ithaca Award of Merit. Dorry still goes to auctions—all for a traveler's haven, her home.

In residence: One dog, Sam, with Dorry's quiet temperament. Grandchildren sometimes visit.
Restrictions: Sorry, no guests' pets. No smoking.
Bed and bath: Four rooms, all private baths. Shower bath for first-floor parlor room (accessible from a grade-level rear entrance) with queen bed. On second floor, full bath for rooms with twin/king-bedded option. Shower bath for room with a double and a single bed. Cot available.
Breakfast: Exotic. From 7:30 to 9:30. May be apricot rose geranium jam on rosemary toast, scrambled eggs with ricotta cheese and chives or herb omelets, homemade granola, local white grape juice, fresh fruit, hot beverages. Served by dining room fire or on sun porch overlooking gardens.
Plus: Iced or hot herb tea (perhaps pineapple sage). Herb bouquets. Flannel sheets in winter. Local historic architectural walking tour information. Front porch. Picnic table.

The Historic James Russell Webster
Mansion Inn

115 East Main Street, Routes 5 & 20, Waterloo, NY 13165
Phone: 315/539-3032
Location: Two blocks from historic village center. In the Finger Lakes area. Four miles from exit 41 on I-90, between Geneva and Seneca Falls. Forty-five minutes from Rochester, Syracuse, and Ithaca.
Hosts: Leonard and Barbara N. Cohen
Open: Year round. Advance reservations required. Two-night weekend minimum.
Rates: $250 per suite. MC, VISA.

"Many who come for B&B say that they should have made dinner arrangements to complete the experience of what we think of as 'living behind the velvet ropes of a major museum.' We are antiques dealers who have furnished the entire Greek Revival mansion with formal museum-quality pieces. Barbara has designed many of the changes including the Palladian-style guest addition, built on the site of a vegetable garden, with many antique architectural items including twelve-foot high Georgian doors. She has also made all the drapes for the suites and canopied beds. All this splendor is set against floors that look like marble of black and white harlequin tile. A tour—in segments with a story behind everything—takes a total of three hours. We have over 600 antique cat figurines, one of the most extensive collections in the world. When not preparing elaborate, haute cuisine dinners, we enjoy visiting with our guests. And we are very interested in metaphysics."

In residence: Five cats. One Russian blue Siamese; a twenty-pound black Angora; a Himalayan seal point; Shiraz, a Balinese seal point; and Radcliffe Worthington, a butterscotch tabby.
Restrictions: No smoking. Sorry, no guests' pets. "We supply paper slippers or guests may bring their own soft slippers or socks for the suites where we request no shoes, boots or bare feet."
Bed and bath: "Ideal for honeymooners." Two air-conditioned guest suites in a separate first-floor wing. Each with a period canopied double bed, working marble fireplace, private bath. One suite has five private entrances, the other, three; some lead to a courtyard or terrace.
Breakfast: 8:30, 9, or 10 sharp. Home-baked breads, imported cheese, fruit, juices, coffee, and tea served on antique china and sterling silver. $15 extra per person for bagels, lox, cream cheese with tarragon eggs, eggs Benedict, eggs Florentine, or quiche lorraine. Served in dining room.
Plus: Tea, wine, imported cheeses and crackers. "Pure luxury with fresh flowers, thick towels, mints on the pillow, and much more." Phone jacks in the suites' hallways. Dinner ($75 per person) with advance arrangements, prepared by Barbara, member of the Master Chefs Institute of America.

Seneca Watch

104 Seneca Street, Watkins Glen, NY
Mailing address: Main Street, Chemung, NY 14825
Phone: 607/535-4490 (July–Labor Day), 607/529-8875 (September–June)
Location: On a large wooded hillside in the village. From driveway, you climb up a series of steps with three landings and assist railings. Just off Route 14, two blocks north of Seneca Market/Harbor and Marina.
Hosts: William and Jan Halaiko
Open: Daily July–Labor Day. Weekends only rest of year. Advance reservations appreciated.
Rates: $32 single. Double $45 twin beds, $45 queen.

There's a magnificent view of Seneca Lake from the 64-foot-long veranda of this big gray Victorian house. With the hills beyond and the harbor and marina below, the setting and surroundings should be shared. So thought two teachers who are planning a people-oriented retirement career. Bill and Jan, longtime area residents, restored and renewed and opened in 1988.

The large estate, a guest house in the late 1940s, was an apartment house when the Halaikos bought it four years ago. There's wonderful woodwork in the many-spindled rail of the large front entrance. The dining room has a grape motif in a stained glass scene. Bill and Jan have furnished with period pieces, lace curtains, and some marble-topped bureaus. Paper and paint give a light and airy feeling. A working fireplace is "almost ready." Depending on the timing of your visit, you may see progress on exterior projects; currently planned are a large roof deck, a rear wildflower garden, and a gazebo beside the small creek that runs along the side of the property. "The view" is complemented by space, peace, and a warm welcome.

In residence: Kate, 18. Grace, a 13-year-old outdoor dog.
Restrictions: No smoking inside. Adults only, please.
Bed and bath: Four second-floor rooms share two new sit-down shower baths. Queen, twins, or single bed available.
Breakfast: 9–10. Juices, fruits, homemade breads and muffins, cold cereals, freshly brewed coffee, tea. On front, side, or second-floor porch or in dining room.
Plus: Hot and cold beverages. Lots of wicker porch furniture. Bedroom ceiling fans. Picnic table. Grill. Lawn games. Swimming at community park on lake. Plenty of information about wineries, antiquing, Mark Twain Drama in Elmira, Finger Lakes.

Rochester Area Reservation Service

Bed & Breakfast Rochester

Box 444, Fairport, NY 14450
Phone: 716/223-8877. Best time to call, 2–7 P.M. Answering machine messages are returned within six hours.
Listings: 15. All are hosted private residences except for one cabin in the woods on the property of a hosted residence. A few are in Rochester, but most are in nearby Pittsford, Bushnell's Basin, Fairport, Irondequoit, Ontario, Webster, and Penn Yan. Two are located at Keuka Lake, in the Finger Lakes area.
Rates: $35–$50 single, $45–$75 double. Some are $5 less per night if stays are more than one night. Family and weekly rates. Some senior citizen discounts. Deposit equal to one night's lodging required plus a $3 booking fee. Full refund if reservation cannot be confirmed. Refund less $10 service charge if cancellation notice is received no less than five days before arrival date.

Beth Kinsman, a mother of five grown children who is also experienced in rental management, realized that she needed a reservation service for empty rooms that were waiting for B&B guests, "so I became one! We try to place guests close to their planned activities or with hosts of like occupation, especially when they are here to interview for jobs, colleges, or for house-hunting. Because all of our hosts are busy, active people, they make great hosts."

Reservations: "We prefer enough advance notice to return confirmation by mail (at least two weeks)." Some phone reservations accepted. Available through travel agents.
Plus: Short-term (up to six months) hosted housing available.

Rochester Area B&Bs

Woods-Edge

Fairport, NY

Location: Quiet and beautiful in a wooded country setting. Twenty minutes to downtown Rochester and museums. Near restaurants. About half an hour to winery tours and Sonnenberg Gardens. Near exit 45, New York State Thruway I-90.

Reservations: Available year round through Bed & Breakfast Rochester, page 179.

Rates: $40–$45 single. $50–$55 double. $65–$75 cabin for two. No charge for crib.

"When you're on the screened porch, you feel like you are in a tree house. Right here or on the trails you can see wood thrush and deer, chipmunks and raccoons. In 1975, when the two youngest of our five children were still at home, we designed and built this contemporary house. It has large barn beams, a chimney of grey lake stones and brick, and rough shelves to hold the duck decoys I have been collecting for over 25 years. With antique pine furniture and new comfortable sofas, it's easy to feel at home here."

The host is a professor in the field of mechanical engineering. The hostess is in rental management and creates stone mosaic pictures using Finger Lakes rocks. She is also a garage sale aficionado and has had more than one guest accompany her on her weekly rounds.

In residence: A 14-year-old calico cat named Scramble "who surprised us all when she learned to roll over at age 10."

Restrictions: Sorry, no guests' pets. No smoking inside. Children should be supervised in woods.

Bed and bath: Two rooms in main house plus a fully equipped "hideaway" guest house on the property. One room with antique double bed shares a full bath with a room that has two antique pine twin beds and a love seat. Charming 650-square-foot guest house has a queen bed plus a queen sleep sofa, living room with fireplace, kitchen, full bath. Cots and cribs available.

Breakfast: At time established the night before. Always early on Thursdays (garage sale day). Fruit. Homemade muffins. Raisin bread French toast, pancakes, or oatmeal with grated apples and raisins. Eggs. Served in dining room or on screened porch. For cabin, eat there or in main house.

Plus: Central air conditioning. Beverages and snacks. Fresh flowers. Refrigerator storage. Laundry facilities. Bicycles. Piano. Guitars. Dulcimer. Chinese checkers too. Hiking right here.

Guests wrote: "What a great feeling to have a friend in Rochester. . . . The cabin in the woods is the most perfect B&B we have found. . . . Delicious breakfast . . . felt like a member of the family."

Strawberry Castle Bed & Breakfast

1883 Penfield Road, Route 441, Penfield, NY 14526
Phone: 716-385-3266
Location: In historic district of a suburb, 15 minutes from downtown Rochester. Set back on hill, on three acres with extensive lawns, gardens, and a cattail marsh. Within walking distance of fine restaurants. Minutes from New York Thruway (I-90).
Hosts: Cynthia and Charles Whited
Open: Year round. Reservations preferred.
Rates: $50–$70 single. $60–$80 double. $15 extra person. AMEX, MC, VISA.

"We have two of the small elaborate boxes that were used for the grapes and strawberries raised and sold by Catherine and George Southworth, who built this 1875 brick Italianate villa. The extraordinary ornate ceiling moldings and medallions are all part of the original design. The amazing thing is that the whole brick mansion—from the marble fireplace imported from Italy to the white cupola—is virtually unchanged. Now the grounds, complete with pool and gardens, are accessible to guests. B&B is a wonderful way to maintain the landmark house that we bought eight years ago. At that time I was working at Xerox, but I have since become full-time innkeeper. Cyndy is still at a Rochester hospital as a clinical microbiologist.

"We are pretty fussy about decorating according to the period and have used Victorian mauve-colored, hand-printed wallpaper and lace curtains in the dining room. We have Oriental rugs, Empire and brass beds, a fainting couch and some wicker. Our collection of antiques is growing. So is our guest list: we have been discovered as a getaway, by honeymooners, and many business travelers."

In residence: Ginger, "a lively boxer who gives an enthusiastic welcome." One host (Chuck) smokes.
Restrictions: Children should be at least 14. Sorry, no guests' pets.
Bed and bath: Three second-floor double-bedded rooms share bath with tub and hand-held shower on second floor and a full first-floor bath. Two guest rooms are large and formal and share a sitting room with color TV. One is a suite with barn-wood sitting room, TV, space for extra beds (available) for additional guests.
Breakfast: 6:30–10. Fresh fruit, filled croissants, jams, coffee and teas served on fine china and silver in the Victorian dining room with original crystal chandelier.
Plus: Bedroom air conditioning. Patio, gas grill, picnic tables, and lounge chairs; 26-by-52-foot swimming pool. Beverages. Laundry facilities. Will meet guests at Monroe County airport or Amtrak train station.

Hill & Hollow

Pittsford, NY
Location: Quiet and peaceful. In a wooded hollow, 20 minutes to downtown Rochester; 7 minutes from New York Thruway, I-90. Less than a mile from Route 490.
Reservations: Available year round through Bed & Breakfast Rochester, page 179.
Rates: $40–$45 single. $50–$55 double.

Thanks to B&B, you will find (discover) this lovely New England-style farmhouse. Interesting inside and out, it was designed and decorated by the owners, both professionals, to reflect their own New England background.
The hostess, a writer and lecturer on 17th- and 18th-century American gravestones, was introduced to the idea of B&B while doing research in Connecticut and Massachusetts. She is also a cookbook author.

In residence: Two cats, "perpetual guests who love company."
Restrictions: Special arrangements can be made for older children. Sorry, no guests' pets. No smoking indoors.
Bed and bath: Two second-floor rooms—one with twin beds, the other with a double bed—share one guest bath. Second room available only to same family or people who are traveling together.
Breakfast: Anytime. Guests' requests filled! Served in sunny octagonal breakfast room overlooking woods and small pond.
Plus: Central air conditioning. Afternoon tea. Patio. Porch. Grill and picnic table.

Guests wrote: "A wonderful experience. . . . Interesting host who is not only a great cook, but a great housekeeper, interior decorator and probably a few other 'greats' as well."

Dartmouth House

215 Dartmouth Street, Rochester, NY 14607
Phone: 716/271-7872 or 473-0778
Location: Quiet. In a tree-lined residential neighborhood. Minutes from the intersection of Monroe Avenue and I-490, exit 18. On Rochester's east side, within walking distance of museums, art galleries, mansions, boutiques, and restaurants. Convenient to universities and colleges, downtown Rochester Convention Center, and Highland Park (lilac festival). Near two bus routes.
Hosts: Elinor and William Klein
Open: Year round. Advance reservations preferred.
Rates: $50 single. $55 double. No charge for crib or cot for child.

The world is finding a path to this lovely English Tudor built in 1905. Home to Ellie and Bill for 40 years, it has been completely redone during the last 8. The den walls are covered with suede cloth. Leaded glass windows flank the massive living room fireplace. And the music room landing has an 18-foot ceiling. Beyond the comfort offered, guests enjoy hearing about (and sometimes seeing Bill's photographs from) the Kleins' travels to more than 20 foreign countries, all 50 states, and most Canadian provinces. They ask about local restaurants, current performances, and walking tour suggestions. (Ellie may direct you to a "horticultural gem with great views of the city.")

Bill, a retired Kodak electrical engineer, teaches at Rochester Institute of Technology. For many years, Ellie taught in both public and private schools. As hosts, they find it great fun to share experiences with all ages.

Restrictions: Children welcome. Sorry, no pets. No smoking.
Bed and bath: Two second-floor rooms with private full baths. One has king bed, window seat, ceiling fan. Other room has two twin beds, bay window. Rollaway and crib available.
Breakfast: Any time. "Three courses, everything from scratch." Entree could be eggs elegante, apple-walnut waffles, or Dutch babies with strawberry chambord sauce. Custard-filled corn bread or lemon-yogurt cashew muffins. Homemade—with 14 ingredients—granola. By candlelight in chandeliered dining room with china, silver, crystal, and linens. Hosts join guests.
Plus: Bedroom air conditioners. Beverages; sherry at bedtime. Terry robes. Cable TV in common living room. Grand piano. Electric organ with headphone adapter. Tour of house. Large front porch. Chaises in back yard. Guest pickup, when possible, at airport, train, or bus station. Laundry facilities.

Highland Bed & Breakfast

Rochester, NY
Location: In a lovely residential area, two blocks off 590 expressway. Close to museums, downtown, Colgate Divinity School, Rochester Institute of Technology, University of Rochester. Five-minute walk to 20-minute bus ride to center of city.
Reservations: Year round through Bed & Breakfast Rochester, page 179.
Rates: $45–$50 single. $50–$60 double. $25 rollaway. $10 crib.

After working with international students for many years, becoming hosts was a natural next step for this sharing couple, a semiretired engineer and a social worker. For the next couple of years, two granddaughters from Kenya (where the hosts' daughter lives) will be in residence.

The well-maintained split-level home is furnished with antiques and traditional furniture. He is the gardener. She's a collector of antique linens (used at breakfast) and enjoys baking.

"B&B has been far more enjoyable than we imagined. We have met many area residents' relatives (who return), business people, travelers who come for hospitals, shoppping, interviews, and the colleges."

Restrictions: Children are welcome. Smoking allowed only in kitchen or outside. Sorry, no pets.
Foreign languages spoken: Swahili and some French.
Bed and bath: Two second-floor rooms. One with double bed, full (sometimes shared) bath. One with king/twin option, private shower bath. Rollaway and crib available.
Breakfast: 7–10. Homemade jams, jellies, and breads. Fresh fruit. Beautifully served in dining room.
Plus: Tea or coffee with dessert. Air-conditioned bedroom. "Forgotten" toiletries. Sometimes, babysitting with advance notice. Offer of picnic equipment for day trips. Will meet guests at airport, bus, or train station. Off-street parking.

Guests wrote: "We felt very comfortable at this home. . . . Extremely warm and gracious hosts who gave good advice for touring Rochester. A wonderful experience."

KEY

Recipes shared, often for house specialties.

Inquiries welcomed about restoration and/or decorating. Symbol indicates that host is willing to share experiences with guests. Tips range from a before-and-after album to rebuilding advice, from furniture refinishing to curtain making. Expertise of hosts ranges from learn-by-doing to professional.

How-to B&B workshop, seminar, or apprentice program offered.

Niagara/Buffalo/Chautauqua Area Reservation Service

Rainbow Hospitality

466 Amherst Street, Buffalo, NY 14207
Phone: 716/283-4794 and 773-1814. Monday–Friday 9–3; Saturday 9–noon.
Listings: Over 40. Mostly private residences. Some guest homes and country inns. Directory $1.
Rates: $35–$50 single, $45–$65 double, $75–$95 suites. Weekly and family rates available. Advance deposit required. Deposit less $10 service fee refunded if cancellation is made with at least one-week notice.

You are "a friend of a friend" when you stay with the hosts selected by Cheryl Biggie and Georgia Brannan. The homes, ranging from modest to spacious, are in residential neighborhoods and in quiet lakeside and riverview communities. Most are in or near Niagara Falls, Buffalo, and Chautauqua Lake. Some are in Lewiston, Youngstown, Wilson, Rochester, Sodus, Mayville, Jamestown, Olcott, and Bemus Point, and in Queenston, Canada (near Niagara-on-the-Lake).

Reservations: At least 24 hours' advance notice required. Available through travel agents.
Plus: Charter sailboats, pleasure boat tours, and airport transportation available by advance reservation. Short-term housing (up to six weeks) available in hosted homes.

Can't find the community you are going to? Check with a reservation service described at the beginning of this chapter. Through the service, you may be placed (matched) with a welcoming B&B that is near your destination.

Back of the Beyond

7233 Lower East Hill Road, Colden, NY 14033
Phone: 716/652-0427.
Location: Quiet and beautiful. A 14-acre country retreat. One hour from Niagara Falls or Chautauqua Institution. One-half hour south of Buffalo. Ten minutes from I-90 and Nordic and alpine ski areas.
Hosts: Bill and Shash Georgi
Open: Year round. Two-night minimum during ski season and summer weekends. Reservations required.
Rates: $40 single, $45 double. $10 child under age 13 in parents' room. Crib, free. $200 weekend chalet (six to eight people).

A find for travelers. A labor of love for the hosts. First it was just land planned for a weekend skiing retreat and organic gardening. After they lived in a tent, cleared the land, and put up the prefab chalet, the Georgis decided to move from their big house in Buffalo and live here year round. So they built the redwood contemporary (main) house with deck and greenhouse, all designed with the herb business in mind. The show gardens grew. People came. The children grew and went to college. B&B guests came.

In addition to being an herbalist, Shash is a writer, lecturer, and physical education teacher. Bill, a physician, also keeps bees and is the photographer for Shash's writings. He also tends the orchard of apple, pear, plum, cherry, and apricot trees and makes wooden flower presses and cutting boards for Shash's Herbtique.

Although many guests come specifically to tour the organic vegetable, herb, and flower gardens, there are lovely woods for hiking. In winter your luggage and supplies go down to the chalet via toboggan (you can too); the pond is cleared for skating, and you can cross-country ski right here.

In residence: Two small dogs and four outside country cats.
Restrictions: Generally, no guests' pets. No smoking, please.
Bed and bath: Four rooms. Three-bedroom chalet (with fully furnished kitchen, fireplace, piano, pool table) has one queen, one double, and two twin beds in separate rooms that share a full bath plus a half bath. A rustic post-and-beam cabin in the woods with bunk beds for two shares chalet bath facilities. Cot and crib available.
Breakfast: 7–10. Served in hosts' adjoining house. Juice. Organically grown fruits. Homemade breads such as applesauce/ mint/nut; maybe peach/mint marmalade or ginger/zucchini conserve; herbal honey, herbal omelets, sausage, applesauce, yogurt, cereal. Garnished with flowers.

Plus: Beverages. Snacks. Tour of hosts' house. Herbtique; Kitchen, Meditation, Potpourri and other gardens. Bedroom fans. Lawn games. Swimming and boating (rowboat provided) in pond.

The Cameo Inn

4710 Lower River Road, Lewiston, NY 14092
Phone: 716/754-2075
Location: On a 60-foot bluff overlooking the Niagara River and the Canadian shore. Along Route 18F, the Seaway Trail. Five miles north of Niagara Falls on the lower Niagara River. Within a half hour of 14 wineries. Five minutes to Canada.
Hosts: Gregory and Carolyn Fisher
Open: Year round. Advance reservations required.
Rates: Double occupancy. $70 queen bed; $90 suite; $60 double or twin beds with shared bath. Singles $5 less. $10 cot. No charge for crib. Weekly rates available.

Guests other than romantics are welcome in this restored Queen Anne, but romance is surely a feature. *Bride's* magazine selected the inn as one of the four most romantic on the eastern seaboard. The Fishers, native Buffalonians, opened here in June of 1987, inspired by the New England B&B they stayed in on their own honeymoon. And now they'll tell you about the year-round breathtaking views of the falls, "even when they are frozen over, and during the Festival of Lights held in December on both the Canadian and American sides."

A professional painting and decorating contractor with 20 years' experience, Greg is known for his radio and TV appearances on the subject. Carolyn, a registered nurse, now is color consultant and office manager for Greg's business. They have furnished the inn with Victorian wallcoverings, Oriental rugs, and antiques—and welcomed many anniversary celebrants, and honeymooners of course, as well as those on getaways.

In residence: Aaron, age 16. Two dogs, Beauregard and Heidi, "absolutely not allowed beyond the family room."
Restrictions: Well-behaved children, please. No smoking inside. Sorry, no guests' pets.
Foreign language spoken: A little French.
Bed and bath: Four second-floor rooms. Private full bath for (brass) queen-bedded room. Private shower bath for suite with double bed, sitting room, view of Niagara. Full bath shared by room with antique double oak bed and one with view of river, two twin white iron beds. Rollaway and crib available.
Breakfast: 8–9:30. Fresh orange or grapefruit juice. Maybe crepes, eggs Benedict, omelets, "Greg's eggs," or Dutch babies (oven pancakes). Fruit salad. Homemade pastries. In dining room or on back deck; both have river view.

Plus: Fireplaced living room. Tea or coffee. Bedroom window and ceiling fans. Picnic tables on grounds.

From Pennsylvania: "Superb! People, rooms, meals and extras! You feel so at home."

Napoli Stagecoach Inn

Napoli Corners, RFD 1, Box 290, Little Valley, NY 14755
Phone: 716/938-6735 or 358-3928
Location: A seven-acre fruit and vegetable farm on Route 242, about five miles west of Little Valley and east of Randolph. Five minutes from Route 17. Twenty-five miles east of Chautauqua.
Hosts: Emmett and Marion Waite
Open: Year round. Reservations required.
Rates: $25 single, $35 double. Discounts for extended stays.

From Colorado: "The highlight of our trip. We're spoiled for all other bed and breakfasts."

That couple from Colorado—who came for two days and stayed for six—experienced hospitality with a heritage. This spacious colonial, now on the National Register of Historic Places, was built as a stagecoach inn by Mrs. Waite's ancestors in 1830. It was converted to a family home in 1880 and has been completely restored by the Waites over the last decade.

Visitors—from the United States, England, Germany, Poland, and Japan in the last year—find that they have come to a real home away from home. "Mom" prepares "a banquet of a breakfast." Mr. Waite, a retired clergyman, reports that he has achieved the status of master gardener. Beyond all the points of interest in the area, conversations often touch on some of the other hobbies "constantly in motion—the building of grandfather clocks, ceramics, china painting, and computer science." For the Waites, "B&B is the most delightful business imaginable."

Restrictions: Children should be at least 10. Sorry, no guests' pets, no smoking, and no alcoholic beverages.
Foreign language spoken: "Limited Spanish."
Bed and bath: Three large second-floor rooms share the three house baths. Two rooms with a double bed; one with two twin beds.
Breakfast: "At guests' pleasure" in the dining room, family room, or kitchen or on the patio. All home cooking and baking. Abundant fruits in season.
Plus: Tour of house, farm and area. Library with 3,000 books. Kitchen and laundry privileges. Will meet guests at Buffalo and Jamestown airports, Buffalo train station, and Jamestown and Olean bus stations; local transportation also available.

Plumbush at Chautauqua

Chautauqua-Stedman Road, Mayville, NY 14757
Phone: 716/789-5309
Location: On 125 acres, set back from the country road. One mile from Chautauqua Institution and most sports. About 20 minutes to wineries and pick-your-own farms; 40 miles from downhill skiing; 90 miles south of Niagara Falls. Three miles from Route 17.
Hosts: Sandy and George Green
Open: Year round. Reservations preferred. Two-night minimum stay preferred on holiday weekends.
Rates: $55–$65 double with private half bath. $75 double with private full bath. Fifteen percent discount for full week. MC, VISA.

> From New York: "Everything about Plumbush is wonderful . . . from the choice of colors to the breakfasts, from the architecture to the hosts."

Sandy knew this 1860s Italian villa–style house from the school bus window as a child. She grew up on a nearby dairy farm, three miles from where George was raised in a family that has been in the lumber industry for five generations. So when the Greens felt it was time to come back home, they sold their acclaimed Hudson Valley B&B and took on this challenge, which became a two-year restoration project. George wired throughout, installed five bathrooms, and designed a sun room with arches that echo the windows of the 11-foot-ceilinged rooms. Sandy substituted painting and papering for church organ playing. Because of the views from each window, she chose shutters rather than curtains. By the summer of 1988 the first guests climbed the beautiful circular staircase to the tower for a commanding panoramic view. Once again the hosts are greeting guests, who enjoy the music room with its piano and organ, the almost-famous Green hospitality, and the country Victorian decor.

Restrictions: Children should be at least 12. Sorry, no guests' pets. No smoking.
Bed and bath: Four second-floor rooms. One with private full adjoining bath; one with private full bath across the hall. Two with half baths and next-door shower. Double or twin beds.
Breakfast: Juice, fruit, homemade muffins and breads, granolas, beverage. Can last a couple of hours.
Plus: Sun room with Franklin stove. Bedroom ceiling fans. Veranda with rocking chairs. Tea and cookies. Meadows and woods for hiking or cross-country skiing right here.

> From Maryland: "Our all-time favorite."

The William Seward Inn

RD 2, South Portage Road (Route 394), Westfield, NY 14787
Phone: 716/326-4151
Location: Overlooking Lake Erie on a hill in a country setting. Minutes from the village, 15 antiques shops, 7 wineries. Four miles to Chautauqua Lake, seven to Chautauqua Institution. Adjacent to cross-country skiing. Half hour to downhill ski resorts.
Hosts: Peter and Joyce Wood
Open: Year round. Reservations recommended.
Rates: Double occupancy. $60–$80. Singles, $10 less. $15 extra person. Ten percent midweek senior citizens' discount. Two-night packages November–May. One-night surcharge, Chautauqua season and summer weekends. MC, VISA.

Although Chautauqua Institution is a major draw, many travelers come specifically to stay at this 1821 antiques-filled inn. The formal but comfortable ambiance created with period antiques (mid-1800s–early 1900s), wallpapers, and decor has been acknowledged in a full-page *New York Times* travel article. Yet, as skiers, honeymooners, business guests, and antiques lovers (and hotel/restaurant management students too) attest, Joyce and Peter make the difference. If you'd like, they'll share the history of the inn, which was given its mansion appearance when William Seward (later governor of New York and Lincoln's secretary of state) added pillars in the 1840s. Full restoration took place in 1982. The Woods made their career change in 1986, when they moved from Philadelphia; there Joyce, a former airline stewardess, had been assistant director of American Red Cross health programs and Peter international marketing director with Westinghouse Electric. The outdoor- and community-minded innkeepers have initiated open houses and many fascinating theme weekends.

In residence: Derek and Deanna during college vacations. A mixed terrier and one cat are usually in hosts' quarters.
Restrictions: Children 12 and over welcome. No smoking inside. Quiet time in common areas starts at 10:30 P.M. Sorry, no guests' pets.
Foreign language spoken: French is understood.
Bed and bath: Ten rooms, all private baths. Six rooms in mansion; four in original carriage house. Two on first floor. Of second-floor rooms, one has porch and one a sitting room. Twin, double, queen (some four-posters), king, and rollaway available.
Breakfast: 8:30–9:30, earlier for business guests and skiers. Juice, homemade muffins and coffee cakes. Garnished entree such as plantation pancakes or Monte Cristos and cheese eggs. Served on century-old English china in dining room with view of birds at feeders or deer in the yard.

Plus: Air-conditioned and fireplaced common areas. Lemonade or sherry and cookies in the library. Wet bar. Grounds with gardens, benches, chairs, trails.

> From Ohio: "A marvelous place. Warm and congenial . . . afforded privacy. . . . The Seward Inn is gorgeous by day and by lights at night. . . . True gourmet breakfasts. Joyce Wood is possessed of a culinary talent without bounds. I envy Peter!"

KEY

 Recipes shared, often for house specialties.

 Inquiries welcomed about restoration and/or decorating. Symbol indicates that host is willing to share experiences with guests. Tips range from a before-and-after album to rebuilding advice, from furniture refinishing to curtain making. Expertise of hosts ranges from learn-by-doing to professional.

How-to B&B workshop, seminar, or apprentice program offered.

Pennsylvania

Eastern Pennsylvania

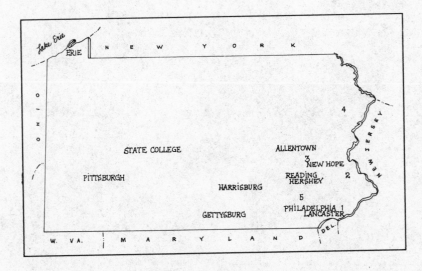

The numbers on this map indicate the regions for which there are detailed sections in this chapter.

Pennsylvania Reservation Services

Philadelphia and Brandywine Valley
Bed & Breakfast Connections. Please see page 198.
Bed & Breakfast of Philadelphia. Please see page 198.
Bed & Breakfast of Valley Forge/Philadelphia. Please see page 199.
Guesthouses. Please see page 200.

Bucks County
B&Bs in Bucks County are represented by several reservation services.
Please see page 221.

Lehigh Valley/Reading Area
Bed & Breakfast of Southeast Pennsylvania. Please see page 235.

Pennsylvania Dutch Country
Bed & Breakfast of Lancaster County. Please see page 252.
Hershey Bed & Breakfast Reservations Service. Please see page 252.

Central and Western Pennsylvania
Pittsburgh Bed and Breakfast. Please see page 282.
Rest & Repast Bed & Breakfast Service. Please see page 282.

EASTERN PENNSYLVANIA

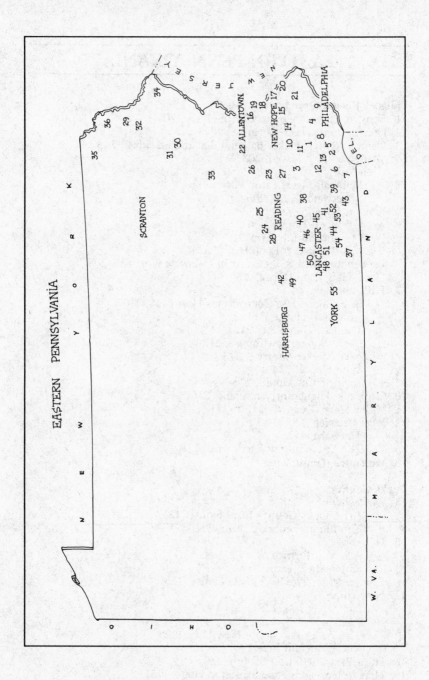

The numbers on this map indicate the locations of eastern Pennsylvania B&Bs described in detail in this chapter. The map for central and western Pennsylvania is on page 280.

Philadelphia and Brandywine Valley Reservation Services

Bed & Breakfast Connections

P.O. Box 21, Devon, PA 19333

Phone: 215/687-3565. Year round, Monday–Saturday 9–9, Sunday 1–9 P.M.

Listings: 50 hosted homes; one eight-room inn. Most are in metropolitan Philadelphia, including Center City, University City, and Society Hill, and in the suburbs of Chestnut Hill, Germantown, Valley Forge, and Main Line. Some in West Chester and Lancaster County. Free computer printout of available listings.

Rates: $25–$110 single, $35–$110 double. $5 one-night surcharge. Weekly rates. Some family rates. One night's lodging or 20 percent of total stay (the greater amount) required as a deposit. $5 booking fee. Deposit, less $15 service charge, is refunded if cancellation is received seven days prior to arrival date. No refund with less notice. Forfeit of deposit can be avoided by rescheduling and staying with the same host within a three-month period. AMEX, MC, VISA.

Ann Goodman and Peggy Gregg personally take care of all bookings—in clean, comfortable, and safe locations. "All of our hosts are hospitable and helpful. Many go 'beyond the call of duty' to offer service to guests. Most homes are located near historic areas and are convenient to public transportation.

Reservations: Two-night minimum required by some hosts. Available through travel agents.

Bed & Breakfast of Philadelphia

P.O. Box 252, Gradyville, PA 19039

Phone: 215/358-4747 or 800/358-4747. Monday–Friday 9–5, Saturday 12–4. Closed Christmas week.

Listings: 110 hosted private homes; two inns. Most are within a 50- to 75-mile radius of Philadelphia and include Center City; the Main Line; Chester, Bucks, Delaware, and Lancaster Counties; Valley Forge, New Hope, and Brandywine Valley. For a sample listing, send a business-sized self-addressed stamped envelope.

Rates: $25–$100 single, $35–$150 double. $5 surcharge for a one-night stay. Some family rates. A few weekly rates. One night's lodging or 25

percent of total stay, whichever is greater, required as deposit. Graduation
and holiday weekend bookings require full payment. Cancellations received at least one week before scheduled arrival date will be refunded,
minus a 20 percent handling charge. Cancellations of graduation bookings require at least 13 days' advance notice, otherwise complete deposit
is forfeited. MC, VISA.

Betsy Augustine and Louise Mullen feature gracious and helpful
hosts who provide convenient and comfortable accommodations. "About
a third of our listings are in historically certified homes. About 20 of our
listings have been B&B hosts for eight years. We receive glowing reports
and many bookings for return visits."

Reservations: Three-day advance notice preferred. Two-day minimum
stay for graduation and holiday bookings. A few hosts will take last-
minute requests.
Plus: Short-term (one to two months) hosted housing available; unhosted
available occasionally.

Bed & Breakfast of Valley Forge/Philadelphia

P.O. Box 562, Valley Forge, PA 19481-0562
Phone: 215/783-7838. Year round, 9 A.M.–11 P.M. daily.
Listings: 112 hosts. Mostly hosted private residences. Seven country
inns. Philadelphia locations include the historic district, University City,
Society Hill, Mount Airy, Chestnut Hill. Others are in the Route 202
high-tech corridor, in the area from Valley Forge to Reading, in West
Chester, in the Chadds Ford to Delaware area, and in Bucks County and
Pennsylvania Dutch country. Send a self-addressed stamped envelope for
a free sample listing.
Rates: $25–$70 single, $35–$100 double. $5 one-night surcharge. Five to
10 percent discount for families and senior citizens. Weekly rates start at
$100. $25 deposit required. Cancellations received at least seven days
before expected arrival, $18 refund; otherwise no refund. AMEX, MC,
VISA (plus a 5 percent fee).

Carolyn Williams, an experienced host before opening her own service, visits each potential home in search of "something special, perhaps
charm and personality. Good hosts like people, like where they live and
want others to like it there too. Often, friendships are formed." Her
facilities include homes on the National Register of Historic Places, garden town houses, restored residences and barns, carriage houses, guest
cottages, country farms and inns, and ski locations. Many have fireplaces,
hot tubs, and/or swimming pools.

Reservations: Last-minute reservations accepted.
Plus: Executive relocation. Multilingual hosts. Handicapped-accessible
facilities. Short-term (weekly or monthly) hosted and unhosted housing
available. Concierge service includes theater tickets, historic house

tours, car rentals, babysitters, day care, restaurant reservations, limousine service, outlet shopping guides. Bed and breakfast for horses and pets.

Guesthouses

Box 2137, West Chester, PA 19380
Phone: 215/692-4575. Monday–Friday, noon–4.
Listings: Over 200. Mostly hosted private residences. Some inns.
Rates: $35–$200 double occupancy. $5 less for singles. Deposits (received within five days of request) or guarantees by credit card for the last night's lodging (including tax) are required. Cancellations must be received 10 days prior to scheduled visit in order to receive full credit as a deposit applied to any future visit within one year. To be eligible for a refund, less 5 percent bank processing fee if charged to credit card, cancellation insurance must be applied for at the time of reservation or on receipt of confirmation. AMEX, MC, VISA.

Although many Brandywine Valley hosts are part of Janice Archbold's personalized service, her widespread listings are in Philadelphia and the Main Line (Wynnewood to Paoli), Valley Forge, Lancaster, Reading, Longwood, Chadds Ford, West Chester, New Hope—all in Pennsylvania. Some others are in Delaware and New Jersey and on Maryland's Chesapeake Bay.

"We best serve those guests who want to savor the experience of being a guest and want more than a bed to sleep in. All of our hosts want to share their part of the world and give their hospitality in return for meeting, however briefly, new friends."

Beyond traditional B&B, Guesthouses has created imaginative weekends that include garden tours, hot air balloon rides with champagne breakfasts, a participatory mystery—"The Manor House Murders"—complete with theater company, and stays on air-conditioned Eastern Shore yachts.

Reservations: At least 10 days' advance notice preferred.
Plus: Complete concierge service. Car rentals, dinner reservations, picnic baskets arranged. Discount tickets to area attractions. And short-term housing (two weeks to three months) available in hosted and unhosted homes.

Berwyn Country Farm House

Berwyn, PA
Location: Serene. On a country road, 10 minutes from Pennsylvania Turnpike Valley Forge exit. Forty minutes to Philadelphia. Within 20 minutes' drive of Haverford, Swarthmore, Bryn Mawr, and Villanova. One mile to historic Waynesborough; 30 minutes to Longwood Gardens.
Reservations: Year round through Bed & Breakfast of Valley Forge/Philadelphia, page 199.
Rates: $65 queen, $75 king. $100 suite. $15 foam mattress. $5 one-night surcharge.

What a setting for this 1700-1800 stone farmhouse! From every room there are pastoral views of horses, geese, bluebirds, and fenced meadows. The hostess, a grandparent who works in marketing, swims, jogs, gardens, and plays tennis. Her home, part of an historic house tour, features stenciling, wall hangings, and wonderful colors—with country furnishings and some early Victorian too. The oldest part is a restored tenant house.

"Guests are wonderful people with a sense of adventure." They include equestrians for Radnor and the Devon Horse Show, artists, other B&B hosts, and one woman who celebrated her 85th birthday here with her children. And if you're headed for Pennsylvania Dutch country, the hostess is happy to share the name of her friends who make and sell quilts.

In residence: Muffin is a lovable Pomeranian.
Restrictions: Children welcome. No guests' pets please. Sorry, no smoking.
Bed and bath: Three (at most) second-floor rooms, all with canopied beds. Two with queen beds, one with a working fireplace, share a full bath. Room with king four-poster (can be coupled with a double room as a suite) has eight large windows, wood-burning stove, private full bath. Two twin foam mattresses available.
Breakfast: 8-10. "Full and good." In brick-floored room overlooking garden and stone wall.
Plus: Bedroom window and ceiling fans. Plenty of thick towels. Guest passes ($4) to local swimming and tennis by advance arrangement.

The Hill House

Creek Road, Chadds Ford, PA 19317
Phone: 215/388-1596
Location: Half a mile from the center of the village. In Wyeth country, on two and a half acres high on a hill overlooking the Brandywine River.
Hosts: Penny and Nick Farley
Open: Year round. Advance reservations preferred.
Rates: $65 single, $75 double.

From Washington, D.C.: "We were bowled over by the house and its proprietor. The house, built about five years before the Declaration of Independence was signed, has been restored to breathtaking simplicity. Mrs. Farley went out of her way to make us feel as if we were relatives. After seeing the area and remembering all the B&Bs we have stayed in, we can truly say that overall The Hill House will remain the best."

Others who echoed these sentiments include a California couple who chose this B&B for their honeymoon; Missouri cyclists who appreciated a ride into town for dinner; wedding attendants who were greeted with fresh flowers, coffee, and fruit; and a mother and daughter who appreciated sightseeing tips.

In the 1960s in England, Penny Farley was a nurse and midwife. While she was wife and mother in a modern nearby Radley residence, she dreamed of living in an old stone house. Ten years ago she and Nick bought this house on the hill, which had painted ceiling beams, wood dating back to the mid-1790s, some dirt floors, and fieldstone walls covered with stucco. The Farleys kept the Indian doors, removed paint, varnished and polished, and added a wood stove and long brick patio—and many English family antiques. "And since 1985 when the children left home, we have been fortunate to host many wonderful B&B guests."

In residence: Sunshine, "a dachshund who thinks this is her house"; Bonkers, a "big, lovable, mostly rottweiler"; and Tigger, a tabby cat "who takes the role of boss among the pets."
Restrictions: Children are welcome. No smoking and no guests' pets, please.
Bed and bath: In private part of house, a second-floor room (with private exterior entrance) and one on third floor, each with two twin beds, share one full bath. Guest rooms have solid stone walls, beamed ceilings, narrow interior staircases.
Breakfast: Flexible hours. Poached eggs or mushroom omelet with sausage or bacon, homemade breads and muffins, fruit, oatmeal, coffee, tea. Served in Penny-designed country kitchen or on patio. Hosts join guests.
Plus: Air-conditioned living room and bedrooms. Tea or wine. Tour of house. Goose down comforters. TV. Bath sheets. Mints. Fresh flowers. Babysitting. Walking paths in woods and along river.

Pickering Bend Bed and Breakfast

Chester Springs, PA
Location: Quiet. In Charlestown Village, a milling town that dates back to the 1760s. Five-minute walk to Swiss Pines Oriental Gardens. Ten-minute drive to Valley Forge National Park; 40 minutes to Philadelphia or Longwood Gardens.
Reservations: Year round through Bed & Breakfast of Valley Forge/Philadelphia, page 199.
Rates: $65 single, $75 double, $90 triple. $5 one-night surcharge.

Now home to a lawyer, the 13-room restored 1790 stucco-over-stone house has a magnificent view of Pickering Creek, a pond, and surrounding meadows. Originally built as two houses to accommodate mill hands, it is a bank house design and listed on the National Register of Historic Places. Furnishings include primitives, antiques and reproductions, and museum quality art. Breakfast is extraordinary.

In residence: Two terriers, one cat, four finches, sheep, and a flock of hens.
Restrictions: Children welcome. Small dogs only.
Foreign language spoken: French.
Bed and bath: One air-conditioned suite (private entrance) with double bedded room, full bath, and small bedroom with twin bed. Cooking fireplace now equipped with a Franklin stove was in original summer kitchen. Desk, sofa, TV, VCR, and stereo; full kitchen; and large brick-floored alcove with wet bar. Private entrance.
Breakfast: 7–9. Elaborate. Exotic fruits and juices. Homemade croissants, pastries, jams, and jellies. Omelets made with home-raised eggs. House specialty—buttermilk walnut pancakes with sauteed apples and whipped cream, with sausage, scrapple, or bacon. Served in formal dining room (winter), in plant porch (spring and fall), or on outdoor patio (summer).
Plus: Stone-covered patio. Intercom to main house. Tour of house.

Guests wrote: "A warm welcome. Beautiful surroundings. Breakfast was a dream. Friendly hospitality. Memorable!"

Glad Haven

Gladwyn, PA
Location: Half a block from Route 23. One and a quarter miles from village center; three miles from Villanova, Haverford, and Bryn Mawr colleges; 20-minute train ride to Philadelphia. Within 20 minutes of Valley Forge Convention Center and Devon Horse Show.
Reservations: Year round through Bed & Breakfast of Philadelphia, page 198. Advance reservations required.
Rates: $45 single, $55 double.

Food is one of the features—another is ironed sheets—at this B&B, a one-and-a-half-story colonial ranch that was built on the site of a 55-room estate mansion. The host, a sous-chef for area galas, sculpts cheese for local shops and caterers. Depending on the time of your visit, you may see one of Philadelphia's historic buildings reproduced in Gouda or cheddar. The long-time resident is a great source for information and frequently makes museum and dinner reservations. "And each of the many antiques in the house has a story. Collections abound here!"

Restrictions: Well-behaved children 12 and over welcome. No guests' pets please. Smoking allowed in public rooms only.
Bed and bath: Three air-conditioned rooms, each with a desk and comfortable chairs grouped for conversation. First-floor (one step) closetless studio has a twin sleep sofa, private full bath with lift bars in the tub and shower. On second floor, room with antique Victorian twin beds and another with a contemporary queen bed share a full bath.
Breakfast: By candlelight at 5:30 or as late as 11. Juice, fruit, special French cereal, homemade jams and breads, Swiss omelets or pumpkin waffles with cider syrup. Coffee, herbal teas, "and much more." Special diets accommodated. Served in colonial dining room or skylit breakfast room, or on patio or Victorian porch. Hosts join guests.
Plus: Tea, wine, cheese, crackers. Bedroom window fans.

Marshall-Myers Farm

Glen Mills, PA
Location: Quiet. On winding rural road in serene countryside. Half hour southwest of Philadelphia. Near Chadds Ford, Longwood Gardens, Winterthur Museum, Brandywine River Museum, antiquing, dinner theaters and supper clubs.
Reservations: Available year round through Bed & Breakfast of Philadelphia, page 198.
Rates: $55 single, $80 double. $5 one-night surcharge.

Charm and comfort are everywhere inside this lovely (and spacious) restoration. It is a wonderful setting for an annual crafts show organized by the hostess. Outside, there's so much to explore that one guest couple "went for a walk at 10 A.M. and returned at 6:30 P.M."

What began as a farmhouse around 1760 has a sawmill owner's 1833 addition with elaborate woodwork. It was still without plumbing or a kitchen when, in 1977, the hosts began their two-year restoration project. Now their living room, dining room, and entrance hall are formal; other areas have a country look. The hostess, a piano teacher and registered nurse, is responsible for all the stenciling and draperies. Her husband is an electrical engineer, manager of a land development company, and township supervisor. Their athletically inclined children raise livestock. It is a home of a welcoming family with many interests.

In residence: In private quarters, three teenagers. Three cats, Spotsie, Sylvester, and Odie. A horse named Feather. "And four cute sheep."
Restrictions: No children or guests' pets. Smoking allowed downstairs.
Bed and bath: A second-floor room double bed, antique Victorian country furniture, nonworking fireplace, stenciled walls, private shower bath. Cot available.
Breakfast: Prearranged time. Homemade muffins, jellies, seasonal fruits, coffee, tea, and special egg dishes or waffles. Served in dining room by the fire, on sun porch overlooking gardens and pool, or at poolside.
Plus: Swimming pool. Afternoon tea or sparkling cider. Tour of house. Fireplaces. Thick stone walls and shade trees keep house cool. Fresh flowers in season. Sheep watching!

Sweetwater Farm

Sweetwater Road, Box 86, Glen Mills, PA 19342
Phone: 215/459-4711
Location: On 50 acres set back from a quiet, winding Brandywine River Valley country road. Surrounded by meadows with split rail fences, cornfields, thoroughbreds, and grazing sheep. Within 15 minutes of Longwood Gardens and Winterthur Museum.
Host: Linda Kaat
Open: Year round by advance reservation. Two-night minimum weekend stay requested.
Rates: Double occupancy. $125 shared bath. $145 private bath. Suite $165. $195 private cottage. $20 extra person. AMEX, MC, VISA.

Word of mouth, starting in 1983, has become word of press. *Country Home* magazine had an 11-page feature. Conde Nast's *Traveler* called Sweetwater Farm "a romantic hideaway," and *Travel & Leisure* referred to "luxurious rooms" in "the quintessential Brandywine Valley bed and breakfast inn."
The 16-room fieldstone house built in 1734 has a history of use by wounded Revolutionary War soldiers and as part of the Underground Railroad. Linda bought it—with falling split-shaker roof—in 1977. Six rehabilitation years later, she opened as a B&B, without a registration desk but with corner cupboards, spinning wheel, grandfather's clock, and wing chairs—early American furnishings purchased with special purposes or places in mind. One attic room, the Fan-Window Room, was made into a magnificent sun-filled space. The grand staircase walls are stenciled. Decor includes primitives, local scenes, Linda's stitched samplers, and grapevine wreaths. Quilts made by her grandmother are on each bed. Garden and dried flowers—all grown here—are everywhere. The sheep provide wool for sweaters that Linda knits. And Linda cooks—together with an assistant innkeeper—using farm-fresh eggs and herbs from the garden. Returnees abound.

Restrictions: Well-traveled children are welcome. Pets allowed by special arrangement. Smoking allowed in common rooms only.

Bed and bath: Nine rooms, most with canopied beds, all with views. On second floor, four fireplaced rooms; private bath for one with queen bed. One large full bath shared by two queen-bedded rooms and one with double bed and crib. Third-floor suites with two queen beds, private baths, sitting areas. In early wing of house, queen-bedded second-floor rooms with private baths. Four guest cottages with private gardens.
Breakfast: 7:30–9 weekdays, 8–10 weekends, Full with help-yourself platters of fresh fruit, farm-fresh eggs, country sausages, and homemade muffins. In country kitchen or dining room.
Plus: Air-conditioned bedrooms. TV, radio, and telephone in rooms. Large swimming pool in summer. Coffee, tea, apple cider. Tour of house and farm. Pillared porch. Total of 10 working fireplaces. Acreage for walks and games.

Campbell House

160 East Doe Run Road, Kennett Square, PA 19348
Phone: 215/347-6756
Location: A country setting on 13 acres just outside Unionville, three-quarters of a mile from Route 82.
Hosts: Judy and Bill Campbell
Open: Year round. Advance reservations required.
Rates: Per room. $55 shared bath, $65 private bath.

> From New Jersey: "A warm greeting . . . a crackling fire, a glass of wine with cheese and crackers . . . a canopied bed with dust ruffle, eyelet embroidery with a blue ribbon finish. That was the ultimate! They made dinner reservations for us at a splendid restaurant. . . . Breakfast was outstanding (and I have been a cooking teacher!). I give the Campbells four stars and would recommend their home to any discerning traveler."

All the antiques—every quilt, mirror, even the bed you sleep in—are for sale in this stucco-over-brick farmhouse, which started with two rooms in 1745. An addition was made in 1794, and a more modern addition was part of the renovation of 20 years ago.

In Oregon Judy was a nurse and an antiques dealer, and Bill a high school teacher. They looked at "just about every old house south of Philadelphia" before finding, four years ago, an old house that was already done over, one that seemed perfect for both the antiques (Queen Anne to Federal periods) and the B&B business.

In residence: One golden retriever and two outdoor cats.
Restrictions: Children over 12 welcome. Smoking allowed downstairs only. No pets, please.
Bed and bath: Three second-floor rooms reached by a steep stairway. Room with canopied double bed has private shower bath. Another with canopied double bed and fireplace shares full bath with room that has a double and a three-quarter bed.

Breakfast: Usually 8–9. Rum-raisin French toast, baked egg with mushrooms and cheese, or ham and cheese souffle with homemade popovers or muffins.
Plus: Tea or wine. Tour of house. Refrigerator space. In-ground swimming pool (in summer). Hints with map for other antiques dealers.

Meadow Spring Farm

201 East Street Road, Kennett Square, PA 19348
Phone: 215/444-3903
Location: On a 200-acre working farm. On Route 926, up a long lane with black and white cows (young stock) on one side and fields of corn and hay on the other. Five minutes from Longwood Gardens.
Host: Anne Hicks
Open: Year round. Reservations required.
Rates: $35 single room. Double, $50 shared bath, $65 private bath. $10 for cot or crib.

From the carrot cake to the granddaughter's handmade baskets (one hangs in my own kitchen), Meadow Spring Farm was very popular in Bloomingdale's "Meet-the-Hosts" program based on this book. Back on the farm, it's hard to tell who is enjoying B&B more—Anne or her guests.

The 1836 farmhouse, the Hickses' family home for over 40 years, is filled with antiques, crafts, and a doll collection. "Although none of our children live here, three sons have taken over the farming. One daughter, [who, like Anne, is a gourmet cook] has become an innkeeper in Vermont. Since we started B&B in 1983, we've met museumgoers, honeymooners, entire families, skiers, canoers. They can take a hayride here in the summer and they enjoy our solarium with its hot tub in the winter. They send their friends. Sometimes they visit our Amish friends in Lancaster. Two B&B guests even had their wedding here. We love every minute!"

In residence: Sparky, German shepherd, "greets guests and gives his approval." Some of the seven grandchildren, ages 5 to 16, may be visiting.
Restrictions: Sorry, no guests' pets.
Bed and bath: Six rooms. In farmhouse, four on second floor. One with queen bed, working fireplace, private bath. Three—with queen canopied, double, or two twin beds—share one full bath. In separate building, two queen-bedded rooms with private baths. Cot and crib available.
Breakfast: Corn fritters, fresh fruit, homemade sticky buns and breads, homemade jams and jellies. Sausage, scrapple, or bacon; French toast or mushroom omelets. Served at guests' convenience in dining room, in glassed-in porch by the pool, or in your room.
Plus: In-ground pool. Welcoming refreshments include home-baked goods. Fresh flowers year round. Fresh fruit. Mints. Beverages. Tour of house and farm. Bedroom ceiling fans. Game room with pool table. TV in every room. Option of dinner ($25 per person). Will meet guests at transportation points. Will plan everything from restaurant reservations to balloon rides. Babysitting. Kitchen and laundry privileges.

From Massachusetts: "A beautiful old farmhouse. . . . Immaculate and furnished in elegant, comfortable taste. . . . Good beds. Highest quality food, deliciously prepared, and generous. . . . A distinguished atmosphere of hominess."

Mrs. K's Bed & Breakfast

404 Ridge Avenue, Kennett Square, PA 19348
Phone: 215/444-5559
Location: On a quiet residential street in the mushroom capital. Three miles from Longwood Gardens; six miles from Winterthur; eight miles from Brandywine River Museum. One hour from Philadelphia or Lancaster; 45 minutes from Valley Forge; 15 miles from Wilmington, Delaware.
Host: Charlotte Kanofsky
Open: Year round.
Rates: $35–$45 single, $45–$55 double. $8 cot or crib.

For her "The only antique is me!" comment that appeared in my first B&B book, Mrs. K has become somewhat famous. That was in the early days of her hosting, following her years of accommodating students, boarders, and travelers while she was employed as a secretary at the Delaware Law School. Now she is "at home" greeting "equestrians, cyclists, judges, doctors, students, business people, retirees, history buffs, house and college hunters, honeymooners, and folks from neighboring towns who knew each other back home. It's really a small world."

Restrictions: No pets please. Children of all ages are welcome. No smoking indoors.
Bed and bath: Four rooms share two full baths. First-floor room has a sleep sofa. Upstairs rooms have a king, double, or two twin beds. Cot and crib available.
Breakfast: 8–9. Full. Traditional foods. Extras on weekends and holidays.
Plus: Central air conditioning. Complimentary wine and cheese, 5:30–6:30. Living room. Screened breezeway. Large backyard. Use of refrigerator and picnic tables.

From Massachusetts: "It's not the Ritz, but it's pleasant, homey, and pin-clean. What makes Mrs. K's worth the visit is Mrs. K herself. She is quite a character—welcoming, warm-hearted, chatty, and cheerful. . . . You feel more like a friend that a paying guest."

Bed and Breakfast of Delaware Host #33

Landenberg, PA
Location: In the rolling hills of lovely chateau country. Very close to Delaware line. Fifteen minutes to Longwood Gardens, University of Delaware, Brandywine River Museum; 20 minutes to Winterthur.

Reservations: Available year round through Bed and Breakfast of Delaware, page 4.
Rates: Double occupancy. $55–$65 double, $85 queen. $5 rollaway. $5 surcharge for a one-night stay.

When the hostess grew up in Wilmington, she always dreamed of living in a Chester County stone house, but she hadn't planned on becoming plasterer, painter, and wallpaperer. Along with those restoration tasks, she became a discoverer, unearthing a brick walk that had been overgrown with grass. That was all nine years ago when she bought the then vacant house, which had been built in the 1700s and expanded three times.

Now the beautiful home with spacious rooms and six fireplaces is filled with antiques and still-growing collections from all over the world, gathered by the hostess, an executive with a large chemical company. She has Persian and Chinese rugs, dolls, and brasses. She still restores furniture, goes to auctions, and loves to ride horses. She mows the lawn, tends the vegetable garden, cooks and bakes. In summer, she shares a 20-by-40-foot swimming pool and hot tub with guests.

"Some guests are enrolled in the sessions at Winterthur. Some just want to sit in peace on the porch. And then there are walkers and joggers who most remember the dogs, who lead them along the old wooded carriage trail for miles and miles and by a very pretty huge lake."

In residence: Two "very friendly dogs and a cat."
Restrictions: No guests' pets. Nonsmokers preferred.
Foreign languages spoken: French and German.
Bed and bath: Five second-floor rooms, all with period furnishings. Two with fireplaces. Four baths. Queen, double, and twin beds available. Rollaway bed.
Breakfast: 8–10. Homemade muffins and other baked goods, seasonal fruits, freshly squeezed orange juice, coffee, many varieties of tea. Served on sun porch or in homey kitchen.
Plus: Living room with two fireplaces. Large porch with wicker furniture (13 chairs). Coffee always on. Turned-down beds. Mints on pillow. Flowers in rooms. Bedroom window fans. Stable for horses (polo field nearby). Suggestion for a favorite nearby gourmet restaurant.

Hamorton House

Lima, PA
Location: High on a hill on 36 acres, close to Brandywine attractions "and a ten-minute walk to nowhere." Five miles to Chadds Ford. A half hour from Philadelphia International Airport. "We offer privacy, peace and seclusion, interrupted only by the sound of birds."
Reservations: Year round through Guesthouses, page 200.
Rates: Double occupancy. $85 shared bath. $95 private bath. $110 suites. $50 additional person.

Memorable. A three-quarter-mile-long horticultural extravaganza leading to an 1850 mansion (with three-foot-thick stone walls), home to the host's family for 138 years. ("I have a plethora of photographic history.") Spacious rooms, no more than three on any one level. Important heirloom antiques and collectibles. Intricate craftsmanship and architectural details in all 30 rooms. Hospitality that is based on 40 years of experience, stemming from the era when this was home of the Master of Hounds to the Lima Hunt.

Many additions have been made through the years, the most recent being a greenhouse built by the hostess, a Philadelphia Flower Show award winner, gourmet cook, and former English literature teacher. With a minimum of help, she maintains the entire house and has created woods to minimize grounds maintenance. Still, there are acres for walking among formal gardens, boxwood—from one, the hostess made 500 cuttings—and meadows.

Although many guests come for the area attractions, a good number come for the experience of being here and meeting this energetic and gracious hostess.

In residence: Two outdoor dogs.
Restrictions: Children should be under 2 or over 12. No guests' pets. Married couples preferred.
Foreign language spoken: French—"un peu—très peu."
Bed and bath: Eight rooms. Private baths for second-floor rooms with king canopy, four-poster queen, or two twin beds. On third floor, oversized bath shared by air-conditioned room with king, air-conditioned suite with two double beds and sofa bed in adjoining room, and one room with a double bed. One air-conditioned suite with king bed, canopied single, private bath, king daybed, two sleep sofas, living room, refrigerator. Cot and crib available.
Breakfast: 7–9:30 Monday–Saturday; 8–10 Sunday. Two fruits, juice, cereal, bacon or sausage, coffee, tea, decaf. Eggs cooked to order; cheese omelet is house specialty. Homemade muffins, breads, croissants, and jams. Buffet in large, gracious dining room with view of lawns.
Plus: In each room, fresh flowers (arranged professionally by hostess), ice, fruit, TV. Beautiful living room. Extensive libraries. Thick oversized towels. Dinners for 10 or more arranged.

Bed & Breakfast Connections Host #128

Philadelphia, PA
Location: In Society Hill. Four blocks from Independence Hall. Close to bus for 15-minute ride to University of Pennsylvania. One mile to commuter train and Amtrak connection.
Reservations: Year round through Bed & Breakfast Connections, page 198.
Rates: $50 single, $65 double. $10 rollaway.

The restored 18th-century town house has random-width floor boards, "some antiques and reproductions and some Oriental rugs." The host couple, a registered nurse and a clergyman, find that "hosting B&B

guests is just like having houseguests who come from all over the country and the world."

In residence: Sometimes Brogan, a quiet Irish setter, visits.
Restrictions: Pets are welcome unless Brogan is visiting.
Foreign language spoken: German.
Bed and bath: Three third-floor rooms. Private bath for one queen-bedded room. Another queen-bedded room and one with a twin bed share a connecting shower bath. Rollaway available.
Breakfast: Usually 8:30–9:30. Juices, fresh fruit, cereal, English muffins, bagels, sweet rolls; sometimes pancakes or omelets. Served in cheerful kitchen or dining room.
Plus: Central air conditioning. Welcoming refreshments. Large thick towels. Garden. Parking garage ($6.75 per night).

Guests wrote: "I stay in B&Bs all the time while traveling throughout the country. This was by far my favorite. . . . Interesting history to the house. . . . Sumptuous breakfast. . . . Beautiful and clean. Lovely, thoughtful down-to-earth hosts; a great location for historic sites."

Cromwell House

Philadelphia, PA
Location: On a quiet street with spring-flowering trees. A five-minute walk from Benjamin Franklin Boulevard and the Philadelphia Museum of Art.
Reservations: Year round through Bed & Breakfast of Philadelphia, page 198.
Rates: Single $45, double $50. $5 one-night surcharge.

George Washington in full regalia greeted one late-arriving guest. Although I never had the opportunity to see him (the host) or the hostess attired in costume, I was delighted to describe my stay on a Philadelphia talk show. Although it was just a one-night stay, I felt richer for the warm experience.

The multifaceted hosts, parents of five grown children, have had many successful careers that have merged into their current work as theatrical producers. They do everything from writing to costuming, lighting to acting—for television and stage. The innovative productions often focus on history and involve the audience.

It is hard to believe that the hosts acquired their 1865 row house as a shell eight years ago. Restored (by them) in full Victorian style, it has reproduced moldings, a formal parlor, a designer kitchen with solarium greenhouse, and an incredible south-facing library with central hearth and windows and plants on the end wall.

Restrictions: Nonsmokers please. Sorry, no pets. No eating in the bedrooms.

Foreign languages spoken: Some French and German.
Bed and bath: One third-floor room with twin beds. Victorian decor. Private full bath.
Breakfast: 7–9. Cereal, fruit, muffins or sweet bread, eggs or pancakes if desired, tea, coffee, juice. Served in dining room or outside.
Plus: Central air conditioning. Ground-level parlor and powder room. Pickup at Philadelphia International Airport, 30th Street train station, or bus station available for an extra charge. Small kitchen with refrigerator next to bedroom. Suggestions for small museums, even the Rare Book Room in the library. The confirmed B&B hosts have been known to drive medical students to exams.

The Earl Grey B&B

2121 Delancey Place, Philadelphia, PA 19103
Phone: 215/732-8356
Location: Quiet. In Rittenhouse Square area of Center City, Philadelphia. In neighborhood that is on the National Register of Historic Places. Fronted by brick sidewalk.
Hosts: Patricia A. and Richard J. Boyle
Open: Year round. Advance reservations required.
Rates: $75–$110 per room. $125 suite. $5 one-night surcharge.

Guests wrote: "Stupendous. . . . This New York City cynic feels enriched by having met hosts who have the secret of life in their souls and the talent to share it with others. . . . A charming place with great attention to detail—sherry, cookies, art, and all those books! . . . Gave us more information on Mexico City than our travel agent . . . gave us useful hints for London . . . wonderful suggestions for Philadelphia restaurants."

Internationally recognized poets and musicians as well as honeymooners are among the many travelers who have appreciated the hospitality in this 1860 brick row house—which is named for the cat, an important member of the household. Dick, a writer, art historian/lecturer, and painter, is former museum director at the Pennsylvania Academy of Fine Arts. Chef Patricia has had considerable experience in public relations and as manager of nonprofit organizations. Their house is "filled with books, art, antiques and things we love—everything from 18th-century to art deco to contemporary. Hosting allows us to share our enthusiasm for Philadelphia. Often we suggest the Rosenbach Museum just a block away, marvelous bookstores, art films, free concerts, and special museum collections."

In residence: "Earl Grey is our charming, friendly cat; Major Grey is his companion."
Restrictions: Children should be at least 16. No smoking inside. No guests' pets, please.
Foreign languages spoken: German, Dutch, and French.

Bed and bath: Four rooms and three baths. Each guest suite on a separate level. All private and very quiet. One large room with queen canopied bed, piano, armoire, sitting area, private full bath en suite. One queen-bedded skylit room with full bath en suite. Two third-floor rooms (can be a suite), one with double bed and one with two singles, share a full bath.
Breakfast: "Intentionally sensational." Fresh fruit, freshly squeezed juice, homemade muffins and breads. Specialty could be apple pancakes, French toast with slivered almonds and apricot sauce, or omelets. Served in dining room, kitchen, or garden.
Plus: Fruit. Sherry. Tea. Chocolates. Fresh flowers. Public parking garage within one block.

Logan Square Townhouse

Philadelphia, PA
Location: In Center City, close to Art, Please Touch, and Rodin museums, Franklin Institute, Academy of Natural Sciences. Half a block from bus stop. Ten-minute walk from train station.
Reservations: Year round through Bed & Breakfast of Philadelphia, page 198.
Rates: $30 single, $40 double. $10 rollaway. $5 one-night surcharge.

Artwork throughout this cozy 150-year-old row house was done by friends of the host, a construction project control technician, and his wife, director of a child care center. There are pressed tin ceilings in the breakfast and living rooms. Still, it's the hospitality that's remembered by sightseers, conferencegoers, and international visitors.

In residence: One teenage daughter.
Restrictions: No smoking. No guests' pets.
Foreign language spoken: French.
Bed and bath: Two third-floor rooms share a shower bath. One with double bed and air conditioning. The other has one twin bed, fan, private roof deck. Rollaway available.
Breakfast: Monday–Saturday 7:30–9:30, Sunday 8:30–10. Blueberry or German oven pancakes, waffles, Monsieur Jacques (cheese covered egg on ham and toast) or sausage strata (casserole of eggs, sausage, and cheese). Served in small, art-filled breakfast room.
Plus: Player piano. Nearby street parking and parking lots.

New Market Surprise

Philadelphia, PA
Location: In historic district, a mix of residential and commercial properties. Within walking distance of most attractions, many restaurants, convenient and good public transportation.

Reservations: Available year round through Bed & Breakfast of Philadelphia, page 198.
Rates: $60 single, $65 double. $5 one-night surcharge.

Although it took more than a magic wand to change the abandoned shell into the warm and inviting private home, you almost have the feeling that the metamorphosis just happened naturally. The historically certified house, built in 1811, retains the original pine floors, some chair rails, and two narrow spiral staircases with pie-wedge-shaped treads. Contemporary furnishings, hand-painted Mexican tile in baths, and many plants and natural fibers give it a very earthy look.

Before the hostess, a psychotherapist also interested in food, arts, and social causes, restored the property acquired from the Redevelopment Authority, she took some photographs. They are shared with guests—as are many suggestions for things to do and places to go. Travelers from all over the world are grateful that a newspaper article (seven years ago) mentioned the need for hosts in this area of the historic city.

Restrictions: No guests' pets. No smoking.
Bed and bath: Two double-bedded rooms, one room on second floor and one on third, each with a working fireplace and private bath.
Breakfast: Usually a full meal. May include oven-baked items such as soufflelike pancake topped with powdered sugar, lemon juice, and orange marmalade; or puffy French toast with bacon, or German apple pancake served with bacon or sausage. If it's a fix-your-own arrangement, homemade muffins provided. Served in fireplaced kitchen that has exposed beams, a brick wall, and a greenhouse leading to garden.
Plus: Tour of house. Metered street parking (or 24-hour lot charge, $10). Small walled garden.

Spite House

Philadelphia, PA
Location: In a residential neighborhood in the northwestern section of Philadelphia called Mount Airy. One block from train; one and a half blocks from 23-minute trolley ride to Center City; five-minute trolley ride to Chestnut Hill.
Reservations: Year round through Bed & Breakfast of Valley Forge/Philadelphia, page 199.
Rates: $50 single. $60 double. $5 one-night surcharge.

Guests in the flower business have named a rose after the hostess. Lots of artists stay here. Museums and businesses like to place their visitors in this semidetached garden row house, an historically certified "spite house" built around 1900.

Home to the hostess for forty years and featured on house tours, this "sparkling clean" home away from home is filled with antiques and a warm ambiance. Whether you are interested in history or genealogy or a suggestion for a nearby area which the hostess thinks is "more exciting than Williamsburg, Virginia," this is a memorable B&B.

In residence: One who smokes (in kitchen only).
Restrictions: Children eight and over welcome. No guests' pets.
Bed and bath: Three rooms—with either a double or two twin beds—on third and fourth floors. One shared full bath.
Breakfast: Flexible hours. Fruit juice, mixed fresh fruit, cereals, eggs, coffee or tea, toast, homemade jelly and sticky buns. Prepared and served by hostess in two-level kitchen.
Plus: Refreshments. Tour of house. Bedroom window fans. Patio. Street parking. If you've been on the road, offer of the washer and dryer.

Taylor-Young House

2106 Delancey Place, Philadelphia, PA 19103
Phone: 215/545-3985
Location: In Rittenhouse Square, "a Center City neighborhood of 19th-century rowhouses that range from great mansions to tiny houses on narrow streets full of charm. Within walking distance of elegant shops, many good restaurants, theaters, concert halls, and art galleries."
Hosts: Mimi and John LeBourgeois
Open: Year round. Advance reservations required.
Rates: Per room. $50 twin bed. $75 double bed with sofa bed or queen bed. $10 additional person. $5 one-night surcharge.

> From England: "Turned my visit to do academic research into a pleasure trip. The accommodation was first rate, the breakfasts filling and nutritious, the New Orleans coffee a welcome discovery! They are people with whom one can often have an extended conversation. I came away feeling I'd made two new friends."

Both hosts grew up in New Orleans. ("We offer coffee and chicory with hot milk.") John, a former history professor and banker, is a dean at Temple University—and a master swimmer. Mimi, a fine seamstress who has worked with many arts and music groups, is currently a volunteer with a Philadelphia tourism organization. Three years ago they moved from Chicago to this restored Victorian split-level brick row house and "only redecorated from top to bottom. It didn't require any of the extensive renovations we had done with a previous residence." They furnished with many 18th- and 19th-century antiques and started hosting when their friends at The Earl Grey B&B sent them their overflow. The guest list now includes artists in town for their show openings, sightseers, medical seminar attendees—and someone who won a night here at a benefit auction.

In residence: "Harlequin, our cat, loves company."
Restrictions: Children should be at least six. Smoking allowed on deck or in garden only. Sorry, no guests' pets.
Foreign languages spoken: "Enough French and Italian to make a guest comfortable."
Bed and bath: Three rooms. Baths (two) with showers are usually private.

On third floor, two large rooms—one with double four-poster bed and a double sofa bed, one with queen bed. On fourth floor, "room with single brass bed and lots of charm."
Breakfast: 7:30–9. (Continental for late sleepers.) Full meal might include sauteed apples, Pennsylvania Dutch bacon or scrapple, French toast ("or Lost Bread as we say in New Orleans"). Homemade muffins. Coffees; teas. Hosts and guests eat together at 18th-century dining room table.
Plus: Air conditioning throughout. Coffee, tea, wine, sherry. Fourth-floor deck. Library with TV. Flowers. Down pillows. Bedroom phone jacks. Robes. Nearby garage parking ($11.50 for 24 hours).

Highpoint Victoriana

Skippack, PA
Location: On five acres along a country road. Four miles from the quaint antiques and craft village of Skippack. Five miles from the northeast extension of the Pennsylvania Turnpike. An hour to Center City; 40 minutes to New Hope. Five minutes from Philadelphia Folk Festival or Spring Mount Ski Festival. Ten minutes to Pottstown.
Reservations: Year round through Bed & Breakfast of Valley Forge/Philadelphia, page 199.
Rates: $50 single. $60 double. $10 rollaway. $5 one-night surcharge.

All Victorian—lighting fixtures, floral wallpapers, wainscoting, tub on legs, and choice of colors. All remodeled five years ago after the hosts, an insurance executive and an antiques dealer, returned from a trip in England. "The 13-room brick house with a wraparound porch has a large barn that is currently, but slowly, being restored to house my antiques business. The guests' parlor of the main house has a wood stove, rococo sofas, and a hand-cranked Victrola which plays 78 rpm records. There are paneled chestnut pocket doors between the living and dining room, and most of the decor is country Victorian. Skiers are greeted with wine and cheese in the late afternoon; champagne is offered for anniversary celebrants. After all the planning and dreaming, hosting is even more interesting and fun than I had thought."

In residence: "An adorable English sheepdog."
Restrictions: Children 12 and over welcome. Smoking allowed in parlor, dining room, sitting room, and porch. No guests' pets, please.
Bed and bath: Five rooms share two full baths. On second floor, rooms with a double bed or three-quarter Murphy bed. Third-floor room has a double bed and a double sofa bed. Rollaway available.
Breakfast: 7:30 weekdays, 9 weekends; but flexible. Hostess cooks. Quiche lorraine, stratas, or French toast. Homemade blueberry wheat and cherry almond muffins. Served by hosts in formal dining room with gaslight chandeliers, at table set with lace tablecloth, floral china, and lace napkins. Hosts join guests.
Plus: Evening tea or wine. Bedroom window fans. Private guest entrance. Porch. Plenty of parking. Grounds for strolling.

Deep Well Farm

Valley Forge, PA
Location: In a pretty residential neighborhood, half a mile from Valley Forge Music Fair, one mile from Valley Forge Park. Half hour to Center City. Two miles from Pennsylvania Turnpike (exit 24) and Route 76 east to Philadelphia; a half mile to Route 202.
Reservations: Year round through Bed & Breakfast of Valley Forge/Philadelphia, page 199.
Rates: $40 single, $60 double. $5 one-night surcharge.

"I always wanted to lie in bed, look out a window and enjoy the scenery," said one city guest, who reveled in the sight of horses grazing and the sound of birds singing on a beautiful morning.

Other guests talk about feeling "restored" after a stay in this painted fieldstone 1880s house, which has 16-inch-thick walls, deep windowsills, and interesting antiques. Once a boardinghouse for itinerant farm workers, it had become a two-family house when the owners bought it—and converted it to a single-family—in the 1950s. (The original main house of the estate is on the adjoining property.) The hosts—she has 16 grandchildren—are seasoned B&B travelers who enjoy sharing both their home and the bounty of this wonderful area.

In residence: "Kitty is a very old fat cat." Two parrots. Two horses.
Restrictions: Children are welcome, but two at most at one time. No guests' pets. No smoking allowed.
Bed and bath: Six second-floor rooms with double or twin beds share three full baths. Crib available.
Breakfast: 7:30–9:30. Coffee, tea, berries in season, juice, hot or cold cereal, Scotch egg rolls. French rolls, Danish, butter croissants, or muffins. "German pancakes are a real conversation piece as well as tasty." Served in dining room "although some guests prefer the kitchen."
Plus: Evening beverages. Fresh flowers. Thick towels. Candy. Nearby school track for jogging or walking. Bedroom ceiling fans. Den. Living room. Back porch and lawn.

The Barn

1131 Grove Road, West Chester, PA 19380
Phone: 215/436-4544
Location: Residential. On a hill overlooking an old springhouse, a pond, and trees. One-quarter mile from Route 100; 1½ miles from town; 20 minutes to Brandywine–Chadds Ford area via lovely country roads. Easy drive to Swarthmore and Haverford.
Hosts: Susan D. Hager and son, Theodore
Open: Year round. Advance reservations preferred.
Rates: For first night, $50 single, $55 double; $90 two rooms for family, $100 three rooms. Subsequent nights, $5 less. Crib free. Long-term rates arranged. AMEX.

Amazing and welcoming. Be sure to see the "before" photo of this B&B created from a half-fallen 1800s stone barn and featured on a holiday house tour.

"Raising three sons and teaching for years in the heart of Greenwich Village, I—with a brand new baby—sought country life six years ago. The beauty and comfort of this incredibly restored barn abetted my decision. The restorers, a husband and wife team, helped by an Amish workforce, preserved the original three stone walls, exposed on the inside and insulated and stuccoed on the outside. Random width pine floorboards, barn siding for doors, and posts and beams were all salvaged from other old barns to create a structure that is both authentic and yet strikingly modern. Bed and breakfast has allowed us to share this neat space with Brandywine Valley tourists, an Englishman here to set up a new company, a transferred family waiting for their own house's completion—and many other now-friends. Often, Teddy leads a merry tour inside and out. And I am collecting wonderful paintings by some very gifted local artists."

In residence: Son Teddy is seven years old. "Pu Yi, a Shih Tzu is a very small gentle creature."
Restrictions: Children as well as small pets welcome.
Bed and bath: Two second-floor rooms—one with a double bed, the other with full four-poster bed—with connecting shower bath. A big third-floor room "great for kids" has a double, two small twin beds, many books, portable TV, couches. Crib available.
Breakfast: Flexible hours. Hot cereal or granola, juice, tea, coffee. Entree could be eggs Benedict or scrambled eggs in crepe with hollandaise; sausage, scrapple, bacon or ham. Fresh fruit or homemade applesauce. Muffins or popovers. Served in living or dining rooms with patio doors overlooking balcony.
Plus: Tea or wine and hors d'oeuvres upon arrival. Classical music. Sunday *New York Times*. Babysitting. Ping-Pong table. Tennis in nearby park.

From New York: "A charming and comfortable B&B with real country flavor, fascinating and unusual antiques. . . . Plenty of privacy, but when you're ready for good food and companionship, Susan and Teddy are marvelous hosts. Excellent cuisine—all homemade and (in season) garden fresh!"

The Log House at Battle Hill

West Chester, PA
Location: Secluded. On a 20-acre estate of manicured lawns, century-old trees, and lakes. Five minutes to Brandywine River Museum, 10 minutes to Longwood Gardens, 20 minutes to Winterthur.
Reservations: Available year round through Guesthouses, page 200. Two-day minimum stay.
Rates: $150 single or double.

"A long sweeping driveway crosses over a bridge to our back acreage, the main house and spring house. Then it wraps around again to the log house and barn. Behind that is the pool and pool house where you have gorgeous views of Brandywine Valley and more ponds. Guests come (and return) for the privacy and the time to savor a special atmosphere. They are welcome to walk on the islands in the ponds. They see bluebirds, herring, ducks, geese, and fish (stocked). The grounds, which we maintain ourselves, have pear and apple trees, osage orange trees, and wildflowers that dry beautifully.

"Because one of the previous owners was married to a DuPont, many of our plantings come from Longwood. The architect of Winterthur did all the additions, overseeing the 1700s log house that was moved from Delaware and reassembled here. It has always been well maintained. We redecorated it with wall to wall carpeting and country furnishings."

Couples who lead rather hectic lifestyles and honeymooners are among those who are thrilled to find these unusual accommodations. If you are curious about the history of the estate, the hostess is happy to share what they have learned since the family moved here 10 years ago. "We love it in all seasons. In winter, it is a wonderland with the European lanterns lighting your way. Sharing the property with B&B guests is wonderful too."

Restrictions: No children, guests' pets, or smoking.
Bed and bath: A separate log house with queen bed, connecting bath, living room, kitchen, and hall. Plenty of closet space. Very private.
Breakfast: In stocked kitchen. Help yourself to extensive continental treats—juice, cheeses, croissants, muffins, fruit, beverages.
Plus: Wine, cheese, and fruit (in guest house) upon arrival. After-dinner mints. Full use of pool (in summer) and grounds.

Lenni

Westtown, PA
Location: Secluded. Three miles from West Chester. Within a 20-minute drive of Brandywine River Museum, Longwood Gardens, Winterthur Museum. Convenient to fox hunts, horse shows, and race meets.
Reservations: Year round (except Thanksgiving weekend, Christmas season, and January) through Guesthouses, page 200.
Rates: Per room. $85 shared bath. $110 private bath.

Guests say: "A warm welcome by gracious hosts who know the area well. We tell our friends that this lovely home is a 'must.' "

A fireplace and fresh flowers in every room, authentic Victorian antiques, and spacious grounds are part of the experience at this 1860 green serpentine Italianate manor house, built by a Quaker family who received their original land grant from William Penn in 1682. House tour visitors, too, have admired the 12-foot ceilings with crown moldings, the parquet floors, and the Jefferson windows that lead to the veranda. For almost four decades this has been home to the hosts, experienced B&B travelers in Alaska and California. Skiing, fox hunting, archaeology, and environmental concerns are among their many interests.

In residence: A German shepherd named Irish. Cat Shaka is named after Zulu warrior.

Restrictions: Children welcome. No pets or smoking allowed.

Bed and bath: Three second-floor rooms. One has two twin beds and shared full bath. Room with king canopy bed and another with queen bed share a full bath.

Breakfast: 7–9. Freshly squeezed orange or grapefruit juice. French toast and bacon, banana pancakes and sausages, or Philadelphia creamed chipped beef. Buttermilk muffins, croissants. Served in dining room, in kitchen, or on veranda.

Plus: Tour of house. Wine and cheese, or tea and cookies. Spacious veranda on three sides of the house. Oak-paneled library with TV and *New York Times*.

Bucks County Reservation Services

Some Bucks County B&Bs are represented by:

Bed & Breakfast of Philadelphia, page 198.
Bed & Breakfast of Valley Forge/Philadelphia, page 199.
Guesthouses, page 200.

Bucks County B&Bs

1819 Bucks County Farm House

Doylestown, PA
Location: On a rolling country road. Seven miles from town; 15 minutes from New Hope.
Reservations: Year round through Bed & Breakfast of Philadelphia, page 198.
Rates: Double $65. Single $55. $10 for children under 12.

From New York City: "What a treat! Easy-going lovely people who know when to give you space. Their home is your home—warm, inviting, very 'country,' beautiful, very comfortable. Chock full of tasteful and unusual antiques. Outstanding homemade breakfasts all from scratch. Couldn't have been better."

Guests are part of family living—"we're not an inn"—in the 1819 white stone farmhouse with beamed ceilings, antique furnishings, and five fireplaces. Because this has been the hosts' residence for 27 years, and because his family has been in the area since 1723, they are well familiar with the local history, culture, and crafts and can suggest almost anything, including historic sites, museums, restaurants, and even places to go canoeing and tubing on the Delaware River.

In residence: One gray Persian cat.
Restrictions: Children of all ages welcome. A cat or small dog would be allowed.
Bed and bath: Two double-bedded rooms, each with a working fireplace, share a shower bath. "A 100-year-old cradle awaits babies."
Breakfast: 7:30–9:30. Full farm breakfast varies according to garden's bounty and whim of cook. Could include homemade scrapple, shoofly pie, or waffles from a 50-year-old waffle iron. Guests sit in the old Windsor chairs at the trestle table set with lovely silver and china.
Plus: Cozy living room. Five acres for walking or cross-country skiing. Badminton and croquet.

The Inn at Fordhook Farm

105 New Britain Road, Doylestown, PA 18901
Phone: 215/345-1766
Location: On 60 secluded acres of meadows and woodlands. Off Route 202, 1.5 miles east of Doylestown, "a town that is more like New England than some in New England." Twelve miles from New Hope. An hour from Philadelphia by train or car.
Hosts: Blanche Burpee Dohan and her husband, Michael; Laurel and Dan Raymond.
Open: Year round. Reservations advised. Two-night minimum stay on weekends.
Rates: $72–$134 double occupancy. $17 cot. AMEX, MC, VISA.

Imagine strolling on the grounds of W. Atlee Burpee's estate. Or sitting at his desk, where he wrote, by hand, the very first Burpee seed company catalog. Today the Burpees enjoy telling how the main house was used as a brooder house to raise game hens before it became—100 years ago—the family residence. Blanche recalls: "As a child, I didn't realize what a great house this was. We used the three stairways going to the second floor for playing tag or hide and seek! B&B is a wonderful way to maintain our family homestead. Fordhook is such a peaceful place, good for unwinding and slowing down. Bring a book to read by the fire, some shoes for long walks through the woods and meadows, or cross-country skis if there is snow."

Blanche, a social worker who worked in adoptions and more recently was a financial consultant, and her brother Jonathan, customer services director for the Burpee Seed Company, are delighted that the Raymonds, their mother's companion tenants during her last year (1984), have stayed on as innkeepers and decorators. Members of the Burpee family are frequently in residence on weekends and during holidays.

There are nine buildings—including the main house with its high ceilings and family heirlooms—on the property recently listed on the National Register of Historic Places. In the carriage house there's an elegant B&B apartment with a chestnut-paneled Great Room, vaulted ceiling, and Palladian windows. There's more, but you will just have to go to experience this national treasure.

In residence: Mark Raymond, age three, and his brother, Kevin, age one. Tammy, a shepherd/retriever, "greets guests, leads them on walks, visits in the inn but sleeps in her own (dog)house."
Restrictions: Children should be at least 12. No guests' pets. No smoking indoors.
Foreign languages spoken: Michael Dohan speaks French, German, and some Russian.
Bed and bath: Two carriage house rooms (king and queen beds) share full bath. In main house, five rooms, three with private baths. King/twin, queen, or double bed available. Some four-posters, antique, and brass beds. Rooms range from master bedroom with working fireplace, private balcony, and large adjoining full bath to a cozy third-floor room under the eaves. Cot available.

Breakfast: 7:30–9:30 weekdays, 8:30–10 weekends. Full. Fordhook (old-fashioned oatmeal) pancakes, cream cheese–stuffed French toast, smoked bacon, local sausage, berries and melons from the farm, homemade jams and freshly baked muffins. Served in the formal dining room with French doors and leaded glass bay windows or on the terrace under 200-year-old linden trees, overlooking acres of meadows. "Can last for hours."
Plus: Bedroom air conditioners. Afternoon refreshments. Tour of house. Large living room with working fireplace. Butler's pantry with refrigerator and teakettle. Study/office with fireplace, phone. Huge tiled terrace. Picnicking on lawn. Badminton. Croquet. Maps of walking trails and buildings. Will meet Philadelphia train or New York bus at Doylestown stations. Weekday tours arranged for greenhouses now used by Delaware Valley College.

Ash Mill Farm

Route 202, P.O. Box 202, Holicong, PA 18928
Phone: 215/794-5373
Location: Pastoral. Set way back off the road on 10 acres of wooded farmland. One-half mile from Peddler's Village. Ten minutes from Doylestown and New Hope.
Hosts: Caroline and Jeff Rawes
Open: Year round. Reservations required. Two-night minimum stay on weekends from April through November.
Rates: Double occupancy $60–$70 semiprivate bath. $70 private bath. $90 suite. Monday–Thursday discounts. MC, VISA.

"When we added sheep for groundskeeping purposes, it worked! And then, as it happened, every lamb seemed to arrive just during afternoon tea. Of course, we can't always guarantee that." Carol, a former teacher, goes on to observe that B&B "in the fourth old house we have restored is a neat way to bring up a family."

The picture-perfect 1800s summer residence of Philadelphia bankers and lawyers has a wide central staircase with stained glass window on the landing, crown moldings, and crystal chandeliers. Quilts and a Rawes-restored hutch are among the many country antiques. Window treatments are beautifully done. Carol has a strong sense of display and is responsible for much of the cross-stitch work and stenciling.

Both Jeff, a steamfitter in the Philadelphia area, and Carol, lifelong Bucks County residents, have hints: back roads into New Hope, 5- to 40-mile cycling loops all through villages, and a hiking route that leaves from the inn and passes the remains of an old mill. "Many of our guests really love the Tuesday flea market. Some just 'stay put' in our peaceful setting. For business travelers, it's a home away from home. Returnees feel like friends or family."

In residence: One host smokes occasionally. Sons, Jonathan, age 13, and Scott, age 11. Two cats, Maggie and Rambo, "our welcoming committee."

Restrictions: Young weekend guests should be at least eight. Younger children welcome midweek. Sorry, no guests' pets.
Bed and bath: Five rooms. On second floor—two with private bath, two share a huge full bath. Queen or double antique bed; the high one has a stool, and two are canopied. Third-floor suite with queen bed, sitting room, private shower bath.
Breakfast: 8:30–10. Fresh fruit, croissants, homemade raisin bran muffins, coffee, tea, juice. Coddled eggs served in porcelain. In dining room, "probably the whole house originally," by walk-in fireplace; or, in warm weather, on patio.
Plus: Bedroom ceiling fans. Federal-style living room. Fresh flowers. Afternoon tea (featured in *Bon Appétit*). Huge wicker-furnished porch. Tour of house. Painted tole on tin (done by a friend) for sale.

Barley Sheaf Farm

P.O. Box 10, Route 202, Holicong, PA 18928
Phone: 215/794-5104
Location: Down a lane, far back from the road on a 30-acre farm 10 minutes from New Hope; about an hour from Philadelphia.
Hosts: Ann and Don Mills
Open: Mid-February through mid-December. Weekends only from first one after New Year's until Saint Valentine's Day. Two-night minimum stay on weekends; three nights on holiday weekends.
Rates: Double occupancy $94–$115. Room with two queen beds, $120. Suite $150. $15 additional person in appropriate rooms.

The family had three teenagers when they first moved into the former home of noted playwright and drama critic George S. Kaufman. In 1979, after traveling the B&B way in England, the Millses opened their own farm to travelers. It was a wonderful lifestyle for everyone, with Don still being president of his New Jersey–based perfume company. Now Don has "retired" to full-time innkeeping and all the children have grown.

What a setting for a recent Mills wedding, which was complete with a hot air balloon send-off for the bride and groom! The gracious 1740 stone house, a designated national historic site, offers a peaceful, elegant, warm ambiance. Throughout, antiques—many refinished by Don—are accompanied by personal touches. Ann is responsible for the decor. Don established the herb garden. The sheep, constantly varying in number, announce their presence. You're welcome to watch the sheepshearing if you happen to be there when the busy itinerant shearer arrives. And chickens add to the pastoral scene.

In residence: Winston, the cat.
Restrictions: No pets, please. "Recommended for children over eight."
Foreign language spoken: Ann speaks French.
Bed: Ten rooms, each with private bath. Seven rooms in main house, three in cottage. Queen, double, or twin beds available. One room with

two queen beds. One queen-bedded suite with fireplace overlooks pool and has adjoining room with trundle bed.

Breakfast: Seatings at 9 and 9:45. Full. Possibilities include apple crepes, souffle, sausage, honey from Barley Sheaf hives, breads, and the freshest of eggs. Served on sun porch (wood stove used in winter) overlooking lawns.

Plus: Air conditioners in all rooms. Swimming pool. Fireplaced living room. Potpourri, soap, and other amenities. New conference facilities (seating capacity: 20) in converted beamed barn.

The Bucksville House

Route 412 and Buck Drive, RD #2, Box 146, Kintnersville, PA 18930
Phone: 215/847-8948
Location: On Route 412 in the pastoral countryside of Bucks County. Thirty minutes north of New Hope. One mile from Lake Nockamixon State Park with swimming, boating, and cross-country skiing.
Hosts: Barbara and Joe Szollosi
Open: Year round. Daily July and August. Weekends only September–June. Advance reservations required. Two-night minimum preferred; three nights on holiday weekends.
Rates: $75 per room. $120 suite. MC, VISA.

Guests comment on the antique basket collection, the huge walk-in fireplace, and the Mercer tile floor. With Joe's handcrafted authentic-looking period furniture, his restoration of the whole house, and Barbara's use of Oriental rugs, canopied beds, quilt collection, and crocks, everything looks so natural that guests often ask if much had to be done to the 1795 structure—which has been a wheelwright shop, a hotel, a speakeasy, a tavern and a private home. The Szollosis' "before" album shows how the place looked five years ago; it was standing vacant when the two New Jersey teachers ended their search for an old house to renovate. Here in Pennsylvania, Joe is a self-employed carpenter. Barbara continues to teach reading.

And guests continue to rave: "A haven. . . . We were shown to a charming room with fireplace, patchwork quilt, flowers and country furniture. . . . The only sounds are crickets and songbirds. . . . Restoration that is a labor of love. . . . Breakfast is a highlight, delicious and plentiful. . . . Warm hospitality."

In residence: "Muffy is our very friendly calico cat."
Restrictions: No smoking. Sorry, no guests' pets or children under 12.
Bed and bath: Three second-floor rooms and one third-floor suite. All double-bedded and with private baths. One air-conditioned room has canopy bed, shower bath, working fireplace. Another has a working fireplace and air conditioning; one has a ceiling fan. In attic suite—a double bed, a sitting room with two twin sofa beds, two ceiling fans, shower bath.

Breakfast: 8:30–10. Fresh fruit cup, bran raisin nut waffles, and sausage; or fresh pineapple with kiwi, egg casserole, ham, and homemade sticky buns. Plus juice and hot beverages. Served in gazebo or by dining room walk-in fireplace.
Plus: Tea, coffee, cider, and homemade cookies. Turn-down service. Mints on pillow. TV room. Living room fireplace. Coal stove. Old puzzles and board games. Tour of house. Deck. Gazebo. Yard and surrounding paths.

Backstreet Inn

144 Old York Road, New Hope, PA 18938
Phone: 215-862-9571
Location: On several acres of parklike grounds—"like a bird sanctuary"—with stream and pool and, sometimes, reindeer. One-quarter mile from town center on a back street. One block off Route 179.
Hosts: Robert Pucio and John Hein
Open: Year round. Two-day minimum stay on weekends; three days on holiday weekends.
Rates: $75–$89 per room. $125 suite. $5 less for single. $20 more for triple. $6 one-night surcharge on weekends. MC, VISA.

"This is home. We'll buy it!" said the two Manhattanites who were "just looking" in New Hope in the winter of 1988. As Bob recalls, "We turned into the driveway into another world—peaceful, serene, a warm place that you can touch, feel, be comfortable with. It's a huge 1750 house that has had several additions through the years. As a B&B, it attracts guests who come here to unwind. They relax around the pool or fireplace and they almost hate to leave, even for dinner."

Bob, an office manager and personnel director, and John, a contractor who is an expert painter, paperhanger, and plasterer, had thought of becoming innkeepers in sunny California. A New Hope relative suggested "just looking here," and that first day ended the search. Thanks to tutelage by the seller, a former restaurant owner, Bob learned quickly about breakfast specialties and how to transfer his joy in preparing large dinner parties to daily morning meals. After installing private baths, John is attending to redecoration. The furnishings are eclectic, and the hosts have added accents of scenic paintings, a German cuckoo clock, a Hummel collection, and some antiques.

Restrictions: No children or pets please. Smoking in parlor only.
Foreign language spoken: "A little Italian."
Bed and bath: On three floors, six double-bedded rooms on first two floors plus third-floor suite. All private shower baths. One second-floor "secret" room.
Breakfast: 8:30–10. Juice, fruit, coffee. Entree might be walnut pancakes with honey walnut syrup. Served in garden room by candlelight with crystal, china linen.
Plus: Air-conditioned bedroms. Afternoon refreshments. Turn-down service. Refrigerator, cable TV, swimming pool, croquet.

Pineapple Hill

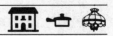

1324 River Road, New Hope, PA 18938
Phone: 215/862-9608
Location: On five acres along a scenic road, 4½ miles south of New Hope.
Hosts: Suzie and Randy Leslie
Open: Year round. Reservations requested. Two-night minimum stay on most weekends.
Rates: Weeknights/weekends $60/$70 double with semiprivate bath, $70/$80 double with private bath. Two-bedroom suites with private bath $80/$90 and $90/$100. Long-term and corporate rates available. AMEX.

From New York: "While visiting our great-grandchild in the area, we enjoyed the hospitality. . . . Interesting hosts. . . . Magnificent quilts. What a delight!"

Honeymooners and corporate guests are among the other guests who have come from 48 states and 22 foreign countries to this inn, which is filled with American folk art and the Leslies' 17-year collection of country and primitive antiques. Even *Country Living* magazine chose this setting (for three pages of photographs showing country linens). The house, built in 1780 with 18-inch stone walls, has additions that ramble all the way to the renovated Victorian attic.

After Randy, an AT&T executive in 1984, was introduced to the concept of innkeeping (on the golf course!), it was all of two months before Pineapple Hill was purchased. That's when Suzie left her position as a teacher of the learning disabled to become a full-time innkeeper—and gardener. Her enthusiasm for the outdoors—hiking, biking, and bird-watching—has inspired studies in the wildlife sciences. Together, the Leslies have created an environment where guests mix easily with one another and where there are many conversations about career choices, nature photography, antiquing, and all the area has to offer.

In residence: "Both Mandy, a Lhasa apso, and our cat, Snuggles, appreciate all the attention guests offer."
Restrictions: Weekdays, children should be at least six. Weekends, no children can be accommodated. No smoking inside. No guests' pets.
Bed and bath: Five air-conditioned guest areas. In 1780 part of house, two second-floor double-bedded rooms share a full bath. In separate wing, a second-floor two-room suite with a double-bedded room and one with a queen bed; private bath. On third floor, a suite with double bed in each room, private bath; a double-bedded room with private bath.
Breakfast: Usually 8:30–10. Fresh fruit salad with yogurt, granola, coconut, sunflower seeds, honey. Croissants with homemade jams and jellies. Hot beverage, juices.
Plus: Swimming pool surrounded by stone walls of former barn. Refreshments. Guests' refrigerator. Fireplaced parlor. Books and games. Bedroom fans.

The Wedgwood Inn of New Hope 🏠 ⫯ 🏮

111 West Bridge Street, New Hope, PA 18938
Phone: 215/862-2570
Location: On a tree-lined main residential street with a horse-drawn carriage on the front lawn, a gazebo near the veranda, and another gazebo on the expansive lawn (two acres) in back. Two blocks from the village.
Hosts: Nadine Silnutzer and Carl Glassman
Open: Year round. Reservations recommended. Two-night minimum preferred for weekends, three nights for holidays.
Rates: Weekday/weekend $55/$65 double with semiprivate bath, $65–$85/$75–$115 private bath, $95/$130 two-room suite, $110–$140 suite with fireplace. $120–$150 carriage house. Single $5 less. $15 cot. Corporate and long-term rates available.

> From New Jersey: "Carl and Nadine love what they are doing and truly enjoy their guests."

Weddings have been held in the gazebo. Sometimes there are art exhibits here. Always, there are returnees at this inn, which was chosen for a Commonwealth of Pennsylvania ad campaign.

Carl, an avocational historian, was working at a social policy think tank, and Nadine was in gerontology when, in 1982, they made their "dream come true." Since opening their restored 1870 Victorian inn (with country decor), they have expanded their B&B to include the next-door 1840 Classic Revival stone manor house (a bit more formal, but very comfortable) and its carriage house. Wedgwood pottery, original art (many works by Dinie's aunt), and antiques are throughout. A delightful brick patio connects the two main houses.

The hosts are well aware of the full range of activities in the New Hope area, and sometimes they create their own right here in the inn. In addition to offering apprentice programs and innkeeping seminars, Carl is a licensed Realtor (specializing in inns) and management trainer.

In residence: Jasper (named after Wedgwood's jasperware), a black Lab/springer spaniel mix.
Restrictions: For the inn, children should be at least eight; no age minimum for the carriage house. Sorry, no guests' pets. Smoking allowed on veranda only.
Foreign languages spoken: French, Spanish, Dutch, and Hebrew.
Bed and bath: Twelve rooms—some with working fireplace—include two suites; secluded two-story carriage house has fireplace, kitchenette, air conditioning. Queen, double, and twin beds; private and semiprivate baths. Cot available.
Breakfast: 8–10. Freshly squeezed orange juice, fresh fruit salad, home-baked goods, hot croissants, yogurt, freshly brewed tea and coffee. Served in breakfast room, in parlor bay window, or in your room. Special Passover menu.
Plus: Bedroom air conditioners. Complimentary horse-drawn carriage rides to and from town at set times. Welcoming refreshments; special Saturday afternoon tea. Almond liqueur (homemade) and mints. Turned-

down beds. Fresh flowers. Veranda. Brick walkways through flowering gardens. Parlors with wood-burning stoves. Pool and tennis club privileges. Workshop and meeting facilities.

The Whitehall Inn

RD 2, Box 250, 1370 Pineville Road, New Hope, PA 18938
Phone: 215/598-7945
Location: Secluded. On 13 acres. Once called a plantation, now a working dressage horse farm with walking trails, gardens, fields, majestic chestnut and maple trees. Ten minutes southwest of New Hope. Five minutes from Peddler's Village.
Hosts: Mike and Suella Wass
Open: Year round. Advance reservations required. Two-night minimum on weekends, three nights on holiday weekends.
Rates: Double occupancy. Weekends—private bath $90–$95; with fireplace $100–$125. Shared bath $90–$100. Weekdays, $10 less. AMEX, CB, Diners, Discover, MC, VISA.

When two Oklahomans, a Sun Oil Company executive (Mike) and his speech therapist wife (Suella), experienced their first B&B, they were inspired—by the disaster. As a result, they have been the ultimate innkeepers for four years. They live in an almost-200-year-old manor house that has a curved walnut staircase, wide pine floors, Oriental rugs, and family heirlooms and other fine antiques. Guests are welcomed into rooms with fresh fruit, flowers, imported English toiletries, homemade potpourri, a bottle of Bucks County wine, velour robes, and thirsty towels. Sometimes a string quartet or woodwind group gives a performance here. There are Chocolate Lovers' or Strawberry weekends. And always, Suella's culinary creations. Mike is the maitre d'/waiter/rose gardener who on his day off is career development instructor and doctoral student. Both hosts delight in fulfilling their idea of a fantasy inn.

In residence: Sarah is 11; Todd is 7. (Guests often feed carrots to horses Amy, Greg, and Miles.)
Restrictions: No smoking, please. No children or guests' pets.
Bed and bath: Six rooms—with queen or double bed—on three floors. Private baths (most have tub and shower) for all but two second-floor rooms. Four rooms have working fireplaces.
Breakfast: At 9. Acclaimed by *Bon Appétit*. Their own blend of coffee; 30 teas. Suella's freshly baked coffee cake, yeast bread, and muffins. Freshly squeezed juice. Wide repertoire of appetizers and entrees; may be raspberries picked that morning with chantilly cream plus herbed cheddar cheese dijon souffle. Or cheddar cheese and corn spoon bread followed by fruit/nut/cheese crepes. And Buck's County sausage. Served by candlelight on linen with European china and crystal, heirloom silver. Suella and Mike always join guests.
Plus: Bedroom and dining room air conditioners. Four p.m. tea with pastries and tea sandwiches. Evening wine or sherry. Spacious fireplaced

parlor with pump organ and piano. Pool. Tennis courts (racquets and balls provided). Picnic area. Flannel sheets in winter. Jigsaw puzzle in sun room. Specialty chocolates.

Tattersall Inn

Cafferty and River Road (Route 32), P.O. Box 569, Point Pleasant, PA 18950
Phone: 215/297-8233
Location: Quiet. Surrounded by lawns and century-old trees. A few minutes' walk to Delaware River and canal towpath. Set a little above the village, 15 minutes north of New Hope.
Hosts: Herbert and Gerry Moss
Open: Year round. Reservations required. Two-night minimum stay on weekends. Three-night minimum on holiday weekends.
Rates: $83–$95 weekends, double occupancy. $10 less Monday–Thursday. $15 third person. Senior citizen rates midweek, 15 percent below midweek rates. AMEX, MC, VISA.

> From New York: "It is a full four-star—how about five—inn with low-keyed, warm and helpful hosts. . . . Beautiful, homey and romantic."

Urbanites know they are "away" when they sit on the second-story porch and hear the nearby carillon through the tall spruce. Or when they have cheese and cider in the beamed-ceiling pub room with huge hearth. Or listen to Herb's vintage phonographs in the Victorian dining room.

Each lovely guest room in this restored 18th-century fieldstone manor house with 18-inch-thick walls is decorated with family antiques and Gerry's paintings and embroideries. Until the Mosses took over the inn in 1985, Gerry was editor of RCA's technical abstracting service. Even today she says, "I still can't believe that we actually own Ralph Stover's house after all the wonderful times we had—while the children were growing up—exploring in the park (once part of the property) that was set up to honor him." Herb, part-time consultant now, was with RCA as a materials scientist until his recent retirement.

In residence: Victoria, "a gentle cat not too sure of people."
Restrictions: No guests' pets.
Foreign languages spoken: German. "A little" Czech and Polish.
Bed and bath: Seven large air-conditioned rooms. All private baths. King or queen beds. One suite with queen bed and sitting room. A first-floor room has a canopied queen four-poster and a sofa bed. Cot available.
Breakfast: 8–10. Sometimes earlier, especially for 7 a.m. Tuesday flea market opening. Juice, croissants, whole wheat bread with raisins and/or walnuts, homemade muffins or cakes (maybe poppyseed or apple), jams, honey, milk, hot beverages. Served in candlelit Victorian dining room, on one of the porches, or in your room.

Plus: Library. Old-fashioned pinball game. That wonderful antique phonograph collection. Jukebox. Upright piano. Chocolates. Apples. Book of guests' comments about area restaurants. Wine for special occasions.

The Bridgeton House

River Road, P.O. Box 167, Upper Black Eddy, PA 18972
Phone: 215/982-5856
Location: On the banks of the Delaware River. In a small historic village. A half block from canal towpath; 18 miles north of New Hope. Within walking distance of shops, restaurants, state park.
Hosts: Beatrice and Charles Briggs
Open: Year round. Reservations and two-night minimum weekend stays required April through December.
Rates: Double occupancy. Midweek $55 single, $65–$85 double. Weekends $75–$85 village side, $95 river side, $110 suite. MC, VISA discouraged; cash or personal checks preferred.

"It's a charming new/old place," said one guest of the 1836 Federal brick house rescued by the Briggses eight years ago. As you view the river from French doors or a balcony, sit by the original fireplace (found behind a closet), or admire the Oriental rugs on refinished old floors (which were hidden under 17 layers of linoleum), you may want to look at the before-and-after album to appreciate the dramatic transformation. Charles, a master carpenter/professional restorer of 18th-century buildings/country furniture maker, made many moldings and even designed a lighting fixture. There are baskets, rag rugs, dried flowers—and throughout, antiques, "the comfortable kind. We want our guests to relax."
        And they do, in a building that was first a private residence, then a bakery, and a general store. Before Bridgeton House, Bea and Charles had 10 years' experience in inns and restaurants. They had also collected antiques; they still buy (and sell). Here they offer warm hospitality complete with a "skip-lunch breakfast." One of Bea's favorite suggestions is the covered bridge tour on a back roads route (map and directions provided).

In residence: In hosts' quarters, Ryan, age three. Bridgeton, a Chesapeake Bay retriever.
Restrictions: On weekends, children should be at least eight. Sorry, no guests' pets. Smoking allowed on the veranda only.
Bed and bath: Eight air-conditioned rooms, all private baths. King/twin option, queen, double four-posters (some canopied), plus one suite with king bed, tub bath, working fireplace, screened porch; two more suites in 1989 two-story addition.
Breakfast: 8:30–9:30. Fresh fruits, juices, homemade breads and pastries, coffee and teas. Entrees might be omelets, shirred eggs, or souffles. Eat by the fireplace, by the riverside, or on the deck, porch, or terrace.

Plus: Sherry. Fresh flowers, fruit basket, chocolates, and English toiletries in each room. Tour of inn. Porches. Swimming or tubing off riverbank. Fishing. Sometimes possible to meet guests who arrive by bus in Frenchtown, New Jersey, three miles away. Canoe and bike rentals nearby.

Woodhill Farms Inn

150 Glenwood Drive, Washington Crossing, PA 18977
Phone: 215/493-1974
Location: Secluded. On 10 wooded acres with walking trails and deer. Twenty minutes to Princeton University; 15 minutes south of New Hope. Two miles north of I-95. Near several private schools and corporations.
Hosts: Mary Lou and Donald Spagnuolo
Open: Year round. Two-night minimum on weekends and holidays.
Rates: Sunday–Thursday—$60 single, $70 double. Weekends and holidays—$75 single, $85 double. $15 per cot. Cribs free. Reduced rates for two or more nights. Corporate rates available. AMEX, MC, VISA.

The only built-to-be-a-B&B (10 years ago) in this historic area is unique for many reasons. Many well-traveled guests say that it reminds them of lodges in Germany and Switzerland. Contemporary in style, it has a large living room with beamed cathedral ceiling, floor-to-ceiling fireplace, indoor garden with small fish pond, and circular staircase to the second floor. Works (for sale) by local artists are on the walls. Furnishings in each very-private guest room vary—with rattan, brass, or a cherry four-poster.

When Donald was transferred from Long Island to Pennsylvania as Internal Revenue Service program manager of data processing, the Spanuolos were long-term guests here—and Mary Lou spent some time as assistant innkeeper—before they bought a house in a nearby town. When the innkeepers planned retirement, the Spanuolos agreed that a new career, "one which allows us to share this wonderful area," was "just right." Ask the hosts about the clockmaker, seminar arrangements (right here), or auctions, flea markets or dinner theater. The enthusiasm of the hosts is matched by the guests—

From Pennsylvania, Colorado, Arizona, New York: "Lavish bedroom with sunken tub . . . elegant breakfast . . . even pleased my "mister clean" husband . . . helpful suggestions. . . . Wonderful honeymoon place. . . . Would recommend it even to our most hard-to-please friends. . . . I work at a four-star hotel and feel you would be doing your readers a service by including Woodhill Farms. . . . A home away from home while working. . . . Gracious hosts."

Restrictions: Children 10 and over or infants not yet walking are welcome. Smoking allowed in guest rooms only.
Bed and bath: Five rooms on two levels with no two bedroom walls adjacent to one another. All private baths. King, queen, double, or twin beds; rollaway and crib available.

Breakfast: Monday–Friday 7–9:30; weekends and holidays, 8:45–9:30. Entree might be eggs Benedict with smoked turkey and hollandaise, blueberry pancakes, cheese strata with chives, almond raisin-filled baked apple. Served with china and crystal.
Plus: Central air conditioning. Private phone lines in each room. Individual temperature control. Wine, soft drinks, cheese, fruit, crackers and nuts. Color TV. Babysitting arranged. Fresh flowers. Thick towels. Hair dryers. Amenities basket in each room. Complimentary champagne for special occasions. Kitchen privileges for long-term guests. Travel and relocation information from New York to Washington, D.C.

Hollileif Bed & Breakfast Establishment

677 Durham Road, Route 413, Wrightstown, PA 18940
Phone: 215/598-3100
Location: On five acres with trees, flowers, a garden, and a stream too. In Bucks County, six miles south of New Hope and Peddler's Village.
Hosts: Jan Sauer and Myra Lenoff
Open: Year round. Advance reservations required. Two-night minimum stay on weekends and holidays.
Rates: $95 per room. $15 rollaway. Ten percent less for senior citizens. MC, VISA.

> Guests wrote: "From the minute you arrive and are greeted by Myra and Jan until you are presented with a farewell gift of handmade chocolates, Hollileif is a wonderful escape from everyday life.... Accommodations couldn't be better.... Immaculate ... romantic ... relaxing ... luxurious.... My husband says that waking up to breakfast there is like waking up as a child on Christmas morning.... The hostesses recommended some great attractions and restaurants.... We have introduced my sister and brother-in-law, several friends and our parents to the Hollileif charm."

It's a plastered stone 1700s farmhouse that had been owned by one family for 100 years when teacher Jan, an Arizona native, and Myra, a computer graphics designer, decided to leave Arizona "to mix business with pleasure." On the way to becoming innkeepers they were restorers and decorators, giving the converted house a country feel and naming it after the 40-foot holly trees at the entrance. Pampering is intentional here. As one New Yorker wrote: "An unsurpassable bed and breakfast experience."

In residence: Rags, "a loving Benji-type dog," and Charlie, a Siamese cat.
Restrictions: Children should be at least 14. Smoking restricted to living room and outside patio. Sorry, no guests' pets please.
Bed and bath: Four double-bedded rooms on three floors. All private baths. Rollaway available.
Breakfast: 8:30–10. Bountiful. Freshly brewed coffee and tea, home-baked

breads or muffins, freshly squeezed juices, fruit, and entree that varies daily. Presented in cozy, many-windowed breakfast room at individual tables set with antique china and crystal.

Plus: Central air conditioning. Afternoon or evening tea or wine with snacks by the fire or on the wicker-furnished arbor-covered patio. Fresh flowers. Candies. Turn-down service. Picnic area, outdoor games, hammock.

KEY

Recipes shared, often for house specialties.

Inquiries welcomed about restoration and/or decorating. Symbol indicates that host is willing to share experiences with guests. Tips range from a before-and-after album to rebuilding advice, from furniture refinishing to curtain making. Expertise of hosts ranges from learn-by-doing to professional.

How-to B&B workshop, seminar, or apprentice program offered.

Lehigh Valley/Reading Area Reservation Service

Bed & Breakfast of Southeast Pennsylvania

146 West Philadelphia Avenue, Boyertown, PA 19512
Phone: 215/367-4688. Live most of the time; otherwise answering machine.
Listings: 38. Most are hosted private homes; a few inns and unhosted private residences. Directory is $2; please enclose a business-sized self-addressed stamped envelope.
Rates: $35–$80 single, $35–$100 double. Some homes have $5 one-night surcharge. Weekly rates; some family rates. Twenty-five percent deposit required. Deposit, less $5 service charge, is refunded if cancellation notice is received at least seven days before arrival, otherwise forfeited. MC, VISA.

The service run by Patricia Fedor matches guests to hosts in an "undiscovered rural area where guests enjoy charming restaurants and ethnic and music festivals. Some of our hosts have been known to take guests to auctions or to craft or antique shops."

Communities represented are Allentown, Bally, Bernville, Bethlehem, Coopersburg, East Greenville, Ephrata/Adamstown, Fogelsville, Kulpsville, Kutztown, Landis Store, Leesport, Macungie, Mertztown, Oley, Orwigsburg, Pennsburg, Plumsteadville, Pottstown, Reading, Rehrersburg, Robesonia, Skippack, Springtown, Sumneytown, Womelsdorf, and Yellowhouse. Also some in Lancaster County.

Reservations: Two weeks' advance notice preferred; will try to accommodate last minute requests. Two day minimum on holiday weekends.
Plus: Short-term (two weeks to two months) hosted and a couple of unhosted housing available. Personal service in directing to antiques shops, with maps and any other reasonable request.

Salisbury House

910 East Emmaus Avenue, Allentown, PA 18103
Phone: 215/791-4225
Location: A country setting within 10 minutes of both center city Allentown and Bethlehem, and within 15 minutes of five colleges—Allentown College of St. Francis de Sales, Cedar Crest, Lehigh, Moravian, and Muhlenberg. Forty-five minutes from Philadelphia, Amish country, and the coal regions.
Hosts: Judith and Ollie Orth
Open: Year round. Reservations required.
Rates: Double occupancy. $125 hall bath. $145 private bath. Fifty percent discount on wedding anniversaries to those who honeymooned here on their wedding night. AMEX, MC, VISA.

At the white picket fence, turn into the driveway and park near the tall barn-wood gate flanked by arborvitae. Enter the grounds, where there are acres of mature trees, a well-manicured lawn, a formal boxwood garden with herbs and wildflowers, a small apple orchard, and a Chinese chestnut grove. Take the winding brick path past the greenhouse to the main entrance of this 15-room stone farmhouse.

For about 100 years, Salisbury House, built in 1810, provided lodging for travelers to Philadelphia. A private residence since 1913, it has been home to the Orths for the past six years. Every nook and cranny is furnished with an eclectic mixture of country antiques, Art Deco, Oriental and braided rugs, and a bit of whimsy too.

Preparing gourmet breakfasts is all part of the chosen lifestyle change for Ollie, who formerly owned a structural engineering company. Judith has traded technical writing for interior decorating in a home that is "not just a place to stay but the reason to come."

In residence: One moderate smoker, Judith. Abby, an eight-year-old border collie. Two indoor and two outdoor cats.
Restrictions: Sorry, no accommodations for children or guests' pets. No smoking in bedrooms, please.
Bed and bath: Four well-appointed double-bedded second-floor rooms. Two with private baths.
Breakfast: 7–9. Five courses. Freshly squeezed orange juice, Chinese chestnuts with maple sugar granules, a fruit dish, homemade baked goods, coffee or tea, "an intermezzo, then the entree which might be Eggs Salisbury with crockpudding potatoes." Served by candlelight in front of huge colonial fireplace; in summer, al fresco.

Plus: Ceiling and window fans. Three fires burning in winter. Electric blankets. Fine linens. Second-floor sitting room. Library. Three patios, nature trails, hammock hung by the creek, a lily pond.

From Connecticut: "We loved the house. Food and hospitality were outstanding."

Bally Spring Farm

Barto, PA
Location: On 100 acres. Midway between Allentown and Pottstown. Near antiquing, farm markets, outlet shopping (half hour away), Doe Mountain ski area. One mile from Route 100; 45 minutes from Philadelphia; 90 from Manhattan.
Reservations: Year round through Bed & Breakfast of Southeast Pennsylvania, 235.
Rates: $55 single, $65 double.

Arrive in your private plane, if you have one! Regardless of your transportation means, you are welcome to explore the grounds of this gentleman's estate, swim in the heated indoor pool, or fish in the six-acre lake. The 1734 stone farmhouse is home to a host who restores antiques, including old radios, and his wife, an educator. The well-traveled couple enjoy meeting other travelers and find that B&B is a wonderful way to share the unique house they have lived in for the last six years.

In residence: Three children, ages five, three, and one. Two golden retrievers. One outside cat.
Restrictions: No smoking. Sorry, no guests' pets.
Foreign languages spoken: Fluent French. Some Spanish.
Bed and bath: Four second-floor rooms, all with queen beds. One with private shower bath. Three share a full bath. Rollaway and crib available.
Breakfast: 7–10. Country breakfast. Fruit, cereal, juice, muffins, sausage, bacon, eggs, home fries, toast, coffee, tea. Served in dining room or on deck overlooking the creek.
Plus: Central air conditioning. Private runway. Tea or wine. Babysitting. Fresh flowers. Bring fishing equipment for lake stocked with bass and stream stocked with trout.

From Maryland: "This was our first B&B experience and we loved it. Lovely setting. And their dinner recommendation was truly outstanding."

Sunday's Mill Farm

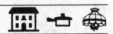

Bernville, PA

Location: Rural. On Tulpehocken Creek, 45 minutes from Amish country. Near auctions, flea markets, wineries, Reading outlets. Five minutes from skiing, 15 minutes to the Appalachian Trail, half an hour to Hawk Mountain. Four miles from Bernville and Womelsdorf.

Reservations: Year round through Bed & Breakfast of Southeast Pennsylvania, page 235.

Rates: Queen bed, $45 single, $55 double. Double bed, $35 single, $45 double. $70 for family of four. $10 child with sleeping bag.

Newlyweds are given a bottle of Sunday's Mill labeled wine and the tradition is repeated when they return on an anniversary. Others "arrive as strangers and leave as friends" at this 1850s Pennsylvania German brick farmhouse, which is on the National Register of Historic Places.

A high school reunion brought the host back just about the time he and his wife began thinking about retiring (from pillow manufacturing, real estate, and interior decorating) and moving from a recently built home to an old one. Now they are involved in having the Tulpehocken Creek designated as a Scenic River. The hostess, a quilt maker, is working on a study of county industry from 1700 to 1850, and her husband, a painter, is working with mentally retarded adults. To add to their collection of antiques, they restore furniture acquired at auctions and flea markets. They have a small Hereford cattle operation. In addition to sharing hints for discovering their fascinating area, the hosts will show you their 1820 mill (on the property), which still has some parts intact. Canoes are delivered for use on the creek. And you can walk in the woods or along the Old Union Canal towpath.

In residence: Some horses and two dogs owned by a tenant on the property.

Restrictions: Smokers are requested to ask before smoking indoors. Sorry, no guests' pets.

Bed and bath: Two second-floor rooms with quilts. One with queen bed and private half bath. The other has a double antique rope bed. Full bath shared by guests and hosts.

Breakfast: Usually 7–9. Juice or fresh fruit, tea, coffee. Deep-dish apple pancake with sausage, homemade muffins, or scrapple and coddled eggs. Served by dining room or kitchen fireplace.

Plus: Central air conditioning. Beverages. TV in living room. Guest pickup (no charge) at Reading airport, Lancaster train, or Reading bus. Kitchen privileges. Fishing on state-stocked Tulpehocken Creek or pond on premises. Cross-country skiing.

The Loom Room

RD 1, Box 1420, Leesport, PA 19533

Phone: 215/926-3217

Location: Rural. Surrounded by two and a half acres of lawn and flower and herb gardens. Two miles north of Reading airport, just off Route 183 in Berks County. Within 25 minutes of antiques shops in Adamstown and Kutztown; 15 minutes to Reading outlets.

Hosts: Gene and Mary Smith
Open: Year round. Advance reservations requested.
Rates: Double occupancy. $40 shared bath, $45 private bath. $15 extra adult. Under age 15, free. Seventh day free.

There's a wonderful story behind this B&B. *Now* the 1812 stone house with two-foot-thick walls is "comfortable and antiquey," with open-beam ceilings, five working fireplaces, and country primitives everywhere. In 1975, when Mary and Gene, teachers and area residents "for years," were looking for a country cupboard, they chanced upon the auction of the neglected house. Two hours later they owned "the perfect place for a weaving studio and shop"—a 10-room center hall colonial that had been a home, tavern, hotel, stagecoach stop, halfway house, general store, and post office. The "buy," which required all of Gene's building expertise, became the site of the Smiths' wedding—by the great summer kitchen walk-in fireplace. Gene opened a tool sharpening business and Mary established her enterprise for beautiful custom classic handwoven fashions (for men and women). The local conservancy awarded the Smiths an historical plaque. And then a 1985 B&B trip to Germany influenced the decision to add hosting to their activities.

This B&B has a very sharing style, with many conversations taking place by the living room fire and with tours of the reconstructed 1760 log house (another Gene job) where Mary weaves and displays the clothing she creates. And from the cupboard that *was* eventually found, for each female guest, the parting gift of a homemade sachet.

In residence: Mimi and Maytag, male tiger "guest-oriented" cats.
Restrictions: Children of all ages welcome. Smoking on first floor only. Sorry, no guests' pets.
Bed and bath: Three second-floor rooms reached by "a stairway that is not steep at all." Two double-bedded rooms, each with working fireplace, share a full bath. Private shower bath for room with a double bed, one twin bed, and a daybed. Rollaway and crib available.
Breakfast: Usually 8:30. (Preceded by a wakeup tray of coffee or tea and juice brought to your door.) French toast with homemade fruit sauce, local sausage or bacon, chipped beef on home fries. Homemade muffins, jams, and preserves. Coffee and teas. Served in kitchen, in dining room, or in Gene-built gazebo. Hosts join guests.
Plus: Air conditioning and ceiling fans in bedrooms. Tea or coffee and pastry. Gene's "incredible before-bed sundaes and banana splits."

Longswamp Bed and Breakfast

RD 2, Box 26, Mertztown, PA 19539
Phone: 215/682-6197
Location: In a rural village. About 15 minutes southwest of Allentown

and east of Kutztown; 40 minutes to Reading outlets. Within 8 minutes of Route 100, Doe Mountain ski area, horseback riding. Excellent restaurant nearby.

Hosts: Elsa and Dean Dimick
Open: Year round. Reservations preferred.
Rates: $50 single, $60 double, $65 "Hideaway." $30 third person in room. No charge for babies. MC, VISA.

> From Massachusetts: "Extraordinarily comfortable home . . . tastefully appointed . . . unbelievable breakfasts. Fresh fruits, vegetables and herbs from the garden, thick cream as I've only seen in England, eggs, waffles, quiches, all prepared with Elsa's unusual skill and creativity. The Dimicks obviously enjoy their enterprise and making their guests feel welcome."

With just one child at home, Elsa, a caterer and psychiatric counselor, and her husband, chief of medicine of the Lehigh Valley Hospital Center, moved six years ago from Allentown to this lovely 200-year-old Federal house "to have a whole new challenge." Grateful guests include business travelers as well as vacationers who appreciate attention to detail. They relax by the fire. They enjoy the collections of books, magazines, games, records, and tapes. Some walk in the woods. "Most want to be part of what's going on. A few value privacy above all." Antiquers love the location—and so do sports-oriented visitors. From the Dimicks' point of view, "guests are terrific."

In residence: One grown son, an artist with a studio in the barn. Clyde is a "loving black Lab." Several outdoor cats not allowed in house.
Restrictions: Sorry, no guests' pets. No smoking in bedrooms.
Foreign language spoken: French.
Bed and bath: Nine rooms with Amish quilts and lovingly restored antiques. Five with private bath; four share two baths. In main house, six rooms on second and third floors with a queen bed, a double, or a queen and a single. "Hideaway cottage" (1700s house that was part of Underground Railroad) has first-floor common room with TV; two bedrooms (one tucked under eaves with skylight), each with twin beds, a working fireplace, and a private shower bath. In west level of cottage, a separate hideaway with queen bed, working fireplace, private bath. Cot available.
Breakfast: 8–11 Sundays, 6:30–10:30 other days. Bountiful and beautiful. From huge repertoire. By fireplace in summer kitchen overlooking lawns and fields.
Plus: Beverages (often before dinner). Bedroom ceiling fans. Second-floor veranda rockers. Potpourri. Current magazines. Shampoos, lotions. Basketball court *in* the barn. Ping-Pong. Bicycles (no charge). Celebrations honored. Use of refrigerator. Horseshoe pits. Bocce court.

Fairway Farm

Vaughan Road, Pottstown, PA 19464
Phone: 215/326-1315
Location: In rural Chester County. Just off Route 422, Pottstown Express-

way. Within 20 minutes of Amish country, King of Prussia, Reading, Valley Forge; 40 minutes to Brandywine Valley's Longwood Gardens, Winterthur, Brandywine River Museum.
Hosts: Katherine and Franz Streitwieser
Open: Year round except for Christmas or Thanksgiving. Advance reservations required.
Rates: $45 single, $60 double. $10 under age 10.

After the "Today" television program featured the world's only Trumpet Museum, the phone rang here for days. And after eight years of inviting museum visitors to tea, the Streitwiesers found B&B a natural next step. "Our large fieldstone farmhouse, built in 1734, has furnishings and artifacts we brought with us when we came from southern Germany in 1978. It's home, like a favorite old sweater that feels good on anybody. Since being restored and named by a golfer in the 1930s, the property has more lawns than fields. It's a very peaceful setting—appreciated by relocators as well as travelers—with an outdoor hot tub overlooking the pond. Guests swim in the spring-fed pool, use the sauna and tennis courts too. But Franz' tour is what is truly special. An internationally recognized lecturer, historian and trumpet soloist, he is a walking encyclopedia about all 650 brass instruments in the 1860 converted pegged barn. It seems that people are constantly discovering us!"
Maybe Franz will be mowing on a tractor when you arrive. Or perhaps Katherine will tour you through her weaving studio. No wonder the hosts mention that they "try to be through with breakfast by 11."

In residence: Hoan assists the Streitwiesers. King, a golden retriever; Geza, a white Hungarian Kuvasz; Striker, a mixed breed; Sparky, a friendly Lhasa apso.
Restrictions: Children should be supervised and well behaved. No smoking inside. Sorry, no guests' pets.
Foreign languages spoken: Fluent German. Limited French and Vietnamese.
Bed and bath: Four rooms with private baths (shower only or full) on second and third floors with queen or king bed. Bunk beds with curtain "door" for children on second level. Rollaway bed and crib available.
Breakfast: 8–10. Freshly squeezed orange juice, fruit, farm fresh eggs, bacon, homemade bread, special coffee blend, cereal. Waffles or crepes. By dining room or kitchen wood stove, on screened porch, or in gazebo overlooking pond.
Plus: Bedroom air conditioners and ceiling fans. European feather beds. Wool fleece mattress covers. Fresh flowers. Fruit. Addresses for homemade quilts. For museum tour and demonstrations, suggested donation ($2.50). Sometimes, Sunday afternoon concerts.

Hiwwelhaus (House on a Hill)

Womelsdorf, PA
Location: Peaceful. In Pennsylvania Dutch country on a hillside with a rural view. Minutes to Amish country of Lancaster County, Reading out-

lets, and Hershey. Near hiking, Heidelberg ski area, and Mount Hope Winery.
Reservations: April–October through Bed & Breakfast of Southeast Pennsylvania, page 235.
Rates: $40 single, $55 double.

The log house with many antiques and locally made handcrafts is located on 26 acres of the host's original dairy farm. She is a painter and quilter who edits a church newsletter. "Having spent a few years teaching in an Amish school, I enjoy sharing my experiences with my guests, people who seem to be considerate, well-traveled or just lovely folks!"

Restrictions: Children five and over are welcome. Smoking outside only. Sorry, no guests' pets.
Foreign language spoken: German.
Bed and bath: Two rooms, each with a king-sized bed. One on first floor with private full bath and access to a small balcony. One on second floor with private shower bath. "Extra" second-floor room with twin bed shares shower bath.
Breakfast: 8–9. Fresh fruit, coffee, tea, omelet, hotcakes, bacon, eggs, fresh biscuits or muffins. Served in dining area adjoining the kitchen or on porch.
Plus: Tea or wine. Bedroom ceilng fans. Living room with quiet music. Porch.

The Beach Lake Hotel

Main Street and Church Road, P.O. Box 144, Beach Lake, PA 18405
Phone: 717/729-8239
Location: In a tiny country village off a main road "in the quiet part of the Poconos." In an area of rolling farmland. Five miles from the Delaware River with its tubing, rafting, canoeing (pickup arranged). Three minutes' walk to lake with swimming, boating, fishing, and ice skating. Near Woodloch Pines resort, Mount Tone and Masthope ski areas.
Hosts: Erika and Roy Miller
Open: Year round. Advance reservations preferred.
Rates: $85 per room. MC, VISA.

> Guests wrote: "A fantasy fulfilled. . . . One of the finer inns in the Northeast. . . . Originally recommended to us by friends who were impressed by the food and the decor. . . . Erika and Roy are a fountain of information on local folklore and roads away from the leaf peepers. . . . Old-fashioned country charm with antiques and accessories all in beautiful condition, and all for sale! . . . An elegant but laid-back kind of style. . . . Clean, clean, clean. . . . We were looking for property and Roy connected us with a Realtor. . . . We had a field day in their filled-to-the-brim country store which has reasonably-priced antiques and collectibles. . . . Loved this place so much we thought of keeping it a secret. . . . Reflects a lot of hard work and intelligent research by an interesting couple. . . . A sense of being transplanted back in time."

Guests' enthusiasm is matched by the Millers, two former health administrators who have fulfilled their own fantasy of combining interests in cooking, interior design, antiques, restoration, music, and theater. After searching all over New England and Bucks County, Pennsylvania, they followed up on a 1986 *Country Living* magazine ad and fell in love with this place, which began as a hotel and tavern around 1859. Through one year's work, they restored wainscoting, made the second-floor porch accessible to all, and put in all private baths. In the basement they found the post office sign, used sometime between 1879 and 1936. Family pictures are in the 15-foot-high living room. And along with "Have you always lived here?" they are often asked about sources for reproduction Victorian wallpapers, woodwork, curtains, and pedestal sinks.

In residence: Two small dogs "who are seldom apparent to guests."
Restrictions: Smoking allowed in common areas. "For your comfort we have no accommodations for children or pets."
Foreign language spoken: Polish.
Bed and bath: Six rooms on second and third floors. All private baths;

most are shower only, one has claw-foot tub. All double beds; two are four-posters, one requires a step stool.
Breakfast: 7–9:30. Entree might be apple pancakes and brandied grape sauce; eggs Benedict; poached eggs in artichoke bottoms with watercress hollandaise; mushroom and onion, or cheese omelets. Homemade popovers, muffins, or coffee cakes and preserves. Juices. Hot beverages.
Plus: Air conditioned bedrooms. Tea, wine, cheese, crackers. Fresh fruit in rooms. Tour of house and area. Dinner ($20–$30) Thursday–Monday. Thick towels. Bubble bath. TV in common room.

Brookview Manor Bed and Breakfast Inn

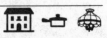

RD 1, Box 365, Canadensis, PA 18325
Phone: 717/595-2451
Location: On Route 447 and the Broadhead Stream "in the heart of the Poconos." On 400 acres with lawns, gardens, tall hemlocks, trout-stocked streams, "and trails that lead to secret waterfalls." Five minutes to Pocono Playhouse, Promiseland State Park, Alpine Mountain ski area, fine dining. About two hours from New York or Philadelphia.
Hosts: Jane and Jim McKeon
Open: Year round. Two-night minimum weekend stays preferred during summer, fall, and winter months.
Rates: Per person. $35–$40 two-room suite with private bath and sitting area. $25 other doubles or studio with twin beds. Carriage house $150 complete (sleeps six). Midweek ski special, $50 per couple. MC, VISA.

"A guest who had scheduled her wedding in another state changed plans after staying here. Another, from Texas, had searched the whole Mid-Atlantic region for a place that would be just right for 24 guests and harp music. This manor house, built as an opulent summer house with heavy paneled doors in 1911, was a guest home for 40 years when we bought and restored it in 1985. We researched everything from architecture to period furnishings, historic paint colors and papers. And we're having a ball in what *Mid-Atlantic Country* magazine called our 'cozy but not pretentious' inn which features European-style hospitality, four working fireplaces, stained glass windows, art work and collectibles."

In New Jersey, Jim was a professional contractor. Jane knows the world of theater as a singer, dancer, manager, and marketing and sales representative. The hosts' interest in foods extends to special cooking weekends and their catering of small affairs. Their interest in informality allowed for an impromptu tempura cooking demonstration by one non-English-speaking Japanese guest.

In residence: In hosts' quarters, Erin Lyn, age 14, and Adam James, age 13.
Restrictions: "Sorry, no facilities for children under 12 or pets. We are a nonsmoking inn."
Bed and bath: Seven rooms. In main house, four double-bedded second-floor rooms with private full baths. One has working fireplace, one a

private porch. In pastel-decorated carriage house, three bedrooms with double or twin beds, sitting room, one full bath, and a ground-floor studio room with twin beds, private full bath, and porch.

Breakfast: 8–9:30. "Country gourmet" might include cinnamon spiced apples, French toast grenadine, baked eggs with Texas cheese sauce, or strawberry crepes. Fresh fruit, home-baked breads, muffins and rolls, apple Betty crunch. Served in fireplaced dining room.

Plus: "Complimentary snacks always on hand." Wraparound porch with rockers and swings. Garden patio. Lawn games. Bicycles. Popular hiking and (ungroomed) cross-country trails here.

Nearbrook

RD 1, Box 630, Canadensis, PA 18325
Phone: 717/595-3152
Location: In the heart of the Poconos. On a state road between I-80 and I-84, on property bounded by rose and rock gardens and, in back, woods and a fresh mountain stream. Within 10 minutes of Pocono Playhouse, downhill and cross-country skiing, hiking, Buck Hill Falls, roller skating, tennis, golf course, indoor pool, state parks, and antiques and crafts shops. Thirty minutes from East Stroudsburg University.
Hosts: Barb and Dick Robinson
Open: Year round. Two-night minimum stay on weekends.
Rates: $25 single. Double $40/$45 shared bath, $50 private bath. Weekly rates available.

Guests wrote: "Delightfully homey and at the same time, a relaxed setting that inspires creativity.... Contagious informality with heartfelt laughter.... Loved the sound of the babbling stream at night."

Winding rock paths through the gardens lead over a tiny arched bridge to the casual comfortable home of two former Philadelphia teachers who have hosted and made many changes here in the last 15 years.

"Among many memorable guests are those who bring a love of life and live it here at Nearbrook. One guest who, after learning that I had taught ninth grade art, returned to study the head in charcoal and clay. [Barb also offers sessions in watercolor and sketching.] Another, a night club pianist who had injured his hand, discovered the tone of our old upright and subsequently returned to his occupation. Other guests find what interests them most with the maps we offer. We started B&B after our sons were grown and have enjoyed every minute of it."

Restrictions: No smoking please.
Bed and bath: Four rooms with sink in each. First-floor double room with private shower bath. On second floor—one double-bedded room shares a full bath with one room that has king/twins bed option. Single room has a private halfbath.
Breakfast: Full and hearty. Menu decided night before. Dick cooks. Barb

serves in dining room or on long porch that overlooks one of the rock gardens. Often, the Robinsons "sooner or later" join guests who are not in a hurry.

Plus: Croquet, toboggan, trunk full of games.

LaAnna Guest House

RD 2, Box 1051, Cresco, PA 18326
Phone: 717/676-4225
Location: Off the beaten path in the town of LaAnna, between Cresco and Newfoundland on Route 191. Nine miles from I-80 and I-84. One mile to shops and restaurants.
Hosts: Kay Swingle and daughter, Julie Wilson
Open: Year round.
Rates: $25 single, $30 double.

This informally run place, which returnees treat like home—"a traditional European-style B&B, not a country inn"—is on a paved road in a wooded area. Kay Swingle acquired the family homestead in 1974, just a hundred years after her grandfather built it as a wedding gift for his bride. It had remained a private home until real estate salesperson Kay, having traveled B&B in Europe, decided to welcome guests in the rural setting.

The trout-stocked pond is used for skating; cross-country skiers track down a country road; downhill skiers go to Camelback or Buck Hill. Summer guests swim (a short drive), hike, and visit in the Poconos.

Bed and bath: Four second-floor rooms with two shared baths. A double and a twin bed in the Blue Room. One double and two twins in the Green Room. The Red Room and Gold Room each has a double bed. All are very large rooms furnished with Empire and Victorian antiques. Two shared baths. Crib available.
Breakfast: 8–12. Juice, muffins, coffee or tea.
Plus: Wonderful mountain views at top of hill about 500 yards behind the house. Waterfalls on the property of Holley Ross Pottery, just across the road.

Academy Street Bed & Breakfast

528 Academy Street, Hawley, PA 18428
Phone: 717/226-3430
Location: In a quiet residential neighborhood. Five minutes from Lake Wallenpaupak. Near blueberry picking and playhouse. Close to Route 6 and I-84. Two hours northwest of New York City.
Hosts: Judith and Sheldon Lazan
Open: May–October, just weekends in spring and fall. Reservations preferred.

Rates: $65–$70 double with shared bath, $75 double with private bath. $35 extra person in a room. MC, VISA.

As Sheldon says, "The lake is the big attraction here. At our home, it sometimes feels like a family reunion, when actually no one knew each other before." That's how it can be in the Italianate-style Victorian house that the Lazans bought in 1983 as a B&B after having a summer residence in Hawley for six years. It was built in 1863 by Joseph Atkinson, a lumberyard owner who used much premium oak and cherry throughout. Judith and Sheldon finished the restoration started by the previous owner, a commercial artist. The eclectic decor of the large airy rooms is fresh and crisp with fresh flowers and plants.

The Lazans, parents of three grown children, have lived in Brooklyn, Long Island, Cincinnati (where Judith had a restaurant), and New Jersey. Sheldon, an engineer, weekend host, "and maintenance man," currently works for a New York real estate syndicator. Full-time innkeeper Judith ("I love to fuss") bakes and cooks the gourmet breakfasts.

Restrictions: Sorry, no accommodations for children. Smoking (with care) allowed.
Bed and bath: Seven air-conditioned rooms on first and second floors. Two with private bath; two with private half bath; three with semiprivate bath. Queen, double, or twin beds. One with queen and a single. One with double and a single. Cots available.
Breakfast: 8–10. Buffet. Varied menu. Repertoire includes strawberry soup, baked eggs, amaretto pudding, quiche, French toast. Juices, fruit compote, homemade muffins, breads, croissants.
Plus: Amaretto coffee, tea, and cakes, 2–4 p.m. Most rooms have cable TV. Lawn games.

The Harry Packer Mansion

Packer Hill, Jim Thorpe, PA 18229
Phone: 717/325-8566
Location: Overlooking a Victorian village center, a national historic district, where three mountains converge in "the Switzerland of America." Ten minutes from Jack Frost and Big Boulder ski areas in the Poconos. Near swimming, rafting.
Hosts: Pat and Bob Handwerk
Open: Year round. Reservations required.
Rates: $65–$75 double, $110 suite. $10 cot. Package rates for murder mystery (just about every weekend now) or Victorian weekends include dinner. MC, VISA.

Some cabin the woods! That's what Bob and Pat were looking for when they took a detour five years ago and explored the town that Bob had never been to even though he grew up a half hour from here. The amazing story of how this B&B "happened" starts with the Handwerks' tour of Asa Parker's mansion next door and their discovery of an over-turned "for sale" sign on this brick property (in shambles then), which was built in 1874 as a wedding present from the founder of the Lehigh Valley Railroad and Lehigh University to his son. Before Pat and Bob moved here, they hired local residents to give tours through the reception room (which has a chandelier purchased at the Philadelphia Centennial Exposition), the solid mahogany handcrafted library, the formal parlors, and the dining room with five different inlaid woods. A community Christmas party proved that the furnace really did work. As Bob, an urban planner and architect, and Pat, a marketing executive, refurbished each room, someone would ask to stay in it. Meanwhile, Taylor was born. The Handwerks sold their big Philadelphia house and moved all their antique furnishings here. Pat left her Philadelphia job. Eventually Bob, too, became full-time restorer, innkeeper, and, in town, shopkeeper.

The completed restoration includes Gentleman's Parlor wallpaper that has been reproduced by Thibault Wallcoverings. Still called "the spook house on the hill" by some of the local children, the setting for mystery weekends and Victorian balls has been discovered by honey-mooners, skiers, and tourists. The whole town of 5,000, once a coal shipping port, has been discovered by architects, historians, and restoration buffs. Pat is historical society president. And the regularly scheduled tours of the Harry Packer Mansion, a National Register landmark, are less than stuffy. ("We don't gild the lily. Harry was a party boy.") Overnight guests might, in addition, hear young Taylor's version of this Second Empire mansion, which was used as a model for Disneyland's haunted mansion. The Handwerks are "having great fun in our cabin."

In residence: Taylor, age five. Bob smokes. Tiger, a Maltese, "is very friendly, does not shed and loves affection."

Restrictions: No guests' pets. Smoking on first floor only.

Bed and bath: Fourteen rooms. Eight in main house with semiprivate baths, working fireplaces. Second-floor rooms are "very Victorian"; third-floor rooms are light and airy. Double or twin beds; cots and crib available. One suite with private full bath, spacious sitting room with hand-painted ceiling. In carriage house, eight queen-bedded "country-decorated" rooms, all with private baths.

Breakfast: Homemade muffins, breads, and jam, eggs or French toast, fresh fruit and beverage. Served in dining room or on veranda.

Plus: Beverages. Bedroom ceiling fans. Kitchen privileges. Laundry facilities. Directions to spectacular waterfalls and a castle ruin, both within walking distance. Tour of house (free to guests). High tea ($5.50) open to public, summer weekends, 3–5 p.m., on beautiful stone porch with tile floor.

Black Walnut Country Inn

509 Fire Tower Road, RD 2, Box 9285, Milford, PA 18337
Phone: 717/296-6322
Location: Up a long winding drive to a 150-acre estate overlooking a four-

acre pond. One mile from I-84 in tri-state area near canoeing and rafting on the Delaware River, antiquing, skiing, horseback riding.
Hosts: Stewart and Effie Schneider
Open: Year round. Two-night minimum on holidays.
Rates: Tax included. Double occupancy. $84.70 weekends and holidays, $60.50 weekdays and December–April weekends. AMEX, MC, VISA.

"When I come to this Garden of Eden, it's a whole new world. You can see stars. You can walk through the fields, see geese, ducks, rabbits, deer. The entire estate, including this Tudor-style stone house, has been renovated in a country motif. A few years ago we added a dining room and a wraparound porch overlooking the pond. Our guests seem to use this as a relaxing base for touring. Often, they go out on the lake in a paddleboat before dinner. When they return from one of the nearby lovely restaurants, they join us for dessert and coffee. Our guests feel like family."
Stu is a New York City supermarket manager during the week. Effie's recipes—for pies and strudel and cakes, made with fruits from the orchard here—are big hits.

In residence: Assisting staff members. Rex, a black Labrador retriever who announces guests' arrival and greets all with wagging tail.
Restrictions: No children or guests' pets. Smoking is not allowed in the main dining room or in bedrooms.
Bed and bath: Twelve rooms, many with antique brass beds, on second and third floors. Four with private baths. Four with private half baths. Two shared baths. Queen, double, or twin beds available.
Breakfast: 8:30–10. French toast, bacon, ham, sausage, bagels, lox, cream cheese, and a homemade streusel cake or muffins. Juice, fruit, coffee and tea. Served in dining room or on wraparound deck.
Plus: After-dinner pie and coffee. Large marble fireplace. Piano. VCR. TV. Pool table. Board games. Ping-Pong. Swimming. Fishing. Hot tub. Lawn games. Cross-country skiing (no groomed trails).

The Nethercott Inn

Main Street, P.O. Box 26, Starrucca, PA 18462
Phone: 717/727-2211
Location: In a tiny Endless Mountains borough with a population of about 150. Ten miles from the Starrucca Viaduct (150-year-old railroad bridge still in use); 35 miles from Binghamton, New York, and 45 from Scranton, Pennsylvania; 19 miles to Elk Mountain and Mount Tone ski areas. Near streams for fishing.
Hosts: Ned and Ginny Nethercott
Open: Year round. Advance reservations requested.
Rates: Per room. $45 shared bath, $60 private bath. $35 room with twin beds. $95 family suite. $10 extra child. No charge for crib or cradle. MC, VISA.

The sign on the front lawn came with Ned and Ginny in 1986 when they moved from their ranch house B&B in California. "We love old houses so when Ned retired from the Air Force, we searched for one in a quiet town. This Victorian—in what was once a thriving tannery and lumber community—seemed right for our dream of a B&B with an antiques shop."

For a hint of the complete renovation, see the before-and-after photo album. The house is carpeted throughout and "furnishings are in the style of 1893 with hands-on antiques so you aren't afraid to touch anything. Our style of hosting means that all our guests are like family when they leave."

Restrictions: Well-behaved children of all ages welcome. Smoking allowed in the kitchen. No pets, please.
Bed and bath: Six second-floor rooms with mountain views. Family suite with private bath has one room with queen bed, one with double bed, youth bed, crib, cradle. Private shower baths for queen-bedded room and a double-bedded room. Full bath shared by one room with queen bed (sink in room) and another with two twin beds.
Breakfast: 8–9:30. Fruit compote, pitcher of orange juice, homemade sweet breads, special blend of decaf and regular coffees. In dining room on crystal and china.
Plus: Use of sleds and bicycles. Wraparound veranda.

Tyler Hill Bed & Breakfast

Route 371, P.O. Box 62, Tyler Hill, PA 18469
Phone: 717/224-6418
Location: Overlooking the Upper Delaware Valley, 2½ miles from the river, north of the Poconos and west of the Catskills. Near auctions, a cider mill, canoeing, train rides, classical music concerts at wildlife sanctuary, horseback riding, and skiing; 20 minutes from Monticello, New York, and Honesdale, Pennsylvania.
Hosts: Wayne Braffman and Roberta Crane
Open: Year round except March. Two-day minimum stay on holiday weekends.
Rates: $75 per room. $20 third person. MC, VISA.

From England: "Of all the holiday homes we stayed in, Tyler Hill was a highlight. . . . From the front porch swing to the best cup of tea we tasted in America, from the magazines in the loo to the lovely paper room with old postcards and advertisements which brought back a lot of memories. . . . Original and beautiful breakfasts with out-of-this-world muffins. . . . A feeling of peace and tranquility."

Many other very detailed letters have been written by getaway travelers, camp parents, and business people, all raving about the hosts at this "jewel" created by a former Newark Symphony Hall director (Wayne's vision made restoration of the hall a reality) and his wife, who was a Newark city photographer and gallery director. They were married on the stage of Symphony Hall following a symphony concert, much to the joy of both the orchestra, which played the wedding march, and the audience.

Until 1986 Tyler Hill was their own getaway. When Roberta and Wayne decided to make a career change and move to the country, they restored and refurnished, using "Mother's attic" and works representing dozens of artists. Wayne has become chef par excellence and cookbook author; Roberta, a design consultant. Their fun-to-read newsletter keeps you up to date on their latest theme weekend or area discovery. Joie de vivre—it's here.

In residence: Roberta smokes. Critter assumes classic cat poses. Loud is pure white and part Siamese. Nice, a long-haired calico, is rarely seen by guests. Nine hens provide fresh brown eggs.
Restrictions: Children should be at least eight. Sorry, no guests' pets. Smoking allowed downstairs only.
Bed and bath: Four rooms share two full baths. King, double, and twin beds and a cot available.
Breakfast: "When you want it!" With classical music playing. Maybe peaches poached in wine, eggs Benedict on homemade English muffins, homemade jams, or French toast with cream cheese and pecan filling. Freshly ground and brewed coffees or teas blended from the herb garden.
Plus: Bedroom air conditioners. VCR and nearly 200 movies. Extensive record collection and library. Evening sherry, port, or brandy. Use of rowboat on quiet, stocked lake. Tyler Hill nightshirts. Laundry. Paper Room gift shop.

Pennsylvania Dutch Country Reservation Services

Bed & Breakfast of Lancaster County

P.O. Box 19, Mountville, PA 17554
Phone: 717/285-7200. Year round, Tuesday–Sunday, 9–2 and 4–9. Closed Monday.
Listings: 40 hosted private residences. Some inns. Directory $2 plus business-size self-addressed stamped envelope.
Rates: $40–$50 single, $55–$75 double. Ten percent discount for senior citizens. Cost of first night required as deposit. If cancellation is received at least seven days before arrival date, deposit (less $10 service fee) will be refunded. MC, VISA.

Pat Reno, a longtime resident and antiques dealer, has been involved in B&B for five years. She selects hosts who are "warm friendly people who also enjoy meeting people." They live in Lancaster County (home of the Amish and President Buchanan); Hershey (chocolate world); Gettysburg (Battlefield); Harrisburg (capital); Honeybrook (countryside, farms, the Maryland line). Among communities represented are Mount Joy, Churchtown, Columbia, Marietta, Ephrata, Mountville, and Strasburg. Many listings are historic homes and/or farmhouses.

Reservations: One week's advance notice required during the summer; 24 hours at other times of year. Two-day minimum stay on weekends.
Plus: Short-term (maximum two weeks) housing available.

Hershey Bed & Breakfast Reservation Service

P.O. Box 208, Hershey, PA 17033
Phone: 717/533-2928. Monday–Friday 10–4. Answering machine at other times.
Listings: 25. Most are private hosted homes; three are inns. Located throughout southeastern Pennsylvania, including Hershey, Middletown, Harrisburg, Lancaster, Lebanon, Mount Gretna, Gettysburg, and Hanover. Send a self-addressed stamped envelope for a directory.
Rates: $40–$45 single, $45–$90 double. Deposit required is 25 percent of total cost of stay. Refunds less $10 service charge made if cancellation is received at least 48 hours prior to arrival date.

Renee Deutel knows her hosts and their homes—and she is fussy! She has places that are perfect for honeymooners, places where kids can milk a cow, places where you can gather your own eggs or just enjoy country living in an atmosphere of friendliness with easy access to many recreation facilities. "Be it a private home, an estate, a Mennonite farm, or country inn, our hosts with a variety of interesting backgrounds are pleased to offer hospitality."

Reservations: Two-week advance notice preferred. Last-minute requests filled if possible. Available through travel agents.

Plus: "Anything needed to make a trip special."

Some B&Bs in Pennsylvania Dutch Country are also represented by:

Bed & Breakfast of Philadelphia, page 198.
Bed & Breakfast of Valley Forge/Philadelphia, page 199.
Guesthouses, page 200.

Can't find the community you are going to? Check with a reservation service described at the beginning of this chapter. Through the service, you may be placed (matched) with a welcoming B&B that is near your destination.

Spring House

Muddy Creek Forks, Airville, PA 17302
Phone: 717/927-6906
Location: Over a running spring in a tiny (population: 17) pre-Revolutionary village. Very rural and scenic, off the beaten track (detailed directions are useful). Five miles from shops; 30 minutes southeast of York; 45 minutes southwest of Lancaster.
Host: Ray Constance Hearne
Open: Year round. Two-night weekend stays preferred.
Rates: Per room. $60 shared bath, $85 private bath. $10 surcharge for one-night weekend stay.

> From Washington, D.C.: "Another nice extra is the information about things to do in the hypnotically beautiful countryside. We happened to be there during the Welsh Festival in a beautiful church in the little town of Delta nearby. What singing! Altogether, Spring House is so special, I just had to let you know."

Both *Country Home* and *Country Decorating* (by *Woman's Day*) have featured this "genuine country inn." Since the spring of 1981 visitors have asked lots of questions about the plastered, whitewashed, and stenciled walls—and the floor cloths, country antiques, Oriental rugs, pottery (some done by the hostess and fired in a kiln Ray made while a student at Antioch College), paintings (some her own) of local scenes, and herb garden too. She lives here "in the way I grew up—with wood heat, cook stoves, cool bedrooms, and good pure food and water." Ray, a dairy-farm girl who became a York County historic preservationist, turned B&B host after a 3½ month backpacking trip in England that followed 10 years of singlehandedly restoring every inch of this 18th-century stone house to its "simple strong character."

In residence: Hadrian, a setterlike dog that gives tours. One Siamese cat, Tachyon.
Restrictions: Sorry, no guests' pets. No smoking.
Foreign language spoken: Spanish.
Bed and bath: Five rooms. A large first-floor room (former parlor) has a double bed, French stove, grand piano, private shower bath. On second floor, private shower bath for one large room with antique three-quarter bed and a double bed. Three double-bedded rooms, one with stove, share a bath with tub, no shower.
Breakfast: Special. By 9; hour arranged night before. Made with locally produced ingredients, including organically grown wheat flour. Many recipes gathered from Ray's travels. Usually two main courses. Maybe

wineberries on buttered buckwheat pancakes with maple syrup or honey
from Ray's bees. Or a frittata with sauteed zucchini and cheese, scrapple,
sausage, or home cured bacon. Jams and jellies (Ray makes her own
pectin from green apples), and syrups from fruits she has picked and
preserved. Served in dining room or on the porch.
Plus: Popcorn at just the right time. Local Amish cheese. Wine from
award-winning winery three miles away. Feather beds, down puffs, and
flannel sheets. Porch swing. Bicycle routes. Trout-stocked Muddy Creek.
Swimming, canoeing, horseback riding, cross-country skiing. River trail
and unused Ma and Pa railroad bed for hiking.

Winding Glen Farm Tourist Home

107 Noble Road, Christiana, PA 17509
Phone: 215/593-5535
Location: Very quiet. In a beautiful valley directly south of Christiana.
One mile from Route 41; 19 miles east of Lancaster.
Hosts: Bob and Minnie Metzler
Open: April until the week before Thanksgiving. Reservations required.
Rates: $32 double. $9 child 6–12, $6 under age 6.

"It's more than 20 years since we started taking the overflow from
motels. Then people started to come back and tell other people. They
really seem to like our farm life. Some just watch or try their hand at
milking cows. Some ask to give a hand if they're here during haymaking.
Oh yes, we're with the guests a lot. They come as tourists and leave as
friends. We're Mennonites and we answer a lot of questions about our
religion. Sometimes our son George sets up two projectors and shows the
slide show, "Our Way of Life," made by our married son Jerry, who lives
next door. It is set to music and the narration talks about how we feel
about things. It shows farm life in different seasons, our neighboring
Amish, and some pictures from his trip to Switzerland.

"There's plenty to do here. You can fish in a stream on our property
and tour Jerry's woodworking shop. Just down the road there's a covered
bridge. Often I draw a map for touring the nearby Amish area that has an
old mill still in use. I enjoy quilting and ceramics. My husband hunts and
fishes. Our 250-year-old farmhouse is simply furnished with family antiques and pieces Jerry has made."

Restrictions: No guests' pets. No smoking indoors. No alcoholic beverages.
Bed and bath: Five rooms. Two shared baths, one with shower, one with
tub. Four second-floor rooms; two with two double beds in each. One
room with queen bed and a single; another with a double bed. A third-
floor room has two double beds and a single. Cot and crib available.
Breakfast: At 8. Full farm meal served family style.
Plus: Air conditioner in hall outside guest rooms. Porch.

Churchtown Inn—Bed & Breakfast Circa 1735

Route 23, Churchtown, PA
Mailing address: Box 135, RD 3, Narvon, PA 17555
Phone: 215/445-7794
Location: On Route 23W, with Amish buggies going by front door (and patio). Across from historic church. Views of Welsh Mountains in back. Five miles from Pennsylvania Turnpike. Twenty miles east of Lancaster; 45 minutes from Philadelphia and Hershey. Two and a half hours from Manhattan and Washington, D.C.
Hosts: Stuart and Hermine Smith and Jim Kent
Open: Year round. Reservations usually required. Two- or three-night minimum preferred on holiday weekends.
Rates: Double occupancy. $49 shared bath, $65 or $85 private. Singles $5 less. Rollaway bed $20. Senior citizen discount 10 percent. Special holiday packages. MC, VISA.

From New Jersey and echoed by many: "Absolutely charming 18th-century stone house filled with exquisite antique furnishings . . . immaculate . . . exceptional food beautifully presented. . . . Even with a full house, we all felt as though we were visiting family. On our first evening we were taken to a nearby Amish farmhouse for dinner. Then it was back to the inn for tea. Stu played the piano and sang so beautifully that I inquired about his background. He has directed choruses that appeared at Lincoln Center and Carnegie Hall and in Europe. It's worth a trip just to hear him perform! We have met some lovely innkeepers in our travels, but there's something special about the warmth here."

When Stu was stationed in Europe as a chaplain's assistant, he liked the idea of B&Bs. Eventually, in 1986, he and Jim restored this history-filled 15-room center hall mansion and decorated with European and American antiques. In New Jersey, Hermine, Stu's wife, was a health food retailer. Jim, an accountant in New Jersey, teaches ballroom dancing. Here the hosts are active in the historical society. They direct guests to back roads and Amish farm stands and crafts, and they plan everything from carriage rides to murder mystery weekends, from holiday weekends with barbecues and accordion music to Thanksgiving dinner.

Restrictions: Well-disciplined children who are at least 12 are welcome. Sorry, no pets. Smoking allowed in brochure room only.
Foreign languages spoken: Limited German and Italian.
Bed and bath: Eight rooms; five with private baths, on second and third floors. Queen or twin beds, some canopied, with handcrafted quilts. On third floor, private full bath for room with a queen and a single bed, cathedral ceiling, skylights. Two queen-bedded rooms share a full bath. Rollaway available.
Breakfast: 9. Five-course meal. Entree might be buttermilk pancakes with fruit, French toast made with Grand Marnier, Scottish oatmeal custard, or egg souffle. Homemade breads and jams. Coffee cake.

Plus: Air conditioning. Often, evening tea or wine, maybe a sing-along and/or the sounds of antique organ, phonograph, and music boxes. Fresh flowers. Victorian parlor. Game room. Den. Courtyard. Garden. Swing. Elaborate Christmas decorations. By advance arrangement, weekend dinner in kitchen of Amish home ($10) where five daughters sing for guests.

The Foreman House in Churchtown

Route 23, Churchtown
Mailing address: Box 161A, RD #3, Narvon, PA 17555
Phone: 215/445-6713
Location: On Route 23. Surrounded by countryside with farms. Buggies pass by. Near auctions, factory outlets, historic sights; 25 minutes from Lancaster.
Hosts: Stephen and Jacqueline Mitrani
Open: Year round. Advance reservations preferred. Two-night minimum on holiday weekends.
Rates: $40 single. $50 double. $10 extra person.

"This carefully maintained house was built in 1919 by the Foreman family, the only other occupants until we purchased it with the original kitchen and baths in 1986. Earlier, all the way back to Revolutionary days, there was a hotel made of logs on the site. To this day we find hotel pottery and clam shells when we are digging in the yard.

"When we lived in the Napa Valley we had friends who hosted. That inspired us when we moved here to my home area. We have furnished with family heirlooms and locally made quilts (for sale). Much to our joy, we have fascinating conversations with B&B travelers—business people, professionals, shoppers and tourists."

Jackie was a teacher and in public relations on the West Coast, and she has lived in Mexico and Puerto Rico. Steve works in real estate management and development.

In residence: In hosts' quarters, Joseph Cline, age six; Mary Beth is three. One parakeet.
Restrictions: Children 10 and over are welcome. Sorry, no pets or smoking allowed.
Foreign language spoken: Spanish.
Bed and bath: In front of house, two second-floor rooms, each with four windows, share a tub bath (which has original pedestal sink). One room with double four-poster and three-quarter pineapple bed and one with a double and a single bed. Rollaway available.
Breakfast: 8–8:30. (After 8:30, continental.) Fruit, freshly ground coffee, specialty teas, juices, home-baked goods. Local specialty such as shoofly pie or Jackie's creation, burrito.
Plus: Bedroom air conditioners. Afternoon or evening lemonade, milk, and cider. Guest refrigerator. TV available. Mints on the pillows. Side porch.

Covered Bridge Inn

990 Rettew Mill Road, Ephrata, PA 17522
Phone: 717/733-1592
Location: Tucked away in Amish country overlooking creek and old millrace. One mile from Route 272. Twenty minutes to Lancaster. Near Ephrata Cloister and antiques shops. Three hours from New York City or Washington, D.C.
Host: Betty Lee Maxcy
Open: Year round. Reservations advisable.
Rates: Single—weekdays $40, business person $38; weekends $50. Two people—$50 double bed, $55 queen canopy. $15 cot or trundle. MC, VISA.

And still the letters come: "A cozy and comfortable atmosphere. Sumptuous breakfasts. . . . Feels like a happy family reunion. . . . And what a delight to hear the clopping of horses and the rumble of Amish buggy wheels crossing over the wooden span. . . . Elsewhere the world has its troubles. At the Covered Bridge Inn it is just peace and contentment. It makes us want to know what the year rate would be."

Betty Lee was a big hit, too, in Bloomingdale's when she participated in the "Meet-The-Hosts" program (based on this book) with her herb bouquets and freshly made muffins. The nurse practitioner turned innkeeper and her industrial engineer husband (who has also been an area tour guide) live in an 1814 limestone house built by a miller from Switzerland. There are wide white pine floors, Indian doors, shutters, and a wide, carved open staircase. And everywhere there are primitives—baskets and trunks, bedsteads and quilts—that the Maxcys have collected over the years.

The house, recently placed on the National Register of Historic Places, was beautifully restored when they bought it—complete with ghost story—in 1984. "For fun" the Maxcys have restored the 1814 barn, acquired "a gaggle of geese," established an 1800 German herb garden, and planted apple trees (1800s varieties) and berry patches.

Restrictions: Children should be at least 10. No guests' pets, please. No smoking inside.
Foreign language spoken: Spanish.
Bed and bath: Four large second-floor rooms share two and a half baths. One canopied queen bed, one double rope bed (and trundle rope bed), another double bed, and one room with white iron double bed plus a three-quarter bed. Cot available.
Breakfast: 8:30. Varies daily. Juice, fruit, meat, homemade muffins or bread, home-preserved raspberry or strawberry jams or jellies. Main dish might be blueberry buckle, cinnamon pancakes, spinach or sausage quiche. Served in kitchen (the gathering place) by the walk-in fireplace, at large dining room table, or on the porch. "It seems to be guests' favorite time—and ours."

Plus: Bedroom air conditioners (plus 20-inch stone walls that keep house cool). Fresh flowers. Living room fireplace. Piano and organ. Lots of books and games. Library with TV. Lemonade and cookies. Wicker-furnished porch. Kitchen privileges. Grill. Picnic tables. Hammock. Croquet. Many locally made items (some by Betty Lee) for sale.

Gerhart House B&B

287 Duke Street, Ephrata, PA 17522
Phone: 717/733-0263
Location: On a corner in this small town surrounded by farms. One mile from Green Dragon (farmers' market), six to antiques of Renningers and Black Angus. Twenty minutes to Intercourse and Bird-in-Hand. Within walking distance of fine restaurant, Playhouse-in-the-Park, Ephrata Cloister.
Hosts: Ray and Shirley Smith
Open: Year round. Two-night minimum stay on holiday weekends.
Rates: Double occupancy. Double bed—$50 shared bath, $65 private bath. Queen bed—$75. Singles $5 less. MC, VISA.

From Indiana, Pennsylvania, New Jersey, Georgia, New York: "I wish everyone traveling through the area could enjoy the Smith family. . . . Extremely knowledgeable about the area, showed us maps, wrote down directions and gave us names of people to contact for quilts and antiques. . . . The best French toast I've ever eaten. . . . Immaculate, tastefully decorated, handmade quilts, hosts who made special arrangements for us to have dinner with Mennonite cousins. . . . A relaxed atmosphere that sets the tone for a whole trip. . . . Friendly hosts who respect guests' desire for privacy."

Restored in 1984 as a B&B, the Lancaster County brick house with Victorian features was built in 1926 by renowned Ephrata builder Alexander Gerhart as his private residence. It was bought three years ago when area natives Shirley, a teacher, and Ray, an avid sailor, ended their search for a "perfect place—with a good layout and original woodwork—for B&B.

"As hosts, we notice that a refreshing cup of tea in the parlor makes many guests forget the pressured city and work. . . . And then there was a grand 90-year-old woman who brought her canaries along." With advance notice, the Smiths will arrange for dinner "and great conversation" at Mennonite homes—with or without electricity—just 20 minutes away.

Restrictions: Smoking allowed everywhere except the breakfast room. Sorry, no children and no guests' pets.
Bed and bath: Five rooms. Private baths for rooms with queen canopied bed (and private entrance and balcony too), double spool bed, and queen cannonball bed (on first floor). One full bath shared by room with two twins and room with a double bed.

Breakfast: Full at 8:30; coffee, juice, and toast at 9. Thick French toast made from homemade bread or eggs with Lancaster County scrapple, or quiche and oatmeal cake; juice, coffee, tea, hot chocolate, and seasonal fruit. Served in breakfast room with fine china, silver, and linens.
Plus: Air-conditioned bedrooms. Coffee and teas. Porch rockers. Gazebo. Collection of 1800s books.

Historic Smithton

900 West Main Street, Ephrata, PA 17522
Phone: 717/733-6094
Location: On a hill overlooking Ephrata Cloister, at the corner of West Main Street and South Academy Drive; 12 miles north of Lancaster.
Host: Dorothy Graybill
Open: Year round. Reservations recommended. Two-night minimum stay for Saturday and holiday reservations.
Rates: $55–$75 double occupancy, Monday–Thursday. $85–$105 Friday–Sunday and holidays. $20 additional person over age eight; 18 months to age eight—$15; under 18 months, free. Singles $10 less. Suite $130 weekdays, $160 weekends and holidays. AMEX, MC, VISA.

> From Canada: "Authentic decor and friendly atmosphere. Gracious hostess. Immaculate. Delicious breakfast. We were able to imagine ourselves back 200 years. There were many imaginative touches such as potpourri. We even wore the nightgowns that were supplied!"

Dorothy is Pennsylvania Dutch and has lived within a mile of Smithton all her life. A director of a local art center, she is a gardener and craftswoman with a strong interest in folk arts. In 1982 a friend suggested that she change from retail store management to innkeeping. Many guests agree with Dorothy's conclusion, "It was a good idea."

Always an inn since it was built in 1763, and owned by the same family until 1979, the stone center hall building, like the buildings of the Cloister, is of German architectural tradition. Guest rooms have the option of being lit entirely by candles.

In residence: Dorothy is often assisted by her sister, June, and her brother, Donald.
Restrictions: "Mannerly children and pets are welcome." Please, no smoking.
Bed and bath: Seven rooms plus a suite, each with private modern bath, refrigerator, working fireplace, chamber music, antique or handmade reproduction furniture. Canopied or four-poster king, queen, or double bed with handmade Pennsylvania Dutch quilt, upholstered chairs, writing desk. Two-floor suite has a kitchenette, living room, queen bed, twin cupboard bed, whirlpool bath. Cot, folding playpen, and antique cradle available.
Breakfast: Served at 8 and 9 in tavern room by the fire. Pennsylvania Dutch waffles with fruit, whipped cream and syrup, orange juice, pastry, fresh fruit plate, hot beverage.

Plus: Air conditioning. In winter, feather beds available. Well-stocked library. Tavern room with tea, snacks (no charge). Gardens with fountain and outdoor furniture. Printed booklet of touring and shopping suggestions. Quilts for sale.

The Osceola Mill House

313 Osceola Mill Road, Gordonville, PA 17529
Phone: 717/768-3758
Location: Peaceful. On a bend in the road along the banks of Pequea Creek. About a mile and a half east of Intercourse; 15 miles east of Lancaster.
Hosts: Barry and Joy Sawyer
Open: Year round. Closed between Christmas and New Year's. Two-night minimum stay on holiday weekends.
Rates: Double occupancy $50–$70, in October $60–$70. Trundle bed or rope bed $10 extra.

Country Living has photographed this B&B for a Christmas issue. The sound of horse-drawn Amish buggies is often recalled in guests' poems. Some visitors walk the country road lined with Amish farms or follow the Sawyers' directions to small step-back-in-time country stores. Honeymooners find privacy here. And some winter guests stay by the fire "to share backgrounds and laughter" with Barry, a banker and musician, and Joy, a former librarian's assistant at Franklin and Marshall College.

As Joy, who grew up in the area, says, "We have researched the history of this large 1766 limestone Georgian-style house which was a private home until 1985 when we purchased it and began restoration. It has 22-inch-thick stone walls and various examples of architectural changes made through the years. I consider it a privilege to share our love for the old homes built by our ancestors. Our keeping room has mushroom boarding on the walls and a large fireplace with antique accessories. Throughout we have furnished with antiques and reproductions. Innkeeping helps us to discover how many wonderful people there are in this world."

In residence: One indoor dog. Outside—cats, two peacocks, one Percheron draft horse.
Restrictions: "Not comfortable for children under 12." No smoking and no guests' pets, please.
Foreign language spoken: German.
Bed and bath: Three second-floor rooms share one tub bath. One high undressed canopy queen bed with a trundle bed beneath, working fireplace. One room with pencil-post double bed, working fireplace. One with canopied queen bed and single rope bed. All with handmade quilts.
Breakfast: Usually 8:30. Specialties include pineapple filled with fruit, baked apple or blueberry pancakes, ham and cheese quiche with cranberry muffins, homemade waffles. Served in fireplaced keeping room or dining room.

Plus: Tea, wine, mulled cider, or cranberry punch. Porch rockers. Tour of house. Bedroom oscillating fans. Use of refrigerator. Picnic facilities. Badminton and croquet. Those peacocks!

Pinehurst Inn

50 Northeast Drive, Hershey, PA 17033
Phone: 717/533-2603
Location: Surrounded by lawns, countryside, and (through the night) the sound of the passing train. Within a mile of the Sports Arena, Hersheypark, Chocolate World, Hershey Museum, Golf Courses, and Rose Garden. One hour's drive to Gettysburg and Lancaster.
Hosts: Jim and Phyllis Long
Open: Year round. Advance reservations preferred.
Rates: Double occupancy. $45 April 15–October 15. $35 off season. $5 extra person. Inquire about golf packages. MC, VISA.

During my three-day stay, I saw an amazing flexibility in this house and its Hershey-born hosts. It offers the perfect arrangement for just a few people around the fire or on the porch, for a family reunion (held while we were there), or for a small conference (the reason I was there). The sprawling brick B&B was originally built by Mr. Hershey as a home (not a dormitory) for orphaned boys attending the Milton Hershey School; currently the school has a coed enrollment of 1,500. There is a warm, welcoming many-windowed living room. The guest rooms with built-in bureaus are decorated minimally as a reminder of their origin.

Phyllis, a substitute teacher at the school in the 1970s, lived here as a young child when her parents were Pinehurst house parents. "As a teenager I entertained some dates on the porch swing, the same one on which my mother read to her grandchildren. Having a B&B was never a dream of mine but Jim came up with the idea three years ago when he saw that the unoccupied house was for sale. We were living in a Cape house right in town, the place where we brought up our four children. Once the decision was made, there were many months when I saw Jim (happily) substitute plastering for golf after coming home from his work as product manager for the international division of an electronics company! Now I am grateful for the career change. In addition to tourists, we meet many visitors who come for the medical center, for weddings (right here sometimes), for theater, symphony, and the annual antique auto show. B&B really does bring the world to your doorstep."

In residence: A cat called Linda.
Restrictions: Children are welcome. No smoking inside. Sorry, no guests' pets.
Bed and bath: Twelve rooms on first and second floors. One with private bath; 11 share four tile (and now stenciled) baths. Queen, double, and twin beds and rollaway available.

Breakfast: Usually 8–9:30. Juice or fruit, homemade coffee cakes, various cereals and teas, coffee.
Plus: All bedrooms have ceiling fans and air conditioning available. Chocolate kiss on each pillow. That swing is on the porch.

White Rock Farm Guest House

154 White Rock Road, Kirkwood, PA 17536
Phone: 717/529-6744
Location: On 150 peaceful acres. A working farm overlooking a scenic stream and an historic covered bridge. Two miles off Route 472. Eighteen miles southeast of Lancaster. Near local Amish and quilt shops.
Host: Les and Lois Hershey
Open: Year round. Advance reservations preferred.
Rates: $45 single. $50 double. Extra person $10 over age 10; $8 ages 2–10; $5 under age 2.

> From New York: "A beautiful, genuine and clean farmhouse away from any commercialized or busy roads. . . . Warm gracious hosts who made us feel as if we were staying with relatives. . . . Comfortable room filled with lovely antiques. . . . Clip clopping (Amish) buggies pass on the way to church on Sunday morning. . . . After a hearty breakfast Les took us on a tour of the farm where they raise cattle and grow their own feed."

It's a stone (quarried from the farm) house with white stucco finish, built in 1860, in the Hershey family for four generations, and recently remodeled and redecorated. Since 1987, Les, a farmer and carpenter, and Lois, a homemaker and substitute teacher, have been "sharing the joy of country living with guests. We are a young Mennonite family surrounded by Amish neighbors. Sometimes guests spend time in our favorite spot, a scenic picnic grove beside a peaceful stream. All year round there is a lot to do in Lancaster County."

In residence: Loren, age five, and Linford, age three. Kisha, a golden retriever; several cats; 150 cattle.
Restrictions: Children of all ages welcome. No smoking. Sorry, no guests' pets. No alcoholic beverages.
Bed and bath: Three second-floor rooms share a full bath. One room with queen bed handcrafted by local Amish. Two are double bedded. All beds have handmade quilts and comforters. Rollaway bed and crib available.
Breakfast: Flexible hours. Any combination of bacon, eggs, quiche, French toast, pancakes, pastries, cereal, juice, milk, coffee, tea, fresh fruit. "Unbeatable" homemade breads and jams. Served family style around kitchen table. Hosts join guests.
Plus: Air-conditioned bedrooms. Babysitting may be arranged. Use of refrigerator. Spacious lawn. Croquet and other lawn games. Front porch. Nature trails. Fishing at covered bridge. Welcome to church services.

The Walkabout Inn Bed & Breakfast

837 Village Road, P.O. Box 294, Lampeter, PA 17537
Phone: 717/464-0707
Location: On Route 741, three miles south of Lancaster. Next to Lampeter Community Park.
Hosts: Richard and Maggie Mason
Open: Year round. Two-night minimum stay on holiday weekend.
Rates: $50 single, $65 double. $15 age 6–15; $5 under age 6. Special weekend packages. AMEX, MC, VISA.

Richard was with the Australian foreign service in Washington, D.C., when he and Maggie, a Baltimore native and former caterer, were searching throughout the Northeast for a B&B, their own favorite style of travel worldwide. They knew Lancaster County from quilt- and food-shopping weekends and happened upon the auction for this house, which was built in 1925 by Ike Herr, a well-known local cabinetmaker who used chestnut for wood trim. The Masons stripped wallpaper, painted, and stenciled. Since furnishing the comfortable rooms with quilts and crafts, they have welcomed tourists (many families) as well as embassy representatives.

Holidays are celebrated here with special package weekends that might include a pumpkin-carving contest or Thanksgiving dinner. Information is a part of the hospitality offered; tea is served while a 28-minute video about the Amish lifestyle is shown. Richard has special maps for guests. He'll direct you to quilt auctions (year round). And all those Australian foods are made by Maggie every morning. If you share one of your own favorite recipes, future guests will hear your name and hometown announced every time your specialty is served.

In residence: Nicholas is eight, Megan is two.
Restrictions: Children of all ages welcome. Smoking allowed on porches. Sorry, no pets.
Bed and bath: Four second-floor rooms and two suites with a double and a single bed in each. Three baths are shared or private depending on arrangements. Rollaway bed and crib available.
Breakfast: 7:30–9. European quiche or banana and apple pancakes with whipped cream and sausage or bacon. Exotic fresh fruit, Australian breads and tea rolls, juice, cereal, imported Australian teas and coffee. Served in dining room by candlelight at table set with silver, crystal, and china.
Plus: Central air conditioning. Tea served during movie shown for guests. Kitchen privileges. Ice machine, barbecue, picnic area, two porch swings, horseshoes. VCR movies, cable TV. Gift shop here. Guided tours.

Buona Notte Bed & Breakfast

2020 Marietta Avenue, Lancaster, PA 17603
Phone: 717/295-2597
Location: In the village of Rohrerstown, on a main road 2 miles west of

Lancaster, 7–10 miles to most tourist attractions (east of Lancaster). Two miles from Franklin and Marshall College, 1½ from Wheatland. Near Park City shopping center.
Hosts: Joe and Anna Predoti
Open: Year round. Two-night minimum on holiday weekends.
Rates: $50 private bath, $40 shared bath. $5 cot.

"It is clean and comfortable, all redecorated and furnished with many older pieces bought at area sales. It is just what we were looking for when we decided to move here from New Jersey in 1985. We wanted to be in the Lancaster area, but not on top of the tourist attractions. I am no longer nursing (although I am still making beds!)."

In New Jersey Anna taught nurses how to use computers. Here Joe is a fifth-grade teacher. Since 1986, when the Predotis started B&B in their turn-of-the-century brick house, they have become well acquainted with restaurants (the number one question) and the ways of the Amish and Mennonites (the next most frequently asked questions). Anna says, "Hosting people from so many different places is fascinating. Sometimes it seems as if the world's problems are being solved around the breakfast table!"

Restrictions: Children should be at least two. Sorry, no pets. Smoking restricted to outdoors. No alcoholic beverages.
Foreign languages spoken: Joe speaks Italian fluently, some French and Spanish.
Bed and bath: Three rooms. The one with private bath is on third floor, with a double bed and room for a cot. One double-bedded second-floor room and one third-floor room with two twin beds share a full bath.
Breakfast: 7:30–9. Fresh fruit, juice, homemade muffins, rolls and buns, homemade toast, jams, granola. Coffee, tea, or milk. Served in cheerful country dining room.
Plus: Beverages. Air conditioning in all bedrooms. Living room with ceiling fan and wood stove. Wraparound porch. Yard and picnic area.

The Dingeldein House

1105 East King Street, Lancaster, PA 17602
Phone: 717/293-1723
Location: On a main road, 10 blocks east of the central Market Square. Near plenty of Mennonite and Amish farms.
Hosts: Keith and Laurie Dingeldein
Open: Year round. Advance reservations recommended.
Rates: Double occupancy. Shared bath, $50 May–November, $45 December–April. Private bath, $60 May–November, $50 December–April. $15 rollaway. Crib free. Weekly rates. MC, VISA.

Guests wrote: " We were skeptical about our first B&B. It was just delightful . . . immaculate, decorated tastefully, conveniently located . . . large enough so that you don't find yourself running into other guests unless you want to. . . . Laurie's and Keith's interests in area history, music, decorating and cooking add an extra measure of what it takes to make their guests comfortable, entertained, *and well fed.* . . . My husband loves food and he was so impressed he booked another night."

Everyone comments about breakfast specialties made by Keith, the Hotel Hershey's pastry chef, who was trained at the Culinary Institute of America before working in four major cities. Even *Gourmet* magazine requested a recipe.

Laurie, a pianist and craftsperson, was a CPA until she and Keith opened the turn-of-the-century Dutch Colonial in 1987. The house was once owned by the Armstrong (floor tile) family and for 50 years by the Leath (Strasburg Railroad and Museum) family. In five months the Dingeldeins painted and papered throughout. Their outside work includes landscaping and a goldfish pond. "We give hints for back roads and good buys on furniture and quilts. Most of all, we feel strongly about giving guests good food and warm hospitality at a fair price."

In residence: Buffy, a red cocker spaniel.
Restrictions: Children of all ages welcome. No smoking or alcoholic beverages, please.
Bed and bath: Four rooms. Private full baths for two third-floor rooms, one with queen and one with double bed. On second floor, room with double bed and one with two twins share a full bath. Rollaway bed and crib available.
Breakfast: 8–9. A highlight with Keith's pastries—maybe croissants, custard flans, fruit Danish, or muffins. Plus locally grown fruit together with eggs, Apfel-Schnitz Pfankuchen (*Gourmet*-requested apple crepes), baked egg casseroles, eggs Benedict, pancakes, or French toast; bacon or sausage; tea or coffee.
Plus: Air conditioning. Tea, coffee, soft drinks, and snacks. Piano in fireplaced living room. Porch with swing and game table. Will meet guests at Lancaster airport, bus, or train station. With advance notice, special occasions honored. Parking.

Hollinger House Bed & Breakfast

2336 Hollinger Road, Lancaster, PA 17602
Phone: 717/464-3050
Location: On an old road that runs parallel and very close to Route 222. Two miles from Lancaster center.
Hosts: Jean and Leon Thomas
Open: Year round. Reservations preferred.
Rates: June–November $35 single, $50/$55 double. Rest of year, $30 single, $40/$45 double. No charge for children under 5. $10 for children 6–12. Age 13 and older $15. (Deposit required for advance reservation.)

Every room was done by a different decorator when the 1870 brick house was a Decorators' Show House in 1985. The Thomases had a season of guests in 1984 and reopened after the decorators were gone and the house tour was over.

Jean is an exuberant hostess who gladly shares the history of the "grand but homey" B&B, originally built as a tanner's private home. ("And we answer lots of questions about the Amish and attractions in the area.") A Pennsylvania resident since her marriage to Leon 42 years ago, she has also led city and county tours and been a rural mail carrier. Leon, a native of the area, is retired.

In residence: One adult daughter. Son and daughter-in-law live in remodeled barn on the property. "Numerous felines and a Samoyed dog named Kenworth."
Restrictions: Sorry, no guests' pets. No smoking indoors. Children of all ages are welcome.
Foreign language spoken: German.
Bed and bath: Five large air-conditioned second-floor rooms. One (sleeps five) with a double bed, a daybed, and a crib, shared bath. Four rooms with double or twin beds share two full baths. Cot and crib available.
Breakfast: At 8. Fruited yogurt, juice, coffee, fresh rolls or donuts. Entree could be French toast, quiche, scrambled eggs, pancakes, or baked oatmeal. Served in spacious dining room.
Plus: All rooms are air conditioned. Beverages. Large family living room with fireplace. Library/TV room. Porches. Tour of house. Will meet guests at the Lancaster airport, train, or bus. Five acres with stream.

The King's Cottage, A Bed & Breakfast Inn

1049 East King Street, Lancaster, PA 17602
Phone: 717/397-1017
Location: In a residential neighborhood on a main road. Ten minutes from either downtown Lancaster or working Amish farms.
Hosts: Karen and Jim Owens
Open: Year round. Two-night minimum stay on Saturdays and holidays.
Rates: Per room. Queen bed $89, with private balcony $99. King bed $99. November–April except holidays, $10 less. MC, VISA.

For meticulously transforming their rare Spanish Colonial/Mission-style house back to its original splendor, Karen and Jim were honored in 1988 by the Lancaster Historic Preservation Trust. Returnees, too, express appreciation for the use of color (a deep green is in the beamed living room); attention to detail (robes, soaps, and shampoos); fine furnishings; "and the warm wonderful hospitality."

The enthusiastic young hosts—Jim, an engineering consultant, and Karen, a former teacher—were inspired by all their own B&B stays before buying the unoccupied house, which had seen several uses. The spacious plant-filled common areas include a Florida Room with ceiling fans, a marble-fireplaced library, a brick-fireplaced living room, and a crystal-chandeliered dining room with original wainscoting and moldings.

Guests speak of being pampered by hosts who (obviously) love what they are doing.

In residence: Kitty is an outdoor cat because of Karen's allergies.
Restrictions: Children over 12 welcome. No smoking. Sorry, no guests' pets.
Foreign language spoken: Spanish.
Bed and bath: Five second-floor rooms, each with private full bath; two can be a suite. King or queen beds. Rollaway available.
Breakfast: At 8:30 or 9:30. Freshly squeezed orange juice, freshly ground coffee, herbal teas, fruit. Entree might be peaches-and-cream French toast, apple pancakes, quiche, or blueberry sourdough pancakes complete with Lancaster County sausage. Pure maple syrup or homemade fruit butters. Cereals always available. In elegant dining room.
Plus: Central air conditioning. Snack and beverage, 4–7 P.M. Liqueur and mints. Cable TV in library. Guest phone. Off-street parking.

Patchwork Inn

2319 Old Philadelphia Pike, Lancaster, PA 17602
Phone: 717/293-9078
Location: Adjacent to an Amish farm. Three miles east of Lancaster, near the village of Smoketown. Two miles from Bird-in-Hand farmers' market and craft shops.
Hosts: Lee and Joanne Martin
Open: Year round. Advance reservations requested.
Rates: Per room. $50 shared bath, $60 private bath. $75 suite. $10 extra person. MC, VISA.

Guest wrote: "A real home away from home. In our extensive travels we have rarely found a place as charming, warm and friendly as this. Antique oak everywhere, touches of potpourri in baskets, books and magazines about quilting and the Amish way of life, and homemade cookies to greet us at the end of the day."

"A grand old farmhouse in Lancaster" was what the Martins had dreamed about ever since they made their first trip here in 1970. It just so happened that B&B was taking hold in Lancaster when Lee was retiring as a colonel from the Marine Corps. Rather than stay in the Washington, D.C., area with their collection of country antiques, 60 handmade quilts, and old telephones (including a booth with working sign and fan), the Martins made their twenty-fourth move in 30 years. They came to a place that had been cared for and updated. Since opening in the fall of 1987, Lee and Joanne, a former field service director, find that many guests are interested in their extensive travels, in auction hints, in the ways of the Amish, "and how do you tell a quality quilt?"

In residence: "Our friendly ten-year-old cat, Precious, seems to know who the cat lovers are.

Restrictions: Children 10 and over welcome. No smoking inside. Sorry, no guests' pets.
Bed and bath: On second floor, three rooms and one suite with quilt-covered queen antique beds. One room with private full bath. Suite has bedroom, living room with queen sofa bed, full bath, kitchen, private entrance. Two rooms share one large full bath with double sinks. Roll-away available.
Breakfast: Usually 8:30. Continental plus with fruit, cereal, juice, home-made pumpkin bread, fresh coffee, herbal teas. Quiche and/or homemade fruit-filled coffee cake on weekends. Served in dining room on antique oak table.
Plus: Air conditioning. Bedroom ceiling fans. Tea or cider. Amish-made wood glider on front porch. Guest refrigerator. Flannel sheets in winter; line-dried sheets in summer.

Witmer's Tavern—Historic 1725 Inn

2014 Old Philadelphia Pike, Lancaster, PA 17602
Phone: 717/299-5305
Location: One and one-half miles east of Lancaster on Route 340, a main road traveled by Amish buggies. Rear yard (with banty chickens) overlooks pastures and cornfields of three farms.
Host: Brant Hartung
Open: Year round. Two-night minimum stay on October and holiday weekends.
Rates: Double occupancy, $55. Larger room with sitting area, $75 for two. $10 extra person. $12 fireplace wood. Prepayment required for advance reservations.

Special U.S. Postal Service stamped envelopes and commemorative coins were issued in 1988 when a Pennsylvania Museum Commission historic commemorative marker was erected on the front lawn here. Inside, a step into the past awaits guests at this 263-year-old pre-Revolutionary inn, where Conestoga wagon trains were made up to start west. Guest rooms with working fireplaces, original paint colors, antique furnishings, and quilts reflect a simple, pioneer style, but up-to-date features include air conditioning, electric heat, and modern baths.

The inn was purchased in 1969 by Marlowe Hartung, Brant's father, a history buff and hotel owner in the advertising business who founded Lancaster's Pennsylvania Dutch Visitors' Bureau in 1957. Through ongoing research the Hartungs have located accounts of visits here by members of the Continental Congress and General Lafayette. When Brant started as a teenager to restore the inn, which is now listed on the National Register of Historic Places, his first task was the removal of the stucco that covered the 22-inch-thick limestone walls. (He has since worked at restoring many old Pennsylvania houses.) He has installed wooden downspouts, using 18th-century methods. Future projects include restoration of the first-floor tavern and the exposure of the spring that still supplies the inn water.

The Hartungs direct guests to "lots of adjacent little towns that are loaded with history and activities" and to country markets, auctions, and craft shops. At the inn, Pennsylvania Dutch quilts are the specialty of the Pandora's Antique Shop, which was started by Pam, Brant's sister (now mother of two children), when she was 18.

In residence: Mother (Jeanne) arranges flowers and is usually in the shop on weekends. Dad (Marlowe) often stops by to chat with guests.
Restrictions: Well-behaved children are welcome. Sorry, no guests' pets. No cigar smoking permitted.
Bed and bath: Seven double-bedded rooms—one with 200-year-old trundle bed—share three baths. Cot and crib available.
Breakfast: 8:30–9:30. Juice, Pennsylvania Dutch sticky buns, fruit in season, cereal. Tea, hot chocolate, milk.
Plus: Sitting room with wood stove. Fresh flowers, popcorn popper, popcorn in each room. No radio or television. Porch with rockers and swings. Tour of inn.

Swiss Woods Bed & Breakfast

500 Blantz Road, Lititz, PA 17543
Phone: 717/627-3358
Location: Off the beaten path among rolling fields and country scenes. On the edge of woods that surround Speedwell Fordge Lake (hiking and fishing). Three miles north of Lititz and pretzel factory; 20 minutes to downtown Lancaster; 25 to Hershey.
Hosts: Werner and Debrah Mosimann
Open: Year round. Two-night minimum stay on April–November weekends.
Rates: Double occupancy. January–March $50; holiday weekends $55. April–December $55, holiday weekends $75. Suites $65 January–March, $70 April–December; $10 rollaway. Under age three, free. MC, VISA.

> From California: "A friendly, beautiful, quiet place where you experience the full meaning of the German word 'gemütlichkeit', a warm, comfortable and relaxed atmosphere among friends." From Pennsylvania: "It's like being in Europe—cozy and warm. And the food—oh my, very good and creative."

Guests are greeted with chilled Swiss-made sparkling cider. There are goose-down covers on the beds, Swiss chocolates at the bedside. All in a Swiss-style house with natural woodwork and a contemporary country feeling—hosted by a Lancaster County native and her husband, whom she met in Austria while working with an interdenominational group.

Debrah explains, "Wherever we lived it seemed that we had visitors who had come a long way. B&B seemed like something I could do at home. While still in Switzerland we drew our own plans for this house to be built—with Werner's help—on family land. [Now Werner is here full time except for one day a week when he works at a family smoked meats and cheese business.] Since opening in June 1986 we have hosted many German-speaking guests, diplomats, a Russian choral director, bankers, health care workers, and vacationers from all over the world."

In residence: In hosts' quarters—Mirjam Anne, age seven; Esther, age six; Lukas, age four; and Jason is a year old. There are two outdoor cats. One golden retriever is kept in her kennel when guests are here.
Restrictions: Children are welcome. No smoking inside. Sorry, no pets please.
Foreign languages spoken: German and Swiss German.
Bed and bath: Five rooms. Four on first floor, each with private full bath, private exterior entrance. Three with queen beds, one with two twins. Rollaway available. Suite sleeps four adults, has large full bath, balcony, crib available.
Breakfast: 8:30–10:30 Monday–Saturday; 8:15–9:15 Sunday. Homegrown fruits, juice, freshly ground coffee, tea, homemade muffins and breads. On weekdays, eggs Benedict or apple waffles with cinammon cream and honey steamed apples. Saturdays, quiche; Sunday, egg sausage souffle.
Plus: Central air conditioning. Fully equipped guest kitchenette. Guest patio. Upon request, evening tea and pastries.

Herr Farmhouse Inn

Route 7, Box 587, Manheim, PA 17545
Phone: 717/653-9852
Location: On 26 acres with panoramic views of farmland. Nine miles west of Lancaster.
Hosts: Ruth and Barry A. Herr
Open: Year round. Advance reservations suggested.
Rates: April–October, $65 double with shared bath, $75 double with private bath. $85 suite. $10 less off season for two-night stay. $10 rollaway. MC, VISA.

"Home," a wonderful 1737 limestone colonial, is the Herrs' fourth restoration. The first was in 1969 in Connecticut, where Barry was in engineering and a building contractor. He and Ruth moved back to their native Lancaster County, and Barry worked in the field of wholesale distribution. While they were dreaming about redoing an old colonial, they found this former working farm, which had been vacant for at least seven years. All the architectural details, including moldings and floors, were intact, but it was a bit big for two people, so the B&B idea seemed just right. "And we love to direct guests away from the tourist traps," Barry reminds me.

Most guests are very curious about the house. Here you are visiting history buffs who are fascinated by the taking apart, seeing what was done, and figuring out why. "The other fun part is decorating," they say. Through the before-and-after pictures you can follow the progress. Today, it's all picture perfect, with chair rails, four-poster beds, Williamsburg colors, and six working fireplaces.

In residence: Clyde, "our friendly gray mostly-outside tiger cat."
Restrictions: School-age children welcome. Smoking allowed in common room only. Sorry, no pets.
Bed and bath: Three second-floor rooms plus a third-floor suite. Private full bath for room with double canopied bed, working fireplace. One room with queen brass bed and one with double canopied bed (with working fireplace) share a full bath. Up a steep stairway is suite with private full bath, two twin beds, sitting room with sofa bed. Rollaway available.
Breakfast: 8–10. Continental. Coffee, tea, milk, juice, fresh fruit, cereal, assorted breads, English muffins, homemade jelly, apple butter. Buffet on island counter in country kitchen with walk-in fireplace.
Plus: Central air conditioning. Bedroom ceiling fans. Tea and lemonade with cookies. Wicker-furnished sun room. Lawn furniture, porch rockers, picnic table, and grill.

Vogt Farm B&B

RD 1, Box 137A, Marietta, PA 17547
Phone: 717/653-4810
Location: Quiet. On a 30-acre farm with barns, a small pond with wild ducks (sometimes), cows in the pasture, and a garden. Fifteen miles west of Lancaster. "Within four miles of all types of dining." Within 30 minutes of Harrisburg, Hershey, and Lancaster.
Hosts: Kathy and Keith Vogt
Open: Year round. Advance reservations requested.
Rates: $30 single, $45 double or twin bed. Children prorated by age.

From Pennsylvania: "Warm, friendly people . . . comfortable, charmingly decorated rooms . . . delicious breakfast . . . impromptu tour of barns. . . . We enjoyed our stay so much that we treated our parents to a night there as a Christmas present."

"Our brick home was a real show place, so we are told, when it was built in 1865. We like to say it is decorated in 'Early Vogt,' the kind of place where you enjoy yourself. Through the years we have had guests from around the world. Now that the kids are getting married, we have official empty rooms for B&B. When guests ask about our country elevator, I am happy to explain the process of storing corn, wheat and soybeans in the big bins. . . . Kathy has lived within five miles of here all her life. I'd like you to know that she is—in no particular order—an excellent cook, the family chauffeur, company gofer, emergency management coordinator at the farm, and wife. I have my pilot's license and we have our own plane. Our fun-loving family hosts with the motto, 'Back door guests are best.'"

In residence: Jennie, 12, and Rebecca, 11. Several outside cats.
Restrictions: "Children are welcome. However, we cannot accommodate

pets." No smoking in the house. "And no long faces, only happy fun-loving people."

Foreign language spoken: A little Spanish.

Bed and bath: Three second-floor rooms—with one double, two twin canopied beds, or a single bed—share a full bath and a half bath. Crib available.

Breakfast: At 8 on Sundays. Other days, agreed-upon time, until 9. Home-baked bread, rolls, coffee cakes, casseroles, and fruit. Served in large farm kitchen at table set with flowers. Hosts join guests.

Plus: Bedroom air conditioners. Tea or some refreshing drink. Use of refrigerator. Living room with baby grand piano. Fireplaced basement family room with TV. Plush robes. Maps provided. Tips, too, for things to see and do. Mints. Fresh flowers. Ice water in rooms.

The Gathering Place

475 Round Top Road, Middletown, PA 17057

Phone: 717/944-2148 or 944-5801 (shop)

Location: Secluded. On nine acres, a half mile down a lane. One and a half miles from Route 283E. Ten minutes via the country route to Hershey; 10 minutes from Harrisburg International Airport and from Pennsylvania Turnpike; 25 to Lancaster.

Hosts: Donna and Lee Killian

Open: Year round. Advance reservations required.

Rates: $45 per room. $5 rollaway. MC, VISA.

"Although it's traditional on the outside, the interior is quite open except for one wall and a three-story fireplace in the center. Built in 1976 on land which belonged to my grandfather, the house has views from each of the 25 large windows. Furnishings are an eclectic collection from Europe, Japan, the west—all places I have lived. As I am an interior designer (who also has a country gift shop), the decor is mine. One guest room is done in country with stenciled walls and antique furniture. The other is contemporary with a platform bed and balcony overlooking downstairs family room; a wall sliding door ensures privacy.

"Lee works for a large company in Harrisburg. He loves hunting and fishing. (A large reservoir stocked with trout is across the street from the end of our lane.) We enjoy reading, traveling and 'working the nine acres.' I started B&B five years ago when the children were in college. It is a fun way to meet interesting people who come for the attractions in this area."

Restrictions: Smoking allowed downstairs only. Sorry, no guests' pets, please.

Bed and bath: Two second-floor double-bedded rooms share a full bath. Rollaway available.

Breakfast: Flexible hours. Usually fresh fruit or juices, homemade breads and jams. Egg dishes or apple dumplings by request. Served in country breakfast room with greenhouse area, in dining room, or on deck.

Plus: Central air conditioning. Tea or wine. A 42-foot rear deck faces woods. In season, garden flowers, fresh fruit. Hershey kisses.

The Country Stay

Route 1, Box 312 (Bull Moose Road), Mount Joy, PA 17552
Phone: 717/367-5167
Location: Rural. "Where the silence and sounds of nature can be heard—the songs of birds, locust, bullfrogs and crickets." Minutes from Routes 743, 441, and 30. Within half an hour of Hershey, Lancaster, York, and Harrisburg.
Hosts: Lester and Darlene Landis
Open: April–November. Advance reservations required. Two-night minimum stay on holiday weekends.
Rates: $35 single, $50 double. For children staying in same room with parent—under age 5, free; ages 6–11, $3; 12 and over, $5. MC, VISA.

From California, Georgia, Virginia, Ohio, New York: "Each room wonderfully decorated with antiques. . . . The grounds are as impressive as the inside. . . . Les gave us tips on roads and eateries. . . . Spotlessly clean. . . . Serene. . . . You can walk the country roads around the farm. . . . Convenient to shops and restaurants. . . . We accompanied them to church on Sunday. . . . Delicious food presented beautifully. . . . Friendly people who shared facts about their home, their life, the area we were in, things to see and do. We felt we were leaving friends we had known for many years. . . . The highlight of our trip to the antique auto show."

Williamsburg and Victorian colors enhance the marble-topped furnishings, the comfortable living room chairs, and the high-headboard rope bed in the 1880 brick farmhouse, home to the Landis family for almost 20 years. Windows are decorated with swags or ruffled curtains. Many guests comment on the impeccable surroundings. Darlene says, "Please remind your readers that we are a working farm. If I am gardening when guests arrive, I may be found with dirty knees and hands!"

In residence: Donavin, age 16, Douglas, age 11, and Katie Joy, age 4. Many farm cats.
Restrictions: No smoking indoors. No alcoholic beverages. No guests' pets, please.
Bed and bath: Three second-floor rooms with private guest entrance share one new full bath. Two carpeted double-bedded rooms, one with handmade Amish quilt. One room with queen canopied bed, Amish quilt. Extra mattresses available.
Breakfast: 8:15 Monday–Saturday; at 8 on Sundays. Fruit, homemade coffee cake, muffins or sticky buns, coffee, tea. Cereal for children.
Plus: Bedroom ceiling fans. Mints. Potpourri. Baskets for carrying towels to bath. Use of refrigerator. A friendship candle in each window. Porch rockers.

Mountville Antiques and B&B

Mountville, PA
Location: On Route 462 in a small town five miles west of the city of Lancaster, "one block from the post office and our friendly corner store." Bus service nearby to Lancaster and nearby towns. Twenty minutes to the heart of Pennsylvania Dutch country; 30 to Hersheypark.
Reservations: Available year round through Bed & Breakfast of Lancaster County, page 252.
Rates: $40 single, $55–$65 double.

The hosts (both pilots), a Chicagoan and his wife, a Mountville native who loves to cook and sail, have been running an antiques shop in this "delightful little town" for 20 years. A few years ago, they added a second floor to the building, designing it to be "comfortable and old looking, furnishing it mostly with art and antiques from the shop." After taking a trip to England in 1984, they were inspired to start a B&B, "not realizing that it would be so interesting and furthermore, so much fun."

Restrictions: No children, pets, or smoking.
Foreign language spoken: Host speaks Italian.
Bed and bath: Four second-floor rooms, each with private bath. Double or twin beds available. Art Deco, country, and Victorian furnishings.
Breakfast: 8:30. A leisurely meal served in the antiques shop at a round table set under a chandelier. Homemade raisin and oatmeal muffins, egg and cheese quiche, fresh fruit in season, juice, coffee or tea, rhubarb cake, zucchini bread. Hosts usually join guests for breakfast.
Plus: Bedroom air conditioners. Beverages upon arrival. Patio. Yard with picnic tables. By request, tour of Lancaster Amish area.

Maple Lane Guest House

505 Paradise Lane, Paradise, PA 17562
Phone: 717/687-7479
Location: Pretty. Set back from the highway surrounded by acres of lawn and rolling valley meadows with winding stream. One mile from Pennsylvania Railroad Museum of Strasburg.
Hosts: Marion and Edwin Rohrer
Open: Year round. Reservations required. Two-night minimum stay on summer weekends.
Rates: $35–$40 single, $40–$48 double. $8 cot. Crib free.

From Massachusetts: "We have stayed at several farms in the Amish Country and found this one to be by far the finest. Our beautiful accommodations included a bedroom hand-stenciled by Mrs. Rohrer, with a handmade quilt and other homemade crafts that provided a comfortable and homey atmosphere. Mr. Rohrer gave us a tour of the farm with a full explanation of the milking machinery. We were invited to partake of the fresh milk and we shared stories of our families. The Rohrers' enjoyment of life and hospitality were our inspiration and joy."

This is home! Marion was born just a mile down the road. She and Ed have been sharing their lifestyle for over 20 years. "Guests ask lots of questions about running a 250-acre farm that has 200 cows." Until 1980, when they built this colonial-style brick home, they lived next door in the 200-year-old fieldstone house that is now occupied by their married son (whom you are likely to meet when you tour the farm). For back roads, unadvertised Amish shops, or covered bridge locations, you have the experts here.

In residence: No house pets. Several outdoor cats. Three grandchildren live next door.
Restrictions: Sorry, no guests' pets. No smoking or alcoholic beverages.
Bed and bath: Four second-floor double-bedded rooms. Two with private shower baths. Two with semiprivate full bath. Cot and crib available.
Breakfast: 7:30–9. Juice, homemade pecan rolls and/or cheese pastry, coffee, tea. Buffet style in dining room. A time when Marion answers a lot of questions.
Plus: Central air conditioning. TV in each guest room. Guests' refrigerator. Guests' Victorian parlor with an organ. Picnic table. Large front porch. Babysitting sometimes available.

The Rose and Crown

44 Frogtown Road, Paradise, PA 17562
Phone: 717/768-7684
Location: Surrounded by Amish farms. Two miles south of Intercourse.
Hosts: Linde and Allan Helmbrecht
Open: Mid-March to mid-December.
Rates: $30 single, $50 double. $15 extra adult. No charge for children under 16 or for crib.

"When we came here two years ago from New York City (where Allan was in commodity operations), we had lots of company who enjoyed this area, so we decided to try B&B. Our guests—all terrific—have come from all over the world. When the timing works out, one interesting activity right here is a visit with neighbors who are hog and dairy farmers. . . . Because this area is Amish, we have decorated our renovated carriage house guest rooms rather sparsely, each with a painting by an American artist. Our added-on-to house was built before the Civil War; we think there's a log cabin under the siding. It seems that half the travelers are real vacationers and the other half want to open a B&B in their own home town!"

In residence: In main house, Sean, age five, and Alana, age three.
Restrictions: Children of all ages welcome. No smoking, please.
Foreign language spoken: Spanish.
Bed and bath: Four rooms on first and second floors; each can accommodate four people. Queen or twin beds with sofa bed, extra twin bed, or space for rollaway or crib. Two rooms on each floor share one bath. Each floor has a separate exterior entrance.
Breakfast: 7–9. Full country meal. Bacon, sausage, eggs, pancakes, biscuits, waffles with maple syrup. On screened porch in warm weather.
Plus: Air conditioners in all rooms. Working fireplace in one. Picnic tables, horseshoes, volleyball, and badminton.

The Decoy

958 Eisenberger Road, Strasburg, PA 17579
Phone: 717/687-8585
Location: "Just off a main road, seven miles south of Lancaster. At night you can hear the clip clopping of buggies in the distance." The second highest point in Lancaster County, surrounded by views of Amish farms. Forty-five minutes to Longwood Gardens.
Hosts: Debby and Hap Joy
Open: Year round. Advance reservations appreciated.
Rates: Double occupancy. $50 Memorial Day weekend to December 1. $30 December 1 to Good Friday. $40 Easter to before Memorial Day weekend. Group rates available.

"Escape from the city was our reason for coming from the Washington, D.C., area four years ago. We had stayed in British B&Bs, always thinking about 'someday.' In the Pennsylvania Dutch area—where we are still discovering marvelous places—we found the perfect house. Ten years ago it was built farmhouse style with large rooms and a huge all-purpose kitchen for an Amish family. We have added electricity, heat, and four bathrooms."

In Washington, the Joys were caterers. Here they have a camp food consulting business and Hap is a food service director for a retreat center. "With so many Amish as neighbors, we have learned about wonderful, friendly, and caring people. We help plan day trips, reminding guests that many shops, farmers' markets and our local restaurants are closed on Sundays. Everyone wants to see everything!"

In residence: Wendy, a recent college graduate. Two cats; one blue-eyed Siamese, Cattiva (Italian for "mischievous"); Orphan is a calico cat.
Restrictions: Children are welcome. No smoking at all inside. Sorry, no guests' pets, please.
Bed and bath: Five double-bedded rooms—one on first floor, rest on second—with private shower baths. In each room, a studio couch that converts to two single beds.
Breakfast: 8:30 (wake-up call is at 8). Meat and potato quiche, baked

oatmeal, or pancakes and waffles with real maple syrup. Homemade
jellies, jams, and fruit syrups. "Family raised bacon and sausage. Eggs
from Amish neighbors' chickens." Served in long narrow dining room at
two large tables.
Plus: Bedroom air conditioners. Tea or wine. Kitchen privileges. Option
of lunch and dinner for groups.

The Apple Bin Inn

2835 Willow Street Pike, Willow Street, PA 17584
Phone: 717/464-5881
Location: In Pennsylvania Dutch country. On a main road, in the center
of town, near restaurants and shops. Four miles south of Lancaster. An
hour north of Baltimore.
Hosts: Debbie and Barry Hershey
Open: Year round.
Rates: Double occupancy. $45 shared bath, $60 private bath. $10 addi-
tional person. AMEX, MC, VISA.

"Take our county maps and get lost for an hour or two. That's what
we tell our guests. And in minutes they are off the beaten track into
beautiful countryside with farms and one-room schoolhouses. We know
these roads from cycling. As area residents, we knew this 120-year-old
house, a local landmark that was originally a candy store and then a
private residence with many additions built on through the years."

The Hersheys' theme is "colonial charm and country flavor," and
they have filled the house with folk art and locally made crafts (many for
sale). Their interest in cycling has prompted plans for another extensive
family B&B/cycling trip. (The last one was 1,100 miles to Florida.) And
now Debbie is learning sign language. Apple Bin—where lots of recipes
are exchanged with guests—is a wonderful example of a "happenstance
lifestyle" that has created friendships and contentment for both the host
family and travelers.

In residence: Michelle, age 18. Lauren is 10. Cocoa, the dog, is not allowed inside. Thumper and Raindrop are rabbits.
Restrictions: Sorry, no children under six. No guests' pets. No smoking
inside. No alcoholic beverages, please.
Bed and bath: Four second-floor double-bedded (pencil or acorn post)
rooms. One with private bath, balcony overlooking grounds. Three rooms
(two connect) share one bath. Cot available.
Breakfast: 7–10; 7–9 Sundays. Fresh fruits, homemade bread and muffins,
egg casserole or German apple pancake, coffee, herbal tea. Served in
country dining room or on one of two patios.
Plus: Evening refreshments. Bedroom air conditioners. Color cable TV.
Dinner offered occasionally. Will meet guests at Lancaster airport, train,
or bus. Piano in living room. Shaded patios. Hershey candy kisses. Secure
bicycle storage. Inquire about cycling tours. (The Hersheys are Lancaster
Bicycle Club members.) Picnic lunches prepared.

From New Jersey: "Cozy, comfortable, and clean. . . . Now I can understand why B&Bs have become so popular." From Maryland: "Made you feel a part of the family . . . I travel frequently for my job and can say that The Apple Bin Inn compares very favorably with fine hotels."

The Inn at Mundis Mills

586 Mundis Race Road, York, PA 17402
Phone: 717/755-2002
Location: Quiet. Down a one-lane country road that runs along a creek. On 30 acres (good for exploring). Ten minutes from downtown York. Near antiquing, craft shops, museums, outlets, canoeing. Twenty-five minutes west of Lancaster.
Hosts: Joseph and Marilyn Korsak
Open: Year round. Reservations preferred.
Rates: $45 single, $55 double. $5 per child. $15 extra adult.

"Joe always wanted to practice in a small Pennsylvania town. We came here twelve years ago from Toledo, Ohio, when he graduated from law school. A trip to Ireland gave us the B&B idea. So that we could try it ourselves, we moved in 1985 to this restored 1840 added-on-to miller's house, a place with lots of room for gathering and for privacy. Our antiques, plants, and dried arrangements fit right in. Because we love to go to auctions, we sometimes sell some of our pieces and rearrange things. This year we had skylights installed in the Great Room, which has an open fireplace. We're a family-oriented B&B. When schedules permit, we all eat together with our guests. It's a nice way to start the day."

Marilyn is a trained nurse. She enjoys York, "a less touristy community where there's always something countrylike going on—maybe a festival or an auction on a farm. All year round the Central Market has crafts, foods, local color. Often we suggest back roads or some special hiking trails or wineries."

Restrictions: Children are welcome and must be supervised in the pool. No smoking inside. No guests' pets, please.
Foreign language spoken: French.
Bed and bath: Two very private rooms, each with full bath. Two antique double beds—one with high headboard, the other is iron—in large first-floor room with bay window. Cozy second-floor room has an ornate antique iron double bed. Rollaway and crib available.
Breakfast: 8–10. Homemade muffins and jams. Eggs, pancakes, or French toast with sausage. Cereals. Fruits. Coffee, tea, milk. Served on deck by the pool, on front porch, or in dining room.
Plus: Bedroom ceiling fans. Late-afternoon or evening tea. Mints. Flowers. Guests' own living room in addition to shared Great Room. Front porch swing facing field. Yard. Spontaneous football or soccer with kids. Swimming pool.

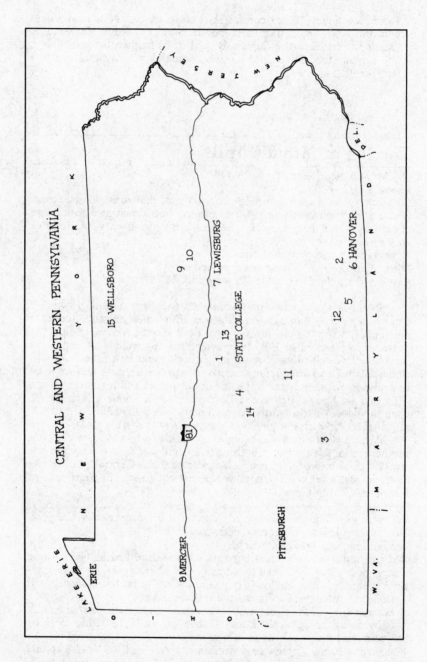

The numbers of this map indicate the locations of central and western Pennsylvania B&Bs described in detail in this chapter. The map for eastern Pennsylvania is on page 196.

CENTRAL AND WESTERN PENNSYLVANIA

Pittsburgh Bed and Breakfast

2190 Ben Franklin Drive, Pittsburgh, PA 15237
Phone: 412/367-8080.
Listings: At least 40 in western Pennsylvania. All hosted private residences, four inns, and one guest house. For a directory, send a self-addressed, stamped envelope.
Rates: $30–$90 single. $34–$99 double. Seventh night free for weekly stays. Deposit required is $20 or 20 percent of long stays. For cancellations received at least seven days before expected arrival, half of deposit refunded. MC, VISA (for deposit only).

Judy Antico accommodates travelers who come for the medical centers, universities, and conventions as well as for the attractions of a city that has interesting architecture, developing riverfront areas, shopping, and "all the updating of just about everything imaginable—even the wholesale produce area." Some guests are en route and appreciate the midpoint stopover.

Many hosts are in suburban communities with good public transportation that includes an underground subway from the South Hills area. Listings cover a 55-mile radius of metropolitan Pittsburgh, north to Mercer and Erie, east to Bedford County and Laurel Highlands, and south to Washington County, which borders West Virginia. Several are near the Pennsylvania Turnpike.

Included are authentically restored houses, Victorians near the city, and some large properties in outlying areas; many are decorated with antiques. One is a working farm.

Reservations: Prefer one or two weeks' notice, "but our hosts are quite flexible and often can take last-minute callers." Also available through travel agents.
Plus: Short-term (up to two months) hosted housing available. Cross-country skiing, hiking, and fishing at some locations. Among the many hosts who are world travelers is one who serves high tea in the afternoon. Another offers guest privileges at a health spa.

Rest & Repast Bed & Breakfast Service

P.O. Box 126, Pine Grove Mills, PA 16868
Phone: 814/238-1484. Monday–Wednesday 9–noon and 6:30–9:30 P.M.

Friday 6:30–9:30. Saturday 9–noon. Closed Thursday and Sunday; as well as December 15–January 1.

Listings: 50 booked through the service. Most are hosted private residences; four are inns. Some available April-November only. Located in north central Pennsylvania, in Centre, Blair, and Huntingdon Counties—in and around Bellefonte, Boalsburg, Spruce Creek, Tyrone (near famous Grier private girls' private school), Holidaysburg, State College, Huntingdon (some are one mile from Juniata College), Potters Mills, and Philipsburg, and near Altoona's PSU campus. A directory ($10) includes information about B&Bs throughout the state, a newsletter, updates, and telephone referrals (for which you make your own reservations).

Rates: $26–$30 single, $30–$45 double. For football weekends, commencement, and the art festival, $40–$65 per room. $10 surcharge for a one-night stay during football weekends. Family and weekly rates. Deposit of $20 per night except for football weekends, when $40 per room per night is required. All cancellations subject to $15 processing fee. Given at least 7 days' notice, balance of deposit is refunded; for football weekends, at least 14 days' notice required.

Linda Feltman and Brent Peters started the reservation service in 1982 to provide needed lodging during peak times in the Penn State area. Because travelers also come for history, culture, and recreation, the service has become active year round. More than 50 percent of the hosts have been on the roster for more than two years. "More than 90 percent attend our January pot-luck host party. They are a bunch of friendly folks, that's for sure!"

Reservations: One week's advance notice usually needed. For big weekends, three months' advance notice recommended.

Plus: Some B&Bs available for up to 14 days. For short-term (4–20 days) housing in private apartments in hosts' homes, breakfast may or may not be included.

Rebecca's House

Bellefonte, PA

Location: High on a hill in a National Register Historic District with mountain views on four sides. Five minutes from Route 80, exit 23, or to Penn State University bus. Ten miles to Penn State. Within walking distance of the county historical library.

Reservations: Available year round through Rest & Repast, page 282.

Rates: $30 single, $35 double. Football weekends $45 per room plus $10 surcharge for a one-night stay.

The family's restoration story is a rebuilding tale that starts with their 1978 purchase of what was a burned-out, water-soaked, and vandalized "place with lots of potential." A year later the local paper headlined, "Operatic Soprano Gets Practice Raising Roof." There are few tasks that the performer/music teacher/choir director hasn't done along with her consulting engineer husband, who is also known for an award-winning Stimson fabric-covered airplane that he rebuilt. (He has also restored a building that houses his office.) Today the parlor is graced by a square 1830 grand piano. The modern kitchen—with fireplace—utilized lumber from an old clothes chute for a bar. The house has been featured in *Victorian Homes* magazine.

The bow-shaped front entrance of the Victorian Gothic leads to a homey atmosphere complete with many original Victorian furnishings—even cat bed warmers—in the 1871 house built for Rebecca Pugh, the young widow of university President Evan Pugh, who had died in 1864. Now, honeymooners, tourists, and Penn State visitors are among B&B guests who "come as strangers and leave as friends."

In residence: One teenaged son. Three cats, Will E. Bear, Tabitha, and Midnight, and a cocker spaniel named Lady. Three young grandchildren who live nearby may be daytime visitors.

Restrictions: Children should be at least 10; exceptions may be made for infants. No guests' pets. No smoking.

Bed and bath: Two second-floor rooms; one with a double bed and one with two twin beds share a full bath. Air mattress and portacrib available.

Breakfast: 7–9. Juice, cereal, milk, coffee, tea, and homemade muffins. Full breakfast on football Sundays. Served in sunny dining room.

Plus: Late-afternoon or evening wine. Large rear deck. Victorian parlor with fireplace and antique harmonium.

The Bechtel Mansion Inn

400 West King Street, East Berlin, PA 17316
Phone: 717/259-7760
Location: In Pennsylvania Dutch country. In the center of East Berlin on Route 234. Eighteen miles east of Gettysburg; 40 miles west of Lancaster. Near fine restaurants, antiques shops, wineries, major weaving center. One hundred miles from Washington, D.C., and Philadelphia; 58 from Baltimore.
Hosts: Charles and Mariam Bechtel
Open: Year round. Reservations preferred. Two-night minimum stay on holiday weekends.
Rates: May 15–November 15 $50–$85 single, $82–$110 double. November 16–May 4 $46–$75 single, $78–$100 double. Suites $80–$95 single, $115–$135 double. $20 rollaway. All rates plus 5 percent service charge. Ski package arrangement with Ski-Roundtop. AMEX, MC VISA.

For honeymooners and anniversary couples, for architecture and history buffs, for arts- and crafts-oriented travelers, and for skiers too, here's a magnificent 28-room Queen Anne Victorian that the Bechtels have restored and furnished with museum-quality antiques and accessories. The mansion, featured in a recent Schumacher wallpaper collection, has original etched glass windows, brass chandeliers, and beautiful woodwork. On the National Register of Historic Places, it is also in the East Berlin National Historic District, which includes 18th-century homes, a restored gristmill, a doll museum (where dolls are restored), an 18th-century school, an 1820 log house, and shops located in period buildings.

The well-traveled Bechtels are weekend hosts. Mariam, a member of Senator Robert Dole's staff, is from Kansas. Charles is a Bell Atlantic manager. His grandparents and great-grandparents were Virginia innkeepers, and his father grew up in a Pennsylvania Dutch family here in East Berlin. Charles has led Smithsonian groups on walking tours. Innkeeper Ruth, an area resident, is also quite knowledgeable about the Amish, Brethren, and local history.

In residence: Ruth Spangler, innkeeper.
Restrictions: Sorry, no guests' pets. No smoking indoors.
Bed and bath: Seven rooms. All have private full or halfbaths. The first-floor suite has a private Victorian parlor. Other rooms on second floor. Twin, double, and queen beds, cot, rollaway, and portacrib available.
Breakfast: 8:30–9:30. Fruit ambrosia, orange juice, coffee cake or home-baked biscuits, muffins or breads, jams and jellies, coffee or tea. Served family style.
Plus: All bedrooms are air conditioned. Beverages. Tour of inn. Living room with oak sliding shutters, bay window, oak and mahogany furnishings. Breakfast room (original cooking kitchen) with exhibits by local artists. Porches, Crafts shop in carriage house includes German nutcrackers and handmade Amish children's and doll furniture.

Newry Manor

Route 1, Box 475, Everett, PA 15537
Phone: 814/623-1250
Location: Rural. On a well-maintained winding road, one mile south of
Route 30, between Everett (three miles) and Bedford (six miles). Across
from the Raystown branch of the Juniata River and the unrestored Juniata
Woolen Mill. Six miles from Bedford historic district with 200 well-
preserved pre-Revolutionary to Art Deco buildings. Near Bedford Spring
Performing Arts Festival (summer). About 12 miles from Breezewood
interchange of Pennsylvania Turnpike; two and a half hours from Pitts-
burgh, Harrisburg, Baltimore, and Washington, D.C.
Hosts: Rosie and Carl Mulert
Open: April 15–November 1.
Rates: Weekdays, single $30–$50, double $35–$55. Weekends, single $35–
$55, double $40–$60.

> From Pennsylvania: "After a long trip by turnpike, to turn into this
> quiet country road with a stream running alongside and see this
> welcoming house . . . was heavenly. And so were our hosts, who
> recommended a restaurant and later relaxed with us in the living
> room where they told us the story of the restored house. We felt as if
> we were visiting old friends."

Rosie is back in her hometown, and Carl, a former federal employee
in Washington, D.C., is leading a group to restore the Juniata Woolen
Mill. Thanks to the Mulerts, both the mill (ruins) and the B&B are on the
National Register of Historic Places. Their home, part stone, brick, and
log, was a five-year restoration project that concluded with refinished
(without a sanding machine) floors, uncovered fireplaces, rebuilt railings,
and converted gas chandeliers that have cranberry glass shades. Furnishings are antiques, reproductions, and family heirlooms. This place to stay
is becoming the reason to go.

Restrictions: Children 12 and over are welcome. Smoking restricted to
first floor. Sorry, no pets. Maximum of two guests per room.
Bed and bath: Three second-floor rooms, each with private bath and
porch. One queen bed, full bath, working fireplace. One queen canopied
four-poster bed, shower bath. Room with two twin beds has bath with
tub, hand-held shower, working fireplace.
Breakfast: 7:30–9:30. Usually continental plus, including orange juice,
fresh fruit, homemade muffins or coffee cake, and beverage. Served in
keeping room or in dining room.
Plus: Tea, coffee, soft drinks, wine coolers. Tour of house. Bedroom fans.
Living room with color cable TV, Steinway baby grand piano. Solarium.

> From Virginia: "Charming, super clean and authentically furnished.
> Breakfast was delicious and attractively served. A real gem!"

Maple Hill Farms

Gatesburg, PA
Location: Quiet. On a hill overlooking field with grazing cows. Twelve miles southeast of Pennsylvania State University, just past state game lands and Scotia Range. On a working family dairy farm with pigs, laying hens, ducks, geese, and a pair of tame turkeys.
Reservations: Available year round through Rest & Repast, page 282. Two-night minimum preferred on football weekends.
Rates: Double occupancy. $30–$40 depending on time of year and family size. $40–$55 on football weekends.

"Some guests enjoy jogging around the farm or walking the back lane to the fields where deer may be seen. One guest who lives in the city expressed delight at hearing rain on the tin roof, seeing the stars shine, and watching the sun come up. For five years now we have shared our country lifestyle and quiet setting with friendly B&B travelers. We bring flowers in from the garden and serve fresh eggs and whole country milk. Our stone house, which is a combination of German and Georgian styles, was built in the late 1820s by Jacob Gates. The village of Gatesburg can be seen across our fields."

The friendly hostess is a busy dairy farmer's wife. Her husband works in the Agronomy Department at Penn State University. Their home is listed on Centre County's Historic Building Project Registration.

In residence: One small long-haired dog. One grown daughter. Grandchildren from next door "love to drop in to say hello."
Bed and bath: Two second-floor double-bedded rooms share a tub bath with hosts. Rollaway available.
Breakfast: Anytime until 9:30. Bacon, farm-fresh eggs, toast, juice, fruit, milk, and homemade muffins. Served in dining room or in summer kitchen.
Plus: Beverages. Tour of farm. Bedroom ceiling fans. Swing on wraparound veranda.

The Brafferton Inn

44 York Street, Gettysburg, PA 17325
Phone: 717/337-3423
Location: In downtown Gettysburg, within walking distance of Battlefield, shops, restaurants, college, and theater. Fifteen minutes to Liberty ski area.
Hosts: Mimi and Jim Agard
Open: Year round.
Rates: $65 shared bath, $75 private bath. $10 additional person. MC, VISA.

A gem! You have to step into this building sandwiched between a stained glass shop and a bookstore to experience the warm hospitality in Gettysburg's first house. It is on the National Register of Historic Places and has been featured in *Country Living*.

"Who has all the talent around here?" guests often ask. When Jim, chairman of the art department at Gettysburg College—and restorer of five Vermont houses—redid this 14-room stone house (which has a 7-room pre–Civil War clapboard addition), he applied magnificent copies of 18th-century stencils on whitewashed walls and decorated with country antiques, prints, samplers, and oil paintings. A potter made bowls for sinks. Guest rooms are separated from the main house by a glass-covered atrium. In the rear of the inn, near where Continental troops gathered, there's another Agard production, an intimate flower garden and deck.

Before moving to Gettysburg, Mimi was in public relations at CBS in New York City. Here she is unofficial tour guide to "wonderful people who come for the Battlefield, to hike, bike, enjoy summer theater and area restaurants."

In residence: Three teenagers, Jason, Melissa, and Brian. "A darling cream color toy poodle," Quincy.
Restrictions: Children over seven preferred. Sorry, no guests' pets. Smoking in designated areas.
Bed and bath: Eight air-conditioned rooms, all with (nonworking) fireplaces. In 1860 addition, private baths for four first-floor rooms (with double bed or a double plus a twin daybed). In original 1786 house, one full bath shared by four rooms with one double or two twin beds. Rollaways and crib available.
Breakfast: 8–9. Seasonal fruit, juice, coffee, tea, and a warm dish such as peaches and cream French toast. Served by Melissa in the dining room, which features a primitive mural of 18 Gettysburg buildings.
Plus: Player piano. Tour of house. Mints. Flowers. Option of picnic baskets. Tips on "how best to see The Battlefield." For area restaurants—menus on hand and reservations made.

Beechmont Inn

315 Broadway, Hanover, PA 17331
Phone: 717/632-3013
Location: On a tree-lined residential street near the intersection of Routes 194, 94, and 116. Fifteen minutes east of Gettysburg Battlefield; 45 minutes from Baltimore. Near wineries, restaurants, farmers' market, state park, skiing, antiques shops, and outlet shopping. Two hours from Washington and Philadelphia.
Hosts: The Hormels—Glenn and Maggie (father and mother); Monna and Terry (daughter-in-law and son).
Open: Year round.
Rates: $64–$79 single, $70–$85 double. $10 third person in room. MC, VISA, personal checks.

All 16 rooms of this gracious Federal house, built by the Hershey family in 1834, were completely redecorated with period colors, artwork, and furnishings (some reproductions) when the Hormels decided to "create a memory that lingers pleasantly long after your stay has ended." Their attention to detail includes 18th-century books in the library, queen-sized pillows on guest beds, and a collection of Civil War and local memorabilia. Gardens and even an old-fashioned glider swing are on the landscaped grounds. It's the kind of place that business guests return to as tourists.

The Hormels, well-traveled B&B guests who have several Hanover-based businesses, share the innkeeping. Maggie and Glenn are full-time residents. Monna hosts and handles many of the household duties. And Terry, an adjunct professor at a local college and a former management consultant, does the cooking. (One of his antique Jaguar automobiles is usually in residence at the inn.)

Restrictions: Children should be at least 12. No pets. Smoking allowed in bedrooms or outdoors.
Foreign language spoken: "College French."
Bed and bath: Seven rooms with queen or double bed; all with private baths. Three large suites; one with working fireplace and two with kitchenettes. Four second-floor rooms reached by a wide spiral staircase. Extra beds for some rooms.
Breakfast: Weekdays 7–9, weekends 8–9. Spiced coffee, a variety of teas, juice, homemade York County Fair prizewinning granola, rice pudding with spiced fruit compote. Entree could be asparagus and ham crepes with Mornay sauce, sausage torte with corn custard, or herb cheese tarts with sweet potato souffle. Freshly baked muffins or sweet breads. Desserts offered on weekends. Served in dining room or outside under the trumpet vine trellis. Guests may also take a tray to their rooms.
Plus: Air-conditioned guest and common rooms. Formal parlor and library. Wicker-furnished back porch. Vine-covered veranda. Flagstone patio with park bench under a 125-year-old magnolia tree. Off-street parking. Bikes.

The Pineapple Inn

439 Market Street, Lewisburg, PA 17837
Phone: 717/524-6200
Location: In the middle of the Susquehanna Valley in a Federal/Victorian town. On a main street (Route 45) corner, four blocks from Route 15. A few blocks from Bucknell University. One hour east of State College and north of Harrisburg. Minutes from Woolrich and Christian Dior outlets. Half hour from Lycoming College and Bloomsburg and Susquehanna universities.
Hosts: Charles and Deborah North
Open: Year round. Two-day minimum stay required during area colleges' special events weekends.

Rates: $45 single weeknights, $55 weekends. $55 double. ($75 private bath.) $88 suite. $15 cot. MC, VISA.

Many guests say, "Just by chance we left the highway only to discover Lewisburg and the Pineapple Inn, our first B&B, a benchmark for future B&Bs. We feel spoiled!"

The 1857 brick Federal home was lovingly restored by the previous owners before the Norths converted it to an inn four years ago. Deborah's natural flair for color and design comes through in the formal parlor and in different guest rooms that feature stenciling, Victorian furnishings, authentic furniture of the Archbishop of Canterbury, equestrian artifacts, or antique quilts. (Her degree is in Middle East archaeology, philosophy, and religion; her professional experience combines digs in Israel and decorating the inn!)

For Charles, fatherhood encouraged the change from being convention director of the Hilton in Washington, D.C. (He was the one who handled the media the day President Reagan was shot while leaving the hotel.) Through 17 years of hotel and restaurant work, he dreamed of finding an undiscovered area filled with history, recreational opportunities, and antiques and craft shops. And here he is, host and antique tub restorer, who, together with Deborah, finds that they are still meeting artists whose studios are "down a lane." A potter, one of the country's 10 best jewelers, photographers, and a "wonderful cycle repair shop owner too" are among the fellow residents who also appreciate this delightful region.

In residence: Marisa is seven. Chad is five. Christopher is almost four.
Restrictions: Well-behaved and well-supervised children are welcome. Sorry, no pets (kennel nearby). Smoking permitted in parlor according to other guests' wishes.
Bed and bath: Six second-floor rooms, most with private full baths. Queen or double beds. Suite with a room with a queen, another with two twins.
Breakfast: 7–9. Amish slab cut bacon, country-fresh brown eggs, cinnamon stack muffins, Walnut Acres granolas (made and packaged nearby), cottage cheese pancakes (like those Charles served to Macy's shoppers in McLean, Virginia, during a very successful Meet-The-Hosts program), or French toast made with homemade bread.
Plus: Fully air conditioned. Complimentary tea, 4–6. Parlor. Turned-down beds. Chocolates on pillows. Walking tour information. Directions to source for beautifully made, reasonably priced Amish quilts. Cross-country skiing/hiking nearby.

The Stranahan House

117 East Market Street, Mercer, PA 16137
Phone: 412/662-4516
Location: In the center of town, steps from historical society with museum, library, and exhibits. Within 20 minutes of Amish country, an-

tiques shops, forges (free tours), Slippery Rock University, and Thiel, Westminster, and Grove City colleges. Five miles from I-79 and one mile from I-80. One hour north of Pittsburgh and south of Erie.
Hosts: Jim and Ann Stranahan
Open: Year round. Reservations required.
Rates: $45 single, $50 double. $10 extra person.

From New York: "Delightful. Immaculate and tastefully decorated with beautiful antiques. Our rooms were charming and breakfasts were delicious and elegantly served. Not only were the hosts warm and gracious, but they were also very knowledgeable about the history of the area. They directed us to Amish farms and antique shops. Mercer is a quiet, pretty little town which has changed very little over the years. We can't wait to 'do it all' again."

Just around the corner is the Apothecary Shoppe with old soda fountain and paddle fans. The old-fashioned band concerts are still a big summer activity. The county courthouse can be seen for miles around. Many craftspeople have discovered the town (population: 2,800), and now more travelers are—thanks to Jim, a fourth-generation Mercer County lawyer, and Ann, formerly in sales and laboratory work. Together with their three children, they are quite immersed in community activities. Every letter of praise (and I have received many) about the hosts and their 150-year-old brick Empire house is very detailed. Some even describe the entire breakfast menu.

In residence: A 16-year-old daughter; one 9-year-old son and another who was a year old in February 1989.
Restrictions: "Babes in arms and well-behaved children are welcome." Sorry, no guests' pets. No smoking.
Bed and bath: Two second-floor rooms, one with private full bath. One room with double bed, Victorian (Philadelphia made) furnishings; the other with two double spool rope beds and working fireplace. Cot and portacrib available.
Breakfast: 7–9. Menu varies. Could include quiche lorraine, German apple pancakes with sausage or cheddar cheese. Fresh eggs, meats, cereal, homemade granola, homemade sweet rolls with cream cheese filling, homemade strawberry jam. Served in fireplaced dining room or on screened back porch.
Plus: Beverages and snacks. Fireplaced living room. Kitchen and laundry privileges. Bedroom ceiling fans.

The Carriage House at Stonegate

RD 1, Box 11A, Montoursville, PA 17754
Phone: 717/433-4340
Location: On 30 wooded acres along the banks of Mill Creek. On Route 87, a minute from I-180. Two miles from Williamsport/Lycoming County airport. Within 30 minutes of Lycoming, Bucknell, and Bloomsburg. Six

miles from Williamsport. Close to Crystal Lake Cross-Country Ski Center, hiking, waterfalls, fishing, and hunting.
Hosts: Harold and Dena Mesaris
Open: Year round. Advance reservations preferred.
Rates: $45 one room, $55 two rooms. $10 each additional guest.

> From Virginia: "Private, comfortable and roomy. Gracious hosts who were helpful with information about the area. More than we ever expected."

A haven at the end of the road—even in a winter's storm! Your own home away from home, a 1,400-square-foot getaway, is in a converted carriage house on the property of one of the oldest farmhouses in the lower Loyasock Creek Valley. Remodeled in 1985, it has wide board floors, some country antiques, and some modern pieces. Harold and Dena usually book one party—up to 10 guests (for a wedding)—at a time.

If you'd like, there are opportunities to "meet the whole family"—Harold, a pilot and aircraft accident investigator; Dena, a teacher who is active in the community; their children; and all the farm animals. For what Harold calls moderately difficult exercise, there are accessible old logging roads. And for a little history, the hosts will tell you about the early valley settlement and direct you to the old family cemetery located about a quarter mile from the B&B.

In residence: In main house, Allison, 14; Meghan, 11; Darcey, 10; and Judd, 8. Two Newfoundlands, several Persian cats, one pony; one sheep, one rabbit, four geese, and eight chickens.
Restrictions: Children of all ages welcome. Guests' pets allowed. No smoking in bedrooms.
Foreign language spoken: Some Spanish.
Bed and bath: Two second-level rooms—one with a double bed and one with a queen—share a full and a half bath. Rollaway and crib available.
Breakfast: Flexible hours. Juice, coffee, fruit, muffins, egg dish with meat. Served in guests' dining room. Host often joins you for tea.
Plus: On first floor, large sitting room with cable TV, dining area, full kitchen, refrigerator stocked with snacks. Babysitting. Swing set. Electric blankets.

The Bodine House

307 South Main Street, Muncy, PA 17756
Phone: 717/546-8949
Location: On a tree-lined street in a National Historic District, three blocks from center of Muncy. Ten minutes from I-80 and U.S. Route 15. Fifteen minutes to city of Williamsport and to Bucknell University. Within 30 minutes of sports, wineries, two state parks in Endless Mountains, summer theater.
Hosts: David and Marie Louise Smith
Open: Year round. Reservations preferred.

Rates: $25 single room. Doubles, $40 half bath, $45 full bath, $50 twin room. $5 less for singles. $10 rollaway. Special historic house tour weekend package.

The Smiths had always thought about living in this "nice little town" whenever they drove through. Twelve years ago they bought this restored Federal town house, which had been owned by the same family from 1805 to 1976. Outside, they mounted a 13-star Betsy Ross flag. Inside, when the living room is lit entirely with candles, there is a feeling of another era—with four working fireplaces and many 18th- and 19th-century antiques.

When the Smiths were bringing up their family, they lived—for 17 years—in the Washington, D.C., area. David was a marketing manager then; now he is host/chef/gift and picture-framing shop owner. Marie Louise is business manager in a surgeon's office.

Restrictions: Children should be at least six. No pets. No smoking.
Bed and bath: Four second-floor rooms, each with individual heat control and air conditioner. Private full baths for one double room and one with two twins. One double with private half bath shares a full bath with a single room. Rollaway available.
Breakfast: 7:30–9:30. Hot and cold cereal, bacon and eggs, toast, muffins, coffee, tea, milk, juices. Served by candlelight; in winter, by the dining room fireplace.
Plus: Wine and cheese, 5–7 P.M. Line-dried sheets. Electric blankets. Free use of bicycles.

Salvino's Guest House

Box 116, Route 522, Orbisonia, PA 17243
Phone: 814/447-5616
Location: "On Route 522 that goes through this sleepy town of southern Huntingdon County, surrounded by mountains, about 20 minutes from exit 13 on the Pennsylvania Turnpike and from Route 22. Three doors down from the only traffic light in town." Minutes to Shade Gap Electric Railway Trolley Museum and to 50-minute ride on one of country's oldest narrow-gauge lines, with steam engine that used to haul coal. Casual eating places in town; 15 minutes to fine dining.
Hosts: Elaine and Joe Salvino
Open: Year round. Advance reservations required during summer months.
Rates: $25 single, $35 double. $10 extra person. No charge for infants. MC, VISA.

Guests wrote: "A homey place. Helpful hosts. Clean. Comfortable. Quiet. . . . While filming the railroad for public television we enjoyed meeting the friendly Salvinos and their guests from anywhere in the country. We shall return! . . . It was wonderful for us and our five-

month-old baby. . . . Makes you feel a part of smalltown America. . . .
Enjoyed our stay while working on the East Broad Top Railroad. . . .
Even made sure that I got up in time to go deer hunting."

A native returns home! Elaine's great-grandparents "and maybe further back then that" were born in Orbisonia. She grew up here, "went to the big cities and vacationed in [B&B capital] Cape May. When Joe retired from bricklaying and working for Conrail a year ago, we thought of doing B&B in Harrisburg, but decided to buy this B&B which had been made from a doctor's home. Because so many people come here for the East Broad Top Railroad and the trolley museum, we have many pictures of the days when 'rails were king.' I teach quilting and have a quilt shop here. Our guests feel as if they have discovered this town, one without shopping malls."

In residence: "Trouble, our black friendly dog, has his chair in the living room."
Restrictions: Children and pets are welcome. Smoking is allowed as long as it doesn't bother other guests.
Foreign language spoken: A little Italian.
Bed and bath: Five second-floor rooms share two baths. Twin or double beds. Some rooms have a sofa bed and/or room for a rollaway or crib.
Breakfast: 8–9. Juice, tea, coffee including decaf, cereal, cinnamon buns. Sometimes, breakfast pie. Larger breakfast served to hunters.
Plus: Air-conditioned bedrooms. Swing on porch.

Hickory Bridge Farm

96 Hickory Bridge Road, Orrtanna, PA 17353
Phone: 717/642-5261
Location: Quiet. On 100 acres in the Appalachian Mountain foothills, with apple blossoms, trout fishing in stream right here, and nearby antiques and flea markets. Eight miles west of Gettysburg. Five miles to Ski Liberty; 60 miles from Baltimore.
Hosts: Robert and Mary Lynn Martin and Dr. and Mrs. James Hammett
Open: Year round. Closed between Christmas and New Year's. Advance reservations required. Two-night minimum on April–October weekends.
Rates: Monday–Thursday, cottage $59; in farmhouse, one room with private bath $59, two rooms (four guests) with one bath $90, three rooms (six guests) with two baths $130. Weekends, cottage $75; one farmhouse room with private bath $75, two rooms $95, three rooms $135. Ten percent discount for families. Cribs free. $10 extra person. MC, VISA.

Mary Lynn explains the unique B&B: "It all began when my mother was researching area history (20 years ago) and found that a franchise was going to buy the local tavern which was located in a true country inn, an old stagecoach stop. My father, who is a *real* country doctor, brothers and friends restored the inn. The business grew and grew! We sold it, because it was more than we wanted to manage, and bought this farm, another business that needed restoring with a personal touch. Our antiques-filled 1700s home, the farmhouse, is where my mother and I prepare and serve breakfast to all B&B guests. In the restaurant, a converted barn decorated with farm antiques, we serve homecooked dinners on weekends. In six years, word of mouth has brought a long list of friends and friends of friends who feel like extended family."

Restrictions: Children of all ages welcome. Sorry, no pets.
Bed and bath: Seven air-conditioned rooms. In farmhouse, private shower bath for one room with queen bed. One room with queen and one with a double bed share a full bath. Four country-decorated cottages with a queen or two double beds, private shower baths, working Franklin fireplaces.
Breakfast: 8:30–9. Farm style. Pancakes, sausage, eggs, bacon, homegrown fruit, homemade jams, apple butter, and potato bread. Served on deck in warm weather.
Plus: Fresh fruit. Flowers. Mints. Wine. Air-conditioned bedrooms in farmhouse and cabins. Weekend dinners (5–9 p.m., $13.50 per person) with homegrown or local produce. Trout fishing (bring your license).

General Potter Farm

Potters Mills, PA
Location: Thirteen miles east of Penn State University. Near Amish country, caves, museums, and state recreational areas.
Reservations: Available March–December through Rest & Repast, page 282.
Rates: $25 single, $35–$45 double, $60 triple. Football weekends, $40–$60 (plus $10 for one-night reservations). $15 cot. Family rates, (not available on football or special event weekends) for two rooms with bath, $45.

After coming to the area for college in 1960, the hosts became permanent residents. In 1979, when the "for sale" sign appeared before the home and on the farmland of the first judge in the county, the couple, a chemist and a teacher of English as a second language, were inspired to take on additional responsibilities and become owners of this 17-room Federal period house. It is on the National Register of Historic Places and has 12 outbuildings, reminders of the variety of activities that were part of farm life here for over a century. Guests often help feed the ducks, chickens, geese, pigs, horses, calves, and bunnies. And all ages are welcome to (learn to) harvest herbs; garden (crops include wheat, corn, alfalfa, asparagus, red raspberries, and black-eyed peas); collect eggs; make flower arrangements; and even "shovel" for creatures. Much of the main house renovation work—a continuous process—has been completed, with each room different. The huge kitchen is "country." The dining room is Victorian; the library is Native American. The farmers will gladly share a before-and-after album as well as history of the farm and area.

In residence: Grandchildren, ages four and six, often visit on weekends. One Persian cat and a calico cat are among their pets.

Restrictions: No guests' pets. No smoking.

Bed and bath: Late spring through fall, five rooms (three in winter); one is on ground floor. Rooms have one or two double beds or a double plus two twins. One room with private bath. Cots available.

Breakfast: At time (usually 7:30–9) prearranged with guests. Full farm breakfast with farm meats, produce, and eggs. In summer the hostess's mother, a retired professional nutritionist, occasionally cooks with her. Served in the library alcove or in the formal dining room.

Plus: Use of "all of downstairs" with its formal parlor furnished with period pieces, judge's parlor, formal dining room, library, and keeping room. Three spacious porches. Dinner by arrangement summers and weekends. Campfires in summer. Picnic area. Hiking and nature paths. Streams for fishing. "Chamber of Commerce" volume of pamphlets and clippings. Suggested routes to see unusual architecture. Bedroom window fans. Sometimes, babysitting.

Guests wrote: "The hosts are the big plus here. They welcome you with an immediate feeling of friendship and spoil you with great food and conversation. It's a beautiful old property being cared for lovingly."

The White House B&B Inn

Tyrone, PA

Location: On main road coming into Tyrone. Two blocks from downtown and Gardners Candy Museum, one-quarter mile from Reservoir Park in Allegheny Mountains.

Reservations: Available year round through Rest & Repast, page 282. Two-night minimum for some Penn State football weekends.

Rates: Per room. $45 queen or double bed. $55 king bed. Rollaway, $15 adult, $10 child.

The hostess, a nursing school student who has studied interior design, grew up in New England and "always wanted a B&B." The host is a Pennsylvanian who lived in New York in the 1950s. They moved here from Florida in 1986 after searching for the perfect place. "We found this well-maintained columned Federal-style house that was built in 1896 with crown moldings and 12-foot ceilings. We furnished with antiques collected in Florida." The hostess designed and made all the drapes as well as the satin and velvet canopies.

"Since opening the inn in the fall of 1987, we have hosted Marriott Hotel executives and the designer of the 1988 Olympic pool. Some guests come for getaways, football weekends, or to visit relatives in a nearby nursing home. It seems that they all enjoy the library, the fireplace in the living room, and the gas fireplace in the ballroom."

In residence: Two teenage sons.
Restrictions: Children welcome. Smoking allowed downstairs only. No guests' pets, please.
Bed and bath: Three second-floor rooms. (Two have French doors leading to balcony with ice cream parlor chairs.) One room has king canopied bed with velvet headboard, a sofa, and a private full bath en suite. Double-bedded room (partial canopy) and room with a queen bed (and small refrigerator) share a full bath. Rollaway available.
Breakfast: Flexible hours. Scrambled eggs, bacon or sausage, toast, blueberry muffins, juice, coffee, tea, sometimes French toast. Served family style in formal dining room, or on balcony by special request.
Plus: Tea, coffee, hot chocolate, cold drinks. Mints. Thick towels. Flowers. Will meet guests at train or bus station. Ballroom with baby grand piano. Library with sofa, chairs, built-in window seat, and desk for letter writing.

Kaltenbach's Bed and Breakfast

Stony Fork Road, RD 6, Box 106A, Wellsboro, PA 16901
Phone: 717/724-4954
Location: On 72 acres surrounded by meadows, pastures, forests (hiking and cross-country skiing), and streams (fishing). "In Pennsylvania's Grand Canyon." Near U.S. Fish Research Laboratory (salmon and trout), lumber museum, paddle-wheeled riverboat, white water rafting, Laurel Festival, logging contests, historical society museum. Twenty minutes from Sawmill and Denton Hill ski areas. Forty minutes south of Corning, New York.
Host: Lee Kaltenbach
Open: Year round. Four-night minimum stay during hunting season.
Rates: $37.50 single. $53 double. $89.50 honeymoon suite. $26.50 third person. MC, VISA.

New Jersey blueberry farmers have been known to arrive with supplies for Lee to bake with. (His recipes are so popular that they are printed for distribution.) Milk is delivered here in big glass jugs from a neighbor who processes it. Son Tim, an active 4-H member, has planted 400 strawberry plants and cares for the pigs, sheep, lambs, rabbits, and steers.

Since opening his sprawling new flagstone ranch house as a B&B eight years ago, Lee, an area native who sells insurance, has organized a Valentine's Day event complete with sleigh rides and hot chocolate. (Three thousand people came.) He meets skiers who come "home" to the cathedral-ceilinged living room with fireplace and mounted elk head. Families also love this place—hosted by the enthusiastic president of the area Tourism Council.

In residence: Timothy, age 16. One 14-pound outdoor cat "looks like Morris." Farm animals.

Restrictions: Children of all ages welcome. No smoking inside. Sorry, no guests' pets please.

Bed and bath: Ten rooms with king or queen beds share seven baths. Honeymoon suite has bath with red tub for two. Some rooms are handicapped accessible. Rollaway available.

Breakfast: Flexible hours. Juices, five styles of eggs, bacon, sausage, ham, whole wheat or white toast, homemade muffins and jams, fruit, cereal.

Plus: Beverages and snacks. Phones available. Cable TV in rooms. Babysitting. Picnic tables, outdoor grill, and playground.

Guests wrote: "Kaltenbach's is missing from your book! Great hospitality. Exceptional location with exhilarating mountain views. Outstanding food in unlimited quantities. . . . The highlight of our trip. Tim gave a wonderful barn tour. . . . I've stayed at about 100 B&Bs and have never written such a letter but I've never had such fine accommodations either."

Virginia

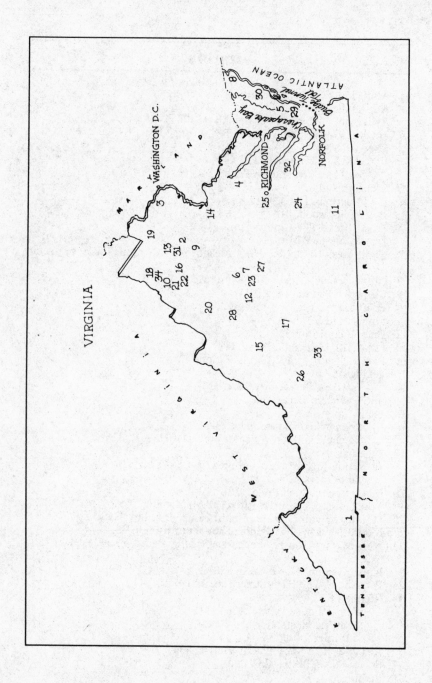

The numbers of this map indicate the locations of B&Bs described in detail in this chapter.

KEY

Recipes shared, often for house specialties.

Inquiries welcomed about restoration and/or decorating. Symbol indicates that host is willing to share experiences with guests. Tips range from a before-and-after album to rebuilding advice, from furniture refinishing to curtain making. Expertise of hosts ranges from learn-by-doing to professional.

How-to B&B workshop, seminar, or apprentice program offered.

Virginia Reservation Services

Bensonhouse

2036 Monument Avenue, Richmond, VA 23220
Phone: 804/353-6900. Monday–Friday, 10–6. Weekend hours vary. Office closed December 15–January 2.
Listings: 30 hosted private residences within 10 minutes of Richmond's sites and attractions. A few are in Williamsburg and Fredericksburg. Some inns. Most are located in historic districts, have private baths, and are air conditioned. They are on or near bus lines. Directory ($3) with SASE.
Rates: $40–$90 single, $52–$102 double. Some hosts offer discounts for families. Deposit of 30 percent of total stay required. Deposit, less $20, refunded if seven days' notice of cancellation is provided; no refund with shorter notice. AMEX, MC, VISA; cash or checks preferred.

As a business woman who travels frequently, Lyn Benson appreciates unique accommodations with hosts who are sensitive to guests' needs. Through her well-established (and respected) service she makes a special effort to match guest to host as well as home "to maximize the B&B experience."

Reservations: Prefer two to three weeks' advance notice but will accommodate last-minute requests if possible. Available through travel agents.
Plus: Fully furnished unhosted self-contained apartments, carriage houses, and homes for relocating executives. Leased for several weeks to several months at a time.

Blue Ridge Bed & Breakfast

Rocks & Rills Farm, Route 2, Box 3895, Berryville, VA 22611
Phone: 703/955-1246. Usually Monday–Friday, 9–1.
Listings: 50, mostly hosted private residences. A few inns and unhosted homes. No charge for directory but please enclose a self-addressed stamped envelope.
Rates: $40–$75 single, $45–$150 double. Family and senior citizen rates. Some weekly rates available. Deposit required is half of total stay. No refunds with less than 48 hours' notice of cancellation. Some hosts accept credit cards.

Rita Duncan's hosts live east and west of the Blue Ridge Mountains in the northern end of the Shenandoah Valley. In Virginia they are in Berryville, Bluemont, Flint Hill, Hinton, Luray, Purcellville, Washington,

Warm Springs, Winchester, and Woodstock. In West Virginia—in Berkeley Springs, Charles Town, Middleway, Shepherdstown, and Summit Point. Also in Mercersburg, Pennsylvania; and Hagerstown, Maryland. Most feature country breakfasts and reasonable rates along with "southern hospitality." They are near canoeing, hiking, fishing, skiing, hunting, golfing, cross-country skiing, swimming, tennis, horseback riding, and riding trails. Most are also close to antiques shops and fine restaurants.

Reservations: One week's advance notice preferred. Available through travel agents.
Plus: Discounts for some theaters and antiques shops. Racetrack passes.

Guesthouses

P.O. Box 5737, Charlottesville, VA 22905
Phone: 804/979-7264. Monday–Friday 12–5. Closed weekends, major holidays and Christmas week.
Listings: 80 regular hosts. More than 200 for major University of Virginia weekends. Almost all listings are hosted private residences. Two inns. Directory is $1.
Rates: $36–$80 single, $48–$160 double. $4 surcharge for a one-night stay. Some weekly rates available. Deposit of 25 percent of total fee required. With seven days' advance notice of cancellation, deposit less $15 service fee refunded. MC, VISA, AMEX for deposits only.

Originally established for America's bicentennial year, Mary Hill Caperton's service has many experienced hosts in the Charlottesville/ Albemarle County area. Some are close to the University of Virginia; a few are in Luray, Virginia. The wide range of rates includes luxurious estates, antebellum homes, and modest comfortable residences. Some homes are on the National Register and have been on the annual Historic Garden Week.

Reservations: Two weeks' advance notice preferred. Two-day minimum stay preferred.
Plus: Short-term (one week to three months) housing available in apartments or efficiency suites with host nearby.

Lamp Lighters Bed and Breakfast

Route 7, Box 96G, Lynchburg, VA 23503
Phone: 804/384-1635. Tuesday–Saturday noon–6:30 P.M. Closed Sundays.
Listings: Four hosted private residences in south central Virginia (Lynchburg and Bedford County). All homes have private baths and air conditioning. For a descriptive list, please send a business-size self-addressed stamped envelope.

Rates: $36–$60 single, $44–$60 double. $2 surcharge for one-night stay. Some family and weekly rates. One night's rate required as deposit. Deposit refunded if cancellation notice is received at least four days before arrival. MC, VISA.

Judy Wynne offers a homestay arrangement with sharing residents who offer a warm welcome to a home away from home. "We take pride in the warmth of our homes, places that range from a very elegant three-storied home in a beautiful section of town to a cottage that is rustic, yet really nice!" Her hosts are all enthusiastic about this area, which includes Thomas Jefferson's summer home, Patrick Henry's home and burial place, Appomattox, Booker T. Washington's birthplace, and Blue Ridge Parkway.

Reservations: For most homes, one week is the maximum stay.

Princely Bed & Breakfast, Ltd.

819 Prince Street, Alexandria, VA 22314
Phone: 703/683-2159. Monday–Friday 10–6.
Listings: 30. Mostly hosted private residences. A few unhosted apartments.
Rates: $65–$75 per room. $10 surcharge for a one-night stay. Monthly rates available. Deposit required is equal to one night's stay. With more than 72 hours' notice of cancellation, full refund made, minus $10 service charge.

"Deluxe accommodations and beautifully served breakfasts" have been offered by E. J. Mansmann's Alexandria hosts since he established the service in 1981 on retiring from the State Department. All have private baths and air conditioning. Many hosts live in Old Town in historically significant houses built between 1750 and 1830; they are near fast, frequent transportation to Washington, D.C.

Reservations: One week's advance notice and two-day minimum stay required. Also available through travel agents.
Plus: Some hosts take guests sightseeing.

Shenandoah Valley Bed & Breakfast Reservations

P.O. Box 6434, Woodstook, VA 22664
Phone: 703/459-8241 or 896-2904. Year round, every day, 9 A.M.–10 P.M.
Listings: 20. Most are hosted private residences. Three inns. Communities represented include Amissville, Dublin, Harrisonburg, Front Royal,

New Market, Orkney Springs, McGaheysville, Rawley Springs, Staunton, Winchester, Woodstock, Roanoke, Luray, Dillwyn. Directory is $1.
Rates: $40–$60 single, $45–$100 double. Family and weekly rates. Deposit of 25 percent lodging rate for entire stay required. $50 annual membership fee. If cancellation notice is received more than 72 hours in advance, deposit less $20 processing fee is refunded. MC, VISA.

Patricia Lee Waldorf says, "By keeping in touch with our hosts, we feel a good camaraderie that contributes to more service and more satisfaction. I am an accountant by profession and have been trained as a European chef. The staff (tiny but accommodating) is in tune with the European way of complete pampering for the traveler. They know the hosts and their homes."

Reservations: As much advance notice as possible appreciated.
Plus: Travel information and advice for plan-it-yourself tours. Many hosts speak German. "And many offer a sumptuous breakfast."

Other reservation services in Virginia:
Bed and Breakfast of Tidewater Virginia, P.O. Box 3343, Norfolk, VA 23514. Phone: 804/627-1983 or 627-9409.
Rockbridge Reservations, P.O. Box 76, Brownsburg, VA 24415. Phone: 703/347-5698.
The Travel Tree, P.O. Box 838, Williamsburg, VA 23187. Phone: 804/253-1571.

Summerfield Inn

101 West Valley Street, Abingdon, VA 24201
Phone: 703/628-5905
Location: In historic district of a town "with seven excellent restaurants" and mountain views. One block from Barter Theatre, the country's oldest continuous repertory theater. Twenty minutes from Appalachian Trail. Near Virginia Creeper hiking and biking trail. One hour west of Blue Ridge Parkway. One-half mile from I-81. Two hours from Roanoke.
Hosts: Champe and Don Hyatt
Open: Year round. Reservations recommended April–October; required for other months.
Rates: $50 single. $60–$70 double. Suite, two rooms sharing a bath, $110. Ten percent discount on stays of three or more nights. MC, VISA.

> From half a dozen states: "Elegant . . . charming . . . hospitable hosts . . . near shops, good place to eat, theater. . . . A pleasant experience for a woman traveling alone. . . . We felt fortunate that there was no room at a nearby inn. . . . A marvelous blend of yesterday and today . . . breathtaking antiques . . . delicious and memorable breakfast served with china, sterling, and crystal . . . a jewel!"

Those comments hint at the praise heaped on the home environment created by the Hyatts, hosts who have enjoyed B&Bs during their own travels in California. They thought about Don's retirement from dentistry and bought a 1920s home in Abingdon, the town where Champe's parents lived for 25 years while her father was manager and president of the Martha Washington Inn. After extensive renovations, Summerfield was opened in 1987, with color schemes—soft pinks and greens—inspired by a living room portrait of the Hyatt children, who are now grown. Those front porch rockers are popular, especially at cocktail time. A jewel indeed.

In residence: "Pepper, our resident miniature schnauzer, the perfect pet, has been called 'the little square dog.' "
Restrictions: Children 12 and over welcome. Smoking in common rooms only. Sorry, no guests' pets.
Bed and bath: Four second-floor rooms, all with fans on 10-foot ceilings, private full baths. King, double, or twin beds available.
Breakfast: 7–9. Juice, fruit, muffins or pastries, coffee, milk. Served in elegant dining room or on porch.
Plus: Sun room with plenty of plants, wicker furnishings. Guest pantry with refrigerator, ice, juice, soft drinks, setups. Laundry facilities.

Bunree

P.O. Box 53, Amissville, VA 22002
Phone: 703/937-4133 or 804/381-5779
Location: On a tree plantation and nature sanctuary, a former horse farm, on east side of Blue Ridge Mountains. Thirteen miles west of Warrenton. Near wineries and a Rappahannock River canoe launching area. A little over an hour's drive from Washington, D.C.
Host: Aileen Laing
Open: Year round. Weekends only September–May. Advance reservations required.
Rates: $35 single shared bath, $45 private bath. $45 double shared bath, $55 private bath. $65 per room with working fireplace. Fifty percent deposit required.

"Designed and built by my grandparents in 1923, this house combines ideas of their native Ireland with Virginia and Cape Cod! It is named after the salmon spawning river that runs past my grandmother's house in Ireland. And the answer to the question that everyone asks: I have lived here all my life. B&B allows me to share this beautiful area with travelers. Some hike, stroll or meander through the fields and woods right here."

This hostess is an art history professor at Sweet Briar College. The family homestead, filled with memorabilia of four generations, has mementos of one uncle who was a well-known horseman, a well-stocked library, cozy corners for reading, and furnishings that range from the 18th to the 20th century. In season, garden flowers are arranged in just about every room.

In residence: Ril and Feinja, Norwich terriers, "important members of the family." One horse and a pony.
Restrictions: Children 10 and over welcome. Smoking discouraged; allowed downstairs only. Sorry, no guests' pets.
Foreign language spoken: Some French.
Bed and bath: Four second-floor rooms, two with private tub baths and two with working fireplaces. Double or twin beds and a rollaway available; one room has additional twin bed.
Breakfast: Usually 7–9. Choice includes juice, fruit in season, cereal, popovers (house specialty), croissants, English muffins, toast, casserole or bacon and eggs. Maybe sausage, grits, muffins, or egg dishes. In dining room or on front porch.
Plus: One bedroom is air conditioned; window fans in others. Late-afternoon tea with homemade breads and cake. Fresh fruit in rooms. Tour of house and farm. Ironed percale sheets. Books and games.

Crystal Bed & Breakfast

2620 South Fern Street, Arlington, VA 22202
Phone: 703/548-7652 (answering service in daytime; calls returned collect)

Location: In a residential neighborhood, within walking distance of Metro. One and a half miles to Washington, D.C. Five minutes from National Airport.
Hosts: Susan and Hal Swain
Open: Year round. Advance reservations required.
Rates: $50 double. $40 single. $15 one child in room, $25 for two. Discounts for seven or more days.

> Guests from all over the country wrote: "The most gracious hosts we have ever stayed with. . . . Immaculate. . . . Excellent food . . . Sue even insisted we take some homemade applespice cake 'for the car.' . . . Quiet and peaceful. . . . Left our car and used the convenient subway. . . . So wonderful that we stayed an extra day. . . . Superb. . . . Recommended to our friends and *The Los Angeles Times*."

The Swains' Dutch Colonial house has country decor, a patio amidst lovely gardens, and friendly hosts who were introduced to B&Bs in Europe. Sue, a native Washingtonian, is a municipal government personnel director. Hal works for the federal government. Among their "wonderful and amazing tourists" in the last five years are families who "see it all" from dawn to midnight, Californians who had never seen fireflies, and a couple who taught Sue the art of drying flowers.

In residence: One who smokes outdoors.
Restrictions: Children welcome (age three and over preferred).
Bed and bath: Six rooms on two floors in two adjacent houses. In Dutch Colonial—two large queen-bedded rooms and one small room with hi-riser (primarily for children) share one bath. Next door—two large queen-bedded rooms share a bath. Private bath for room with single bed. Rollaway available.
Breakfast: At 7:30. Weekdays—croissants, homemade muffins and jams, fruit, cereal, juice, coffee, tea. Full on weekends; perhaps fruit salad with omelets, blueberry pancakes, oregano sausages, or raisin French toast.
Plus: Off-street parking. Tea, iced tea, or lemonade. Central air conditioning. Gardens.

Old Mansion Bed & Breakfast

Box 845, Bowling Green, VA 22427
Phone: 804/633-5781
Location: Off the beaten path. Set one-quarter mile back from Routes 2 and 301. Twenty minutes from I-95. Twenty miles from Fredericksburg, 32 from Richmond; 1½ hours from Williamsburg and Washington, D.C.
Host: Peter Eric Larson
Open: Year round. Reservations preferred.
Rates: $55 per room. No charge for crib, cot, or sleeping bag for child in same room. $85 family rate (with two children) for two rooms. $10 for use of bedroom fireplace.

The chance to stay in what may be the oldest house in the country open for occupancy is coupled with the opportunity to meet a restorer of antiques who shares much—including information about area historic houses and antiques shops. His own remarkable antiques-filled home has private guests' quarters in the 1670 section, still with its original floor plan and walls and connected by a door to the host's section, which was built in 1750. Always a working plantation owned by public notables, it has been this young family's home for five years. If guests visit Peter's workshop on the premises (and most are *very* curious) they see both fine museum-quality restoration work in process as well as the making of architectural pieces such as doors or moldings.

You enter the grounds via a circular driveway that was among the first quarter-mile race tracks in the country. Centuries-old boxwood, cedar, and holly are on the 126 acres. Peter maintains—and shares plants from—his extensive and beautiful wildflower garden. He continues the tradition of hosting "as it was in colonial days."

In residence: Lars Peterson, age eight. Border collies Gypsy and Meg.
Restrictions: Sorry, no pets. No smoking indoors.
Bed and bath: Three second-floor rooms, two accessible by a "hidden" staircase. Two shared baths. One large room with queen four-poster bed and a cannonball double bed, working fireplace. A smaller room with cannonball double bed, working fireplace. Third room, furnished with circa Civil War antiques, has double bed. Cot and antique crib available.
Breakfast: At hour set by guests. Swiss eggs, sausage, fresh fruit, homemade bread or biscuits, freshly ground coffee, for example.
Plus: Air conditioning. Tea. Two parlors. Tour of house (from attic to basement). Croquet on the entrance greensward. Kitchen and laundry privileges. Host's favorite dinner theater nearby. An invitation to stay right here by the fire or on the grounds (with bluebirds). Marked one-mile trail through woods.

Nottingham Ridge

P.O. Box 97B, Cape Charles, VA 23310
Phone: 804/331-1010 or 442-5011 if no answer
Location: High on a hill at the end of a tree-lined country road. Four miles north of Bay Bridge Tunnel, halfway between (one hour from) Williamsburg and Chincoteague, just off state highway 13. Near winery. Ten minutes to golf course, tennis courts, charter fishing boats.
Hosts: Bonnie and Slick Nottingham
Open: Year round. Advance reservations preferred.
Rates: $45 single. $60 double. $10 extra person. Family rates available.

Excerpts from many guests' letters: "We plan to return when we want a quiet place with a beautiful view of the bay in lovely pine woods, well off the beaten track.... I travel all over the world and would rate this B&B the best—a magnificent home, charming hostess and unbelievable breakfasts.... Shared flavor of the community, information about local activities and eating places. . . . A short walk over the dunes to secluded private beach. . . . Breathtaking sunsets."

"Might there be nearby property for sale?" ask many guests, enchanted with the peace and quiet at this unique spot overlooking the lights of Chesapeake Bay.

In 1975, when the family was younger, the Nottinghams had the two-storied brick colonial house built by skilled local craftsmen. It's warm and cozy, with antiques, reproductions and collectibles. A welcoming fire glows in the family room during chilly months. For Bonnie and Slick, B&B is a sharing experience. Often, they suggest Eastern Shore back roads.

In residence: Son Slick is 18. The cat, Tootie, and Colonel, a dog, are outside pets.
Restrictions: Children over 12 welcome. Smoking allowed only downstairs. No pets, please.
Bed and bath: Three rooms with private baths. One private-entrance first-floor room with queen canopied bed, shower bath, bay view. Upstairs, room with two twin beds, full bath, bay view; room with queen bed, shower bath. Rollaway and sleeping bag available.
Breakfast: 6–9:30. Bonnie loves to cook; menu varies. Maybe Virginia baked ham, sweet potato biscuit, bacon quiche, waffles, homemade bread and (sometimes hot) jam. Served in country kitchen or on porch.
Plus: Central air conditioning. Evening wine, cheese, and dessert. Fireplaced family room. Large private beach. Kitchen privileges.

Sea Gate Bed & Breakfast

9 Tazewell Avenue, Cape Charles, VA 23310
Phone: 804/331-2206
Location: In a small (pop. 1500) Eastern Shore Victorian town, a designated historic district as of August 1989. Two houses from the beach. Within walking distance of shops, restaurants, golf course, dock, marina, fishing charters. Ten miles north of Chesapeake Bay Bridge and tunnel; 35 miles northeast of Virginia Beach and Norfolk; 20 miles south of Tangier Island ferry.
Hosts: Chris Bannon and Jim Wells
Open: Year round.
Rates: Per room. Queen bed, $70 private bath; $65 half bath, $60 sink. Twin beds $65.

The hosts call Cape Charles *Camelot*, "the perfect place to live." Some of their first guests, who first discovered Sea Gate while Chris and Jim were restoring it, returned to enjoy hospitality in the transformed Victorian—and to buy nearby property.

Now the 1910 house has French, English, and American antiques throughout with Persian and Chinese rugs in most rooms. The exceptional rag-rolled (faux finish) and raised relief painting was done by Jim, an interior designer, a Manhattanite who searched the entire east coast for a shore location. He and Chris, a manager of conference centers and small retreat houses, opened in 1988, a year after they moved from Connecticut. Already Chris is director of volunteers for county social services and Jim is on the zoning board. They share their big wonderful house with delighted guests. In summer, the breezes come on cue. Year round, there are sunsets too.

In residence: One host smokes
Restrictions: No pets. No smoking in bedrooms.
Bed and bath: Four second-floor guest rooms. Private full bath for room with queen-sized antique brass bed, semi-private porch overlooking bay. Four-poster queen with half bath, semi-private porch. Twin beds with half bath. Queen with sink. Three rooms share a shower bath.
Breakfast: Usually 8–10. Maybe French toast made with homemade bread or European style scrambled eggs. Bacon, sausage, or ham. Fresh fruit, cottage cheese, cereals, juices, hot beverages. Served in kitchen, formal dining room with gas burning fireplace, or on year-round enclosed or screened breakfast porch.
Plus: Afternoon tea. Central air conditioning (seldom needed). Ceiling fan in every room. Living room fireplace. Fresh flowers. Thick towels. Custom handmade quilts on all beds. Beach towels. Outdoor hot and cold shower. Use of bicycles. No parking problem. Pickup service arranged from marina.

Alderman House

Charlottesville, VA
Location: Just a mile from the university, with no other house in sight.
Reservations: Year round except December 15–February 1 through Guesthouses, page 304.
Rates: Per room. $72.

Elegance. Southern hospitality. And history. *Country* magazine and the *Washington Post* have featured this formal Georgian house, which was built in the early 1900s as the retirement home of the first University of Virginia president. It is now the residence of a gracious hostess and her physician husband, parents of a grown family. Seminar leaders, international visitors, and students' parents are among those who have appreciated their hospitality, the flower-filled brick-walled terrace, and a delightful balcony with pink awnings, lounge chairs, and hanging plants.

In residence: One grown daughter. One black poodle.
Restrictions: Children 12 and over welcome. No smoking. No guests' pets. Married couples preferred.
Bed and bath: Two second-floor rooms, each with private full bath. One with canopied double four-poster bed. One with two twin beds.

Breakfast: 7:30–9:30. Cheese souffle, English muffins, homemade preserves, fresh fruit, coffee or tea. Served in crystal-chandeliered dining room or on the terrace.
Plus: Bedroom air conditioner and window fan. Tea or wine. Tour of house.

Bollingwood

Charlottesville, VA
Location: In a convenient neighborhood, within walking distance of the University.
Reservations: Year round through Guesthouses, page 304.
Rates: $60 per room.

The fence-enclosed city gardens and slate terrace of this handsome colonial were featured during the 1988 Historic Garden Week. Built in 1927 with many windows, the house is furnished with antiques throughout.

Word has it that Albemarle County natives are rare in Charlottesville. Here you have one, a woman who has returned after living in New Orleans, New York, and Washington, D.C. She has experience as a stockbroker and as a presidential personnel staffer. Several of her guests have been journalists who wrote articles about area gardens, starting right here.

In residence: Bear, a very friendly terrier who loves guests.
Restrictions: Children 10 and over welcome. No guests' pets, please.
Bed and bath: Two second-floor rooms, each with private full bath. One with two twin beds. Another with two antique three-quarter beds (one canopied, one in connecting room).
Breakfast: Flexible hours. Homemade breads and muffins. Raisin bread French toast. Served in formal dining room or on terrace.
Plus: Bedroom air conditioners and ceiling fans. Tea or wine. Tour of house. TV. Extensive library. Sun room.

Clifton—The Country Inn

Route 9, Box 412, Charlottesville, VA 22901
Phone: 804/971-1800
Location: Tranquil. On 35 acres overlooking the Rivana River. Three miles west of Charlottesville and three miles south of Monticello. In a secluded area on Route 729.
Host: Nancy Keel
Open: Year round. Advance reservations required.
Rates: Double occupancy. $135 main house and suite. $95 cottage. $10 extra person. MC, VISA.

Keep coming up the long wooded drive until you finally see the 18th-century white frame colonial, originally the estate of Thomas Mann Randolph, an early governor of Maryland and husband to Thomas Jefferson's daughter, Martha. High on a cliff, with private lake frontage (also without another building in sight), tennis courts, a lap pool, and those sheep, is the setting pictured in a full-page *Southern Bride* feature. The main house has antiques throughout, and the bathroom floors are hand-painted. The carriage house was rebuilt with historic Meriwether Lewis (Lewis & Clark) estate architectural salvage. The many fireplaces beckon. The food is a highlight.

"A friend told us about this quintessential inn when we wanted to leave the corporate world in 1987," explains ebullient Nancy. A former department store buyer, she is now an innkeeper who loves the outdoors, the sheep, spinning, taking classes at the university, and tap dancing too. Lots of business people come here. Some families do too. And couples find it the perfect getaway.

In residence: "The world's gentlest spirits, our dogs, Lucy and Ethel." Four (soon to be more) sheep—Ruth, Naomi, Rebecca, Elvis.
Restrictions: Smoking and guests' pets discouraged.
Bed and bath: Seven spacious rooms, all with private baths and working fireplaces. Five main house rooms with queen beds (some canopied); some with sofa beds too. In carriage house, a queen-bedded loft suite with queen sofa bed in living room, full wall-sized brick fireplace. In cottage, double four-poster bed. Crib available.
Breakfast: Flexible hours. Fresh fruit. Homemade muffins or breads. Maybe pineapple wedge with bacon or sausage and vegetable quiche; Belgian waffles with fruit, cream, and Vermont maple syrup; or Virginia smoked ham and cheese grits. "Our own blended coffee and the famous Clifton (fruit) Smoothie."
Plus: Bedroom air conditioners. Tea or wine. Library. Dock, swimming, fishing. Croquet. Woods for walking. Weather permitting, line-dried (all-cotton) sheets. Down comforters. Fresh flowers everywhere.

Recoletta

Charlottesville, VA
Location: Within walking distance of University of Virginia, restaurants, theaters, and shops. Ten-minute bus ride to downtown.
Reservations: Year round through Guesthouses, page 304.
Rates: $56 single. $60 double.

By the time most guests rise for breakfast, this hostess has probably walked many laps around the university track. Guests feel very much at home in this Mediterranean-style villa built with flair and imagination, with a red tile roof and a walled garden complete with pools. The comfortable and rather elegant living room filled with books gives the feeling of an Italian library. There are American antiques and many from Central America as well as from Europe.

The effervescent and welcoming hostess, an administrator in education, is active in the Society for the Prevention of Cruelty to Animals. (For an epitaph, she once chose "Born a dog, died a gentleman.") Many seasoned travelers write that this is their favorite B&B.

In residence: One cat.
Restrictions: "Sorry, no room for children." No guests' pets.
Bed and bath: One second-floor room with brass double bed, private hall bath with shower.
Breakfast: Until 9:30. Juice, fruit, eggs, bacon or sausage, muffins, gourmet jams, yogurt, cereals, coffee, tea.
Plus: Bedroom air conditioner and fan. Beverages. Fireplaced living room.

From Washington, D.C.: "The hostess is as interesting as her house, the house as hospitable as the hostess."

High Meadows . . . Virginia's Vineyard Inn

Route 20, Charlottesville South, VA
Mailing address: Route 4, Box 6, Scottsville, VA 24590
Phone: 804/286-2218
Location: Pastoral. On 22 acres along a scenic byway. Twenty minutes to Charlottesville, 15 to Monticello and Ash Lawn. Near 10 wineries. Two and a half hours from Washington, D.C.
Hosts: Peter and Mary Jae Abbitt Sushka
Open: Year round. Advance reservations required. Two-day minimum weekends April–May and mid-September–mid-November.
Rates: Double $75–$85. Singles $15 less. $15 extra person. Senior citizens, 10 percent discount.

First came four years of living in England while Peter was a navy officer. As retirement years approached, the "restoration gem" newspaper ad beckoned. Then there were three years of commuting from Washington jobs (Jae still works as a Securities and Exchange Commission analyst) to complete the monumental task, "the dream," two interconnected houses, one built in 1832, the other in 1882.

The inn is on the National Register of Historic Places. Antiques and 19th-century botanicals are in every room—and so is printed information about the furnishings as well as the restoration. There are many suggestions for day trips, but some guests choose to explore the pathways and discover the gardens, the gazebo by the pond, and the 1¼-acre vineyard of Pinot noir grapes right here.

In residence: Kali, a golden retriever, and Snickers, a dachshund.
Restrictions: Well-behaved children over eight welcome. Small trained pets accepted with advance notice. No smoking inside.
Foreign language spoken: French.

Bed and bath: Seven rooms. All private baths. Garden level rooms have a private entrance. Whirlpool tub for room with a double bed and a three-quarter bed. Bath with sitting bench in shower-bath for double or twin-bedded rooms. Claw-footed tub in bath for room with floor-to-ceiling lace at posters of queen bed. Suite, up a narrow steep stairway, has room with two double beds that shares a tub bath with twin-bedded room.
Breakfast: 8:30–9:30. Freshly squeezed juice, homemade muffins and toast, fruits, baked egg and meat dishes, coffee, tea. In fireplaced dining room or on terrace.
Plus: Tea on arrival. Evening wine tasting with hors d'oeuvres. Fresh flowers, fruit, and brandy in room. Tour of house and vineyard. Candle-light dining, Saturday–Sunday ($25 per person). Weekdays, gourmet picnic basket ($30 per couple). Guest refrigerator. Croquet. Horseshoes. Rose garden with 25 varieties.

From Colorado: "We felt like we were old friends of the owners. . . . Charm, cleanliness, excellent food, comfort and history, all in a beautiful rural setting."

Miss Molly's Inn

113 North Main Street, Chincoteague, VA 23336
Phone: 804/336-6686
Location: In downtown Chincoteague Island, four miles from the Chinco-teague Wildlife Refuge (300 species of birds and a famous herd of wild ponies) and Assateague National Seashore (30 miles of beach).
Hosts: Dr. James C. and Dr. Priscilla J. Stam
Open: April–November. Advance reservations required. Two-night mini-mum on weekends.
Rates: Memorial Day–Labor Day—shared bath, $79 twin beds; $65–$69 double bed; $85 with ocean view. Private bath, $95 king bed. Off season, $69 twin; $59–$63 double; $75 ocean view; $85 king bed.

"We restored a 22-room Victorian for a summer house and then our children all moved west!"
Jim, chef and host, was president of Salem College in West Virginia. Priscilla, an art and interior design major, has worn the hat of department chairman at Fontbonne College in St. Louis, Missouri. Miss Molly, the daughter of the original owner, lived all of her 84 years here. An inn for the last six years, the house is filled with the Stams' 30-year collection of antiques and art. Oriental rugs are on the first floor. A hat rack and a marble-topped table are in the front hall. The dining room has a lace tablecloth. Window treatments are simple and summery. Often, guests talk about restoration (there's a full collection of *Old House Journals*), photography (Pris's interest), wildlife, or the world (Washingtonians love it here).

Restrictions: Children 12 and over welcome. Smoking allowed in public rooms only. Sorry, no pets.

Bed and bath: Seven air-conditioned rooms on second and third floors. Private full bath for room with king bed. Six rooms with either one double or two twin beds share three semiprivate full baths. (Two more baths are on first floor.) Rollaway available.

Breakfast: 8–10. Juice, fresh fruit topped with rum raisin yogurt sauce (recipe has appeared in *Virginian* Magazine), quiche with fresh pineapple slices, hot apple strudel, hot croissants with French blackberry jam, homemade coffee cake. Served on back porch with attached gazebo overlooking the bay.

Plus: Afternoon tea. Sun deck. Sitting rooms. Bike storage. Clothesline for bathing suits. Five porches; one is screened.

Fountain Hall

609 South East Street, Culpeper, VA 22701
Phone: 703/825-8200
Location: Quiet residential street that is on a walking tour. One block from Main Street. Six blocks from Amtrak. Within half hour of seven wineries and historic Montpelier. Less than an hour from Charlottesville, Fredericksburg, and Skyline Drive. Seventy miles from Washington, D.C.
Hosts: Steve and Kathi Walker
Open: Year round. Reservations required.
Rates: Shared/private bath. $45/$60 single. $55/$70 double. $65/$75 or $85 suite. $10 additional person. Special holiday weekends and seasonal getaway package rates. Gift certificates available. AMEX, MC, VISA.

"Walk out the front door and you're in town. Walk out the back and you're in the country. That's what our guests—both tourists and business people—always say.

"After looking at more than 50 properties, in 1985 we discovered Culpeper, laid out in a grid by George Washington as his first surveying job. We found this grand 1859 Colonial Revival house, with six fireplaces and ten-foot ceilings, in excellent condition, situated on an acre and a half of landscaped gardens. Through a couple of months of auction going, we furnished each room differently—Victorian, Empire, Art Deco and one from the 50s. The breakfast room is done in primitive country. The sitting room—where no one really sits—is formal Victorian. The den with fireplace and TV is where people from all over the world gather. Some guests choose to be quite private, but most like the chance to meet other people—as we do."

Steve has a degree in hotel administration and has worked in the corporate world and in his own electrical business. Kathi works in the data processing field. Together they conclude, "B&B feels just right to both of us."

In residence: Oscar, a 10-year-old "friendly, gentle and mellow yellow Canadian Labrador allowed into guest area by invitation only."
Restrictions: Sorry, no guests' pets. Smoking in conservatory only.

Bed and bath: Five large rooms. One first floor double-bedded room, private bath, screened porch and entrance. Second floor—suite with queen and bunk beds, private bath, and porch. Suite with two double beds (antique and brass) shares a bath with a double-bedded room with own vanity. Fifth room has one queen bed and one twin bed, private bath. Cot and crib available.

Breakfast: 6–10:30. Freshly baked croissants, cereals; jams and jellies, fresh fruit, cheese, coffee, teas, and juice. Family-style buffet in breakfast or dining room.

Plus: Bedroom air conditioners and ceiling fans. Refreshments. Library. (Okay to take unfinished paperback with you.) VCR. Porches. Spacious grounds for picnics. Tour of house.

Mary's Country Inn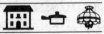

218 South Main Street, Route 2, Box 4, Edinburg, VA 22824
Phone: 703/984-8286
Location: In the Shenandoah Valley, just off Route 81. Next to the historic Edinburg mill (now a restaurant). Near "easy access to an absolutely awesome view of the Seven Bends of the Shenandoah."
Hosts: Mary and Jim Clark
Open: Year round. Reservations required.
Rates: $50 double, shared bath. $45–$55 double, private bath. $45 single. $7.50 rollaway. No charge for portacrib.

The miller's house grew from a simple rectangular frame structure in 1850, to a bay-windowed place with massive Jeffersonian French doors leading to a wraparound porch in 1890, to a house with the addition of a schoolroom in 1910. A miller's residence until 1982, it then became an inn, with Mary and Jim doing just about all the conversion work. The most recent changes include a new patio, "a Victorian breakfast garden."

"Down-to-earth, country comfortable without airs" is the feeling enjoyed by guests, who come for hiking, fishing, or hunting in the George Washington National Forest. Some come for the caverns, museums, antiquing, vineyards, or "solitude and inspiration."

Mary, a photographer, and Jim, a retired electronic engineer and part-time Realtor, are both stained glass artists. And they conduct photo safaris—to the tops of mountains for sunset shots, to valleys for waterfalls, to covered bridges. Participants develop their own film and give slide shows right here.

Bed and bath: Seven rooms. Six with double beds and one with two twin beds. Two first-floor rooms (one with fireplace) have private baths. Second-floor suite accommodates three people, has wood stove, private bath with claw-foot tub. Four other second-floor rooms share one full bath. Rollaways and portacrib available.
Breakfast: 8–10. Fresh fruit, cereals, homemade muffins or fruit breads, sweet rolls, biscuits, eggs, sausage/bacon, juices, coffee, tea, or milk.

Served buffet style in the sitting room or dining room or on wraparound porch overlooking the green.

Plus: Air conditioners and ceiling fans in five rooms. Iced tea or lemonade/coffee or tea. May–October, area carriage rides ($10 per couple) from the inn. Inquire about weekend photography or country real estate seminars. Swing, wicker chairs on wraparound porch. Flower and vegetable garden. Inner tubes and fishing poles available for use in large creek next to property. Art and antiques gallery.

---

105 1/2

105 Goodwin Street, Emporia, VA 23847
Phone: 804/634-2590 or 634-6325
Location: In a lovely residential neighborhood in the middle of town, a small community at the crossroads of Routes I-95 and 58. Three hours to Washington, D.C. Sixty-five miles to Richmond, 40 to Petersburg, 75 to Williamsburg, 90 to Virginia Beach.
Hosts: June and Robert Little
Open: Year round. Reservations preferred.
Rate: $50.

From Virginia: "Such a comforting place to settle in after a trying highway trip! The privacy of our own little guest house was special fun. The (Williamsburg) colonial decor, the fresh spray of new daffodils, the wine—all such special touches! After a sound sleep, the warmth of the kitchen and homemade bread made a perfect finale to our visit."

The perfect overnight stop for travelers is in Robert's hometown. (He left to go to college, where he met June. They have lived here since they were married.) When their five children grew up, they converted the garage into this marvelous guest house, decorating it as they have their own Cape Cod–style home—with 18th-century antiques and reproductions, Oriental rugs, and original art. Robert, semiretired from manufacturing, enjoys painting and photography. Although he is definitely a "people person," B&B began as homemaker June's idea. In warm weather, guests enjoy the gardens and an expanse that extends to a pond with ducks. All this and hospitality too. Perfect indeed.

Restrictions: No guests' pets.
Bed and bath: One large room in a private brick (painted white) guest house with double four-poster bed, phone, TV, full bath, air conditioner, sitting area, fireplace.
Breakfast: Guests choose the hour. June "loves to cook." Could include seasonal fruit, homemade bread, eggs any style, bacon, sausage, country ham, cheese souffle.
Plus: Evening drinks. Mints. Thick towels. Living room. Patio.

Acorn Inn

RR 1, Box 192, Faber, VA 22938
Mailing address: P.O. Box 431, Nellysford, VA 22958
Phone: 804/361-9357
Location: Rustic, rural, peaceful. In orchard and vineyard country in the foothills of the Blue Ridge Mountains. Forty-minute drive to Monticello, 40 minutes south of University of Virginia, 12 miles east of Wintergreen Resort skiing, golf, dining.
Hosts: Kathy Plunket Versluys and Martin Versluys
Open: Year round. Reservations preferred.
Rates: Friday, Saturday, and holidays, $40 single, $45 double, $75 cottage. Sunday–Thursday, $32 single, $36 double, $65 cottage.

The original horse stall doors are still used—now for each of the 10 guest rooms in this converted tin barn. The hosts, two world travelers, lined and painted the rooms and made many other changes (all the new trim woodwork was made by Martin) so that guests would have "a clean, warm, comfortable place to stay." Major structural work was done by local builders.

Martin, a carpenter, photographer, and conservationist, has worked on microfiching books around the world. A native of Holland, he has bicycled through almost 100 countries. Before settling down here in 1987, Martin and Kathy (a photographer, writer, and printmaker) lived in South America for four years. Their own residence, the old farmhouse, is just fifty yards from the inn. "Sometimes we show slides from our travels—complete with music and stories. Fun!"

Restrictions: Nonsmokers preferred. Sorry, no pets.
Foreign languages spoken: Dutch, German, Spanish, and Portuguese.
Bed and bath: Ten carpeted rooms, each about 12 feet square, with a double bed, a wardrobe, chair and desk, five-foot-high screened window, individually controlled baseboard electric heat. Two baths, one for men and one for women, each with two sinks, two separate toilets, and handicapped-accessible showers. Cottage with one bedroom, living room with TV, bath, kitchen, sleeps four or five.
Breakfast: 6:30–10:30. Orange juice, fresh fruit, homemade whole wheat breads, sweet loaves, and cobbler in season. Teas and coffee.
Plus: Central air conditioning. Strobe alarm system for hearing impaired. Big carpeted hall/lounge with practical furnishings, color TV, woodcuts and photographs. Tea, hot chocolate, and instant oatmeal and soups always available. Microwave and toaster. Refrigerator space. Outdoor table and gas barbecue. Hose for washing cars. Laundry facilities.

Caledonia Farm

Route 1, Box 2080, Flint Hill, VA 22627
Phone: 703/675-3693
Location: Next to the Shenandoah National Park and the eastern edge of

Blue Ridge Mountains. On a 52-acre cattle farm bordered by stone fences. On Route 628, 4 miles north of Washington, Virginia; 68 miles southwest of Washington, D.C. Near Skyline Drive, battlefields, caves, wineries, antiquing, golf, riding, climbing, hiking, tennis, swimming, skiing, and "one of the world's finest restaurants."
Host: Phil Irwin
Open: Year round. Advance reservations requested. Two-night minimum on holiday weekends and in October.
Rates: $70 main house room. $100 suite.

Phil, a retired Voice of America broadcaster who has visited hundreds of B&Bs throughout North America and Europe, raises Angus cattle. His Federal manor house, built with two-foot-thick stone walls in 1812, has wide board floors and many fireplaces. It was completely restored in 1965 and, in 1985, redecorated throughout.

As host, Phil is prepared with suggestions for walking, jogging, and scenic drives—as well as with information about the history of the house and the family cemetery. When possible, he offers the treat of a hayride to a clearing in the national park.

In residence: "One gregarious outside cat." Beef cattle herd.
Restrictions: No smoking inside. Children over 12 welcome. Sorry, no guests' pets.
Foreign languages spoken: (Minimal) German and Danish.
Bed and bath: Two rooms plus a suite, each with working fireplace, individual heat control, and air conditioning. Entire second floor of main house has two double-bedded rooms that share a full bath. Converted summer kitchen (connected by portico to main house) has double-bedded room and full bath upstairs, and on the first floor a living room with huge original cooking fireplace. Handicapped-accessible room available.
Breakfast: On the hour, 7–11. Choose from full menu that includes fruit, eggs, smoked salmon, omelet, grits, and eggs Benedict. Served by candlelight and always with "unannounced extras."
Plus: Evening social hour. House tour. Antiques-filled parlor. Three porches with spectacular views. Weeknight candlelight dinners ($30 per person) or box lunch ($5) by reservation. Laundry facilities.

La Vista Plantation

4420 Guinea Station Road, Fredericksburg, VA 22401
Phone: 703/898-8444
Location: Surrounded by farm fields, herb and vegetable gardens, pond for fishing, woods with paths for walks, cycling, bird-watching. Eight miles south of Fredericksburg, just off Route 1. Five miles from I-95. On the East Coast bicycle trail. Near Civil War battlefields, antiques shops, pick-your-own farms. An hour to Monticello and Mount Vernon.
Hosts: Michele and Edward Schiesser
Open: Year round. Reservations suggested.
Rates: $65 per room or suite. Children 12 and under free. $5 each child 13–17. $10 additional adult, 18 or older. Seventh night free. MC, VISA.

From Massachusetts: "A warm welcome. Plenty of space and privacy. Lovely antiques and art works. Morning brought the rooster's crow, sunlight streaming in from all sides, and a delicious hot breakfast. ... A feeling for the period of the lovely house. ... We left with Mickey picking peas from the garden—and wished we could have stayed longer."

Mickey, a former junior high school teacher, and Ed, chief of exhibits and design at the Hirshhorn Museum, will gladly show you their restoration in progress. Guests also appreciate hearing some history and anecdotes about the 1838 Greek Revival manor house, which was occupied by both armies during the Civil War.

The Schiessers had experience renovating their previous residence, a Victorian house in Maryland. When they came here six years ago, they renovated the sunny English basement (with cathedral-type windows) for B&B by updating the former winter kitchen and furnishing the spacious rooms with antiques, Ed's limestone sculptures, and many books. This arrangement of a home-within-a-home provides as much privacy or company as you wish and is appreciated by honeymooners, families, cyclists, tourists, and business travelers too.

In residence: William, age nine, and Julia, age seven. Gretchen, "a clean, beautiful, well-behaved and quiet English setter." Chickens and rabbits on the farm.
Restrictions: Sorry, no guests' pets.
Bed and bath: Rooms on two floors. A four-room ground level, handicapped-accessible suite with private shower bath; double bed in huge room; living room with queen-sized sofa bed; fireplace; large fireplaced kitchen; two private entrances. On first floor, a huge fireplaced room with king four-poster bed, private full bath. Crib available.
Breakfast: 6–11. Danish with coffee or tea, La Vista's fresh brown farm eggs, toast, bacon, homemade jams from fruit trees here, orange juice, milk. Varied menus for extended stays. Mickey serves by the fire in suite kitchen.
Plus: Bedroom air conditioner, TV, radio. Beverages. Fresh flowers. Plenty of wood on hearths. Flannel sheets. The family's living room. Today's newspaper. Use of two bicycles. Porch swing. Option of dinner (no charge) to those arriving on bicycles. Babysitting if arranged in advance.

Fassifern Bed & Breakfast

Route 5, Box 87, Lexington, VA 24450
Phone: 703/463-1013
Location: On a country road, surrounded by century-old maples and oaks. Two miles from town center, three-quarters of a mile from I-64. Half mile from Virginia Horse Center; 15 miles from Blue Ridge Parkway; 11 from Natural Bridge.
Hosts: Patricia and James Tichenor
Open: Year round.

Rates: Shared bath $35, $40 single; $40, $45 double. Private bath $45–$60 single; $50–$65 double. $10 extra person in Ice House.

After staying in B&Bs on several continents, the Tichenors now have the world coming to their doorstep. Their 1867 Victorian home reflects living in six countries. There's an Austrian burled walnut bedroom set. The stairwell has Korean windows. In the dining room there's a collection of paintings of houses, mostly old ones, that Pat and Jim have lived in. Oriental rugs, antiques, and art works, many by family members, enhance the ambiance. Pat's talents range from being "a consummate cook" to the making of all the swags and draperies. Jim, a retired colonel, is a candle maker who specializes in sand-casted driftwood candles.

The Tichenors restored the entire house (all themselves except for plumbing and electricity) before opening in 1986. On the 3½ acres of pastures and lawns there's a pond with pier, a spot chosen by some for enjoying wine and cheese.

In residence: Lucky, a friendly dog.
Restrictions: Sorry, no guests' pets. Children should be at least 16. Smoking in conservatory only.
Bed and bath: Six rooms. On second floor, private baths for one double-bedded room and one with two twins. On third floor, a shared bath with claw-foot tub for one room with twin beds and another with a double bed and a sitting room. One shared first-floor half bath. Converted ice house has queen, private full bath. Converted farm office building has double bed, shower bath, private entrance, and deck.
Breakfast: 8–10. Freshly squeezed orange juice; fruit; homemade bread and/or muffins; jelly made from their own grapes, raspberries, and pears; tea, freshly ground coffee, hot chocolate. Served in dining room or on patio.
Plus: Central air conditioning. (Ice House and Office individually air conditioned.) Fireplaces in living room, dining room, and conservatory. Games. Refreshments before and after dinner. Tour of house. Fresh flowers. Fluffy towels. Custom made chocolates. Baskets of toiletries in rooms.

From New York: "The good taste, the privacy and the hosts—unbeatable."

Llewellyn Lodge

603 South Main Street, Lexington, VA 24450
Phone: 703/463-3235
Location: In a lovely old residential neighborhood of this historic Shenandoah Valley community, "a New England town in Virginia." Ten minutes' walk to downtown historic area. Five-minute drive to Virginia Military Institute; three to Washington and Lee University; Virginia Horse Center.
Hosts: Ellen Thornber and John Roberts
Open: Year round. Reservations requested.

Rates: April–December 15, $45 single, $55–$60 double, $65 king, $7 extra person. December 15–March, $38 single, $48 double, $53 king. $5 extra person. AMEX, MC, VISA.

From Connecticut: "Our daughter-in-law made all the arrangements and we really weren't sure about staying at a B&B. Llewellyn Lodge was clean, comfortable and cool (the weather was in the 90s). Ellen made us feel very much at home. We definitely will stay there again."

Ellen says, "I've been in the hospitality business for 20 years, working in New York City for Pan Am and Finnair, and in Washington, D.C., with Finnair, Washington Circle Inn and Fourways Restaurant. From all my worldwide travels, I fell in love with the concept of B&B. Although this half-century-old brick Colonial (painted oyster gray) was built as a single family residence, along the way it was a tourist house. I added some new plumbing and closets and furnished it with antiques and period pieces, and with things I have collected from different parts of the world. Interesting people travel to B&Bs. Some guests are Civil War buffs. Some come for Historic Garden Week, the Quilt Show, or the universities. And they meet John, a native who knows the surrounding area—particularly where fish are hiding."

Restrictions: Well-behaved children welcome. No guests' pets.
Bed and bath: Five second-floor rooms, all private baths. King (with TV), queen, twin four-posters, or two double beds.
Breakfast: 7:30–9:30. Juice, omelets, sausage or bacon, French toast or Belgian waffles, homemade coffee cakes or muffins or biscuits with homemade jellies, coffee or tea. In summer, garnished with produce from the garden. Served in the dining room or on the deck.
Plus: Beverages and canapes. Fresh summer flowers. Central air conditioning. Bedroom ceiling fans. Will meet guests at the Greyhound bus stop. Laundry facilities ($2.50 per load).

From Virginia: "Delicious breakfasts! A lovely but relaxed environment."

Shenandoah Countryside

Route #2, Box 370, Luray, VA 22835
Phone: 703/743-6434
Location: On a hilltop surrounded by 45 acres with panoramic views of the Shenandoah Valley and Blue Ridge Mountains; 20 minutes from Shenandoah National Park entrance and Shenandoah River canoeing and tubing; 10 minutes from Luray Caverns; two miles from swimming beach; two hours from Washington, D.C.
Hosts: Phil (Phelma) and Bob Jacobsen
Open: Year round. Reservations preferred.
Rates: $55 single, $60 double. Tax included.

"I could have stayed there forever," reported a previous guest. We concur.

As we pedaled up the winding lane, we could see the chimney smoke from the Finnish sauna and Phil, Bob, and the dogs waiting to greet us outside of the dream (brick) house that the Jacobsens designed and built—with some help—in 1980. There are enough decorative and imaginative touches (all Phil's), blending country and traditional themes, to fill many magazine pages. It's spacious and gracious, and, like the hosts, welcoming.

We were there during Bob's last year as superintendent of the Shenandoah National Park. They were starting the Christmas tree farm. Their organic garden was thriving. After enjoying a refreshing drink on the screened porch, which overlooks Luray in the distance, we visited in the keeping room with wood burning stove. Somehow theater, music, family, and environmental concerns became part of the unfinished conversation. By departure time, we understood why their photo album was filled with pictures of guests, who come for a getaway, for the area's activities—and for the Jacobsens themselves.

In residence: Trill, a six-pound Yorkshire terrier. Buffy, an outdoor dog.
Restrictions: Children accepted only when there will be no other guests. Pets not encouraged. No smoking indoors.
Foreign language spoken: Limited Finnish.
Bed and bath: Three rooms. First-floor room with queen bed, private shower bath. Two large second-floor rooms share one full and one half bath and sauna shower. One with brass double bed (Phil's grandmother's), balcony; the other with king/twins, dressing room.
Breakfast: 8–10. Homegrown berries (four varieties) in season. Homemade breads, jams, and jellies. Sausage or bacon. Entree might be eggs Benedict, Finnish pancake, or fruit waffles. Sweet rolls or coffee cake. Hosts usually join guests at beautifully set harvest table or on huge cathedral-ceilinged screened porch. Views everywhere.
Plus: Beverages. Often, evening dessert. Bedroom ceiling fans. Sauna bath; robes provided. Tour of house. Two five-speed bicycles; one tandem. Will meet guests at Luray airport for car rental in Luray. Dinner option ($20 per person) on Thanksgiving and Christmas.

Shenandoah Valley Bed & Breakfast Host R

Luray, VA
Location: On an 18-acre farm between the Shenandoah and Massanutten mountain ranges. Minutes from Skyline Drive, antiques shops, Luray Caverns; 88 miles west of Washington, D.C.
Reservations: Year round through Shenandoah Valley Bed & Breakfast, page 305.
Rates: Private bath, queen bed, $80–$90 single, $85–$95 double; twin beds, $75–$85 single or double. Shared bath, $45–$55 single, $55–$65 double; with porch, $10–$15 more.

"Peter Ruffner, the first settler of Luray, discovered the cave near Luray Caverns. His descendants have been very enthusiastic and pleased with our restoration. Family members have shared old photos as well as history with us. Our business, a tannery, is on adjacent property. Long-time residents of Luray are full-time innkeepers; some one of our own family is at the inn from time to time. Together with area antique dealers, we have furnished the main house with museum quality pieces; the guest house is more rustic with country prints. This has been a wonderful project that we are delighted to share."

Enter through the farm gates and follow the tree-lined drive to the two-storied 1739 brick manor house with its 12-inch-thick walls, 10-foot-wide hall, and carved mantels. Eat in the elegant Victorian dining room furnished with red velvet upholstery and an Oriental rug. Stroll on the grounds. Feed (host-supplied) carrots to the Arabian horses. Enjoy!

Restrictions: Children 12 and over welcome. Sorry, no pets. Smoking in designated areas only.
Foreign languages spoken: German, Russian, French, Polish, Czech.
Bed and bath: Seven (total) second-floor rooms in main house and guest lodge. Queen and twin-bedded rooms have private baths (some full, some tub only). Two double-bedded rooms share a tub bath.
Breakfast: 8–10. Eggs, pancakes, or French toast. Meats, homemade muffins or bread. Juice, coffee. Served in Victorian dining room in main house.
Plus: Afternoon or evening tea. Basket of fruit. Bedroom ceiling fans. Library. Daily newspaper.

Lamp Lighters Bed and Breakfast Host ⌐ᛡ #1

Lynchburg, VA
Location: Quiet. Rural. Off Route 501. Eight miles from downtown Lynchburg, historic homes, and Poplar Forest. Five miles from shopping center and dining.
Reservations: Year round through Lamp Lighters Bed and Breakfast, page 304.
Rates: $38 single. $44 double. $10 crib. $2 one-night surcharge.

"We have had some guests ask if they could babysit. Others have inquired about housesitting for their vacation at a later date! We are really a homestay B&B, a home away from home. Guests are welcome to join in with our family or have privacy if they wish. . . . Our contemporary but rustic house is only eight years old. We have three stone fireplaces—and a shaded deck that is very popular with guests. . . . We started because of my mother-in-law's good experiences as host in the Charlottesville area. . . . Already we are thinking of hosting more when my husband retires from the bank."

In residence: Two children, ages two and three. "Sir Thomas Frazier Fur, our cat, is very lazy, fat, and gentle."
Restrictions: Children welcome. No smoking inside. One dog at a time allowed.
Foreign language spoken: A little French.
Bed and bath: Two first-floor rooms, each with private full bath. One with a double bed; the other with two twins. Crib available.
Breakfast: Full 7–9:30; continental at other times. Juice, bacon or sausage, eggs, fruit, pastry, coffee. Sourdough bread or homemade coffee cake (with homegrown blackberries in summer). In fireplaced kitchen or formal dining room.
Plus: Central air conditioning. Evening refreshments. Outside deck.

Sojourners

P.O. Box 3587, Lynchburg, VA 24503
Phone: 804/384-1655
Location: On a cul-de-sac with acres of woodland. Ten minutes from downtown; 16 miles east of Blue Ridge Parkway; 25 miles west of Appomattox. Near restaurants and small shopping areas.
Hosts: Clyde and Ann McAlister
Open: Year round. Advance reservations required; map sent.
Rates: $38 single. $45 double. $10 child age 6–12; older charged at single rate. $2 one-night surcharge.

> Guests wrote: "Our favorite B&B. . . . Breakfast is out of this world. . . . We appreciated their openness and cordiality. . . . Interesting conversations. . . . We especially enjoyed watching the birds at the feeder outside the breakfast window. . . . Very helpful hosts who go the extra mile. . . . A well-stocked mini-library that left us with a greater appreciation of the area."

For traditionalists, this is the ultimate B&B. There's just one (quite private) guest room. Mac is a retired college business administrator; both hosts are professional genealogists. They live in a 30-year-old brick ranch house furnished with "our style of comfort and simplicity, with memories of favorite friends and places and Ann's father's oil paintings." Although not natives—they came from New Jersey 13 years ago—the McAlisters are prepared with area suggestions for cyclists, art aficionados, nature lovers, and history buffs. For 8 years now they have hosted "friends"—extending the British style they were introduced to when their own daughter was an exchange student in England.

Restrictions: One child age six or older welcome at any given time. No smoking or pets allowed. Please check in by 9 P.M.
Foreign language spoken: Very minimal French.
Bed and bath: One large first-floor room with a double and a twin bed, private full bath, private entrance. Completely separate from family quarters.

Breakfast: You choose the hour. Homemade breads, home-canned local apples or fresh fruit. Filled omelets, sausage strata, or homemade muesli. Fresh eggs from farmers' market. Special diets accommodated. Hosts join guests.
Plus: Central air conditioning. Tea or wine. "Meander in the woods, sit in sun, join us for TV, or talk in living room." Tour of area.

Good Intent

Route 1, Box 435, Maurertown, VA 22644
Phone: 703/459-2985
Location: In rural northern Shenandoah Valley. On 20 acres (to explore). Two hours west of Washington, D.C.; 6 miles north of Woodstock on Route 623; 25 miles from Skyline Drive.
Hosts: Fran and Woody Rohrbaugh
Open: Year round. Reservations required.
Rates: $35 single, $45–$50 double. Washhouse cottage $75 double, $10 extra person.

We really thought we had the countryside to our anonymous selves when someone called out from his porch rocker, "Just a mile to the Rohrbaughs'!" The neighbors knew that Fran and Woody were expecting their first cycling guests.

It is country at its best in the house where Fran's grandparents brought up nine children. Fran's parents made changes when they retired here; so did Woody and Fran when they retired (from school administration in Bucks County, Pennsylvania, and the Educational Testing Service in Princeton, New Jersey). The 1890 farmhouse is surrounded by beautiful grounds and views—with the summer kitchen now Woody's workroom, the bath done over with refinished pine flooring from the old pigpen, and the washhouse now a cozy private guest house. It's warm, inviting, and immaculate—furnished with family antiques and collected functional pieces.

Beyond B&B, Fran has become quite a potter and is, as she says her brother-in-law says, "a decent docent" at Belle Grove Plantation. To boot, we can tell you she is a fabulous cook. Woody, a Civil War buff, has chaired the committee that administers the Shenandoah Valley Music Festival. They are a sharing couple who invite guests to use Good Intent as a touring base or for total relaxation. We left after a prolonged parting discussion and a hug.

In residence: Fran smokes "but can do without."
Restrictions: Sorry, no children. No pets allowed indoors. No smoking in the bedrooms.
Bed and bath: Two second-floor rooms share one full bath. One room with queen bed; double bed in other room. The washhouse, a separate air-conditioned studio cottage, has queen bed, private bath, fireplace, sitting area, deck.

Breakfast: Whenever guests wish. Seasonal fruits, juice, bacon, ham, sausage, eggs any style, homemade hot biscuits, muffins, jams and jellies, coffee and tea. Served in dining end of country kitchen or on deck.
Plus: Beverages. Bedroom air conditioners and ceiling fans. Front porch swing and hammock. TV in family room. Deck for stargazing.

"The Briar Patch" at Middleburg

Route 50, P.O. Box 803, Middleburg, VA 22117
Phone: 703/327-4455, 327-4465
Location: In hunt country on a 90-acre working farm surrounded by cultivated fields, grazing horses, old boxwood, and mountain views. Near vineyards and historic sites. One hour from Washington, D.C.; 25 minutes from Dulles International Airport.
Hosts: Jean and Jay Gold, Arch and Katrina Randolph
Open: Year round. Advance reservations required.
Rates: $65 shared bath. $85–$95 private bath. $115 suite. Personal checks welcome.

It's just as the local paper's headline reported, "Good As Gold." Today their imprint is there, but Jay and Jean are in and out since building their contemporary home up yonder on the acreage and since Jean has become director of the local community theater with Jay working on special effects. He was one of the founders of Time-Life Records. They both were *Life* magazine staffers during World War II and worked on Time-Life Books. They moved from New York City and Long Island to Jean's country residence, The Briar Patch, in 1984. A spacious family home that belies its beginnings as a log cabin, it is filled with family pictures; early American, French provincial, and English antiques; and memorabilia from Jean's extensive travels. The Randolphs are here full time greeting guests, who come for getaways, race weekends, Foxcroft parents' weekends, and, sometimes, for weddings at a spot that is perfect for joyous celebrations.

Restrictions: Children 10 and over welcome. Smoking allowed in downstairs public rooms only. Sorry, no guests' pets.
Foreign language spoken: A little French.
Bed and bath: Eight rooms. Private shower baths for two first-floor rooms—one with two twin beds, the other with canopied double bed—each with private outside entrance. On second floor, two twin-bedded rooms and two double-bedded rooms, each with semiprivate full (tub and shower) bath. A suite with king bed, full bath, fireplaced sitting room. (Crib available when a group rents entire inn.)
Breakfast: 9–10:30. Juice, croissants, coffee or tea. Served in glass-enclosed dining room with wood stove in winter.
Plus: Air conditioning. Tea or wine. Flowers. Large veranda overlooking Bull Run Mountains. Swimming pool. Tour of house and farm. Common rooms with fireplaces.

The Pumpkin House Inn, Ltd.

Route 2, Box 155, Mount Crawford, VA 22841
Phone: 703/434-6963
Location: On a 43-acre farm "in the heart of the Shenandoah Valley."
Across from the corncrib with a pumpkin mural pictured in a 1976 *National Geographic* magazine; close to antiquing and Massanutten Peak skiing. Four miles south of Harrisonburg.
Hosts: J. Thomas Kidd, Jr. and Elizabeth K. Umstott
Open: Year round. Advance reservations requested.
Rates: Queen bed, private bath, and fireplace, $65 single, $70 double. Double bed, shared bath, and fireplace, $55 single, $60 double. Double or twin bed, shared bath, $45 single, $50 double. Business rates available Sunday–Thursday except holidays. $5 rollaway. AMEX, MC, VISA.

This really is the family homestead. Tom and Liz, brother and sister, grew up in this "simple brick Victorian farmhouse," which still has a crib used by five generations and still has "friends" at the table. Things were changed more than a bit during the restoration days of 1986, when the extended family, including the Umstott teenagers, helped and a local artist stenciled borders.

Now the refinished floors have Oriental or hooked rugs. Everything is fresh and immaculate. The hatbox of the original 1847 owner is in the red room. The front hall has a ceiling fixture once fired by kerosene. One room is filled with cat designs and whimsy. Instead of pumpkins for sale across the road (hence the name), now every room has some antique furnishings (on consignment from local dealers) for sale.

Tom formerly worked in public accounting in Culpeper and now does some part-time bookkeeping in addition to his full-time innkeeping. Liz is a registered nurse, wife, and mother in Newport News and works at the inn two or three weekends a month.

Restrictions: Children welcome; guests provide own infant equipment. Sorry, no pets.
Bed and bath: Six rooms; two on first floor. Private shower baths and fireplaces for queen-bedded second-floor rooms. Semiprivate bath for double-bedded rooms (one with working fireplace), twin-bedded room, and room with canopied double bed and a trundle bed. Rollaway available.
Breakfast: 7–9:30 weekdays; 8:30–10 weekends and holidays. Pumpkin bread, Danish, mixed fruit bowl, cereal, juice, tea, coffee. Buffet style.
Plus: Bedroom air conditioners. Lemonade or cider. Pumpkin mints. Flowers. Garage space for bicycles and skis. Ice maker with ice buckets. TV.

Guests wrote: "We felt as if we were welcome neighbors."

The Widow Kip's Country Inn

Route 1, Box 117, Mount Jackson, VA 22842
Phone: 703/477-2400
Location: Rural setting (cows grazing 10 feet from swimming pool).
Shenandoah River is 50 yards from house which is visible from I-81. A
few minutes from village center. Two hours from Washington, D.C.
Host: Rosemary Kip
Open: Year round. Advance reservations preferred.
Rates: $45 single. $55 double. Guest house, $65 for two, $85 for four
people. Ten percent discount for seniors.

From Florida: "Its ambiance, charm and warmth made our stay a
memorable one. It is decorated with flair and imagination, and nos-
talgia greeted us in every room. As avid readers of your book, we felt
your readers should know about this delightful and special B&B."

Marvelous combinations of color, prints, and locally made quilts are
part of the flair. Rosemary has succeeded in providing a memory—with
Cousin Marjorie's picture here, Uncle Em's game table there. She restored (almost fully) this 1830 home, once part of a 300-acre farm. Now,
in addition to sharing hints about things to do just minutes away—hiking, canoeing, downhill skiing, antiquing, caverns, and a good chef-owned
candlelit restaurant—she has hints about adding new bathrooms where
there doesn't seem to be space or can tell you about creating a guest
house from an outbuilding. "The city lady with a country heart" was, for
many years, private club manager (mostly women's) in New York City
and Washington, D.C. She now offers "old-fashioned hospitality" surrounded by antiques and collectibles, mostly Victoriana, that are all for
sale! In addition, there's a working fireplace in each main house guest
room, a 32-foot swimming pool, a cool veranda, and picnicking by the
waterfall.

In residence: One cat.
Restrictions: Children welcome. Pets allowed in cottages. Smoking permitted except in dining room.
Bed and bath: Eight rooms with double or queen beds; all private baths.
Six main house rooms are on first and second floors. In guest house, one
room with double, one with a double and a trundle twin bed, sitting
room.
Breakfast: 8–9. Pure apple cider, local homemade sausage patties, homemade southern biscuits, real butter, scrambled eggs, blueberry jam, apple
butter, cereal, fruits, beverage. Served in dining room at tables for six.
Plus: Tea or sherry. Bedroom air conditioners. Fireplaced living room
with VCR, game table, books. Porch rockers. Picnic table area with gas
grill. (Do-it-yourself dinner or light picnic, lunch, or supper provided at
reasonable rates.) Bicycles (no charge).

Shenandoah Valley Bed & Breakfast Host SQ

New Market, South, VA
Location: In a rural area between New Market and Harrisonburg with views of mountains and creeks. A mile from I-81 and Highway 11. Within half an hour of Civil War history, caverns, wineries, crafts, outdoor and dinner theater, golf, hiking, and a private small-craft landing field. Fine restaurants 10 minutes away.
Reservations: Available year round except Thanksgiving, Christmas, and New Year through Shenandoah Valley Bed & Breakfast, page 305.
Rates: $30 single, $56 double. $10 cot or crib.

"Our home was built in 1960 when we moved back to the farm from Alabama with our three children. The house, traditional in design, was on a Historic Garden Week after we remodeled it to include a 32-foot greenhouse and spa. Through the years we have had a variety of stock including short-horned cattle, turkeys, and chickens. Hosting is much more fun than we ever expected. Among our guests have been west coast people looking for wide pine flooring planks, a retired Foreign Service couple on tour, and anniversary celebrants—each one memorable."

The host, retired from the U.S. Forest Service, teaches safety classes to motorcyclists and conducts promotional tours for farm-related groups. The hostess grows vegetables and fruits and is learning about raising orchids.

In residence: A daughter in her twenties. The host and hostess smoke. Pets include Lessa, a cat who tends to hide from guests, and Curly, a Border collie who spends most of his time outside.
Restrictions: Twenty-four hours' notice needed to provide a cot or crib. Pets allowed if friendly and housebroken.
Bed and bath: A second-floor room with a king bed, full bath.
Breakfast: Time determined night before. Fruit or juice, assorted cheeses and meat, croissants, homemade jam or jelly, beverages. Served on sun porch surrounded by ferns and flowers.
Plus: Refreshments upon arrival. Air-conditioned guest room. Chocolates. Fresh flowers. Soft music. Kitchen, laundry facilities. Year-round use of six-foot spa on the sun porch. Take a walk, fish, picnic, or just observe the wildlife; sometimes, see deer, wild geese, hummingbirds.

North Garden

North Garden, VA
Location: Pastoral. On a small farm with beautiful views. Twenty minutes south of University of Virginia, 30 to Wintergreen ski resort.
Reservations: Year round through Guesthouses, page 304.
Rates: $52 single. $60 double. $4 one-night surcharge.

"I might be feeding a calf or two when you arrive. We serve home-cooked homegrown foods in our green room, so-called because it was added to the house for lots of plants—and people."

It's a century-old, meticulously restored farmhouse. Home to the host family for a decade, it is filled with family pieces and a country feel. "Some guests feed the calves. Others just relax. This is a very low-key place."

In residence: Three young adults. Inside, one bird. Outside, cats, dogs, rabbits, a small herd of beef cattle.
Bed and bath: Three second-floor rooms. One double-bedded with private full bath. One with a double and one with two twins share a full bath. Rollaway and crib available.
Breakfast: Flexible hours. Home style. Fruit or juice, homemade bread and jelly, eggs and bacon; cereal. Hostess joins guests.
Plus: Tea or wine. Bedroom window fans. Tour of house and farm. Babysitting available. Hiking.

The High Street Inn

405 High Street, Petersburg, VA 23803
Phone: 804/733-0505
Location: "Just off I-95" in historic district with homes built from 1735 to 1900. Two blocks from museums, shops, and restaurants. Thirty minutes from downtown Richmond or James River Plantations. Within an hour of Williamsburg and Busch Gardens.
Hosts: Bruce and Candace Noé
Open: Year round.
Rates: $50–$55 double with shared bath, $55–$60 with private bath. $70 suite. Singles $5 less. $7.50 rollaway. MC, VISA.

Guests wrote: "In completing our revitalization study of Petersburg, I had the pleasure of staying at High Street Inn, an opportunity to step into history. . . . An experience not to be missed by avid inngoers . . . unique . . . a jewel . . . exquisite with every detail from the lace curtains to the furnishings. . . . Impeccable . . . a warm welcome."

And all because the Noés fell in love with the neighborhood and its old houses four years ago. "An instant education" is the way Candace describes the extensive restoration process. Their 18-room yellow brick 1891 Queen Anne house had been used commercially since 1932. Now each high-ceilinged guest room reflects a different style, from Empire to Eastlake. There are still some gas/electric fixtures and fireplace mantels have their original beveled mirrors. Since opening as a B&B in 1986, the house fronted by an iron fence has been on a Virginia Historic Garden Week tour and the Noés received the 1987 Historic Petersburg Foundation Preservation-Restoration Design Award.

In residence: In hosts' private quarters, Amanda, age four. "Charlie is our ten-year-old cat."
Restrictions: Children are welcome. Smoking in first-floor rooms only. Sorry, no pets please.
Foreign languages spoken: Some Spanish, German, French.
Bed and bath: Five second-floor rooms. All baths have shower and claw-footed tub. Private bath for suite with queen bed and sitting room, room with double bed and balcony, and room with two twin beds. Two double-bedded rooms share a bath. Rollaway and crib available.
Breakfast: 7–10. Juice, fresh fruit, croissants, home-baked muffins, Virginia ham biscuits, coffee or tea. In dining room, sun room, or guest room.
Plus: Bedroom air conditioners. Tea or wine. Fireplaces. Parlor with a playable melodeon. Tour of house. VCR with classic and foreign films. Stereo. Books and games. Off-street parking.

Bensonhouse Host #2036

Richmond, VA
Location: In historic district, one and a half miles from I-64 and I-95. Ten minutes from downtown. Within minutes of most sites and attractions.
Reservations: Year round through Bensonhouse, page 303.
Rates: $66–$84 single. $75–$95 double. $10 rollaway or portacrib.

"Relaxed and at-home, but not forgotten" is how guests feel in this grand Italian Renaissance home, which has just been totally restored—close to the single-family residence it was when built in 1914, far from the rooming house and apartment building it had become. Once again, books fill the bookcases that flank the marble fireplace in the mahogany-paneled living room. Once again, friends made in the hostess's previous residence come for hospitality and comfort.

The hostess (and restorer) collects watercolors and folk art painted by a Virginia artist. She has a real estate license and since the early 1980s has worked to spread the bed and breakfast concept. Earlier, she was a social worker and a volunteer coordinator for the state of Virginia.

In residence: A 13-year-old Abyssinian cat named Russ.
Restrictions: Children eight and over welcome. Nonsmokers only, please. Sorry, no guests' pets.
Bed and bath: Four second-floor rooms with private baths; two with working fireplace. Furnished with queen (one with Jacuzzi), double, or two antique sleigh twin beds. Rollaway available.
Breakfast: Usually 7:30–9. Eggs, homemade breads, juice, natural cereal, coffee and tea. Served in formal dining room. Hosts join guests.
Plus: Central air conditioning. Tea or wine. Tour of house. Elevator to second floor.

Hanover Hosts

P.O. Box 25145, Richmond, VA 23260
Phone: 804/355-5855
Location: In the Monument Avenue/Fan District. Within walking distance of restaurants, shopping, museums, historic sites. Two and a half miles from I-95 and I-64.
Hosts: Barbara and Bill Fleming
Open: Year round. Advance reservations recommended. Two-night minimum preferred April–June, September, October.
Rates: Private bath—$45 single, $65/$75 double. Shared bath, $10 less. $125 suite (with one bath). $15 extra person.

They are still living in an early-1900s Richmond Colonial Revival house, but the Flemings (experienced hosts at another location) moved to this much larger and grander version in 1988. Their first guests here, Californians who just couldn't wait, loved seeing the transformation in progress and are planning to come back. They want to take a full tour—and see just how Barbara, an interior designer, decorated the two parlors flanked by Doric columns and how she treated the hall stairway that leads up to a stained glass skylight and the large guest rooms with $10\frac{1}{2}$-foot ceilings. They will find a rococo mirror from an older Richmond building. There are Oriental rugs, antiques, and some reproductions too. The dining room is Barbara's "magic room," aviarylike with trees and plants in the bay window.

Bill is very much co-host here. Since the move, he has reduced his management consulting and plays every role from chef to firetender. "This is home," as they say, "the kind of place where our cat just might meow at your door, the kind of place where you're welcome in the living room, but it's okay if you wander into the kitchen too."

Restrictions: Children should be at least 12. Sorry, no guests' pets. Please restrict smoking to the porch.
Bed and bath: Seven rooms; option of suites. Three second-floor rooms, two with private full baths; extra shower room in hall. Four third-floor rooms share a large full bath. Working fireplaces in queen and double-bedded rooms. Lavatory sink in rooms with two twin beds and queen beds. Rollaway available.
Breakfast: 7–9. Fresh fruit compote in season. French toast, poached eggs, or Belgian waffles with peaches. Homemade bran muffins.
Plus: Air conditioning. Tour of house. Tea. Fruit in rooms. Plenty of thirsty towels. Great porch for rocking. Small gift shop with Virginia products.

Summerhouse

Richmond, VA
Location: On historic Monument Avenue. Two-block walk to 15-minute bus ride to Center City. Forty-five minutes to Williamsburg.

Reservations: Year round through Bensonhouse, page 303.
Rates: Second floor, $80 single, $90 double, $110 suite. Third floor, $68 single, $75 double. Suite (two rooms plus bath), $115 for family with children, $130 for two couples. $10 rollaway.

Southern Living readers will recognize this 1908 house richly appointed with Oriental rugs, French crystal chandeliers, and oil paintings. The hosts, antiques collectors, began in 1987 by gutting a burned-out residence and finished with the installation of recessed lighting and authentically reproduced millwork. Still—after renovating six houses—their enthusiasm is high. They find hosting, too, "absolutely wonderful!"

In residence: A five-pound dog who barks only when you knock at the door.
Restrictions: Children eight and over welcome. Nonsmokers only, please. Sorry, no guests' pets.
Bed and bath: Three carpeted rooms. Private full bath for second-floor queen-bedded room with optional adjoining suite, which has a working fireplace. Two adjoining third-floor rooms share a full bath. One has two twin four-poster beds; the other a queen bed, wet bar, and refrigerator. Rollaway available.
Breakfast: 7–9:30. Fresh juice, muffins, butter, coffee, tea. Served on silver trays with starched napkins, sterling flatware, silver coffee service, fresh flowers.
Plus: Central air conditioning. Beverages. Cable TV in each room. Tour of house. Courtyard.

The Mary Bladon House

381 Washington Avenue, S.W., Roanoke, VA 24016
Phone: 703/344-5361
Location: In Virginia's largest congruent historical area (National Registry). Within walking distance of downtown, Center in the Square, Farmers Market, antiques, crafts, Transportation Museum, "a special restaurant." Ten minutes from Blue Ridge Parkway entrance. Twenty minutes from airport; 15 minutes south of I-81. Near wineries.
Host: Sally Pfister
Open: Year round. Reservations preferred. Three-day minimum stay on holidays.
Rates: Double occupancy. $55 upstairs room with shared bath, $65 larger rooms, $75 with kitchen. $3 less for singles and Parents Without Partners members. Ten percent discount for senior citizens.

Guests wrote: "What an incredible experience! Being serenaded by a concert violinist while sipping tea on the porch, having the bed turned down while you are out, eating a delicious breakfast by candlelight. We will always remember our 10th anniversary weekend."

When Sally restored the high-ceilinged house with its gingerbread and three porches, she retained many original brass light fixtures, ornate fireplaces, and crown and bull's-eye moldings. The Victorian where "Mother Bladon," wife of a railroad worker, took in boarders in 1892 is furnished with some iron beds, some bedsteads with tall headboards, and other antiques as well as flea market finds. Original paintings and crafts done by Virginia artists are for sale. Recently Belle/Leggett photographed their 100th anniversary catalog here.

Before opening this B&B in 1985, Sally was a nurse in Winston-Salem, North Carolina. Now she arranges fresh flowers, writes poetry, and offers warm hospitality with a "terrific" breakfast appreciated by both business travelers and tourists.

In residence: Maybe grown children on holidays. Samantha (Sam), "a perfect black B&B cat." Valentine, a Border collie, and Sheba, a small stray, not allowed in guest areas.
Restrictions: Children should be at least 12 and accommodated in own room. Sorry, no guests' pets. Smoking in kitchens and on porches only.
Foreign language spoken: "Moderate Spanish."
Bed and bath: Four rooms. The large first-floor room has double bed, private entrance, private shower bath. Second-floor rooms include one with double bed, sitting area, private shower bath. Two double-bedded rooms (when a suite) share a full bath (private if guests choose to use additional bath off dining room) and kitchen.
Breakfast: 7:30–10. Casseroles, homemade breads and muffins, freshly ground coffee. Served in candlelit dining room.
Plus: Coffee in rooms for early birds. Tea or local wines. Three bedrooms with air conditioners; one with ceiling fan. Sunday night dinner by advance notice only.

Chester

Route 4, Box 57, Scottsville, VA 24590
Phone: 804/286-3960
Location: On a seven-acre estate just off Route 20. Forty-five minutes from Skyline Drive; within half an hour of Monticello, Ash Lawn, Charlottesville, and University of Virginia.
Hosts: Gordon Anderson and Richard Shaffer
Open: Year round. Two-day minimum during UVA graduation and parents' weekends July 4, December 22–January 2. (Advance reservations necessary for weeks after major press coverage.)
Rates: Per room. Private bath $70. Shared bath $55, with fireplace $65. $70 queen bed with adjoining sitting room. $30 sofa bed (one or two people).

"We have returned to a marvelous place that really should be in your book. The hosts are wonderful with guests. They serve beautifully—with Waterford, and their meals are extraordinary," reported the Jacobsens, popular Shenandoah Valley hosts (page 324).

Dick was a legal administrator in Manhattan and Gordon a Wall Street investment banker before they spent a year restoring the gracious 1847 Greek Revival frame house built by a landscape architect from

England. It has a columned portico, four porches, eight fireplaces (now working), expansive lawns (perfect for weddings), and English boxwood. Many of their furnishings were acquired during their own extensive travels—trips that inspired them to host. It's "home" with Oriental rugs, comfortable chairs, traditional furnishings, classical music, and artwork.

In residence: "We breed and show borzoi (Russian wolfhounds) who love people and often are visited by guests." Johnny Weismuller and Esther Williams are outside cats. One host (Dick) smokes.
Restrictions: Well-mannered children, preferably over eight, welcome. "Guests' dogs allowed in our kennel" ($3.50/night).
Bed and bath: Five rooms; four with working fireplaces, all with heated towel racks. Private full bath for first-floor room, four-poster three-quarter bed. Four second-floor rooms with semiprivate baths have queen four-poster bed, pedestal sink, sitting room with double sofa bed; double bed, pedestal sink, twin beds; one smaller room with double bed. Rollaway available.
Breakfast: 7:30–10. Fresh fruit. Eggs (maybe sherried) or omelets or five-grain pancakes, local sausage or bacon. Homemade breads. Cereals. Juices. Coffees, teas. Served on large screened porch or by fireplace in dining room.
Plus: Beverages. Flowers. Bedroom fans. Use of bicycles. Laundry room with ironing facilities. Tour of house, kennels, greenhouse. Picnic baskets prepared. Dinner ($15) with advance reservation.

Frederick House

18 East Frederick Street, P.O. Box 1387, Staunton, VA 24401
Phone: 703/885-4220
Location: In downtown historic Staunton, across from Mary Baldwin College. Within walking distance of Woodrow Wilson Birthplace. Near Skyline Drive, Blue Ridge Parkway, and the new Museum of American Frontier Culture.
Hosts: Joe and Evy Harman
Open: Year round.
Rates: Double occupancy. $60 suite, $15 extra person. $55 large room, $10 extra person. $40 small room. Breakfast $3 per person. AMEX, Diner's, Discover, MC, VISA.

When the inn was "created" in the downtown area, it was intentionally designed to be very homelike, furnished in antiques and period pieces. The three adjoining houses, built in 1810, 1850, and 1910, had become offices when the Harmans bought them in 1983. Then Washingtonians Joe, a banker, and Evy, an auditor, became award-winning restorers, supervising a crew and recording the progress in a before-and-after album (now available to guests).

In true B&B style, they offer assistance to sightseers, business travelers, and college-related guests. They can tell you about restaurants, a walking tour of the historic area, mountain hiking trails, or back roads for driving or cycling. The hosts also have a jewelry store and operate a farm.

Restrictions: Sorry, neither smoking nor pets permitted.
Bed and bath: Five suites and six rooms, each with private bath. All suites have sitting rooms. Seven of the accommodations have private entrances. King, queen, double, and twin-sized beds available. Cot and crib available.
Breakfast: Available in dining room or delivered to your room by Joe at any hour requested. Traditional menu.
Plus: Each room has TV, phone, air conditioning, and ceiling fan. Robes provided. Tour of the house (unoccupied rooms). Backyard of flowers and herb gardens. Extra charge for exercise facilities and indoor swimming pool (both at athletic club next door), and for laundry facilities or babysitting.

Thornrose House at Gypsy Hill

531 Thornrose Avenue, Staunton, VA 24401
Phone: 703/885-7026
Location: On spacious grounds with arbors. Across from 300-acre Gypsy Hill Park with golf, tennis, swimming, ducks, and swans. Six blocks from the center of "Victorian Staunton" (walking tour territory).
Hosts: Carolyn and Ray Hoaster
Open: Year round. Three-day minimum for July Fourth.
Rates: Double occupancy. $45 double or queen bed, $50 king bed. Singles $10 less. Rollaway $5 per child, $15 adult. Personal checks accepted.

> Guests wrote: "As close to Great Britain as one could expect without an actual airline ticket."

That being the case, goal fulfilled! Inspired by their own stays in more than 60 British B&Bs, these two musicians started hosting in 1985 when they moved here from Washington, D.C. Both continue to be active with area musical and theater productions.

Their 1912 two-storied modified Georgian brick house is comfortably furnished in what Carolyn calls "unfussy Victorian." (The late-1800s carved cherry living room set is a family heirloom.) Some guests return for A Victorian Sampler (see "Plus" below). Two who met here planned a trip to Europe together. And another concluded, "Comfort, hospitality, cleanliness, breakfast, and location—all 10 on a scale of 1–5."

Restrictions: No smoking inside. Sorry, no pets.
Bed and bath: Three second-floor air-conditioned rooms. All private baths. Private exterior entrance. Room with king bed, full bath. Queen bed with shower bath. Double four-poster bed, bath with footed tub. Rollaway, crib, and bassinet available.

Breakfast: Usually 8–9. Birchermuesli (a hit called "the unpronounceable cereal" by guests) made with oats, apples, raisins, fruit, almonds, whipped cream. Juice, eggs, bacon, sausage, tomatoes, toast, coffee or tea. Served in fireplaced dining room.
Plus: Afternoon tea or evening sherry in fireplaced living room. Wraparound porch. Tennis racquets. VCR with movies and British imports. Use of health club facilities ($5). A Victorian Sampler, a three-day, two-night package with dinner, breakfasts, admission tickets, games, afternoon tea, and entertainment.

Pickett's Harbor

Mailing Address: Box 97AA, Cape Charles, VA 23310
Phone: 804/331-2212. (Please try 6–7:30 A.M. and 5–10 P.M.)
Location: Rural. On 17 Chesapeake Bay acres directly across from Virginia Beach. Four miles north of the Chesapeake Bay Bridge Tunnel. Two miles from Route 13 on Virginia's Eastern Shore.
Hosts: Sara and Cooke Goffigon
Open: Year round. Reservations are helpful.
Rates: $45 single, $60 double. $10 cot.

A real find: on a secluded wide beach marvelous "for family, guests, seagulls, brown pelicans and sandpipers," with spectacular sunsets. A 12-year-old colonial home that has a kitchen with cupboards, doors, and floors made from old barn lumber. It's decorated with antiques, reproductions, and country pieces and, in season, has wildflower arrangements in every room. The breakfast jams and jellies have received such rave reviews that they have become a mother (Sara)-and-daughter (Sarah) business that now produces about seven varieties in addition to pickles and relishes.

Cooke, an avocational pilot who "works for the ABC Commission and manicures the yard," and Sara, a secondary school teacher, built the home on family land. (Sara grew up on the farm, just a half mile away down a country lane.) Now that all five Goffigon children are grown and gone, the world comes to this wonderful doorstep. They come for a retreat, for auctions, for nearby nature tours. Some come to beachcomb (acres), to swim, to fish, or to crab (a skill Sara has taught to many, including an anthropologist who had been with a camel caravan in the Sudan for about a decade). Others come to research old homes or to take day trips to Norfolk, Williamsburg, or Virginia Beach.

Restrictions: Sorry, no guests' pets. No smoking indoors.
Bed and bath: Four rooms. All with views of bay, pines, and beach. First-floor room has queen bed, shares full bath. On second floor, two cozy dormer rooms, each with a double bed, share a full bath. Third room has queen bed, private bath. Cot and sleeping bags available.
Breakfast: 6–9. Juice or fresh fruit, sweet potato biscuits, popovers, rolls, cinnamon buns, bran muffins, ham, sausage, cheese/egg/sausage casse-

role, scrapple, eggs, and, in season, fish. In kitchen, on porch overlooking bay and pines, or in Williamsburg-style dining room.
Plus: Fireplaced living room. Dining room with open fireplace. Bedroom air conditioning and fans. Beverages. Use of refrigerator. Porch ceiling fan. Dinner sometimes available by advance arrangement. Paths through woods "where deer, squirrel, quail, foxes and rabbits roam freely."

The Burton House

11 Brooklyn Street, Wachapreague, VA 23480
Phone: 804/787-4560 or 787-4848
Location: One block from the waterfront. In a fishing village on an undeveloped peninsula that has a winery. Bordered by Chesapeake Bay and Atlantic Ocean. Overlooking the Barrier Islands. Within walking distance of restaurant, rental and charter boats; 45-minute drive to Chincoteague Island.
Hosts: Pat, Tom, and (son) Mike Hart
Open: Year round. Reservations advised. Two-day minimum on summer holidays.
Rates: $60 per room.

"It was always called 'Mrs. Burton's house,' so there was no need to change the name. There are 350 year-round residents in this town where we have lived 'forever.' For many years I worked in the supermarket. Our son, Mike, works for the post office and loves his flower gardens and the yard. Tom and I love fishing, outdoor life, and antiques. After reading about B&Bs in magazines, we got 'the bug' in 1986 and completely restored this 1883 house, leaving everything as original as possible. We repaired and refinished locally-found furniture—brass beds, rockers, china cabinets, you name it. [Other pieces can be purchased in their small antique shop.] Tom is a carpenter whose pride and joy is the screened gazebo made with posts and trim from a 1902 hotel. *Self* magazine writers and photographers have returned several times. Honeymooners, too, have discovered us. It's fun—for everyone!"

Restrictions: Smoking on first floor only. Sorry, no guests' pets.
Bed and bath: Seven rooms on three floors; each with private half bath. Shared shower baths; two rooms share a full bath. Rooms have a queen bed, a double, two twins, or a double and a daybed.
Breakfast: Usually 8–10. Family style. Locally made sausages. Juice, fruit, bacon, eggs, muffins or biscuits, coffee. Sometimes waffles, Latvian pancakes, or French toast. Served at oak table in dining room or in gazebo.
Plus: Afternoon tea, wine, coffee, soda. Always, cake or brownies. Central air conditioning plus individual units in bedrooms. And bedroom ceiling fans. Laundry facilities. Bicycles (no charge). Large deck with rockers next to gazebo.

The Foster-Harris House

Main Street, P.O. Box 333, Washington, VA 22747
Phone: 703/675-3757
Location: "On land that George Washington surveyed in a wonderful town (pop. 250), six blocks long and two blocks wide." Three blocks from The Inn at Little Washington, a five-star world-famous restaurant rated among the country's top 10. Near antiquing; vineyards; country fairs; swimming holes; little-known hiking trails. Fifteen minutes from Skyline Drive; 65 miles west of Washington, D.C.
Hosts: Camille Harris and Pat Foster
Open: Year round. Reservations suggested, especially for weekends.
Rates: $50 single. $60 double. Suite $75 single, $85 double. $5 under age 12. $10 over age 12. $10 use of fireplace wood stove. Less beyond three nights or for three-night stays that start on Monday or Tuesday. MC, VISA.

> From Washington, D.C.: "Many little touches. . . . .A meticulous sense of each guest's interests and needs. . . . I felt truly welcomed into the family atmosphere."

It's just as Camille hoped when she suggested that they buy the turn-of-the-century house, which had been, in the 1940s, a tourist house, and which was, in 1983, in need of care. Pat, born on a farm located 10 minutes from here, is responsible for all the major changes. The country Victorian decor is Camille's touch. For some guests, the home away from home has become a home exchanged for home!

Camille, a Mississippi native, has experience as both a school director and a fund-raiser. All the flower arrangements reflect her newest creative venture as a home-based flower broker and designer.

In residence: Elise, age 8, and Ariele, age 10—two daughters who have grown up as assistant innkeepers.
Restrictions: Children are welcome (age six is minimum for rooms with shared bath). Inquire about pets.
Foreign languages spoken: Some Spanish and German.
Bed and bath: On air-conditioned second floor. Two queen-bedded rooms, one with a fireplace stove, share a full bath. Four-room suite with queen bed, sitting room with double sofa bed, private tub bath, kitchen.
Breakfast: Until 10. Three fresh rolls such as croissants, orange-nut muffins, and cherry turnover. Fruit, juice, coffee or tea. Served in kitchen; suite guests eat in their own kitchen.
Plus: Refreshments. Mints. Fireplaced parlor. Use of bicycles. Babysitting available. Kitchen privileges. Picnic table, lawn chairs, front porch swing.

Liberty Rose Colonial B&B

1022 Jamestown Road, Williamsburg, VA 23185
Phone: 804/253-1260

Location: One mile from restored area. On a hilltop acre of old trees.
Hosts: Brad and Sandra Hirz
Open: Year round. Two-night minimum on major event weekends.
Rates: Per room. $95 private bath. $70 shared bath. $20 child or third person.

> From Georgia, North Carolina, Illinois, Oklahoma, New York: "While on a business trip, I had the good fortune to discover this B&B. . . . Kind, enthusiastic and helpful, just like my neighbors here in my own small town. . . . 'Magnolia's Peach' was the perfect honeymoon suite. . . . Breakfast was a banquet. . . . The entire house has great warmth and charm."

A millstone from one of Williamsburg's old mills is on the entry porch of the 1930s clapboard house. Much of the brick used in the porch came from Jamestown Colony before it became a historic lanemark. Slate is on the roof. And inside there's a new/old kitchen, the Hirzes' specialty. There's a tin ceiling in the common room. And a grand piano in the fireplaced living room. The collectibles, quilts, and refinished antiques are all placed with a strong sense of display and color—and comfort and fun too.

The way Sandi tells the story, "Brad was pulling out of farming in the state of Washington. I was in interior design in California. We got married, moved to Williamsburg in 1986, and did the whole restoration on this house that looks older than it is. And we learned a lot about great places to eat while we were without a kitchen for four months."

In residence: Mister Goose, "our gorgeous outdoor kitty."
Restrictions: Well-behaved children welcome. No smoking. Sorry, no guests' pets.
Bed and bath: Three second-floor rooms with queen or double beds; adjoining dormer rooms (with twin or three-quarter bed) for extra persons in same party. Private or shared bath depending on room arrangement. Crib available.
Breakfast: Usually 7:30–9. The repertoire of both hosts includes waffles, hotcakes, or French toast with bacon, sausage, or Virginia baked ham. Homemade croissant filled with eggs, bacon, cheese, tomato, and spices. Coffee, tea, juice, fresh fruit, homemade muffins, scones, fritters. Served in dining room or on glass-enclosed porch.
Plus: Air conditioning. Chocolate chip cookies. Tour of house. Refrigerator space. Laundry facilities. Tandem bicycle. Small gift shop. Courtesy B&B referral service.

Sheldon's Ordinary

Williamsburg, VA
Location: In a quiet wooded area, one mile from Colonial Williamsburg. Adjacent to College of William and Mary. Near swimming pool.
Reservations: Year round through Bensonhouse, page 303.
Rates: $72 single. $80 double. $10 child.

"When we built the house six years ago, we copied a Connecticut 18th-century tavern. (The original is pictured in Richard Pratt's *The Golden Treasury of American Homes*.) It features oak paneling from an old church in Indiana, our home state; a large Palladian window; hand painted tiles from the Caribbean in the living room mantel; and antique heart pine wide plank floors. The overall floor plan just lends itself to entertaining—and for guests, lots of privacy."

The home has been on a Historic Garden Week tour. The hostess is a community activist, physician's wife, and mother.

In residence: The children, ages 9–15. One golden retriever who greets all guests. One cat with a pink nose.
Restrictions: Children and pets welcome. No smoking inside.
Foreign language spoken: Some Spanish.
Bed and bath: One room, selected from two quiet third-floor rooms. Adjoining private full bath. One with queen bed, working fireplace, phone, cable TV. The other has two twin beds, a queen sleep sofa, game table. Portacrib available.
Breakfast: Flexible hours. Fresh juice, homemade ham rolls, fruit, cereal and eggs on request, coffee or tea. Buffet style in dining room with fine china, silver, and linen.
Plus: Central air conditioning. Beverages. Electric blankets. Pickup at train or bus station. Use of bicycles, trampoline, piano. Honeymoon package ($40) with breakfast in bed, champagne, fruit, and cheese.

Guests wrote: "The house is delightful, exuding warmth and Virginia hospitality . . . decorated in just the Williamsburg style we had anticipated. The fireplace in the cozy and private third-floor room was a perfect touch. . . . A gracious hostess. Delicious breakfast, elegantly served. A treat!"

War Hill Inn

4560 Long Hill Road, Williamsburg, VA 23185
Phone: 804/565-0248
Location: On a 32-acre farm with miles of white fences around pastures where cows and horses are grazing. Three miles west of historic Williamsburg. Two miles off Route 60, within easy access of I-64.
Hosts: Shirley and Bill Lee
Open: Year round. Advance reservations suggested.
Rates: $45 or $55 double bed. $60 room with double and a twin bed. Suite—$65 for two, $75 for three, $85 for four. $10 additional person. AMEX, CHOICE, MC, VISA.

The black Angus show cattle make for a perfect picture in front of the 18th-century-style house built by the Lees 20 years ago with bricks salvaged from Norfolk's "reurbanized" waterfront area. And because so many features of the inside—mantels, stairs, even floors—are from old buildings, most guests think that the large house is restored. It is furnished with period pieces and antiques.

Both Shirley, a fabric consultant who collects colonial antiques, and Billy, a veterinarian, skilled builder, and basket maker, grew up on farms. For hosting, inspired by their empty nest, the Lees installed a sprinkler system and redecorated the children's rooms. As guests "pick one for the road"—from the orchard with its apples, pears, peaches, and plums—they leave with the feeling of having visited family.

Restrictions: Children are welcome. No smoking inside. Sorry, no guests' pets.
Bed and bath: Five rooms, each with cable TV, private full bath. On first floor, private entrance for room with a double and a twin bed, individual temperature control. On second floor, two double-bedded rooms. Suite has a bath and dressing room between a room with a double four-poster bed and a room with a double and a twin bed. Rollaway and crib available.
Breakfast: 8–9. Homegrown fruit in season, juice, homemade breads or muffins, casserole, cereal. Served at large family table in dining room with ladder-back chairs and corner cabinet.
Plus: Central air conditioning. Babysitting can be arranged.

The Manor at Taylor's Store

Route 1, Box 533, Wirtz, VA 24184
Phone: 703/721-3951
Location: In Piedmont region, with magnificent mountain views. On 100-acre historic estate with ponds and trails. Five minutes from Smith Mountain Lake for swimming, boating, dining; 20 minutes to Blue Ridge Parkway and Roanoke.
Hosts: Lee and Mary Lynn Tucker
Open: Year round. Reservations preferred.
Rates: Per room. $50–$70. Ten percent discount for senior citizens and other B&B hosts. MC, VISA.

"Renovating is like having a three-dimensional canvas to paint on," says Mary Lynn, a registered nurse specializing in nutrition who, together with Lee, a pathologist, tackled the circa 1820 Federal-style colonial mansion just after they had restored a house in Roanoke. Beyond repairing, refinishing, and decorating with their collection of lovely antiques, the Tuckers added a sun room, a hot tub, an exercise room, and a "great room" with pool table and stereo. Since their first guests arrived in 1986, "hosting has been more fun than we imagined!"

In residence: All outdoors—Saint George and Basil, Newfoundlands; cockers Gandalf and Pippin; and cat Grizebella.
Restrictions: Children welcomed in the cottage. Sorry, no smoking in the manor house. No guests' pets.
Foreign language spoken: A little German.

Bed and bath: Four rooms, all private baths. On lower level, double bed, shower bath, private sitting porch with wicker furniture, private entrance. On main level, suite with two antique canopied double beds, full bath, working fireplace, sitting area. Second level—"romantic Victorian suite" with double bed, shower bath; another with canopied queen bed, full bath, private balcony. Three-bedroom cottage also available.

Breakfast: At time arranged with guest. "High fiber, low fat, fresh and nutritious." Pancakes, waffles, muffins, quiches, souffles. In dining room with picture window overlooking mountains, in plant-filled sun room, or in guests' rooms.

Plus: Central air conditioning. Tea, wine, or lemonade. Fireplaced "great room" and formal parlor with baby grand piano. Library. Terry robes. Mints. Flowers. Champagne for honeymooners. Picnic lunches and dinner with advance reservations. Guest kitchen. On the premises—swimming, fishing, hiking, canoeing, cross-country skiing, and skating.

> From North Carolina: "Elegant charm. . . . Having stayed in inns and B&B in North America and Europe, we would give this outstanding B&B and its hosts the highest rating."

The Country Fare

402 North Main Street, Woodstock, VA 22664

Phone: 703/459-4828

Location: In Shenandoah Valley, within walking distance of village and of hiking path that leads to a view of the Seven Bends of the Shenandoah River. Near Belle Grove, the National Trust Plantation, breathtaking caverns, Bryce Mountain, wineries.

Host: Bette Hallgren

Open: Year round. Two-night minimum fall weekends.

Rates: Double occupancy. $55 private bath, $45 shared. $10 third person in room.

"Everyone in town has a story to tell about this marvelous 1771 log and brick house that I found through *Preservation News*. The woodwork is beautiful. So is the stenciling. Two previous owners did all the impeccable restoration and redecorating with Williamsburg colors and wallpapers. There are inside window shutters and four fireplaces. My grandmother's furniture fits right into many of the rooms, all of which have been part of historic and Christmas house tours. The log cabin on the property was originally an auction house for antiques. And the garden shed was a barbershop that was rolled here from down the street. There are auctions every weekend around here and lots of places to walk and hike."

Bette discovered Virginia in 1985 after having a career in management for a library subscription agency in Massachusetts. She is an accomplished craftswoman who shares ideas and supply sources—and her home.

Restrictions: "Children at innkeeper's discretion." Sorry, no guests' pets. No smoking on the second floor.
Bed and bath: Three hand-stenciled second-floor rooms. The one with adjoining private full bath has a double bed. One with twin beds shares a full bath (with footed tub) with double-bedded room. Rollaways and air mattresses ("kids love these!") available.
Breakfast: 8–9. Continental plus. Homemade breads (rhubarb, in season, or poppy seed), fresh fruit, beverages, "plus grandmother's treats and surprises." Served in dining room with sterling, crystal, and candlelight and, in season, by wood-burning stove.
Plus: Bedroom air conditioners. Fireplaced common rooom with reading material. Fresh flowers in season. Large brick patio. Old-fashioned swing and rocker on second-floor porch. Off-street parking.

From South Africa: "A joy to share this home."

Shenandoah Valley Bed & Breakfast Host W

Woodstock, VA
Location: On a country road just outside Woodstock at the base of Massanutten Mountain. On one of the famous Seven Bends of the Shenandoah River, with a spectacular view of mountains and George Washington National Forest.
Reservations: Available Memorial Day–December 31 through Shenandoah Valley Bed & Breakfast, page 305. Advance reservations required.
Rates: $55–$95 single or double occupancy. $5 crib or cot. $10 for use of fireplace in bedroom.

Although it's an elegant antiques-filled Victorian mansion with architect-designed wings and a formal living room, "guests feel very much at home here. They come to escape the city or to stay overnight while they are passing through. They can relax in a hammock beneath our towering oak trees or take in the many Valley attractions. We meet a lot of embassy staff, government personnel and just plain lovely people.
"I'm still hoping to write the history of this house that we have had for 18 years. In preparing the property as a family gathering place, we gutted it and spent about ten years restoring everything including the woodwork in the 14 enormous rooms. When it was all done and fully decorated, it evolved, at the suggestion of friends, into a very small personalized inn with European-style service."

In residence: A cat named Mother Cat.
Restrictions: No guests' pets. No smoking upstairs. Hosts' permission required for use of fireplace or wood stove.
Foreign language spoken: German.
Bed and bath: On second and third floors, seven very large rooms, each

with private bath. Each decorated differently; each with fireplace or Franklin stove. King/twin, queen, and double beds available. Features in one room or another include cathedral ceiling; four-poster bed; a dressing room; sitting area; English antiques; Tiffany chandelier; sunken tub.
Breakfast: At 9. German full. Quiche, scalloped tomatoes, seasonal fruits, country ham, bacon, sausage, coffee cakes with homemade jams, egg bakes, toasted dark bread. Served on antique dishes with fine crystal and with Victorian flatware, in the paneled dining room in winter and on the 60-foot veranda in the summer.
Plus: Central air conditioning. Heated swimming pool. Whirlpool ($10) for two. Grand piano. Great Room (40 by 28 feet) with floor-to-ceiling fireplace. Flowers. Turned-down beds.

West Virginia

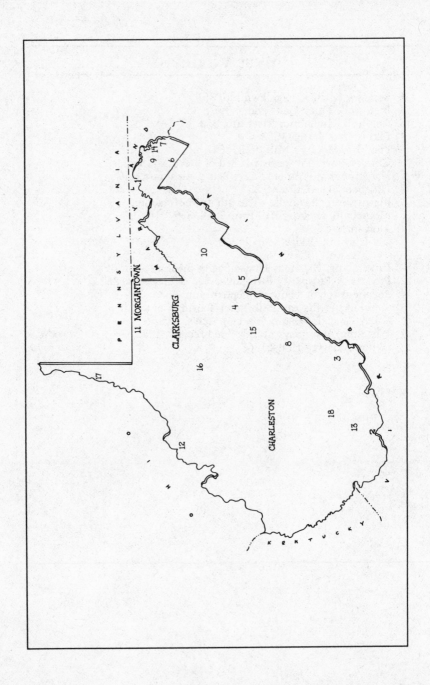

The numbers of this map indicate the locations of B&Bs described in detail in this chapter.

Highlawn Inn

304 Market Street, Berkeley Springs, WV 25411
Phone: 304/258-5700
Location: On a quiet side street. At the top of a steep hill, three blocks from the center of town.
Hosts: Sandra Kauffman and Timothy Miller
Open: Year round. Reservations required. Two-night minimum stay on October, holiday, and special events weekends.
Rates: $70–$80 per room. $90 suite. MC, VISA.

From Virginia: "Original Victorian elegance recreated. Antique furnishings. (Pastel) green and rose color scheme throughout . . . luxurious linens, quiet and restful atmosphere. We really felt pampered. . . . The innkeeper has a rare talent for making each visit a memorable one. Enchanting . . . an oasis."

"Peace and comfort" is what Sandy set out to provide when she restored the late 1890s house. In preparation for becoming an innkeeper, she had visited many B&Bs and even started an antiques business. Since opening Highlawn, the former urban law firm legal administrator (manager of 60 staff members) who was president of the Association of Legal Administrators has continued her interest in historic research, has become quite an expert in resources for restoration supplies, and has even had experience stripping seven layers of wallpaper! Her efforts were recognized in 1986, when the inn was on the Berkeley Springs Home and Historic Tour.

An extension of Sandy's cooking expertise is her catering for weddings and conferences at Berkeley Castle, a national and West Virginia historic landmark overlooking Berkeley Springs. Timothy specializes in planning conferences and unusual weddings.

In residence: "Jackie, the friendly porch cat who adopted our inn."
Restrictions: Children should be at least 14. No guests' pets.
Bed and bath: Five second-floor rooms plus a first-floor suite with private entrance and porch. All private baths, all but one with claw-foot tub and shower. Double or twin-sized beds that are brass, carved walnut, or white iron-and-brass.
Breakfast: 8:30–10:30. "Unforgettable." Could be freshly squeezed orange juice, egg and cheese casserole, locally produced country sausage and bacon, grits, lemon curd topping on "mile high" biscuits, hot glazed cinnamon rolls, prizewinning locally made apple butter. Special Sunday casserole. Sandy joins guests most mornings.
Plus: Air conditioning and TV in rooms. Rockers and swing on wraparound veranda. Picnic table. Large lawn. Tour of house. Shower caps,

shampoos, and other toiletries; English soaps. Option of dinner by reservation for full house rental and on Thanksgiving and Victorian Christmas weekends.

Three Oaks and a Quilt

Duhring Street, P.O. Box 84, Bramwell, WV 24715
Phone: 304/248-8316
Location: Off the beaten path. In a town of about 1,000 people. Eight miles north of Bluefield, West Virginia. In a residential section atop a hill across from the Thomas Mansion "Carriage House."
Host: "B.J." Kahle
Open: May–October. Reservations preferred.
Rates: $47.50 or $55 double. $5 less for single occupancy. Discounts for stays of three or more nights.

"Most people come here to see the coal operators' mansions in this town which is on the National Register of Historic Places. They fall in love with the area and want to return. One is quickly renewed in the restful, relaxing atmosphere. My grandfather bought this house in 1919 and it has remained in the family ever since. I restored it, using and reusing everything possible. The oaks are to keep you cool. The quilts are to keep you warm."

A magnificent "Whig Rose" appliqued quilt, one of B.J.'s collection (of three dozen), is hanging on the front porch wall. Inside, the homestead is freshly painted and papered.

B.J. was born and raised in Bramwell and has returned after many years away. She has been a teacher in five states. Her husband is an executive administrator with the U.S. Department of Labor in Atlanta. They are parents of three grown children.

Restrictions: Children should be at least 12. No guests' pets. Nonsmokers preferred because smoke smell lingers in fabrics (quilts).
Bed and bath: Three second-floor rooms. Two shared baths, one with tub, the other with shower. Two rooms with double beds (one is grandparents' cherry bed, the other a spool). One room with twin beds. Handmade quilts, traditional patterns, in each room.
Breakfast: 8:30–9:30. Juice, pigs in blankets, Christmas Eve Plum Pudding Bread, glazed apples, hot beverages. Menu varies according to guests' tastes and B.J.'s schedule. Served in the dining room amidst a quilt collection.
Plus: Late-afternoon beverages. Bedroom fans. Mints. Fresh flowers. Thick towels. Tour of house and area. Refrigerator space. Laundry facilities (fee charged).

From Delaware: "Gracious hostess. Clean, homey, filled with functional antiques, an assortment of beautiful quilts. . . . We were given a walking tour of the community. A delightful experience."

Greenbrier River Inn

P.O. Box 133, U.S. Route 60, Caldwell, WV 24925
Phone: 304/647-5652 and 647-5712
Location: On 25 acres of lawns and woods with a half-mile nature walk, tennis and basketball courts, boat launch, and fishing. On the Greenbrier River. Five miles from The Greenbrier Hotel. Near caves, white water rafting, fish hatchery.
Hosts: Joan and Jim Jeter; Rand Schoolfield
Open: Year round. Advance reservations appreciated.
Rates: $50 single. $55 double. $10 extra person. No charge for infants. Ten percent discount for West Virginia Public Radio donors. AARP midweek discount. MC, VISA.

"We decided to put our love of restoration, antiques, crafts, art, and fruits of farm labor together into the style of B&Bs we knew from our own travels," said Jim, a lawyer who had experience restoring his own home and office. Joan, the decorator, is a registered nurse who is now a sheep farmer. In 1986 the Jeters uncovered fireplaces, removed false ceilings, and retained the great circular doorway of this columned Greek Revival brick house built in 1824 as an inn with tall ceilings and large rooms. It is now on the National Register of Historic Places. President Martin Van Buren was honored here. The house figured in the Civil War. And in 1987 it was the site of the 50th anniversary celebration of the former owners, the Caldwells, after whom the town is named.

The Jeters still live nine miles away on the farm (tours given to guests), but they are at the inn every day, working with Rand, who knows the area; greeting old and new friends; sharing the history of the house and area; and giving hints for restaurants, antiques shops, and "a park that is a photographer's wonderland."

Restrictions: Children welcome. Inquire about guests' pets. No smoking in hall.
Bed and bath: Seven rooms with private baths. On first floor, one room has double bed, working fireplace, full bath; the other has a king bed, shower bath. Upstairs, rooms have one or two double beds, twin beds, or one double with one or two singles (some baths with shower only). Roll-away and crib available.
Breakfast: 8–10. Homemade breads, juice, homemade jams made from farm berries and fruit, grits casserole, coffee, tea. Buffet in dining room or on glass-enclosed porch.
Plus: Bedroom air conditioners. Tour of house. Babysitting. Cable TV in all rooms. Ice machine. Mints on the pillow.

The Retreat

214 Harpertown Road, Route 2, Box 214-1, Elkins, WV 26241
Phone: 304/636-2960
Location: On wooded grounds, half a mile from downtown Elkins and

U.S. Routes 33, 250, and 219. About 40 miles from I-79. Between Canaan Valley/Timberline and Showshoe/Silver Creek ski areas.
Host: Jim Lynch
Open: Year round. Advance reservations preferred.
Rates: $25 single. $32 double. $10 extra person.

"I call it 'country elegant.' Most furnishings are from estate auctions. After repairing, wallpapering, and painting, I still have ideas for projects in this old house. . . . An 85-year-old granddaughter of the original owner has provided me with turn-of-the-century pictures. . . . It is a pleasure to host people who come for the college; skiing; hunting and fishing; all sorts of workshops—and good food!"

Jim grew up 50 miles from Elkins, visited state parks and ski areas, and then went to Boston for college. During his 20 years in New England he was introduced to friendly B&Bs "and, eventually, I realized that the thing I most enjoyed was entertaining guests." He has worked at a private psychological consulting firm and done research at Harvard Business School. He restored an 1860 house, went to law school, and did law firm work. Now he assists developmentally disabled adults on their way to independent living. And his joy of cooking may lead to a catering business.

In residence: Penny, a wheaten terrier, "the boss." Nick, a sheep dog "who follows you around until you shake hands with him."
Restrictions: No firearms in house. Storage area for sports equipment.
Bed and bath: Four second-floor and one third-floor double-bedded rooms (most with in-room sinks) share two full baths and one half bath. Two-room third-floor suite has connecting bath. Rollaways available.
Breakfast: Maybe buckwheat cakes and fried cornmeal mush (made with locally milled grains) with maple syrup; omelets; French Canadian pork pie; eggs Benedict; Portuguese baked egg soup; bacon, eggs and toast for people in a hurry. Seasonal fruits. Homemade coffee cakes or muffins. Special diets accommodated.
Plus: Five o'clock sherry and hors d'oeuvres. Coffee and tea always available. Dinner (about $15 per person) or supper (about $6) by reservation. Babysitting. Diesel plug-in. Cable TV. Cordless phone. Candy. Fresh flowers. Bird feeders at guest room windows. Porches, lawns, and gardens.

McCoy's Mill B&B

Thorn Creek Road, Box 610, Franklin, WV 26807
Phone: 703/740-8943 or 304/358-7893
Location: Where Thorn Creek rushes into the headwaters of the south branch of the Potomac River. Just off Route 220 at the foot of mountains. Three miles south of Franklin.
Hosts: Glen and Iris Hofecker
Open: March–December. Advance reservations requested.
Rates: Single, $40 shared bath, $50 private. Double, $45 shared bath, $65 private. Less for three or more nights.

Guests wrote: "A fantastic experience. . . . A combination of a step back into history, into a mill that is being restored; a memorable evening and morning visiting with fascinating folks; a stick-to-the-ribs breakfast with the best homemade applebutter we've ever had. . . . Sleeping next to the sound of a rushing stream. Waking up to one of the most picturesque scenes in West Virginia. What more could one ask for?

And all because of the great flood of 1985. Glen, a cabinetmaker who reproduces clocks and Chippendale furniture—mostly Newport style—had restored a 1756 mill in Virginia. While working with the West Virginia flood disaster relief, he found McCoy's Mill and felt it would be a great place to share with others via B&B.

On one of the oldest landmarks (1758) in West Virginia, the present mill of post-and-beam construction was built in 1848. The adjoining miller's house was built in 1909. Glen has created a small hydroelectric plant that uses the mill and mill wheel to produce electricity for heat and lighting in the B&B and shop.

Restrictions: Children are welcome. Pets not allowed in guest rooms. No smoking inside.
Bed and bath: Six second-floor rooms. In mill, three, each with queen bed, private full bath. In miller's house, two double-bedded rooms (one with a twin bed too) share a full bath. Queen-bedded room has a private bath and kitchen.
Breakfast: 7–9. Iris's full country breakfast includes homemade breads and rolls. Served on deck overlooking waterwheel or in country kitchen.
Plus: Tour of house and mill. Barbecue, picnic tables, fishing on premises. Some fishing equipment available. Babysitting arranged.

Prospect Hill Bed & Breakfast

P.O. Box 135, Gerrardstown, WV 25420
Phone: 304/229-3346
Location: Secluded. On a 225-acre working farm. At the foot of North Mountain. Four miles from I-81. About a 90-minute drive from Washington, D.C. Near Harpers Ferry, Antietam, Gettysburg, and Winchester.
Hosts: Hazel and Charles Hudock
Open: Year round. Advance reservations required. Two-night minimum preferred.
Rates: Double occupancy. $75 for two nights. $95 Saturday night alone. $85 cottage for two. $20 each additional person. MC, VISA.

"A discovery," say guests, who drive between the stone pillars, cross over the stone bridge, and pass ducks and geese before arriving at the Georgian mansion. The grand main hall has a graceful open three-storied stairway. And just off the hall is a room with a hand-painted mural of 19th-century country scenes. Built between 1789 and 1802 by a businessman who outfitted wagon trains going west, the elegant residence was restored 10 years ago when the Hudocks came here for what B&B guests also seek: peace and quiet. With five children grown—now visiting grandchildren come—"B&B just sort of happened."

The house on the Register of Historic Places is filled with antiques collected through the Hudocks' 28 years of traveling when Charlie was a meteorologist with the U.S. Navy. Still, it's the kind of place where you can be very private or "wander into the kitchen for tea and talk." It's the kind of place where you can browse through a library of 2,000 books. Or go for long walks through the woods. Discover herb, vegetable, and fruit gardens. Enjoy the scene of cows and calves.

In residence: Charlie smokes a pipe. Shannon is a golden retriever; Tanga, a gentle Doberman; Elmo, "a "Morris-like" cat. Ducks and geese.
Restrictions: Children accepted in guest cottage only. Smoking in living room only. No guests' pets, please. Arrival time, 3–10; departure by 11 A.M.
Bed and bath: Two large mansion rooms, each with a private full bath, working fireplace, sofa, and comfortable chairs. One with a double bed; the other, a queen. Brick cottage, former servants' quarters, has one second-floor room with double bed plus a double hide-a-bed in the keeping room, full bath, kitchenette, living room, working fireplace, and breakfast room.
Breakfast: 8–9. Juice, fruit, baked omelet or apple pancakes with sour cream and maple syrup, homemade biscuits, jams and syrups. In formal dining room with china, silver, and crystal.
Plus: Tea or wine. Tour of house. Fish (and release catch). Country roads for cycling.

Fillmore Street Bed & Breakfast

Fillmore Street, Box 34, Harpers Ferry, WV 25425
Phone: 301/377-0070 or 304/535-2619
Location: On a quiet side street in the historic area. Within walking distance of all historic attractions.
Hosts: Alden and James Addy
Open: Year round. Advance reservations required. Closed Christmas and New Year's.
Rates: $54 single, $64 double.

They say that before the last edition of this book, this B&B was a well-kept secret! The antiques-filled Victorian with blue shutters and picket fence has been home to two teachers for the last 10 years. "We do B&B for fun and to make practical use of our house that is in a wonderful area. Although most guests come to visit the Harpers Ferry National Historic Park, many come, particularly in winter, for a getaway from urban areas."

The Addys often share their interests in history, antiques, art, theater, and gardening. Fillmore Street is definitely a B&B where the hospitality is remembered at least as much as the country Victorian decor. As one guest from Maryland said, "Superb host and hostess. Alden has a career waiting in interiors. I especially loved breakfast—served by the most charming butler, waiter, PhD!"

Restrictions: Young people 12 years and older who would be comfortable in a separate room at full rate are welcome. Sorry, no guests' pets.
Bed and bath: Two second-floor air-conditioned rooms. One has a king bed and private full bath; the other has a queen and private shower bath.
Breakfast: 8:30 or 9. Link sausages, herbed scrambled eggs with mushroom and/or tomato garnish, buttered chili potatoes, spiced applesauce, corn muffins and homemade preserves; or poached eggs and ham on English muffin, cheese and bread souffle, steamed buttered apples, breakfast cake. Juice, fresh fruit, coffee and tea. In formal dining room.
Plus: As a Pennsylvania guest wrote, "The finest details to the letter." Fresh flowers. Chocolates. Mints. Turn-down service. Guests' upstairs sitting room with library. As the Addys say, "Guests are free to tour the house." Garden. Extensive sightseeing material. Will meet guests at Harpers Ferry train station.

The Current

Box 135, Hillsboro, WV 24946
Phone: 304/653-4722
Location: In the Allegheny Mountains, within sight of the Greenbrier River. Five miles from the Pearl S. Buck Birthplace. Near cross-country skiing and hiking in Cranberry Wilderness, Droop Mountain, and Watoga state parks.
Hosts: Leslee McCarty and John Walkup
Open: Year round.
Rates: $30 single, $40 double. $10 extra person.

After pedaling along the incredibly beautiful Greenbrier River Trail on our first mountain-bike B&B-to-B&B trip, we approached The Current to find a hot tub on the near side, a Morgan horse farm across the way, and beyond, the spire of a white church against a mountain backdrop. The whole visit was a wonderful introduction to West Virginian hospitality.

Leslee and John had just purchased the church. Now they are in the process of restoring it for meetings—and maybe even for more guest rooms. Their 1905 farmhouse, owned by one family until 1985, has refinished woodwork. The furnishings and collections, arranged with flair, include John's great-grandfather's walnut and cherry bed with six-foot headboard; Leslee's grandmother's quilts; Raggedy Ann and Andy dolls; and West Virginia crafts and photographs.

The easy-to-be-with hosts met while organizing a local festival for world hunger. They married and continued their work on what has become a very successful annual benefit festival. John, a native who can trace his family's arrival in Greenbrier Valley back to about 1760, is a photographer and guitar player and runs a cattle farm that you are likely to pass "15 miles down the river." Leslee, a community activist, teaches English as a second language. We left well fed and supplied with "don't miss" suggestions as well as fond memories.

In residence: Leslee's parents, retired teachers and avid golfers, summer residents in the first-floor suite. Honey, a golden retriever. Another dog, Squeaky. Four outside cats, "all named Kitty." Some chickens.
Restrictions: No smoking.
Foreign languages spoken: Spanish fluently. German haltingly.
Bed and bath: Four spacious double-bedded rooms. One upstairs and one downstairs shower bath. First-floor suite. Three second-floor rooms. Enclosed porch with two "especially nice for kids" daybeds. Rollaway bed.
Breakfast: Until noon. Freshly baked bread, homemade jelly, omelet or cottage cheese pancakes with strawberries, cereal, juice, fruit. Served in dining room or in large fireplaced country kitchen.
Plus: Beverages. Deck (for stargazing too). Hot tub. Wildflower arrangements. Canoe and bicycle rentals arranged. Semivegetarian dinner ($7 per person) by request. Babysitting. Kitchen and laundry privileges.

Boydville—The Inn at Martinsburg

601 South Queen Street, Martinsburg, WV 25401
Phone: 304/263-1448
Location: On 10 acres. In historic district. One block from outlet center. One and a half miles to I-81 exit; 80 miles from Washington, D.C.
Hosts: Owen Sullivan and Ripley Hotch
Open: Year round. Advance reservations requested. In October, two-night minimum stay.
Rates: Per room. $75 shared bath, $95 private bath. $20 extra person. AMEX, MC, VISA.

Saved by President Abraham Lincoln minutes before it was scheduled to be burned. And, after a three-year search, found by Owen, a designer in Alexandria, Virginia, and Ripley, an editor for *Nation's Business* magazine. Built in 1812 as the home of General Elisha Boyd, the stone Federal plantation house—the roadside historic marker reads, "mansion noted for its fine workmanship"—remained in the same family for 150 years. When the hosts acquired it in 1987, they spent seven weeks on restoration, "thanking previous owners every day because the original woodwork, hand-carved mantels, French brass chandeliers *and* entry hall wallpaper are still here." The summer kitchen and ice- and smokehouses are too. The hosts, experienced B&B travelers, brought their 10-year collection of antiques, including oil paintings, furniture, and, for Christmas, 800 tree ornaments. "Our guests come for business reasons; for antiquing; apple blossoms and fall foliage; within an hour's drive—Antietam Battlefield, Harpers Ferry, Berkeley Springs, and white water rafting. And they come for this house!"

In residence: In hosts' quarters, one Himalayan cat.
Restrictions: Children should be at least 14. Please, no smoking in the house. Sorry, no guests' pets.
Foreign language spoken: Some French.
Bed and bath: Seven rooms. Private baths for two first-floor rooms; one with double bed and old-fashioned tub bath, the other with queen bed and shower bath. On second floor, private baths for two queen-bedded rooms. Three rooms with double or queen bed share a full bath.
Breakfast: At 9. Full. Includes casseroles, fried apples, homemade muffins and biscuits. Served family style in dining room.
Plus: Afternoon wine or sherry. Fireplaced drawing and music rooms. Books, games, TV in garden room. Wide front veranda with rockers (two are original). Croquet. Garden enclosed by ivy-covered brick walls. Special receptions arranged.

Hickory Hill Farm B&B

Route 1, Box 355, Moorefield, WV 26836
Phone: 304/538-2511
Location: On a bluff with spectacular views. On Route 220, three miles north of Petersburg in historic South Branch Valley of Potomac Highland.
Hosts: Frances and John (Jack) C. Welton
Open: Year round. Advance reservations, please.
Rates: $35 single. $45 double. $10 children under 12.

"Guests sit on the wide back veranda that faces corn fields, pastures with cows, and the river. Some go wading or swimming. Or they walk through the ancient oak grove to the top of the mountain and view the valley. There are ponds to fish in and an old family cemetery to visit. This is a working farm, a getaway place without pressures rather than a place with excitement, bright lights and fine food. For 25 years we have lived in this 1809 Federal brick house that is listed on the National Register of Historic Places. It has hand-carved woodwork and family furnishings that mean a lot to us. After the great flood of 1985, we took in three construction workers, and that started us as a B&B. I paint watercolors, have a West Virginia crafts shop here, and raise horses. Jack drives a truck part-time so he can continue his love of farming."

In residence: A deaf collie, "an excellent lip reader." A basset hound "who thinks she's a person."
Restrictions: Children are welcome. Smoking allowed in kitchen. No guests' pets; kennel three miles from B&B.
Bed and bath: Two rooms share a full bath and a half bath with hosts. One room with double bed, crib, and nonworking fireplace. In east wing, up steep stairs, room has a double bed and a three-quarter bed.
Breakfast: Hour and menu chosen by guests. "The works, if you'd like." Possibilities include fruit, cinnamon ring, sausage or ham, egg casserole, sourdough pancakes, waffles. In country kitchen by wood stove.
Plus: Iced or hot tea. Bedroom fans. Chocolate kisses by the bowlful.

From New Zealand: "Our attention was drawn to it by a *Washington Post* writeup. We found the hosts very hospitable, the guest facilities all that we desired, and the house and area of considerable historic interest."

Chestnut Ridge School

1000 Stewartstown Road, Morgantown, WV 26505
Phone: 304/598-2262
Location: On the outskirts of Morgantown. On a high hill with beautiful view. Four miles from I-48; two minutes from airport and medical center. Five-minute drive to downtown or main West Virginia University campus. Near lake, arboretum, nature walks.
Hosts: Sam and Nancy Bonasso
Open: Year round.
Rates: $48 single. $54 double. $7 extra person in room.

Until seven years ago, this was an elementary school. Built in the 1920s and gutted when the Bonassos bought it in 1987, the brick building still has large windows and an arched entranceway (fronted by flowers in summer). An old quartermaster's book, sitting on an old butcher's block, serves as the guest register. Rooms, separated by a hallway-turned-parlor, are decorated without clutter in green and pink with antique armoires, wicker, and rockers.

After living in town for 20 years and being "totally involved in the conversion," the Bonassos have taken up residence on the second floor "in a neighborhood and area that we enjoy sharing with guests." Sam is a civil engineer, known, perhaps, for some more elaborate projects.

Restrictions: Children are welcome. Nonsmokers preferred; no smoking in guest rooms. Sorry, no guests' pets.
Foreign languages spoken: A little French and Italian.
Bed and bath: Four first-floor queen-bedded rooms, each with vanity in room and adjoining private marble and brass full bath. Rollaway and crib available.
Breakfast: Usually 7:30–9:30. Juice; fruit; grain muffins (recipe often requested) with bran, corn, raisins, and nuts. Coffees and teas. Eat in parlor, in your room, on deck, or in hosts' kitchen.
Plus: Central air conditioning. Beverages. Deck overlooking mountain backdrop of suburban Morgantown.

From an astronaut now working in Washington, D.C.: "I would recommend it to any traveler, explorer, bon vivant, or anyone in search of 'the good life.' " From Colorado: "Immaculate, cozy, bright, quiet, very pleasant. Terrific hosts!"

Maxwell's B&B

Route 12, Box 197, Morgantown, WV 26505
Phone: 304/594-3041
Location: Quiet. At Ridge Way Farm, surrounded by woods and fields overlooking Cheat Lake. Two miles from I-48, exit 10. Eight miles east of Morgantown and West Virginia University. Two miles from Lakeview Sheraton Conference Center.
Hosts: Emma B. Maxwell and Pat Keith
Open: Year round. Advance reservations with one night's deposit required.
Rates: $30 single, $40 double. $70 suite. One (at most) 10 percent discount for stays of seven nights or more, for senior citizens or foreign tourists.

If meeting people is what B&B is all about, you've come to the right place, an organic farm where Pat, a former social worker and now a rural mail carrier, raises Scotch Highland cattle and tends the vegetable garden and fruit orchards. Emma Maxwell, her mother, is a retired social worker who, at age 69, put a pack on her back for a round-the-world trip. She rode elephants and camels, took canoe and rapids trips, stayed in African villages . . . and visited 137 countries before returning home in 1980.

And now, with the motto of "I Bid Ye Fair," Emma meets travelers in the farmhouse dating from 1895. (Pat has lived here for 20 years.) Among the many changes—"We're do-it-yourselfers"—is an attached solar room with rocking chairs from which you might see white-tailed deer and wild turkey. "For those with time to wait and watch, the surrounding woods abound with wildlife."

In residence: Two dogs, Mollie and Pondi. Three cats—Miss Elie, Pansy, and Grey Kat.
Restrictions: Please, no guests' pets. No smoking in bedrooms. Inquire about children as guests.
Bed and bath: On second floor, two rooms, each with king bed and raised fireplace, plus a sitting room with wood stove and bed nook. All can be a suite for five.
Breakfast: Guests select hour and menu. Choice of continental or full farm breakfast.
Plus: Ceiling fans in bedrooms.

Harmony House Bed & Breakfast Inn 🛏 🏮

710 Ann Street, Parkersburg, WV 26101
Phone: 304/485-1458
Location: In downtown Parkersburg. Within walking distance of Art Center; Actors' Guild; residential district with historic homes, and stern-

wheeler boats on the Ohio River to historic Blennerhasset Island. Near glass and doll factory tours and outlets. Three and a half miles from I-77. Ten miles south of Marietta, Ohio; 72 miles north of Charleston.
Hosts: Rich and Deborah Shaffer
Open: Year round.
Rates: $37 single. $40 double. $50 triple. Seventh night free. MC, VISA.

"Parkersburg, our hometown with great community spirit, has some concert, exhibit, or production available almost every weekend of the year! In fulfilling Rich's dream of restoring an historic house, we returned here in 1987 after living in Pennsylvania and New Jersey. [Deborah was a church program director; Rich, a system and purchasing manager for manufactured housing.] We repaired, patched, replaced and updated. Rich restored all the original gas/electric light fixtures. Auction finds have been added to our collection of Victorian antiques. We serve a variety of evening snacks—homemade apple pie or cookies, even good old-fashioned hand-cranked ice cream!"

Business travelers, too, have discovered this three-story brick Queen Anne residence, on the National Register of Historic Places, which has original oak mantels and pocket doors. At least one music box is in every room. There's also a Kimball player piano, a console piano, a crank Victrola, and a violin—all available to guests. And if you become curious about the history of the house, Shaffer research has produced some fascinating detail.

In residence: "Shep, age 16, is a very docile mixed terrier."
Restrictions: Sorry, no guests' pets. No children. Smoking allowed on porches only.
Bed and bath: Two second-floor rooms, each with private bath. One has a double bed and adjoining shower bath. The other has a double and a twin bed, hall bath with claw-footed tub and marble sink.
Breakfast: Flexible hours. Juices and fruit. German sausage (personally blended and seasoned). Belgian waffle topped with fruit and whipped cream. Homemade muffins, breads, and pastries. Coffee or tea.
Plus: Central air conditioning. Bedroom ceiling fans. Refreshments. TV, stereo, and VCR in family room. Mints. Fresh flowers in season. Front porch swing. Free parking in nearby lot. By request, tour of house. Airport and bus station pickup arranged. Shop with restored lighting fixtures, stained glass items, and collectibles.

Prosperity Farmhouse Bed & Breakfast

Box 393, Prosperity, WV 25909
Phone: 304/255-4245
Location: On 80-acre cattle farm off a country road. "In an unpopulated, beautiful area that we love." Near West Virginia White Water Rafting Company, Winterplace ski area, Prosperity Speedway. Five minutes from

shopping mall, theaters, restaurants, bowling alleys, parks. Five minutes from I-77; fifty miles southeast of Charlestown.
Hosts: Tara and John Wooton
Open: April–October; weekends only April, May, September, October and possibly rest of year. Reservations appreciated.
Rates: $30 single. $40 double. $5 additional person. Children under six, free. MC, VISA.

What was a granary for 100 years has become a very private B&B—a perfect arrangement for two couples traveling together or for families—on the grounds of (just 10 yards from) the hosts' century-old farmhouse. For the conversion, barn wood was installed on the inside walls. Floors and ceilings are original. There are crisp white curtains, Laura Ashley fabrics, some antiques, and local crafts.

Tara, a teacher, is delighted with the outcome—and with hosting. "Many come for white water rafting. We had one family reunion here. And some travelers find us a perfect stopover as we are four hours from both Cincinnati and Raleigh. Sometimes they join us for fishing, basketball, haying, gardening—or walking on the dirt road that leads up to a knoll where there used to be a school. Children love the pond that is full of frogs, turtles and fish. . . . John, a lawyer and lifelong resident of the area, is a great storyteller, local historian, and very likable guy!. . . . We butcher our own pig and beef and serve our own eggs. . . . We love to share this beautiful area."

In residence: In hosts' quarters, Jody, age nine; Clint, age seven. Two golden retrievers, one cat, a pony, two horses, 40 cattle, 50 pigs.
Bed and bath: Two sleeping areas. Beds for seven people. One shower bath. First floor has queen sleep-sofa, kitchenette. In large upstairs room, canopied double bed and two trundles that can be a king. Rollaway and crib available.
Breakfast: Flexible hours. Fruit (some homegrown). Juice. Waffles, crepes, or pancakes with ham or bacon. Homemade muffins. Served in farmhouse, in B&B kitchen, or on deck.
Plus: Private deck. Bedroom ceiling fans. Mints. Laundry facilities. Tour of house and farm.

Thomas Shepherd Inn

Box 1162, German and Duke Streets, Shepherdstown, WV 25443
Phone: 304/876-3715
Location: Downtown—with landscaped yard—in the state's oldest community, which has a college-town aura and a 1738 gristmill. Eight miles from Harpers Ferry, four from Antietam Battlefield. Ninety minutes from Washington, D.C., and Baltimore. Within walking distance of excellent restaurants and the Chesapeake and Ohio Canal towpath and old lock houses.
Hosts: Edward and Carol Ringoot
Open: Year round. Reservations preferred.

Rates: Per room. $65 private bath, $60 shared bath. $10 more, Fridays, Saturdays, and holidays. MC, VISA with 5 percent processing fee. Gladly accept personal checks.

The stately 1868 Federal brick house, once a parsonage and then a doctor's residence and office, was meticulously restored by the Ringoots in 1984 as a spacious B&B filled with American antiques and items collected from around the world. Although the ambiance with a sense of personalized attention as well as privacy is appreciated by first-timers and returnees alike, the conversations, too, are well remembered. Ed, a retired Foreign Service officer with a financial background, was Shepherdstown's town clerk/treasurer. Carol's background is in international health, primarily in health programming in the developing world. Their last foreign assignment was in West Africa. "With all our travels and entertaining, innkeeping was a natural evolution."

Guests come to experience "the country" and for antiquing, historical sites, and even white water rafting. The Ringoots, too (after a search that took them as far as England), feel that they chose the right house in the right place.

Restrictions: Young people 12 or older who are comfortable in a separate room are welcome. No smoking indoors. No pets, please.
Foreign languages spoken: French and Flemish.
Bed and bath: Six large second-floor rooms with queen, double, or twin beds. Private baths for four rooms. Two interesting rooms with old floor-to-ceiling windows share a large full bath.
Breakfast: 7:30–9:30. Full breakfast with favorites such as puffed fruit pancakes, ham and cheese souffles, Belgian waffles, and a variety of griddlecakes. Served in formal dining room. Option of continental breakfast in guests' room.
Plus: Air-conditioned bedrooms. Coffee or tea on arrival. Before-dinner wine by living room fireplace. Belgian chocolates (Ed was born in Belgium) at bedside. Thick towels. Local restaurant menus in each room. Library. TV. Special soaps. Rockers on treetop-level porch. Tour of house. Will meet guests at the Harpers Ferry train. Bicycles and picnics available with 24-hour notice.

Willis Farm/Elk River Touring Center

Highway 219, Slatyfork, WV 26291
Phone: 304/572-3771
Location: Pastoral. Way up on a huge plateau. Across a small bridge surrounded by mountains. Sixteen miles north of Marlinton; eight miles after you cross Elk Mountain. Twelve miles from the Greenbrier River. Near Snowshoe ski area.
Hosts: Gil and Mary Willis
Open: Year round. Advance reservations recommended.
Rates: $30 single. $45 double. $55 triple. MC, VISA.

Gil met us at the Lewisburg airport. While some fellow airline passengers rode off in the Greenbrier Hotel limousine, Gil, with map in hand, oriented us to our first day's cycling route, which included gorgeous sections of the level 75-mile-long Greenbrier River Trail, a former railroad built for the timber industry at the turn of the century. Eventually we pedaled—and walked—up to the Willises'.

Before Gil established his cycle (mountain bike) and ski touring center here in "paradise country," he lived "bachelor style" at this former sheep farm. His wife, Mary, a trained marine biologist turned friendly innkeeper and creative chef, has changed all that. Now the cozy living room has lots of plants and a big wood stove. Rooms are comfortable, not fancy. The food is delicious, plentiful, and pretty to look at.

Thanks to Gil and Mary, we learned about a bakery in a Mennonite residence, Sharp's Country Store in Slatyfork (worth a special stop), and a wonderful route to Cass, home of the scenic railroad where the steam locomotive pulls passengers seated on refurbished logging cars.

In residence: In hosts' quarters, 50 feet from B&B—Thurston, age two. "Tima, a husky/shepherd whom kids love and Michelle, our cuddly fat tabby cat."
Restrictions: Please, no pets. No smoking inside.
Bed and bath: Four ground-level rooms, each with one double and one twin bed, share two shower baths (located off the kitchen). Rollaway and crib available.
Breakfast: 8–9. Maybe herbed cream cheese omelets made with farm-fresh eggs; blueberry pancakes and local maple syrup, sausage links or bacon, grits or fried potatoes; homemade muffins and cornbread, fruit salad or baked pears from homegrown fruit. Coffee, teas. Served in sunny new fireplaced dining room in converted barn.
Plus: Outdoor hot tub. Tea or coffee. Option of dinner by reservation ($6–$10 per person). Babysitting by reservation.

Ingeberg Acres

P.O. Box 199, Millstone Run Road, Valley Chapel, Weston, WV 26446
Phone: 304/269-2834
Location: On a 450-acre farm overlooking a private valley with brook, meadows, and woodlands. Eight miles from Weston along a paved road; one mile along gravel road from Valley Chapel post office. Near glass blowers, craft outlets, lakes, state 4-H camp at Jackson's Mill.
Hosts: John and Ingeborg Mann
Open: March–December. Advance reservations required.
Rates: $39 single. $59 double. No charge for crib. Ten percent senior citizen discount. $100 per day/full board in hunting season.

"My husband, our children, and I designed and built the Dutch Colonial ourselves during six summer vacations. Both John and I taught when we lived in the Washington D.C./Maryland area. For eight years now, we have been here full time, raising horses and cows where there's not even another house in sight. B&B was something I knew from Europe. We started hosting in the fall of 1987. It's a traditional style: We share our living room, dining room and fireplaced recreation room. Guests may watch and, if they'd like, participate in our farm activities. For the most part, they just relax!"

In residence: Moby, a collie. Three barn cats.
Restrictions: Children are welcome. Sorry, no pets. Nonsmokers preferred.
Foreign language spoken: German.
Bed and bath: Two second-floor carpeted rooms share a full bath. One with one double bed; one with two double beds.
Breakfast: Flexible hours. Homemade pastries and jams. Egg dishes and breakfast meats, homegrown fruits and berries, honey, juice and coffee. Served in dining room or kitchen. Hosts join guests.
Plus: Above-ground swimming pool, deck, patio. Tea, coffee, or wine. Candy. Reading material. Dinner (German specialties) during hunting season or by special request. Kitchen privileges. Extensive flower and vegetable gardens; honeybees; fruit trees.

Yesterdays Ltd. Bed and Breakfast

651 Main Street, Wheeling, WV 26003
Phone: 304/232-0864
Location: In historic urban area with a city street in front and Ohio River in back. Three blocks from downtown.
Hosts: Julie and David Sapper
Open: Year round. Advance reservations preferred.
Rates: Double occupancy. $50 shared bath, $60 private bath, $80 whirlpool suite. $10 third person.

Almost two years later, the Sappers have sustained excitement about their move from Chicago to this city of Victorian homes on the Ohio River. They were among the first guests here, only to find themselves in residence as hosts six months later. Julie, happy to be an at-home mother (and part-time student in music education), is an innkeeper known for her French toast and for her newsletter to guests. David commutes to his insurance company in Pittsburgh. They both are active with the local restoration group. And whether it's a neighborhood walking tour, restaurant suggestions, or events information, guests find that the Sappers are well informed.

And then there's the B&B itself, a town house restored by Bill Fields, a local businessman who sees Wheeling emerging as the Victorian capital of the country. Built in 1895, the house still has pocket doors, stained glass, and some natural woodwork. Fresh wallpaper is striped and floral. Comfortable antiques are all part of the home away from home.

In residence: Jori, age two.

Restrictions: Smoking allowed in public areas only. Children are welcome.

Bed and bath: Three second-floor rooms and a third-floor suite, all with eyelet bed ruffles. Private full bath for room with queen bed, screened porch overlooking river. One queen-bedded room shares a full bath with room that has 150-year-old high-headboard double bed. The large suite has queen brass bed, beamed ceiling, private bath with whirlpool tub, separate shower. Rollaway and crib available.

Breakfast: Usually 8:30–9:30. Perhaps French Quarters (house specialty). Homemade muffins or coffee cake, juice, fruit, coffee. Served on an enclosed porch overlooking river and hill beyond. "Definitely not meant for eat and run."

Plus: Air conditioners in most rooms. Bedroom ceiling fans. Wine and cheese or finger sandwiches. Two parlors with piano, stereo (chamber music), and collections of diaries (which kept David up when he was a guest), old autograph books, antique hats, and rocks and minerals. Turned-down beds. Mints on pillow.

> From Pennsylvania: "Enjoyed refreshing drinks and tasty canapes while watching barges and an old sternwheeler reminiscent of long-gone days. . . . We were treated royally."

Garvey House

P.O. Box 98, Winona, WV 25942
Phone: 304/574-3235
Location: "Out of the way but easy to get to." On a mountainside, surrounded by trees and gardens. Near abandoned mining towns that you can hike to. About nine miles from the intersection of U.S. 19 and Route 60.
Host: Valerie Ritter
Open: April–October. Advance reservations preferred.
Rates: Double occupancy. $54 shared bath, $58 private bath. $8 extra person. Late charge for checkout after 11 A.M. MC, VISA.

"I loved West Virginia as soon as I got here," says Valerie. Six years ago she came from Cincinnati, where she was director of training for a hotel management company. Now she's a white water rafting guide "with not one regret. It is very rewarding when people go away pleased and even more so when they return."

Adventurous people come here. For a special treat, Valerie recommends an unmarked trail that brings you to the edge of New River Gorge, where you can see seven rapids on the river and look into the distance for miles and miles.

Her large and airy adjacent houses, built in the early 1900s by a coal company superintendent, are "I don't know what you'd call it" style.

"Furnishings are a mix—from the early 1900s to contemporary. Comfort is the main objective." Goal attained! As travelers have said, "Excellent. Lots of fun. Goes all out for her guests."

In residence: Mat, a cat "who sleeps with any guest who will have him." Alice, Mat's mother, "a little more aloof." Lem, the dog, "loves everyone, accompanies guests on a hike to the river."
Restrictions: Children are welcome. Smoking in living room only. Sorry, no guests' pets.
Bed and bath: Eight rooms. The larger Garvey House has private bath for one first-floor room with two double beds. On second floor, three double-bedded rooms share a bath. Smaller house has two upstairs double-bedded rooms with private baths and two downstairs double-bedded rooms that share a bath.
Breakfast: Until 9:30. Apple Garvey, house specialty; scrambled eggs with cream cheese; or sausage and cheese–stuffed mushrooms, potato wedges. Orange juice blended with fresh banana, strawberry, egg, and vanilla.
Plus: Bedroom ceiling fans. Tea, wine, chocolates on pillow. Fresh flowers everywhere. Terraced gardens. Stone paths leading from gazebo to two tiny ponds.

Index

New York

Pennsylvania

Virginia

ABOUT THE AUTHOR

Bernice Chesler, the "Bed and Breakfast Ambassador," is known for her personalized approach and her attention to detail. Guests from all over the world write to her about their B&B experiences. She shares their impressions—and her own gathered through hundreds of stays and extensive interviews—in her books, unique Meet-The-Hosts programs, workshops, lectures, and by speaking at bed and breakfast conferences. She is a member of the Professional Advisory Board of the Professional Association of Innkeepers International.

BBB—Before Bed and Breakfast, Ms. Chesler conducted thousands of interviews throughout the country for documentary films seen on national public television. As Publications Coordinator for ZOOM, she edited twelve books that emanated from the Emmy Award winning television program. She is also the author of the classic guide, *In and Out of Boston with (or without) Children*, and co-author of *The Family Guide to Cape Cod*.